Jesus Christ

Jesus Christ

The New Face of Social Progress

Edited by

Peter J. Casarella

WILLIAM B. EERDMANS PUBLISHING COMPANY
GRAND RAPIDS, MICHIGAN / CAMBRIDGE, U.K.

Published 2015 by
Wm. B. Eerdmans Publishing Co.
2140 Oak Industrial Drive N.E., Grand Rapids, Michigan 49505 /
P.O. Box 163, Cambridge CB3 9PU U.K.

Printed in the United States of America

21 20 19 18 17 16 15   7 6 5 4 3 2 1

Library of Congress Cataloging-in-Publication Data

Jesus Christ: the new face of social progress / edited by Peter J. Casarella.
       pages   cm
   ISBN 978-0-8028-7113-8 (pbk.: alk. paper)
   1. Christian sociology — Catholic Church.
   2. Social justice — Religious aspects — Catholic Church.
   3. Catholic Church. Pope (2005-2013 : Benedict XVI). Caritas in veritate.
   4. Charity.   5. Love — Religious aspects — Catholic Church.
   I. Casarella, Peter J., editor.

   BX1753.J28   2015
   261.8 — dc23
                                                2014015189

www.eerdmans.com

Contents

PART II: REIMAGINING SOCIAL AND POLITICAL ORDER

PART III: RETHINKING THE ECONOMY AS GRATUITOUS

Preface: Integrating Discourse in a Divided World

Daniel K. Finn

We live in a divided world. This has always been the case, of course, but in several respects the divisions today have become sharper and deeper than in any other time in recent memory. Terrorism, environmental catastrophe, the loss of social cohesion, the breakdown of the family, the death of innocents, and a billion people mired in crushing poverty can all be understood as both cause and effect of these divisions. There are many reasons to be discouraged about the future of humanity.

In the midst of all these temptations to despair, Pope Benedict XVI offered to the church and the world a vision of hope in his encyclical, *Caritas in Veritate (CV)*. It holds out to us a notion of truth in Christ that animates a deep faith and a lively commitment to transforming this divided world in charity and justice. As this volume of essays reminds us, the pope teaches that Jesus Christ is indeed the very face of the social progress that our world needs so badly.

The moral task faced by Christians today is in one very important way more complicated than that faced by our spiritual ancestors in the pre-modern world. With the rise of anthropology and sociology over the past two centuries, people today better understand the social structures within which daily life is lived, whether political, social, or economic. Traditional Catholic moral theology has always articulated the moral requirements faced by kings, princes, and others charged with the oversight of human organizations. But today we understand both how the choices of every individual — from the lowliest to those with greatest authority — are conditioned by those social structures and how we together have a (limited) capacity to shape those structures in more humane ways.

Pope Benedict advanced the magisterium's articulation of this insight into "sinful social structures" when he spoke of "the presence of original sin in social conditions and in the structure of society" (*CV,* no. 34). He recognized that any social progress against current threats to humanity must address both personal and structural transformation. In this, the pope implicitly reiterates the traditional Catholic position of providing a countercultural witness against the errors and abuses of the world without becoming a sectarian force that so rejects the world that it withdraws in hopes of establishing a simpler and more perfect community.

This leaves us, of course, with the very Catholic necessity of living life amid moral ambiguity in striving for social progress. Consider two of the broad themes addressed by authors in this volume: political order and economic life.

There has been much discussion about international governance in light of Pope Benedict's call for "a true world political authority" (*CV,* no. 67). Even his insistence that such an authority would need to be designed in light of subsidiarity has not quieted critics who find such a call to be romantic and unthinkable in the world today. Similarly, his call for including "the logic of gift" in daily economic life has raised eyebrows, and his pointing to small hybrid firms has led some to wonder what he has in mind for the other 99.9 percent of businesses in the world today.

It is one of the great strengths of this volume, and more fundamentally of the group of scholars gathered by editor Peter Casarella, that such issues, and the theological underpinnings necessary to debate them, are engaged with energy, integrity, and mutual respect. Thus, it is no surprise that the ambiguities of life, even those generated by the inevitable conflicts among the many priorities that Christians hold, leave the reader with a volume of essays that implicitly question and challenge each other.

We live in a world where so much public discourse exhibits a disrespectful fracture between conflicting points of view. The diversity embodied in this volume promises to leave the attentive reader better able to live out a gospel commitment — and better prepared to embody the person of Jesus Christ in the social progress that we his followers are called to make.

Introduction: Why Does Social Progress Need a New Face?

Peter J. Casarella

> *In Christ, charity in truth becomes the Face of his Person, a vocation for us to love our brothers and sisters in the truth of his plan. Indeed, he himself is the Truth.*[1]

Pope Benedict XVI's long-awaited economic encyclical *Caritas in Veritate (CV)* was greeted around the world with both critical acclaim and outright puzzlement. Some Catholic loyalists awaited a radically new vision of social order. Others found it highly unlikely that a learned Bavarian theologian could say anything new about global development in the immediate wake of an unexpected economic crisis. What emerged in the encyclical took everyone by surprise. The message of *Caritas in Veritate* is a critique of economic globalization that, at first glance, sounds much like progressive thought, allowing the generally progressive newspaper *The Chicago Tribune* to publish a side-by-side comparison of "Obamanomics" and "Popeanomics." But this intriguing comparison also left out quite a bit. Pope Benedict's undiminished enthusiasm for the renewal of evangelization, the end of abortion, and the *necessary* promotion of ethical entrepreneurialism receive equal attention in the new social encyclical. Liberals and conservatives can continue to pick out their choice topics, but both sets of readers were challenged by the shift of focus to funda-

---

1. Pope Benedict XVI, *Caritas in Veritate*, no. 1. Translation at http://www.vatican.va/holy_father/benedict_xvi/encyclicals/documents/hf_ben-xvi_enc_20090629_caritas-in-veritate_en.html.

mentals in both theology and principles for thinking about politics, society, and the economy. Anyone who wishes to encounter the new face of social progress touted by Pope Benedict has to learn to read the encyclical as a whole.

For this reason, the Center for World Catholicism and Intercultural Theology at DePaul University gathered scholars and distinguished Church leaders on April 20-21, 2010, and invited them to see beyond bifurcations that typically separate liberals from conservatives. These scholars eschewed the normal party lines to explore the deeper meaning of the encyclical. The papers presented at that conference are included in this volume. The presenters set an agenda to move beyond intellectual inquiry and social commitment, between the social gospel of North America and the cry for liberation of the South, and between confronting in love the person of Jesus Christ and calling in truth for a global assessment of economic structures.

Such a reorientation of thought and action begins with the encounter with the person of Jesus Christ. "In Christ," writes Pope Benedict at the very beginning of the encyclical, "charity in truth becomes the Face of his Person." The face of Christ *is* the new face of social progress. The subtle novelty of this move presents challenges for both social progressives of all stripes and Christians of diverse political persuasions. The simplicity of the message belies its stunning radicality. The pope is plumbing the depths of the Scriptures to discover a new idiom for thinking about reality. First and foremost, this hitherto unexplored "Johannine twist" in Catholic social teaching (see Horacio Vela's essay) is no marketing ploy. The pope is not advertising Jesus as a revamped promoter of a social gospel for the twenty-first century. He is actually reverting to the palpable presence of a divine person in our very midst.[2]

What can progressives learn from this encounter? Why should they believe that this time there really is a new face? How can this face be new, given that Christianity has, for more than a century, presented itself as a force for modern progress and has done so with such mixed results? Social progressives in our day are wary of the Christian category of charity. One common criticism is that Christian charity is inherently individualistic and otherworldly. In this view, a charitable deed performed on behalf of the poor actually blinds the proud

---

2. The theme of encountering Christ face to face is hardly limited to the encyclical. In *Jesus of Nazareth,* vol. 1, Pope Benedict XVI makes the search for the face of the Lord the common thread to how all people of good will might approach the Scriptures. For details, see my "Searching for the Face of the Lord in Ratzinger's Jesus of Nazareth," in *The Pope and Jesus of Nazareth,* ed. Adrian Pabst and Angus Paddison (London: SCM, 2009), pp. 83-93. On the historical development of this theme, there is no better source than Emery de Gaál, *The Theology of Pope Benedict XVI: The Christocentric Shift* (New York: Palgrave Macmillan, 2010).

Christian to the social structures of sin. Another concern is with the category of the poor itself. Those working side by side with the victims of global out-sourcing do not know "the poor"; they know particular women and men who have been treated unjustly by market forces beyond their control. The new face of social progress is also a renewed call to see the link between charity and justice. Quoting Pope Paul VI, Pope Benedict XVI writes: "the individual who is animated by true charity labors skillfully to discover the causes of misery, to find the means to combat it, to overcome it resolutely" (*CV*, no. 30).[3] Pope Benedict's reclaiming of justice is not window-dressing. In other words, the Catholic authority whose reputation is linked most closely to the critique of the theology of liberation actually shares with the theologians of liberation an in-terest in social justice inspired by Jesus' preaching and his lucid message that intelligence and love are not in separate compartments (*CV*, no. 30).

But the encyclical was not aimed solely at social progressives. It was writ-ten by a pope who wanted to place himself in a tradition of Catholic social thought that has animated Christians of many denominations. Here, the con-cern is quite different. Why should Christians care about the new face of social progress? Is their faith not one of learning to know the Lord on an individual basis? Is this new Christ of social progress going to dispense with the priority of a personal witness? The encyclical takes the encounter with the Lord of history as an indispensable condition for the witness of the Christian in soci-ety. No social agenda can circumvent that task. At the same time, Christians can also learn that the orientation to the person of Christ is not an individu-alistic affair. The encyclical contains concrete and novel directives regarding, for example, the ethics of the corporation and the practice of micro-financing that are corroborated by the message of salvation that Jesus preached. The writing of the encyclical was a patient interdisciplinary labor that wove to-gether theology, metaphysics, and the latest fruits of social scientific research. Reading the face of the Lord in the light of the wisdom collated therein will offer fresh inspiration to all those followers of the gospel who have become numbed by the hackneyed trivializations that pass for contemporary Christian social thought.

Accordingly, this volume brings together nineteen essays written from a variety of disciplines. On the whole, they highlight the Christological and Trinitarian underpinnings of *Caritas in Veritate*. But experts from the social sciences and from practical disciplines like finance and marketing have also contributed richly to the offerings.

---

3. Citing Pope Paul VI, *Populorum Progressio*, no. 75.

In part I, we consider historical context, use of Scripture, and the new areas of theological development in the encyclical. Archbishop Celestino Migliore is as of this writing the Apostolic Nuncio to Poland but wrote his overview of the encyclical in his capacity as the head of the Permanent Observer of the Holy See to the United Nations. As such, Archbishop Migliore was able to address cogently the fundamental question of why a Roman pontiff would even consider speaking about the global economy. Migliore's piece shows that new realities such as the emergence of a post–World War II and post–Cold War balance of powers in the United Nations and in the world require a fresh way of thinking about global order and social questions. The biblical scholar Horacio Vela then examines the novelty of Benedict's use of Scripture. Previous social encyclicals focused on the Synoptics; Benedict offers a novel reading of the Gospel of John in order, Vela opines, to offer a genuinely new and creatively Johannine prologue to Catholic social teaching itself. J. Brian Benestad's essay goes into much greater depth about how Benedict reads Paul VI's *Populorum Progressio*. Never before, Benestad argues, has a pope explored the social thought of a predecessor with the same detail. The results of this historical analysis are impressive. Benedict is extending the teaching of his two predecessors while still breaking new ground. Roberto Goizueta's piece also highlights the encounter with Christ as the guiding theme of the new encyclical. For Goizueta, Pope Benedict has introduced the very principle that the personal and ecclesial relationship with Christ *constitutes* Catholic social teaching. David L. Schindler links this Christocentrism to a new theological anthropology and thereby draws out the implications of this new starting point for a new understanding of the human person.

Part II demonstrates the novel thinking regarding the social order found in the encyclical. William T. Cavanaugh shows that the pope's thinking about politics and economics begins where both state and markets typically fail to provide comprehensive solutions. He focuses on the phrase "dispersed political authority" in the encyclical in order to show how the idea of subsidiarity is carried forward in the encyclical and allows for spaces that require creative new ways for the active participation of local communities in the social order. Julie Hanlon Rubio looks specifically at how the vision of the family in the encyclical is thought-provoking. She defends Benedict's prophetic contention that gratuity is to be the animating principle not only of family ethics but also of social ethics and describes what this might mean for ordinary Christians. The doctrine of love has mutually implicated consequences for individuals, for the family, and for society.

Patrick Callahan, Michael Budde, and Maryann Cusimano Love consider the hotly contested issue of what is meant by global governance in the encyclical. Did the pope actually intend to encourage a transnational entity to intervene in global affairs? Callahan considers the question in terms of the history of Catholic social teaching. Budde raises important questions about the ambiguity of the variant configurations of global order in *Caritas in Veritate* as well as in other encyclicals. Budde asks, "Is the encyclical as coherent as its defenders want to claim, or could Pope Benedict have drawn on an even deeper sense of ecclesial identity and solidarity in cogently addressing matters of global politics?" Cusimano Love then argues that what Benedict is trying to do is to expand our moral imaginations to make it easier to see how peace and justice can be brought into the world. This pragmatic task of moral reimagining needs to begin within the Church with its firm mandate to educate the faithful on social matters, but also extends to intermediate institutions of nongovernmental organizations (NGOs), diverse communities across the globe, transnational companies, presidents of nation-states, and the heads of other influential bodies such as agencies of the United Nations.

Part III examines the specific proposals regarding economic theory and practice in the encyclical. D. Stephen Long makes the link between Christology and economics. He argues that, for Pope Benedict, economics opens us to the metaphysical and theological order that antedates our existence, an existence founded on a generous act of *creatio ex nihilo* where God creates solely out of the Love and Truth that defines God's being. Accordingly, even this theory of relations grounded in a newly assimilated Christian vision of reality must be present whenever economic calculations are made. Paulo Fernando Carneiro de Andrade writes as a Brazilian theologian who has labored for many years on behalf of the preferential option for the poor that defines Latin American theology of liberation. Carneiro de Andrade shows that the issue of the malaise in our contemporary political, economic, and cultural situation — especially when seen from the perspective of the poor — is intimately bound to justice and the very future of humanity. Far from departing from this course, Pope Benedict in the new encyclical lends new weight to the arguments initiated decades ago by theologians from Latin America. Lorna Gold addresses the issue of an economy of communion highlighted by Pope Benedict in his encyclical. Rather than just one of several items on a laundry list, she shows the integral place of this well-tested economic initiative within the spirituality of communion of the Church and of the pope. Simona Beretta, an economist and consulting member of the Pontifical Council for Justice and Peace, situates the economic theory in the encyclical within the realm of contemporary economic thought. She shows that dualisms are never value-free in spite of the attempt by economists to hide their not-so-veiled preconceptions. Dualisms arise when efficiency is juxta-posed to justice, population growth to environment protection, and foreign aid to national policy space. The subtle and dangerous claim underlying each of these convictions consists in conceiving ethical issues as mere additions to the result of scientific inquiry and application, a technological form of reason that, from the vantage point of the supposedly neutral scientist, can also be repre-sented as wholly neutral. Michael Naughton examines economic dualism in terms of current thinking about the ethics of the corporation. Like Gold, he is able to demonstrate that there are companies that have incorporated what Pope Benedict calls "the logic of the gift" into their daily business. In that light, the application of this novel way of thinking about reality is hardly abstract. The-odore Tsukahara Jr. is an economist, an investment banker, and a professor in a great books program for undergraduates. As such, he brings the economic implications of the encyclical down to the very concrete level of pedagogy based on a rich set of experiences. What kind of new perspective can be brought into the classroom so that the communication of the wisdom in the encyclical is neither merely theoretical nor cold and technical? His insights provide much food for thought about how economic teachings can be brought to life in the classroom and beyond.

Part IV uncovers a hidden dimension in the thought of Pope Benedict. The noted journalist John Allen spoke during the DePaul conference on *Caritas in Veritate* about Benedict as a "Green Pope," and the contributions from Sister Damien Marie Savino and Keith Lemna explore that theme in the terms out-lined in the encyclical itself.[4] Drawing on the wisdom of Philip Sherrard, Lemna shows how the ecological thinking of the encyclical coheres with a broader theological cosmology. Employing this same point of departure, Savino focuses on the fundamental insights put forward in the encyclical on the ancient cos-mogonic and theological question of how humanity arises from dirt. She proves that the "Green Pope" brings science and wisdom together in exciting ways.

The epilogue to the volume was written by the much revered president of the Pontifical Council for Justice and Peace, a biblical scholar who taught and promoted social justice for many years in his native Ghana. Cardinal Peter Kodwo Appiah Turkson offers a synthetic overview. In the end, he argues, the central theme of loving in truth is not just directed at faithful Catholics. It represents a renewed vocation for all the disciples of Jesus Christ, and, by the same token, it is a way of loving the world by remaining faithfully at the heart

---

4. See, for example, John Allen, *The Future Church: How Ten Trends Are Revolutionizing the Catholic Church* (New York: Doubleday, 2009), pp. 298-337.

of the world's own rightful demand for progress and development for all peoples on the globe.

These essays are not intended to be the final word on *Caritas in Veritate* or even less to the urgent debates it has provoked. As Daniel K. Finn notes in his preface, we are faced today with the promise and threat of fragmented knowledge of global proportions. The rise of the social sciences in the modern era can hardly be ignored. In that light, there are important questions raised by the encyclical that need to be posed and answered. For example, what are the minimum conditions and what is the theoretical framework for achieving the common good in human society today?[5] How do we morally evaluate unjust contracts and what resources are available in the Anglo-American legal tradition for translating these ethical principles into law?[6] Does social capital play a structural role in creating and sustaining wealth?[7] Can the current dysfunctional state of the global economy be civilized and what would a "civil economy," as called for explicitly by *Caritas in Veritate,* look like globally and regionally?[8] What does the economic situation of women mean for the economic justice envisioned in the encyclical?[9] These questions exemplify the kind of additional work that is being done with the encyclical as its point of departure. They cannot be ignored. Only the revelation of a disincarnate Messiah would sanction the avoidance of critical social analyses.

The essays in this volume could aid in the healing process by allowing Jesus' face to emerge while recognizing at the same time the new scientific analyses of sinful social structures that are causing threats to humanity today.

5. See, for example, Albino Barrera, O.P., "What Does Catholic Social Thought Recommend for the Economy?: The Economic Common Good as a Path to True Prosperity," in *The True Wealth of Nations: Catholic Social Thought and Economic Life,* ed. Daniel K. Finn (Oxford: Oxford University Press, 2010), pp. 13-36.

6. See, for example, Daniel K. Finn, "The Unjust Contract: A Moral Evaluation," in *The True Wealth of Nations,* pp. 143-64, and Vincent D. Rougeau, "Just Contracts and Catholic Social Teaching: A Perspective from Anglo-American Law," in *The True Wealth of Nations,* pp. 117-41.

7. John A. Coleman, S.J., "Wealth Creation, Social Virtues, and Sociality: Social Capital's Role in Creating and Sustaining Wealth," in *The True Wealth of Nations,* pp. 199-225.

8. See, for example, Stefano Zamagni, "Catholic Social Thought, Civil Economy, and the Spirit of Capitalism," in *The True Wealth of Nations,* pp. 63-93, and Paulinus I. Odozor, C.S.Sp., "Truly Africa and Wealthy! What Africa Can Learn from Catholic Social Teaching about Sustainable Economic Prosperity," in *The True Wealth of Nations,* pp. 267-87.

9. Cf. Simona Beretta, "What Do We Know about the Economic Situation of Women, and What Does It Mean for a Just Economy?" in *The True Wealth of Nations,* pp. 227-65, and Maylin Biggadike, "An Ecofeminist Approach to the True Wealth Project," in *The True Wealth of Nations,* pp. 319-40.

The impetus of this volume is to retrace scientific reasoning about new social realities back to the person and message of Christ. The sense of "retracing" here is that of St. Bonaventure's *reductio,* a leading back to an original font of revealed wisdom that still requires in-depth critical scrutiny with complex social realities.[10] Pope Benedict XVI, writing not as pope but as a theologian, expressed his own sense of this retracing in commenting on the second beatitude of Matthew's Gospel: "Blessed are the poor in spirit" (Matt. 5:3):

> The Sermon on the Mount is not a social program per se, to be sure. But it is only when the great inspiration it gives us vitally influences our thought and our action, only when faith generates the strength of renunciation and responsibility for our neighbor and for the whole of society — only then can social justice grow, too. And the Church as a whole must never forget that she has to remain recognizably the community of God's poor.[11]

The witness of such a community living in the historical present becomes the place of the encounter — not just for Catholics but for anyone who is already on the path of seeking the face of the Lord.

So why does social progress need a new face? This question brings to light the urgency of the encyclical and its message. It is not only a question of revamping time-worn themes of Catholic social teaching. The encyclical deploys the professional expertise of leading social scientists regarding the global economic crisis that delayed its promulgation by several years. At the same time, it draws on wisdom as old as the gospel. Old and new are brought together into a novel synthesis. The results need to be tested by theologians and social policy experts, by believers and nonbelievers. The contributions to this volume show why the new face of social progress proclaimed by Pope Benedict is more than a new spin on an old theme. There are seeds of wisdom in the encyclical that envision a whole new approach to thinking about social questions, an approach that previous encyclicals have treated only in a piecemeal fashion. Herein lies the novelty and urgency of *Caritas in Veritate* for the Church and for the world.

Last but not least, the editor would like to thank Dr. James Hang Koon Lee as well as the Institute for Scholarship in the Liberal Arts at the University of Notre Dame and the Center for World Catholicism and Intercultural Theology at DePaul University for their generous support and assistance.

---

10. St. Bonaventure, *On the Reduction of the Arts to Theology,* ed. Zachary Hayes, O.F.M. (St. Bonaventure, N.Y.: St. Bonaventure University, 1996).

11. Pope Benedict XVI, *Jesus of Nazareth,* vol. 1, *From the Baptism in the Jordan to the Transfiguration* (New York: Doubleday, 2007), p. 77.

PART I: HISTORICAL AND THEOLOGICAL APPROACHES

Caritas in Veritate: A First Glance at the Encyclical

Archbishop Celestino Migliore

While many people are somewhat familiar with the jargon of the Catholic Church, I begin this essay with a few words on what an encyclical is and why this blunt title: *Caritas in Veritate (CV)*.

An encyclical, or circular letter, is an extended message from the pope addressed to all the bishops of the world and sometimes to all people of good will. Why this almost cryptic title, *Caritas in Veritate*? The title of an encyclical is usually taken from its *first few words*, its *incipit*. And usually those very first words contain or summarize the topic of the document. Charity and truth "is the principal driving force behind the authentic development of every person and of all humanity" (*CV*, no. 1).[1]

In this essay, before trying to answer questions like why a new encyclical and what is the new encyclical all about, I would like to deal with another basic question that arises quite often in our minds. Why does the pope, who is above all a religious and spiritual figure, venture into the minefield of economics, finance, trade, and technology? With this document, Pope Benedict writes to us not as a politician or an expert in finance and economy, but as a man of faith trying to read the signs of the times in light of God's wisdom. He does so not to give out recipes and solutions, but to shed light on different human situations and to help people make sense of and find hope and the necessary resilience to confront new situations and events. The fact that we share the same faith in Jesus Christ does not entitle us to speak of a "Catholic economy"

1. Translation at http://www.vatican.va/holy_father/benedict_xvi/encyclicals/documents/hf_ben-xvi_enc_20090629_caritas-in-veritate_en.html.

or a "Catholic finance system." The term "Catholic" is not an appropriate label to attach to any sector of human activity. We may speak of a Catholic perspective, a Catholic point of view, or Catholic tradition. In our current language, we do speak of a Catholic or Christian school, university, or hospital. But we know that they stand for schools, universities, or hospitals run by people who treasure their Christian values and try to implement them in teaching, education, or caring.

It is precisely against this background that Pope Benedict, in the context of a stringent and critical analysis of the contemporary society that has produced the worst economic crisis of recent times, introduces the categories of charity and truth, capable together of interpreting and reviving development, economics, labor, and the environment. Christianity or Catholicism represents a faith, faith in God who is Triune, that is, whose specificity is the bond of love who links God the Father with Jesus the Son and the Holy Spirit. Jesus came on earth and lived among us to show us and to allow us to share in the same culture of love that exists in the Trinity. But he never intended to set up either a political or a social system. He came to share his culture of love with as many women and men as possible so that they could change their hearts and minds, conform them to the values and ideals that he preached and lived, and be the salt and light of the world. In turn, they would be able to take the initiative, discerning and promoting in all human institutions what is good, and critiquing and changing what is destructive and harmful.

It helps to look back at history in order to understand the impact that Christian values have had on human history. Jesus Christ was born and Christianity emerged in the context of the Roman Empire. But around the year A.D. 500, this empire collapsed and left behind chaos, and a political and social vacuum. For centuries warlords fought among themselves throughout Europe and the Near East. During that time the Christian community tried to do one thing: to implement the commandment left by Jesus, "love one another as I have loved you." This simple principle was translated into what we call the seven corporal works of mercy: feed the hungry, give drink to the thirsty, clothe the naked, shelter the homeless, visit the sick, visit those in prison, bury the dead. So, soon after the collapse of the Roman Empire and its administration, and well before the creation of the modern state administration, the seven corporal works of mercy inspired Christian communities to organize hospitals, schools, universities, centers of agricultural education and formation, and humanitarian and social institutions for orphans, destitute people, girls, and women often neglected by society.

This specific commitment to and involvement in the works of mercy has provided the Church through the centuries with a unique perspective in dealing with social issues and also with a wealth of social thought and doctrine.

The Church shapes its social thought by carefully reflecting on the realities of human existence, in society and in the international order, in the light of faith and the Church's tradition. Its main aim is to interpret these realities, determining their conformity with or divergence from the lines of the gospel teaching on man and his vocation. Its aim is thus to guide Christian behavior.[2]

It is precisely in this light that Pope Benedict XVI issued his encyclical *Caritas in Veritate,* "charity in truth." It is inserted in the tradition of the social encyclicals initiated with *Rerum Novarum* (1891) of Leo XIII, and continues with, among others, *Quadragesimo Anno* (1931), *Pacem in Terris* (1963), *Octogesima Adveniens* (1971), the Vatican II document *Gaudium et Spes* (1965), and the encyclicals *Sollicitudo Rei Socialis* (1987) and *Centesimus Annus* (1991).

Why a new encyclical? As we know, the social doctrine of the Church has one dimension that perdures and one that changes with the times. This is the encounter of the gospel, which endures, with the ever-new problems that humanity must confront. They change and today do so at astonishing speed.

If we look backward in time and travel over again the years that separate us from *Centesimus Annus* we notice what great changes have entered into human society. First, take into account the clash of ideologies that dominated the political landscape prior to the fall of the Berlin Wall. After 1989, they occupied less and less attention. In their place we have seen greater and greater confidence in technology. The hopes attached to technology developed into an ideology that challenges notions of what it means to be a human being. It caught public attention with the specter of human cloning and it continues with nanotechnology. Already in 1967 Pope Paul VI warned against entrusting the entire process of development to technology alone because in that way it would lack direction. As technical capabilities advance, those who raise philosophical and theological questions are told not to stand in the way of progress since relativism does not admit of such concerns. *Caritas in Veritate* takes up this theme in chapter six on development of peoples and technology.

Second, consider the change effected by globalization. Every aspect of social life has been affected by it. Just try to imagine what would be different without the Internet. As such, the encyclical treats it not just as a single subject but as a theme throughout the entire discussion. One of the main thrusts of the encyclical rests on a concise but pregnant statement: "As society becomes

2. See Pope John Paul II, *Sollicitudo Rei Socialis* (Washington, D.C.: United States Conference of Catholic Bishops, 1988), no. 10.

ever more globalized, it makes us neighbours but does not make us brothers" (*CV*, no. 19).

Religion accounts for a third dimension. In the nineteenth century Karl Marx said that religion was the opium of the people, in the sense that it can easily be used to control the population, to divert their attention from the need to start a social revolution by simply promising a paradise in the next world. Today, on the contrary, religion is said to be the vitamin of the poor. It gives a precise identity, a sense of belonging, to those who otherwise can be left behind on the road to globalization.

The divisive influence of religion has long been recognized; its more helpful aspects have not. While modern morality, particularly as expressed through the doctrines of human rights and humanitarian intervention, is marked by the tendency to reject and dismiss religion from public discourse as an opium, an illusory happiness for the people, intercultural dialogue and interreligious dialogue are much talked about and pursued as indispensable tools and vitamins for the promotion of a culture of peace.

The encyclical of Pope Benedict explores a somewhat unusual aspect of religious liberty, that is, the inseparable and directly proportional relationship between respect for religious liberty and development.

A fourth development concerns the rise of several states from poverty. With new opportunities come new challenges, especially to the balance of power between countries and the role of international organizations. Energy and other aspects of development can enable corporations sometimes to exercise an influence previously enjoyed only by governments.

Today we often speak of a stagnation or even of a decline of multilateralism. Perhaps things are not so serious. The real problem is that multilateralism is in a period of transition. Until now the word connoted interaction between governments, which were the bodies to indicate priorities, conduct negotiations, reach consensus or majority, and make decisions and implement them in collaboration with nongovernmental organizations. Today, with the emergence of many other actors in national and international public life, multilateralism can no longer ignore these new players at any stage: debate, decision, or implementation. In United Nations environments we speak of "messy multilateralism." Pope Benedict maintains that "globalization certainly requires authority. . . . This authority, however, must be organized in a subsidiary and stratified way, if it is not to infringe upon freedom and if it is to yield effective results in practice," a principle that operates on a national level as well as on a global and international one (*CV*, no. 57).

The United Nations Security Council, one of the most authoritative forums in the context of international organizations, was composed in 1946 of five countries, four of which were victors in a world war. Today we have other countries that are considered equally victorious. They are called emerging powers, not because they won a devastating war, but because they have placed themselves firmly on the path that leads them back from poverty and under-development. As such, they expect to have their say.

These significant new trends, among others, happened in the years that separate us from the 1967 social encyclical and have changed profoundly the social dynamics of the world, sufficient on their own to prompt the writing of a new social encyclical.

Let us look at some specific points raised by Pope Benedict's encyclical. The first point is the idea that

> the world is in trouble because of the lack of thinking. . . . A new trajectory of thinking is needed in order to arrive at a better understanding of the implications of our being one family; interaction among the peoples of the world calls us to embark upon this new trajectory, so that integration can signify solidarity rather than marginalization. (*CV*, no. 53)

That the world is in trouble because of the lack of thinking is a remark taken from Pope Paul VI in his encyclical *Populorum Progressio* (1967). Actu-ally, *Caritas in Veritate* was initially conceived as a commemoration of the forty years of *Populorum Progressio*. But, then, the editing of *Caritas in Veritate* demanded more time also in view of the ongoing economic and financial crisis. There is an evident connection and continuity between the two pontif-ical documents, however, inasmuch as the former focused on the development of peoples and the latter on the integral development of the human person and society.

Pope Benedict points out that a new trajectory of thinking is needed today to defuse the seeds of crisis embedded in our current economic and social systems. In other words, to overcome our current financial and economic crises we need intellectual clarity and creativity. In the months following the publi-cation of the encyclical, he returned to this point with clear emphasis.

While the financial system seems to be regaining stability and increasing production in some sectors offers signs of economic recovery, still in many places the level of unemployment continues to worsen. In this context, in order to promote economic and social growth along with employment, it seems that the patterns of consumption should be focused on relational goods and ser-vices that promote greater connection between people. By investing in relational goods, such as medical care, education, culture, art, and sport — all things that develop a person and require unique human interaction rather than machine production — the state, through its public intervention, would be addressing development at its root, while also promoting employment and long-term development.

The second point the pope makes is the idea that there will not be a true humanism — and therefore a human economy — if it is not open to the Absolute (*CV,* no. 16). The various recent world crises that intertwined bring to the discussion presuppositions of thought and principles of individual, social, and international behavior, which extend well beyond the financial or economic field. The idea of producing resources and assets, that is, the economy, and strategically managing them, that is, politics, without also wanting the same actions to carry out the good, that is, ethics, has been proven to be a naïve or cynical and fatal delusion.

In this light, the two fundamental rights to life and religious liberty find in *Caritas in Veritate* a new approach. That is, without neglecting the moral aspect of these two rights, Pope Benedict links them directly and irreversibly to a correct policy of development. Consider the following two examples:

> Openness to life is at the centre of true development. When a society moves towards the denial or suppression of life, it ends up no longer finding the necessary motivation and energy to strive for man's true good. If personal and social sensitivity towards the acceptance of a new life is lost, then other forms of acceptance that are valuable for society also wither away. (*CV,* no. 28)

> When the State promotes, teaches, or actually imposes forms of practical atheism, it deprives its citizens of the moral and spiritual strength that is indispensable for attaining integral human development and it impedes them from moving forward with renewed dynamism as they strive to offer a more generous human response to divine love. (*CV,* no. 29)

This brings to mind another similar moment in recent history. At the very beginning of communism in the Soviet Union, the Church expressed its opposition on the ground that it was atheistic, that it excluded and opposed God. But this argument did not seem to be able to rally the masses. When the Church started criticizing communism for being against God because it trampled the basic private, social, and political rights of the image and likeness of God on earth — the human being — its points were well understood.

Benedict's third point is that "in order to defeat underdevelopment, action is required not only on improving exchange-based transactions and implanting public welfare structures, but above all on gradually increasing openness . . . to forms of economic activity marked by quotas of gratuitousness and communion" (*CV,* no. 39). In other words, we need to infuse solidarity and fraternity into economics.

Paragraph 19 of the encyclical sheds some light on this point. The pope writes:

> The causes of underdevelopment are not primarily of the material order. . . . [We need] to search for them in other dimensions of the human person: first of all, in the will, which often neglects the duties of solidarity; secondly in thinking, which does not always give proper direction to the will. . . . Underdevelopment has an even more important cause . . . it is 'the lack of brotherhood among individuals and peoples.' . . . As society becomes ever more globalized, it makes us neighbours but does not make us brothers. Reason, by itself, is capable of grasping the equality between men and of giving stability to their civic coexistence, but it cannot establish fraternity. This originates in a transcendent vocation from God the Father, who loved us first, teaching us through the Son what fraternal charity is. (*CV,* no. 19)

The media demonstrated itself to be interested above all in how the pope would assess the current capitalistic system. Newspapers wondered whether the new encyclical would condemn capitalism as such. The encyclical does not condemn capitalism as such; rather, it clarifies that confusion of thought that identifies the market economy with the capitalist market economy. Indeed, there are the capitalist markets — those tied to the logic of profit — and there are the civil markets, that is, economic systems that tend to include the social responsibility of businesses, cooperatives, associations of responsible consumers, and the nonprofit world along with the redistributive activity of the state.

The current crisis concerns a particular version of market economies — the capitalist version — but not the market economy as such. In other words, the social doctrine of the Church has never spoken against the market economy. Rather, it has spoken beyond it — in favor of the civil markets, more than the capitalist market. What we realize now very clearly is that after the crisis of the Soviet model the capitalist economic market has not kept its promises and is not able to deliver, to resolve a number of problems. What we are called to do now is to "civilize the market," that is, to make it so that once again inside the economic systems blow the winds of gratuity, of solidarity and subsidiarity, of reciprocity. But this change has to emerge from within the economic systems and not as an aside, that is to say, from Monday through Friday I follow the logic of profit and at the end of the week, in a metaphorical sense, I engage in philanthropy. This model, today, is in irreversible crisis.

From the encyclical emerges a positive vision that offers encouragement to humanity because it seeks to find the resources of truth and will to overcome difficulties. This is not a sentimental encouragement, given that in *Caritas in Veritate* all the principal problems of development in the various areas of the planet are enumerated with clarity and concern. This is rather a well-grounded encouragement, aware that in the world there are at work many protagonists and agents of truth and of love.

In the title *Caritas in Veritate* there appear two fundamental terms in the magisterium of Benedict XVI: charity and truth. These two terms marked his entire magisterium in the years of his pontificate in that they represent the very essence of Christian revelation. In connection with each other, these constitute the fundamental motive in the historical and public dimension of Christianity; they are at the origin, therefore, of the social doctrine of the Church.

Pope Benedict XVI's Use of Scripture in *Caritas in Veritate*

Horacio Vela

As is well known, modern Catholic social teaching began with Pope Leo XIII's 1891 encyclical *Rerum Novarum*. It is interesting to note that this same pope also influenced Catholic biblical studies through his encyclical *Providentissimus Deus*. Pope Leo certainly held deep reservations about the kind of biblical studies that emerged out of the Enlightenment. While he encouraged the study of the Bible in its original languages, he also privileged the Vulgate. Though he recognized that biblical authors sometimes spoke in the language and figures of speech of their day, he defended the inspiration of Scripture and denied that it contained any real errors. Leo XIII argued that Scripture and faith, when properly understood, were compatible with new scientific findings that seemed to contradict Scripture. While he demanded that priests and seminarians study the Bible and defend it, he also demanded that biblical scholars be thoroughly acquainted with the church fathers and systematic theology.

I mention these two encyclicals together, *Rerum Novarum* and *Providentissimus Deus,* because they represent two of Leo's important contributions to the Church. Much progress has been made in social teaching and biblical scholarship since then. Nearly every pope since Leo XIII has written a social encyclical. In addition to its sacramental worldview and emphasis on the incarnation, the Church's social teaching is often what appeals most to average Catholics. Yet many questions remain: issues regarding the role of justice, capitalism, and life ethics and politics are points of contention among Catholics. With respect to biblical studies, although some of Leo's successors took a more restrictive and punitive approach, Pope Pius XII's *Divino Afflante Spiritu* is credited with fully authorizing the use of historical criticism. Yet in recent years, some within the Church have expressed concern about the purpose and theological significance of historical criticism. Pope Leo XIII never envisioned the wide gulf that sometimes separates exegetes and theologians. While Scripture scholars often criticize theologians for a naïve use of Scripture, they themselves can be prone to a naïve understanding of the nature and task of theology. The discipline of biblical studies has become so specialized that the acquisition of the necessary historical and linguistic tools often precludes the study of other branches of theology.

Over the years as prefect of the Congregation of the Doctrine of Faith, and as pope, Benedict praised the work of internationally renowned Catholic biblical scholars such as Raymond Brown and John Meier. Yet, like Pope Leo XIII, he expressed concerns over a scientific, secular approach that mummifies Scripture and divorces Scripture study from the life and tradition of the Church. Pope Benedict expressed these concerns in *Jesus of Nazareth* and in his 1988 Erasmus lecture "Biblical Interpretation in Crisis."[1]

We should not be surprised then that Pope Benedict's own approach to Scripture places biblical interpretation squarely within the task of theology and the Catholic tradition. The Bible is not an archaeological relic; it is the living word of God, the soul of theology. Thus, the pope reads Scripture informed not only by Rudolf Bultmann and Raymond Brown; he also reads Scripture with a great cloud of witnesses from the early church, most notably Augustine.

In what follows, I comment briefly on the use of Scripture in *Caritas in Veritate (CV)*, focusing mostly on the introduction to the encyclical. The encyclical is marked by a thoroughly Johannine bent that distinguishes it from previous encyclicals. The relationship between this encyclical and its predecessors can be likened to the relationship between the Synoptic Gospels and the Gospel of John. The pope's theological moves in *Deus Caritas Est* and *Caritas in Veritate* form a kind of Johannine prologue for a new era in Catholic social teaching.

First, it will be helpful to review ever so briefly some of the major scriptural themes in previous social encyclicals. *Rerum Novarum* appeals strongly to natural law theory and human anthropology. "Every man has by nature the right to possess property as his own."[2] The human mind separates humanity

---

1. Published in *Biblical Interpretation in Crisis: The Ratzinger Conference on Bible and Church,* ed. Richard John Neuhaus (Grand Rapids: Eerdmans, 1989).

2. See Pope Leo XIII, *Rerum Novarum* (Boston: Pauline Books & Media, 1999), no. 6: "It

from other animal creatures and permits human beings to hold possessions for purposes other than the temporary procurement of nourishment or livelihood. Genesis 1 and 2 confirm this ideology. Human beings are the culmination of the creation accounts, and God has given authority to human beings to dominate the earth. In Genesis 2:15, Adam is given the task of tilling and keeping the garden. While these passages confirm that humankind has the inherent right to own property and to work, Genesis 3:17 does put a negative spin on it. "Cursed be the ground because of you! In toil shall you eat of its yield the days of your life."[3] Pope Leo XIII writes:

> In like manner, the other pains and hardships of life will have no end or cessation on earth; for the consequences of sin are bitter and hard to bear, and they must accompany man so long as life lasts. To suffer and to endure, therefore, is the lot of humanity; let them strive as they may, no strength and no artifice will ever succeed in banishing from human life the ills and troubles which beset it. If any there are who pretend differently — who hold out to a hard-pressed people the boon of freedom from pain and trouble, an undisturbed repose, and constant enjoyment — they delude the people and impose upon them, and their lying promises will only one day bring forth evils worse than the present. Nothing is more useful than to look upon the world as it really is, and at the same time to seek elsewhere, as we have said, for the solace to its troubles.[4]

This passage would seem to indicate that Leo was ambivalent about real social change. Christ's redemption is of a supernatural order; our lives were not designed for riches on earth. He cites 2 Timothy in *Rerum Novarum,* no. 21: "if we suffer with him we shall also reign with him." Yet this does not prevent him from criticizing the rich. He echoes the message of Jesus in Matthew 19:23-24 that it is difficult for the rich to enter the kingdom and also the Lukan woes against the rich in the Sermon on the Plain (Luke 6:24). Those who are wealthy beyond their needs are ordered to give from their abundance. Their generosity

---

is the mind, or reason, which is the predominant element in us who are human creatures; it is this which renders a human being human, and distinguishes him essentially from the brute. And on this very account — that man alone among the animal creation is endowed with reason — it must be within his right to possess things not merely for temporary and momentary use, as other living things do, but to have and to hold them in stable and permanent possession; he must have not only things that perish in the use, but those also which, though they have been reduced into use, continue for further use in after time."

3. Scriptural translations from the New American Bible.

4. Pope Leo XIII, *Rerum Novarum,* no. 18.

with the poor is a condition for salvation according to Matthew 25. Perhaps anticipating later views on the preferential option for the poor, he cites Jesus' occupation as a carpenter as evidence that work has an intrinsic value and that poverty is not cause for shame. Jesus declared the poor blessed in the Sermon on the Mount. Jesus himself was rich and became poor for our sake (2 Cor. 8:9). Leo does not expect the poor to remain poor always, however. They can rise above poverty. Charity, according to Leo, has been at the heart of the church's mission from its very beginnings, when church members held all in common and shared wealth (Acts 4:34).[5]

The encyclical *Quadragesimo Anno* comments on *Rerum Novarum* quite heavily. The main Scripture verses used are from Matthew, Luke, and Pauline writings. Thus, the preaching of Jesus and the apostles is utilized to advocate for the poor.

Mater et Magistra follows the same pattern, but it places a greater emphasis on the ecclesial dimension of social teaching. The Church itself is the pillar of truth, and it follows the example of Jesus, the way, the truth, and the life. Jesus was concerned primarily with our eternal salvation, but that did not mean he neglected the everyday concerns of the poor. Even Jesus' multiplication of the loaves, which temporarily fed the hungry, was a foreshadowing of the Last Supper and the gift of himself as spiritual bread from heaven in the Eucharist. The Church is called to emulate this twofold mission of care for both soul and body. *Pacem in Terris* emphasizes a natural law perspective and the implications of the image of God in each human being.

Paul VI's *Dignitatis Humanae* emphasizes the preaching and teaching of Jesus. *Populorum Progressio,* the encyclical praised by Pope Benedict XVI, does not appeal to Scripture that often. When Paul cites Scripture, he tends to focus on Matthew and Luke. According to Pope Paul, the Church is committed to preaching the gospel to the poor as Jesus' inaugural sermon in Luke 4 indicates. In Luke 7:22, it is one of the marks of Jesus' ministry (the blind regain their sight, the lame walk, lepers are cleansed, the deaf hear, the dead are raised, the poor have the good news proclaimed to them). The encyclical also alludes to the Matthean Sermon on the Mount, Matthew 16:26, "What profit would there be for one to gain the whole world and forfeit his own life?" and the parable of the sheep and the goats. The encyclical also draws briefly from the parable of the rich fool (Luke 12:20), and the parable of the rich man and Lazarus (Luke 16:19-31).

Moving forward to *Laborem Exercens,* Pope John Paul II's second social

5. Pope Leo XIII, *Rerum Novarum,* no. 28.

encyclical presents a sustained reflection on Genesis 1–3. The pope declares the book of Genesis to be the first "gospel of work."[6] God's own work in the act of creation of the world grants dignity to human work. Human beings, created in God's image, are thus able to imitate God. They have been commanded by God to engage in meaningful work and to rest on the Sabbath just as God did. God's creative work is ongoing, as Jesus declares in John:"My father is working still" (John 5:17). Additionally, God's creative power holds the cosmos together and brings humankind toward salvation (as indicated in Heb. 4:1; 9:10). Jesus himself was a man of work, a mere carpenter, who also spoke many parables that incorporated numerous images about work. Jesus' work continued in his suffering and death on the cross. Work is good, but all work has an element of suffering and toil on account of Adam's sin (Gen. 3:15). The pope urges modern Christians to unite their own work, toil, and suffering to the "work" and suffering of Jesus on the cross. While the pope sees toil and labor as a part of everyday life, this does not obviate the need for concrete social change. The poor can find dignity and transformation in the resurrection of Jesus. The fullness of the kingdom, however, is not realized in this world.

In this all too brief survey of the use of Scripture in previous social encyclicals, about which much more can be said, the emphasis is on the preaching and parables of Jesus and Genesis 1–3. It is not the case that John's Gospel never appears, but there does tend to be a preference for the Synoptic Jesus. It is clear that the encyclicals are not commentaries on Scripture, nor are they always supposed to negotiate between conflicting opinions in scholarship. The style is more homiletic, and popes, after all, read Scripture in light of previous encyclicals and in light of the broader history of interpretation of the Bible.

Now turning to *Caritas in Veritate* itself — there is a kind of Johannine twist to this encyclical. The most sustained reflection on Scripture occurs in the introduction, the prologue. Indeed, we may even call it a Johannine prologue. Nowhere else in the rest of the encyclical does the pope comment on Scripture so thoroughly. Scripture supports and punctuates the rest of the encyclical, but explicit Scripture citations are more sporadic. This should not surprise us. *Caritas in Veritate* is ultimately a commentary on *Populorum Progressio.* In his use of Scripture, the pope universalizes and recontextualizes certain features of Johannine and Pauline texts that were originally intended for particular communities. I think, however, that his Scripture citations are

6. Pope John Paul II, *Laborem Exercens*, no. 6. Translation at http://www.vatican.va/holy_father/john_paul_ii/encyclicals/documents/hf_jp-ii_enc_14091981_laborem-exercens_en.html.

fair within their given context and remain, more or less, faithful to the spirit of the text. First I comment on the use of Scripture in the introduction to the encyclical and then make a few observations about Scripture in the rest of the work.

The encyclical begins with these words: "Charity in truth, to which Jesus Christ bore witness by his earthly life and especially his death and resurrection, is the principal driving force behind the authentic development of every person and of all humanity" (*CV*, no. 1).[7] These important words form the theological, Christological core of the encyclical. In all of the New Testament, the words "love" and "truth" appear most frequently in the Johannine literature (at least in English translations). Charity in truth is the driving force for human development. Again, the pope gives a theological core to *Populorum Progressio*. Pope Paul VI noted the problem, but Benedict seems to have given a theological assessment.[8] Love, the pope says, drives each person to pursue justice and peace; by fidelity to God's calling, each person can find the truth and become free. The first explicit citation of Scripture is John 8:32, "you shall know the truth, and the truth shall set you free."

As most New Testament scholars might indicate, strictly speaking, the verse is taken out of its narrative context. In John 8, Jesus debates with several Jews who, according to John, seek to kill him because, they say, he has made himself God's Son. Jesus declares that those Jews who seek to kill him are slaves to sin and sons of Satan rather than sons of Abraham.[9] This is one of the more controversial texts in the Fourth Gospel. The setting is sectarian, the church's

---

7. Translation at http://www.vatican.va/holy_father/benedict_xvi/encyclicals/documents/hf_ben-xvi_enc_20090629_caritas-in-veritate_en.html.

8. *Populorum Progressio* begins with this paragraph: "The progressive development of peoples is an object of deep interest and concern to the Church. This is particularly true in the case of those peoples who are trying to escape the ravages of hunger, poverty, endemic disease and ignorance; of those who are seeking a larger share in the benefits of civilization and a more active improvement of their human qualities; of those who are consciously striving for fuller growth." Translation at http://www.vatican.va/holy_father/paul_vi/encyclicals/documents/hf_p-vi_enc_26031967_populorum_en.html.

9. John 8:42-47: "If God were your Father, you would love me, for I came from God and am here; I did not come on my own, but he sent me. Why do you not understand what I am saying? Because you cannot bear to hear my word. You belong to your father the devil and you willingly carry out your father's desires. He was a murderer from the beginning and does not stand in the truth, because there is no truth in him. When he tells a lie, he speaks in character, because he is a liar and the father of lies. But because I speak the truth to you, you do not believe me. Can any of you charge me with a sin? Whoever belongs to God hears the words of God; for this reason you do not listen, because you do not belong to God."

debate with and separation from Judaism in the post–Second Temple period, perhaps the early second century, when the figure of Jesus himself has replaced the Temple definitively for the Johannine church. Of course, depending on whom you read, there are nuances to that generalization. The pope has lifted a polemical statement from John 8 and universalized it. This is not without good reason. John 1:14, 14:6, and 18:37 all portray Jesus as truth itself or a witness to the truth. What Jesus said to several people in a debate is one of the central themes of John's Gospel. As the prologue and John 3:16 and following indicate, all those who reject the Son are already condemned. But those who acknowledge God's word and the truth to which Jesus testifies can become adopted by God and become free.

The pope goes on to say, "to defend the truth, to articulate it with humility and conviction, and to bear witness to it in life are therefore exacting and indispensable forms of charity. Charity, in fact, rejoices in the truth" (*CV*, no. 1). Thus, he alludes to and universalizes the hymn to love in 1 Corinthians 13. Many New Testament scholars are quick to point out that this hymn to love, often read at weddings, is not a definition of love as such, but rather a guide to the proper exercise of ministry. "If I speak in human and angelic tongues but do not have love, I am a resounding gong or a clashing symbol" (1 Cor. 13:1). This citation of Scripture might seem far-fetched, but Benedict links the idea of charity rejoicing with the truth to the overall vocation of everyday people. Concluding the first paragraph, the pope leaves us with a sort of icon of Christ. Our search for charity and truth, blemished by original sin, is sanctified and guided by the person of Jesus Christ. The pope writes, "He reveals to us in all its fullness the initiative of love and the plan for true life that God has prepared for us. In Christ, *charity in truth* becomes the Face of his Person, a vocation for us to love our brothers and sisters in the truth of his plan. Indeed, he himself is the Truth (cf. John 14:6)" (*CV*, no. 1). This "true life" prepared for us by God calls to mind the divine life and dwelling that the Father prepares for all believers (John 14:1). This further alludes to Philip's demand in John 14:8, "Lord, show us the Father," to which Jesus replies, "Whoever has seen me has seen the Father." The life, death, and resurrection of the incarnate word reveal the Father to all believers. The idea that the Son is the visible image of the Father was an especially important theme in the early church (although Augustine later revised that exegetical tradition in *De Trinitate,* interpreting the image of God as the entire Trinity rather than one figure). Already in one paragraph Benedict has set the core of the encyclical with themes that are thoroughly Johannine — love and truth. Before he ever begins to quote Jesus, he has grounded the encyclical in the incarnation and the paschal mystery.

Moving on to section 2, the pope quotes the Matthean Jesus who, in a response to a lawyer's question in Matthew 22:36, declares that the first and greatest commandment is to love God; the second is to love one's neighbor as oneself. Thus, charity, the love of God and neighbor, is the heart of the Church's social teaching. As some New Testament scholars might do, the pope does not discuss here the Lukan parallel. In Matthew, the question is which of the commandments is the greatest. In Luke 10:27, the question is "what must I do to inherit eternal life?" In Matthew, Jesus does not abrogate the law; in Luke (and especially the Acts of the Apostles), the law at times seems to pass away. The early Christian debate over the practice of the Jewish law is not at issue here. Rather, the pope simply recontextualizes the passage and applies it to current moral theology and social thought — love of God and neighbor becomes the core of the moral code as such.

Again referring to Johannine literature, the pope reminds us that God is love (1 John 4:8, 16). "Everything has its origin in God's love, everything is shaped by it, everything is directed toward it. Love is God's greatest gift to humanity, it is his promise and our hope" (*CV*, no. 2). The allusion to 1 John again lifts a scriptural passage from its historical context. Whereas John's Gospel deals primarily with the situation between church and synagogue, 1 John deals head on with a fractured, disintegrating Johannine church. Christology, community praxis, and charity are at the heart of 1 John. The epistle's reflection on love is meant to strengthen and to reunite a splintered group. "The way we came to know love was that he laid down his life for us; so we ought to lay down our lives for our brothers. If someone who has worldly means sees a brother in need and refuses him compassion, how can the love of God remain in him? Children, let us love not in word or speech but in deed and truth" (1 John 3:16-18). The pope applies the exhortations from a broken community to the broader context of a world broken by the lack of charity. These themes were developed more fully in *Deus Caritas Est*.

The pope then moves on to his principal concerns over charity and truth and maps out the rest of the encyclical. "Only in truth does charity shine forth" (*CV*, no. 3). The ghost of relativism haunts this encyclical. Without truth, charity can descend into emotionalism and relativism. Love without truth can lead to false forms of charity — euthanasia for the suffering, reproductive services for impoverished countries (when the problems are much deeper than population control), love of self that neglects the other. Or, charity might be completely dismissed from public discourse as a mere religious concept incapable of solving society's problems. On the contrary, the pope insists that charity in truth can lead to genuine dialogue among peoples. Love, insofar as it is a gift given and received, can help to heal the obsession with self-centeredness, power, and greed that has produced the global economic crisis. Charity in truth precedes and is the basis of all efforts for justice and peace. Charity is not mere almsgiving; it is not an afterthought. Perhaps one could say that the pope argues, "if you want justice, work for charity."

This leads to us to the title and maxim of the encyclical: charity in truth. It is drawn from the Epistle to the Ephesians. The concept itself can be found in the Johannine epistles, as in 1 John 3:18, "Children, let us love not in word or speech but in truth and action." Also, 3 John 1:1, the incipit: "The presbyter to Gaius whom I love in truth." The pope cites here explicitly Ephesians. Although Paul probably did not write the letter (and the textual tradition indicates it was probably not addressed to the Ephesians), the pope makes an interesting use of Ephesians 4:15. Chapter 4 (seemingly combining elements of 1 Corinthians 12 and Romans 12) uses body of Christ imagery to exhort its audience to live together in unity and to exercise ministry properly. In 4:15 the author declares, "Rather, living the truth in love, we should grow in every way into him who is the head, Christ, from whom the whole body, joined and held together by every supporting ligament, with the proper functioning of each part, brings the body's growth and builds itself in love." The author invokes the principle of "veritas in caritate." The pope offers a complementary principle, "caritas in veritate." This is not simply a clever spin on Ephesians 4. Love must be grounded in truth, and truth must be grounded in charity. It is intrinsically linked to the spiritual development of the church. Ephesians 4 commands ministers to "build up the body of Christ" until all "attain to the unity of faith and knowledge of the Son of God, to mature manhood, to the extent of the full stature of Christ, so that we may no longer be infants, tossed by waves and swept along by every wind of teaching arising from human trickery, from their cunning in the interests of deceitful scheming" (Eph. 4:12-14). The pope has chosen Ephesians 4:15 precisely because the broader context of the passage echoes his own fears about relativism and "new doctrines" that do not conform to the Catholic faith. The pope thus duplicates the rhetoric of the passage, written perhaps to help claim and define Paul's legacy in a transitional period in early Christianity. Ephesians speaks of the development only of the church itself. Yet the pope applies this language to the spiritual and earthly development of all peoples on earth, both Christian and non-Christian. While this development is clearly rooted in Christ, he does not seem to argue that evangelization or conversion is a precondition for the exercise of charity. All human beings can be transformed by Christ's love. Again, the pope has universalized an image and metaphor from a text that refers specifically to a Christian community. It is the grounding principle of the "development of peoples" and the hermeneutic for his rereading of *Populorum Progressio*.

Much more can be said about the rest of the encyclical's use of Scripture. I have focused on the introduction, which grounds and sets the agenda. In general, I think we can see a shift in thinking. Charity is not mere almsgiving; it is not an afterthought. It is the center of Catholic social teaching and the basis of justice in the world. It is specifically Christ's own charity that is at the heart, not a mere secular humanism or global ethic.

It is well known that the church fathers regarded the Fourth Gospel as the more spiritual Gospel. Yet, they also recognized that the Johannine chronology was longer and that it filled in the gaps of the Synoptic account. The differences between the Synoptics and John, at least according to Origen, were intended to reveal spiritual truths, the most important of which was the divinity of Jesus. Mark begins with Jesus' baptism and preaching. Luke and Matthew begin with a birth narrative. John begins with creation itself. For instance, in John, the cleansing of the Temple, an event that one could probably not have committed and lived much longer to tell about (unlike Jesus, who goes on for three years of ministry), occurs at the beginning, not the end, of Jesus' ministry, thereby establishing Jesus as the Temple, the dwelling place of God. There is no trans-figuration in John, for the entire Gospel is a transfiguration. A case in point is the nature of the Last Supper. In the Synoptics, the Last Supper is a Passover meal. In John it is not; Jesus dies on the feast of preparation when the lambs are slaughtered. Jesus is the Lamb of God in John. In the Synoptics, Jesus' preaching takes center stage. His identity is hidden in Mark, and in Mark, Matthew, and Luke he speaks in parables. In John, there is no doubt who this Jesus is. His identity is not hidden. He does not speak in cryptic parables but speaks about himself, his relationship with God, and his relationship with his followers quite openly. Bultmann famously characterized the Johannine Jesus as a revealer without a revelation. The revelation is himself, of course, as Ray-mond Brown has suggested.

It is tempting to posit extreme differences between *Caritas in Veritate* and previous social encyclicals. However much *Caritas in Veritate* coheres with the previous tradition, it is noticeably different. Whereas previous encyclicals point to the eschatological preaching of Jesus, *Caritas in Veritate* takes a step back and points to the very figure of Jesus himself. Previous encyclicals made heavy use of Genesis 1–3 to speak of human beings as God's image and of the dignity of work, perhaps also appealing to natural law theory on the side. *Caritas in Veritate* points to creation and zooms in on the Logos, the ultimate divine principle behind creation and the natural law (hinted at by God's creative *speech* in Genesis 1). Thus, the pope focuses on the Logos and the charity inherent in the incarnation, seen most visibly when the word (made flesh) was nailed to the cross. While Mark associates Jesus' messiahship in some way with his baptism, and Matthew and Luke trace his messianic identity to his birth, John goes straight to the beginning: "In the beginning was the word" (John 1:1). Like John himself, Benedict focuses on the Logos. In reframing and re-centering Catholic social teaching on the Logos, the pope follows a very old Johannine move, and sets the stage for further social teaching and theology in this new century.

Reading Paul VI's *Populorum Progressio* through Benedict XVI's *Caritas in Veritate*

J. Brian Benestad

This essay explains how Pope Benedict XVI interpreted and used Pope Paul VI's *Populorum Progressio* (1967, *PP*) in his *Caritas in Veritate* (2009, *CV*). No pope in the twentieth century ever spent so much time explaining a social encyclical written by a predecessor. Pope Benedict refers to nearly every major point made by Pope Paul VI; he also uses *Populorum Progressio* as a springboard to build on his predecessor's thought. Pope Benedict expresses no explicit or implicit disagreement with anything that he draws from *Populorum Progressio*. Pope Benedict's *Caritas in Veritate* also makes observations and presents teachings not found in *Populorum Progressio*. The parameters of this essay only allow me to highlight selected aspects of all this material.[1]

Hardly any English-speaking reader, I contend, could have fully understood Pope Paul VI's *Populorum Progressio* before the publication of *Caritas in Veritate*. The first reason is that the English translation published by the United States Catholic Conference in 1967 contains a number of significant errors. The translation currently on the Vatican website is better, but on occasion is still misleading. Pope Benedict's citations from *Populorum Progressio* in English translation accurately reflect the meaning of the authoritative Latin text. Second, Pope Benedict XVI explains Paul VI's profound vision of development in a clear and compelling way, thereby revealing "the principal reason why that encyclical is still timely in our day."[2] It presents a perspective on

---

1. For my reflections on the whole of *Caritas in Veritate*, see Brian Benestad, "Pope Benedict XVI's *Caritas in veritate*," *Josephinum Journal of Theology* 16, no. 2 (2009): 411-28.

2. Pope Benedict XVI, *Caritas in Veritate*, no. 16. Unless otherwise noted, the translation

development that is countercultural, not at all on today's radar screen, but "valid for today and for all time" (*CV*, no. 18).[3] Pope Benedict is so impressed with the teaching of *Populorum Progressio* that he calls it "the *Rerum Novarum* of the present age" (*CV*, no. 8).

Introduction to Catholic Social Teaching

Before presenting *Populorum Progressio,* Pope Benedict XVI provides an illuminating description of Catholic social teaching. "Charity is at the heart of the Church's social doctrine. Indeed, all the responsibilities and all the duties spelled out by that doctrine are derived from charity" (*CV*, no. 2, modified translation).[4] This is not a new thought for Pope Benedict XVI. In 1986 the Congregation for the Doctrine of the Faith issued the *Instruction on Christian Freedom and Liberation* under the signature of its prefect, Cardinal Joseph Ratzinger. The *Instruction* says that Catholic social teaching had to emerge from the practice of the Christian faith. "The Church's social teaching is born of the encounter of the Gospel message and of its demands (summarized in the supreme commandment of love of God and neighbor in justice) with the problems emanating from the life of society."[5] Catholic social teaching helps people to know what love and justice require in the various circumstances of life, knowledge that would escape many without instruction. In his book on the morals of the Catholic Church, St. Augustine had underscored the difficulty of carrying out the commandment to love's one's neighbor: "From this commandment, arise the duties pertaining to human society, about which it is difficult not to err."[6] In other words, it is easy for human beings to love one another badly both in personal encounters and in devising proposals for the common good of society.

---

follows the Vatican website, http://www.vatican.va/holy_father/benedict_xvi/encyclicals/documents/hf_ben-xvi_enc_20090629_caritas-in-veritate_en.html.

3. Pope Benedict XVI actually explains the vision of development in *Populorum Progressio* more clearly and more compellingly than Paul VI.

4. "Caritas praecipua est Ecclesiae socialis doctrinae semita. Omnis quidem responsabilitas offciumque, quae ex hac doctrina oriuntur, ex caritate depromuntur."

5. Congregation for the Doctrine of the Faith, "Instruction on Certain Aspects of the 'Theology of Liberation' *(Libertatis Conscientia)*," no. 72. Translation found at the Vatican website, http://www.vatican.va/roman_curia/congregations/cfaith/documents/rc_con_cfaith_doc_19860322_freedom-liberation_en.html.

6. St. Augustine, *The Catholic and Manichaean Ways of Life (De Moribus Ecclesiae Catholicae et de Moribus Manichaeorum)* (Washington, D.C.: Catholic University of America Press, 1966), p. 40, no. 49.

Pope Benedict's new encyclical, dated June 29, 2009, builds on the earlier Congregation for the Doctrine of the Faith's *Instruction* by emphasizing that love has to be guided by truth. "*Only in truth does charity shine forth,* only in truth can charity be authentically lived. Truth is the light that gives meaning and value to charity" (*CV,* no. 3). In short, "*Caritas in veritate*' is the principle around which the Church's social doctrine turns" (*CV,* no. 6). Both faith and reason discern the truth by which charity takes its bearings.

Pope Benedict next makes an argument dear to the heart of St. Augustine: "practicing charity in truth helps people to understand that adhering to Christian doctrine[7] is not merely useful but essential for building a good society and for true integral development" (*CV,* no. 4). Augustine thought that the knowledge given to us by divine revelation cannot be fully grasped unless it is also loved. The love of Christian truth, of course, grows when it is put into practice.

Christians practicing charity in truth "make themselves instruments of grace, so as to pour forth God's charity and to weave networks of charity" (*CV,* no. 5). Examples of these networks would be the institutions of Catholic charities, Catholic schools, and Catholic hospitals. The establishment of various institutions is necessary to allow Catholics to love their neighbors more effectively on the macro-level.

In another seeming response to the Marxist objection that the Christian emphasis on charity causes Christians to neglect justice, Pope Benedict says, "If we love others with charity, then first of all we are just towards them. . . . Justice is inseparable from charity and intrinsic to it" (*CV,* no. 6). Charity upholds all that is required by justice, such as the respect for rights and the fulfillment of duties, but demands more. Pope Benedict specifically refers to "relationships of gratuitousness, mercy and communion," about which he has much more to say in chapter three (*CV,* no. 6). Suffice it to say for now that the pope expects these three qualities to be characteristic of citizens as they go about their work, interact with their neighbors, do volunteer work, and participate in the political process.

Practicing charity in truth also requires a commitment to the common good. To clarify what he means, Pope Benedict first explains the relationship of love to the good: "to love someone is to desire that person's good and to take effective steps to secure it" (*CV,* no. 7). Steps that people could take depend on their talents and their opportunities. Effective steps could refer to those initiatives directed toward establishing the common good, namely, "the sum total

---

7. Translation modified; "doctrinae christianae adhaesio" is mistranslated as "adhering to the values of Christianity."

of the conditions of social life which allow people, either as groups or individuals, to reach their own perfection more fully and more easily."[8] Without these conditions individuals would not be able to achieve the good for themselves. For example, without jobs, hospitals, and schools, people will not be able to take care of their health, their families, and the education of their minds. Every Christian is called to make feasible contributions to the common good "in a manner corresponding to his vocation and according to the degree of influence he wields in the pólis" (*CV,* no. 7). Think of what teachers, doctors, nurses, lawyers, senators, and presidents can do to promote the common good.

Another way to understand Pope Benedict's reflections on the common good is to think about what must happen in society so that persons will have the opportunity to perfect their dignity. Every element of society should promote respect for human dignity and its perfection. As Vatican II specifically says, "it devolves on humanity to establish a political, social, and economic order which will to an even better extent serve man and help individuals as well as groups to affirm and perfect the dignity proper to them" ("ad dignitatem sibi propriam affirmandam et excolendam").[9] This means that the family, mediating institutions, the law, and the Church all have a role to play in helping individuals perfect their dignity. For example, the education a mother and a father give to their children will help them recognize and achieve their dignity. Schools, primary mediating institutions, to a greater or lesser extent, form the character of students so that they might be inclined to act in accordance with their dignity. The law encourages people not to act beneath their dignity by driving while drunk or acting in a discriminatory manner toward racial minorities. In *Centesimus Annus* Pope John Paul II says that the Church contributes to the enrichment of human dignity when she "proclaims God's salvation to man, when she offers and communicates the life of God through the sacraments, when she gives direction to human life through the commandments of love of God and neighbor."[10] These examples show that a correct conception

8. *Catechism of the Catholic Church,* no. 1906: "summam eorum vitae socialis condicionum quae tum coetibus, tum singulis membris permittunt ut propriam perfectionem plenius atque expeditius consequantur." English translation available on the Vatican website, http://www.vatican.va/archive/ENG0015/_INDEX.HTM. See also Pope John XXIII, *Mater et Magistra,* no. 65; Pope John XXIII, *Pacem in Terris,* no. 58; Vatican II, *Gaudium et Spes,* nos. 26, 74; and Pope Paul VI, *Dignitatis Humanae,* no. 6.

9. Vatican II, *Gaudium et Spes,* no. 9, my translation and emphasis.

10. Pope John Paul II, *Centesimus Annus,* no. 55. Translation at http://www.vatican.va/holy_father/john_paul_ii/encyclicals/documents/hf_jp-ii_enc_01051991_centesimus-annus_en.html.

of the human person provides guidance to all educators and to all legislators, and also enables all people to recognize that they must strive to perfect their dignity in order to be good persons and, even, good democratic citizens.

The Introduction of *Caritas in Veritate* on *Populorum Progressio*

After his brief description of Catholic social teaching, Pope Benedict presents Paul VI's main point in *Populorum Progressio:* "life in Christ is the first and principal factor in development" (*CV,* no. 8).[11] Union with Christ is the culmination of all that goes into the work for development, that is to say, the perfection of the human person. Echoing Paul VI, Pope Benedict describes this "development of the whole man and of all men" (*PP,* no. 42) as *"integral human development"* (*CV,* no. 8). Otherwise stated, development properly understood seeks the complete good of everyone in the world, from health, housing, and a job to good family life, education, and life in Christ. This work to achieve better living conditions for all and the union of every person with Christ will require the dedication of many hearts and minds, that is to say, "the ardor of charity and the wisdom of love" (*CV,* no. 8).[12] In other words, charity will have to be *"illumined by the light of reason and faith"* (*CV,* no. 9). Without such illumination, how could development at the highest level be understood as life in Christ?

Anticipating a possible objection to papal teaching on development as a breach of the separation between church and state, Pope Benedict says the Church is not in the business of proposing "technical solutions" to the problems of development and is not asserting a right "to interfere in any way in the politics of states" (*CV,* no. 9, quoting *PP,* no. 13).[13] While only individuals, churches, missionaries (lay, religious, and clerical), and nongovernmental or-

---

11. See Pope Paul VI, *Populorum Progressio,* no. 16. "United with the life-giving Christ, man's life is newly enhanced; it acquires a transcendent humanism which surpasses its nature and bestows new fullness of life. This is the highest goal of human self-fulfillment." Translation at http://www.vatican.va/holy_father/paul_vi/encyclicals/documents/hf_p-vi_enc_26031967_populorum_en.html. Note that Pope Benedict's reformulation of Paul VI's point is simpler, clearer, and even more compelling.

12. See Pope Paul VI, *Populorum Progressio,* no. 82.

13. The United States Conference of Catholic Bishops edition of *Populorum Progressio* has "The Church [is] completely independent of every political party." See Pope Paul VI, *Populorum Progressio* (Washington, D.C.: United States Conference of Catholic Bishops, 1967). The Latin text confirms the correctness of the English translation in *Caritas in Veritate.*

ganizations (NGOs)could take their bearings by the goal of life in Christ, states could respond favorably to the popes' argument that progress should be measured by movement "from less human conditions to those which are more human" (*CV*, no. 8, quoting *PP*, no. 20), and remain open and supportive in various ways of the work of NGOs to bring Christ to people in the developing nations.

Chapter One: "The Message of *Populorum Progressio*"

Chapter one of *Caritas in Veritate*, entitled "The Message of *Populorum Progressio*," is entirely devoted to reflecting on the implications of saying that "life in Christ is the first and principal factor of development" (*CV*, no. 8). Inspired by Vatican II's vision of the Church serving the world by truth and love, Pope Paul VI, according to Pope Benedict, makes two important points in his 1967 encyclical on development. First, when the Church is faithful to her threefold mission of proclaiming the word, celebrating the sacraments, and performing works of charity,[14] she is also *"engaged in promoting integral human development"* and is thus serving the world in the best way possible (*CV*, no. 11). In other words, the Church helps people develop a life in Christ by teaching the truth, communicating God's love in the sacraments, and living that love in her works of mercy. Second, *"authentic human development concerns the whole of the person in every single dimension"* (*CV*, no. 11).[15] In other words, it must include the material, intellectual, and spiritual needs of the person.

While there is no specific reference to the Church's threefold mission in *Populorum Progressio*, there is mention of the Church doing the work of Christ, exhorting the faithful to love their neighbors, proclaiming the gospel of Christ, and doing works of charity.[16] And while there is no specific mention of the Church celebrating the sacraments in *Populorum Progressio*, there is the clear implication that the Church promotes development by being faithful to its complete mission. Pope Paul VI explicitly emphasizes the relation between evangelization and the sacraments in his 1975 apostolic exhortation *Evangelii Nuntiandi (EN)*, where he says: "The role of evangelization is precisely to educate people in the faith in such a way as to lead each individual Christian to

14. See Pope Benedict XVI, *Deus Caritas Est*, nos. 19-25, for his reflections on these three activities that constitute the life of the Church.

15. See Pope Paul VI, *Populorum Progressio*, no. 14.

16. See Pope Paul VI, *Populorum Progressio*, nos. 3, 12, 13, and 82.

live the sacraments as true sacraments of faith" (*EN*, no. 47).[17] Since many Catholics do not readily see that the Church's fulfillment of her threefold mission promotes the achievement of development — and other initiatives recommended by Catholic social teaching — Pope Benedict appropriately and wisely brings out this point.

To those who would argue that getting the right structures and institutions in place would solve the development problem, Pope Benedict says that "institutions by themselves are not enough, because integral human development is primarily a vocation and therefore involves a free assumption of responsibility in solidarity on the part of everyone" (*CV*, no. 11). In other words, virtuous and competent individuals must both direct and man the institutions and work outside them with a sense of their "vocation" to promote their own development and that of others. While Paul VI does not touch on this issue in *Populorum Progressio*, he does address it pointedly in his *Evangelii Nuntiandi*:

> The Church considers it to be undoubtedly important to build up structures which are more human, more just, more respectful of the rights of the person and less oppressive and less enslaving, but she is conscious that the best structures and the most idealized systems soon become inhuman if the inhuman inclinations of the human heart are not made wholesome, if those who live in these structures or who rule them do not undergo a conversion of heart and of outlook. (*EN*, no. 36)

As Pope Benedict XVI points out, Paul VI certainly recognized the importance of having the right institutions and structures in place, but nevertheless "proposed Christian charity as the principal force at the service of development" (*CV*, no. 13).[18]

In his May 2007 "Meeting and Celebration of Vespers with the Bishops of Brazil," Benedict XVI takes up the question of the relation of the Catholic faith as a whole to the work for justice. He says, "Wherever God and his will are unknown, wherever faith in Jesus Christ and in his sacramental presence is lacking, the essential element for the solution of pressing social, political problems is also missing."[19] Catholics, he added, must have a thorough knowledge of their faith, as presented in the *Catechism of the Catholic Church* and its

---

17. Translation from the Vatican website, http://www.vatican.va/holy_father/paul_vi/apost_exhortations/documents/hf_p-vi_exh_19751208_evangelii-nuntiandi_en.html.

18. See Pope Paul VI, *Populorum Progressio*, nos. 67 and 82.

19. Pope Benedict XVI, "Meeting and Celebration of Vespers with the Bishops of Brazil," May 11, 2007, no. 2. Translation from the Vatican website, http://www.vatican.va/holy_father/

abbreviated *Compendium*. They must also receive an "education in Christian personal and social virtues"[20] as well as an education in social responsibility. One example of this kind of education is the formation of "a genuine spirit of truthfulness and honesty among the political and commercial classes."[21] In short, the work for justice requires that the minds and the hearts of Catholics must be educated and formed to know and practice the whole faith.

Anticipating a likely objection to his emphasis, Benedict asks, how can one justify "the priority of faith in Christ and of 'life' in him" when there are so many pressing political, economic, and social problems in Latin America? He answers that both Marxism and capitalism promised that just structures, as the indispensable condition for promoting justice in society, could be established and maintained without "individual morality," that is, without individuals formed by the virtues. Benedict XVI implies that people now see that both political and economic systems failed to live up to their promises. In fact, he argues, just structures depend on a moral consensus in the body politic, and on lives lived by citizens in accordance with the virtues. He further holds that the necessary moral consensus cannot develop where God is not acknowledged. A great effort is constantly needed in order to maintain belief in God. "In other words, the presence of God, friendship with the Incarnate Son of God, the light of his word: these are always fundamental conditions for the presence of justice and love in our societies."[22] This, of course, is the teaching of St. Augustine and St. Thomas Aquinas, as well as that of the social encyclicals from Pope Leo XIII until Pope John Paul II.

Benedict XVI next refers to *"the strong links between life ethics and social ethics"* (*CV*, no. 15) in Paul VI's *Humanae Vitae* (1968). Benedict directs his readers' attention to the split that has occurred today between life ethics and social ethics, of which social justice is the main component. In many Catholic and secular circles, social justice is understood to be more or less the program of the political left, including, of course, the right to abortion and same-sex unions, embryonic stem cell research, and the like. The split between life ethics and social ethics is, of course, the primary reason for the divide between pro-

---

benedict_xvi/speeches/2007/may/documents/hf_ben-xvi_spe_20070511_bishops-brazil_en .html.

20. Pope Benedict XVI, "Meeting and Celebration of Vespers with the Bishops of Brazil," no. 4.

21. Pope Benedict XVI, "Meeting and Celebration of Vespers with the Bishops of Brazil," no. 7.

22. Pope Benedict XVI, "Address at the Inaugural Session of the Fifth General Conference of the Bishops of Latin America and the Caribbean," May 13, 2007, no. 4.

life and social justice Catholics. Even when the latter do not support the right to abortion, they are likely to justify their inattention to this evil in the name of the so-called consistent ethic of life.

What does this "consistent ethic of life" entail? Generally, it is a term used in social justice circles to describe the position that those who object to the taking of life at one stage or in one form must object to the taking of life at all stages or in all forms. Practically speaking, this means that those who oppose abortion should in practice oppose capital punishment and most wars. It is also generally understood to mean that Catholics should promote a respect-life attitude by supporting government spending on what are called the "social justice" issues, and embrace a host of progressive priorities. This is a position articulated by the late Cardinal Bernardin, the former archbishop of Chicago, who argued in his much discussed Fordham address of December 6, 1983, that a consistent ethic of life not only opposes abortion but also endorses policies designed to increase a people's well-being, that is, their quality of life. Cardinal Bernardin argued, "A quality of life posture translates into specific political and economic positions on tax policy, employment generation, welfare policy, nutrition and feeding programs and health care."[23]

Anyone who is consistently pro-life and on the side of justice should favor the kind of governmental policy that will help everyone, especially the poor. Reasonable Catholics, nevertheless, might disagree as to which policies will do the most good. Cardinal Bernardin interprets "the consistent ethic of life" to mean both opposition to clear evils about which there is no dispute in Catholic circles and the endorsement of specific positions on such matters as tax policy, about which there will inevitably and legitimately be disagreement among Catholics. His approach implicitly places debatable policy positions on the same level as Catholic doctrine on faith and morals. Under the influence of this paradigm, Catholics are able to tolerate the endorsement of abortion, embryonic stem cell research, and same-sex marriage by political candidates as long as they have the right positions on enough of the so-called social justice issues.

To show the absurdity of celebrating justice while tolerating or defending the legal right to abortion, the pope quotes from Pope John Paul II's *Evangelium Vitae*, no. 101: "a society lacks solid foundations, when, on the one hand, it asserts values such as the dignity of the person, justice and peace, but then radically acts to the contrary by allowing or tolerating a variety of ways in

---

23. Cardinal Joseph Bernardin, "Call for a Consistent Ethic of Life," *Origins* 13, no. 29 (1983): 493.

which human life is devalued and violated, especially when it is weak or marginalized" (*CV,* no. 15).[24] Otherwise stated, how can people speak passionately of social justice and the dignity of the human person without embarrassment, when they have no problem either with *Roe v. Wade* — which allows for the killing of unborn children for the whole nine months of pregnancy — or the recently passed health care law, which provides for the use of federal tax dollars to pay for abortions?

The defense of life ethics by John Paul II and Benedict XVI does not in the least imply any neglect or downplaying of social justice. Benedict cites two passages in Paul VI's *Evangelii Nuntiandi* in order to show the connection between evangelization and social justice.[25] In his own summary of Paul VI's point, Benedict writes, "*Testimony to Christ's charity, through works of justice, peace and development, is part and parcel of evangelization,* because Jesus Christ, who loves us, is concerned with the whole person" (*CV,* no. 15). This means that the effort to understand and to implement Catholic social teaching is part and parcel of living one's faith.

Besides the temptation to give short shrift to life ethics, social justice advocates face another challenge, according to Paul VI. This is the temptation to reduce the content of the faith to social justice alone. "We must not ignore the fact that many, even generous Christians . . . would reduce [the mission of the Church] to a man-centered goal; the salvation of which she is the messenger would be reduced to material well-being. Her activity, forgetful of all spiritual and religious preoccupation, would become initiatives of the political or social order, but if this were so, the Church would lose her fundamental meaning" (*EN,* no. 32).

This is a caveat with which Pope Benedict wholeheartedly agrees, but chose not to mention at this point in the encyclical. I cite it so that Pope Benedict's connection between evangelization and development cannot be misunderstood. Still today, many people, including Christians, are inclined "to reduce [the Church's] mission to the dimensions of a simply temporal project" (*EN,* no. 32). In other words, a narrow view of social justice is embraced, which has little or no connection to the Church's mission to be an instrument of salvation for all.

Pope Benedict XVI does discuss the elevation of social justice *über alles* in his *Jesus of Nazareth.* The modern form of Jesus' third temptation, Bene-

24. Translation from the Vatican website, http://www.vatican.va/holy_father/john_paul _ii/encyclicals/documents/hf_jp-ii_enc_25031995_evangelium-vitae_en.html.

25. See Pope Paul VI, *Evangelii Nuntiandi,* nos. 29, 31.

dict XVI argues, is "the interpretation of Christianity as a recipe for progress and the proclamation of universal prosperity as the real goal of all religions, including Christianity." God disappears! "Faith and religion are now directed toward political goals. Only the organization of the world counts. Religion matters only insofar as it can serve that objective."[26] Pope Paul VI was prescient to notice this destructive tendency back in 1975. At the time he even warned the Jesuits to be on guard against succumbing to this beguiling temptation.

In his well-known address at Santa Clara University in the fall of 2000, Father Hans Peter Kolvenbach, the father general of the Society of Jesus at the time, first explains that the Thirty-second General Congregation of the Society of Jesus (henceforth GC 32), held in 1975, declared that "the overriding purpose of the Society of Jesus, namely 'the service of faith,' must also include 'the promotion of justice.'"[27] The latter is to guide every single Jesuit and every Jesuit work, not just Jesuits working in the so-called social apostolate. The Jesuit father general can claim that work for justice is a "new direction" for the Society because he believes GC 32 is endorsing a new understanding of justice, one focused predominantly on changes in the political and social order. Father Kolvenbach explains that the word "promotion" has the "connotation of a well-planned strategy to make the world just." Because St. Ignatius wanted love expressed in words and deeds, "fostering the virtue of justice in people was not enough," says Kolvenbach. "Only a substantive justice can bring about the kinds of structural and attitudinal changes that are needed to uproot those sinful oppressive injustices that are a scandal against humanity and God." While "substantive justice" is not a term used in the Catholic philosophical or theological tradition, Father Kolvenbach seems to mean that view of social justice prevalent in many Catholic circles that reduces it to a set of political and social conditions brought about by law and public opinion.

Father Kolvenbach's reference to needed "attitudinal changes," on the other hand, seems to imply some kind of interior transformation in the souls of individuals. Since Father Kolvenbach acknowledges that attitudinal changes are indispensable in the struggle against injustice, he is implicitly directing his readers' attention to the virtues. Christian virtues are all about transforming hearts and inclining people to do the right thing, including work for good public policy.

26. Pope Benedict XVI, *Jesus of Nazareth*, vol. 1 (New York: Doubleday, 2007), pp. 42-43, 54-55.

27. The address may be found at http://www.loyola.edu/Justice/commitment/kolvenbach .html.

In reading about the newness of the Jesuit promotion of justice, I could not help but think of the many Jesuits who labored to instill the virtue of justice in the lives of an untold number of individuals since the time of Ignatius. I also thought of the Jesuit educational institutions that did an admirable job explaining the nature of justice and the common good to their students, with beneficial consequences for the life of society. Surely, many Jesuit alumni have made the world more just because of their Jesuit education. Obviously, Father Kolvenbach knows better than I the great work done by Jesuits to promote faith and justice since the Society's founding. The promotion of justice advocated by Father Kolvenbach and GC 32, therefore, can only be reasonably described as a "new direction" in a limited sense, insofar as the Society of Jesus is directed to focus on making the world more just through the promotion of structural changes in the political and social order.

The Vatican response to GC 32's decree 4 on faith and justice seemed to understand it to be breaking new ground, but was critical in two important respects. Writing on behalf of Pope Paul VI, J. Cardinal Villot, the secretary of state, said, "the promotion of justice was unquestionably connected with evangelization,"[28] but then quoted from a papal address to the 1974 Synod of Bishops in order to show that decree 4 did not make all the proper connections. The key passage quoted by Villot reads, "Human development and social progress in the temporal order should not be extolled in such exaggerated terms as to obscure the essential significance which the Church attributes to evangelization and the proclamation of the full Gospel."[29] Cardinal Villot then added, "This applies to the Society of Jesus in a special way, founded as it was for a particularly spiritual and supernatural end. Every other undertaking should be subordinated to this end and carried out in a way appropriate for an Institute which is religious, not secular, and priestly."[30]

The second criticism of the decree at least implied that distinctions between the roles of the clergy and the laity in the promotion of justice were not sufficiently clarified. "Moreover, we must not forget that the priest should inspire lay Catholics, since in the promotion of justice theirs is the more demanding role. The tasks proper to each should not be confused."[31] Pope Paul VI and Cardinal Villot undoubtedly understood that the promotion of

28. Letter of the cardinal secretary of state to the father general, Pedro Arrupe, S.J., May 2, 1975, in *Documents of the 31st and 32nd General Congregations of the Society of Jesus* (St. Louis: The Institute of Jesuit Sources, 1977), p. 547.

29. Letter of the cardinal secretary of state to the father general, p. 547.

30. Letter of the cardinal secretary of state to the father general, p. 548.

31. Letter of the cardinal secretary of state to the father general, p. 548.

justice recommended by GC 32 would necessarily involve the Jesuits and their institutions in the kind of lobbying for social reform that would be more properly and efficiently carried out by the laity. In other words, Paul VI was asking the Society of Jesus to think more carefully about the way it was planning to promote justice. Not that Paul VI had anything against making the world more just through good law and public policy! This is especially the role of the laity, not that of religious orders, whose work for the salvation of souls provides the indispensable foundation for the promotion of justice. On the basis of these two criticisms I would have to conclude that Pope Paul VI thought that GC 32 was attempting to give the Society of Jesus a new direction without an adequate compass.

After contemplating the deviations from the proper understanding of social justice described by Benedict XVI and Paul VI, we are ready to explore their thought on work for *"development as a vocation"* (*CV,* no. 16). The former quotes the latter as saying, "in the design of God, every man is called upon to develop and fulfill himself, for every life is a vocation" (*CV,* no. 16, quoting *PP,* no. 15).[32] A more literal translation of the Latin would read, "in God's plan every man is born to promote his own development, for the life of every man is destined by God for some vocation" *(aliquod munus).* To call work for development a vocation is to say that all human beings have received a call from God. Prior to the publication of *Caritas in Veritate* hardly any reader of an English translation of *Populorum Progressio* could have understood that work for one's own development and that of others is a vocation. The two available English versions of *Populorum Progressio* translate the Latin words *aliquod munus* as "some task" or "some function," both expressions a far cry from "vocation." The Italian, French, Spanish, and Portuguese translations of *munus* all have "vocation."

Pope Benedict notes that Paul VI spoke of vocation at one other point in his encyclical when he was describing humanism: "There is no true humanism but that which is open to the Absolute, and is conscious of a vocation [*munus*] which gives life its true meaning" (*CV,* no. 16, quoting *PP,* no. 42).[33] True humanism teaches us to pursue development for ourselves and others as a God-given vocation with life in Christ and union with one another in Christ as our ultimate goal. Pope Benedict comments, "This vision of development is at the heart of *Populorum Progressio* [and] is also the reason why that encyclical is

32. The Latin text is as follows: "Ex divino consilio, quilibet homo ad sui ipsius profectum promovendum natus est, cum cuiusvis hominis vita ad munus aliquod a Deo destinetur." *Munus* is translated as "vocation" in this context.

33. Again, the English translations of *munus* do not have "vocation," but "duty" (United States Conference of Catholic Bishops edition) and "task" (Vatican website).

still timely in our day" (*CV*, no. 16). It should now be obvious that hardly any readers of *Populorum Progressio* in English translation could have arrived at Pope Benedict's interpretation of Paul VI's encyclical.

If the pursuit of development is a vocation, then there has to be "a free and responsible answer" to the call (*CV*, no. 17). Individuals and peoples must freely decide to pursue their own integral human development and freely respond to a request for help from others who ask for assistance in acquiring the basic necessities of life, in addition to life in Christ. Pope Benedict adds that "no structure can guarantee this development apart from and beyond human responsibility" (*CV*, no. 17, modified translation). As noted previously, Benedict XVI and Paul VI do not think that any structure or institution, however well conceived, can take the place of individual virtue.

Benedict XVI logically adds, "Besides requiring freedom *integral human development as a vocation also demands respect for its truth.* The vocation to progress drives us to 'do more, know more and have more in order to be more'" (*CV*, no. 18 quoting *PP*, no. 6).[34] In other words, development should be more about being a certain kind of person than having health and sufficient possessions, although such goods are necessary for integral development. To be more ultimately requires that all achieve life in Christ. That is the truth that the two popes are explaining and defending. "The truth of development consists in its completeness: if it does not involve the whole man and every man, it is not true development. This is the central message of *Populorum Progressio,* valid for today and for all time" (*CV*, no. 18).

Living the quest for development as a vocation not only requires freedom and truth, but also charity. Without this virtue underdevelopment cannot be overcome. To explain this point more at length Pope Benedict directs attention to Paul VI's thoughts about the three reasons the work for development fails in the world. The will "often neglects the duties of solidarity"; the mind "does not always give proper direction to the will"; and more important than deficient thinking, "brotherhood" or solidarity "among individuals and peoples" does not develop. These reasons direct attention to the underlying theme of the encyclical *Caritas in Veritate.* The mind needs to attain the truth in order to love correctly, and the will needs the determination and fire to carry out what the mind correctly perceives.

---

34. The English translations of *Populorum Progressio* do not have "in order to be more" but "to enhance their value" (United States Conference of Catholic Bishops) and "so that they might increase their personal worth" (Vatican website). The Latin is "ut ideo pluris valeant." The French, Spanish, and Italian translations all have "to be more."

Deficient thinking would, of course, include counsel to rely exclusively on structures and institutions to promote development, the failure to see the importance of charity and truth, the rejection of technology altogether, not seeing the link between social ethics and life ethics, not realizing that openness to new life is required by development, and the inability to grasp that integral development includes "being more" or life in Christ for every single person in the world. The two popes both imply that the virtue of charity would strongly incline people to overcome weakness of the will, deficient thinking, and the lack of brotherhood or solidarity. Later in the text, Pope Benedict quotes Paul VI's explicit statement on the power and indispensability of charity: "Deeds without knowledge are blind, and knowledge without love is sterile. Indeed, 'the individual who is animated by true charity labors skillfully to discover the causes of misery, to find the means to combat it, to overcome it resolutely'" (*CV*, no. 30, quoting *PP*, no. 75).

In several places in *Populorum Progressio* Pope Paul VI makes an urgent call for reform to overcome the injustices of underdevelopment. Pope Benedict comments: "This *urgency is also a consequence of charity in truth*. It is Christ's charity that drives us on: '*caritas Christi urget nos* (2 Cor 5:14)'" (*CV*, no. 20).

Chapters Two through Six of *Caritas in Veritate* on *Populorum Progressio*

Chapter one, "The Message of *Populorum Progressio*," does not at all exhaust Pope Benedict's reflection on Paul VI's encyclical. Benedict refers to *Populorum Progressio* twenty-six times in chapters two through six, and then twice in the conclusion. In chapter two, "Human Development in our Time," Pope Benedict refers to Paul VI's mention of the "scandal of glaring inequalities" (*CV*, no. 22, quoting *PP*, no. 9). Paul VI was referring to the disparities in the ownership of material goods and in the exercise of power. In his comment, Pope Benedict refers to the contrast between the consumerist, wasteful super-development in some rich countries existing side by side with "dehumanizing deprivation." Another sign of the glaring inequalities is the shortage of food in various parts of the world (*CV*, no. 27, and *PP*, no. 47). Both popes refer to Lazarus being deprived of a place at the table of the rich man (see Luke 16:19-31). Paul VI notes that the quest for super-development is sought as the highest good and is the result of avarice, which causes "stultified moral development" (*PP*, no. 19). Pope Benedict takes up this theme, pointing out that the developed nations sometimes corrupt poor countries by inducing them to accept a "reductive vision of the person and his destiny" (*CV*, no. 29). That reductive vision leaves no place for God and focuses only on the material side of development. Deprived of a relation with God, persons do not have the understanding or the spiritual energy to pursue integral human development; instead, they are led to accept moral underdevelopment.

Pope Benedict embraces Paul VI's view that underdevelopment is partly caused by a "lack of wisdom and reflection, a lack of thinking capable of formulating a synthesis, for which a 'clear vision of all economic, social, cultural and spiritual aspects' is required" (*CV*, no. 31, quoting *PP*, no. 13, and referring to *PP*, nos. 40 and 85). Both popes insist that development work has to be guided by the proper "doctrine" and fueled by charity. In Benedict's words, "Deeds without knowledge are blind and knowledge without love is sterile" (*CV*, no. 30). Otherwise stated, people in underdeveloped nations need a vision of integral human development, which necessarily includes life in Christ and freedom from every kind of physical, material, and intellectual deprivation.

One might wonder what Pope Paul VI thinks about the role of government in addressing the problems of development just mentioned. Pope Benedict says *Populorum Progressio* assigned a central, albeit not exclusive, role to "public authorities" (*CV*, no. 24, quoting *PP*, nos. 23 and 33). Paul VI argues that the public authorities, in consultation with individuals and social groups, should intervene in some fashion when rights are exercised in such a way as to be in conflict with "basic community needs" (*PP*, no. 23). Later in *Populorum Progressio* Paul VI says the public authorities should not only support and stimulate individuals and intermediary agencies in their work for the common good, but also make up in various ways for their deficiencies. Whatever kind of leadership steps the governing authorities take, "they must also see to it that private initiative and intermediary organizations are involved in this work. In this way they will avoid total collectivization and the dangers of a planned economy which might threaten human liberty and obstruct the exercise of man's basic human rights" (*PP*, no. 33). These caveats, and others expressed in *Octogesima Adveniens* (1971),[35] regarding the exercise of governmental power show that Paul VI did not succumb to the statist temptation. He never wavered in his support for protecting the freedom of individuals and groups acting in the area of civil society.

Chapter three, "Fraternity, Economic Development and Civil Society," directs our attention to Paul VI's point that an economic system, guided by justice, would contribute to the development of poor countries and thereby

---

35. See Pope Paul VI, *Octogesima Adveniens*, nos. 26, 28, and 31.

benefit the rich countries. In other words, the economy is not a zero-sum affair. The prosperity of poor countries contributes to the further well-being of developed lands. A model market economy, then, would benefit all participants. If everyone in the economy benefits, "all will be able to give and receive, without one group making progress at the expense of the other" (*CV*, no. 39 quoting *PP*, no. 44). Persons perfect their dignity by both receiving and giving. To deny the poor the opportunity to contribute to the common good is demeaning to them. Both popes note that the economy of poor countries can be damaged when individuals, pursuing their own interests, transfer capital to other countries without regard for any detrimental effects on their own native lands (*CV*, no. 40, and *PP*, no. 24).

Pope Benedict also directs attention to Paul VI's thought that "business activity has a human significance, prior to its professional one" (*CV*, no. 41, and *PP*, no. 25). What Paul VI seems to mean is that workers have the opportunity to be creative, and to display courage, generosity, and fidelity to duty in the accomplishment of their tasks. The practice of these virtues is more important than the product they produce.

Chapter four, "The Development of People — Rights and Duties — the Environment," refers to *Populorum Progressio* seven times and actually begins with a line from it indicating that we have duties because we are social and political animals: "The reality of human solidarity, which is a benefit for us, also imposes duties" (*CV*, no. 43, quoting *PP*, no. 17, modified translation). Pope Benedict's commentary on this line develops Paul VI's thought in a remarkable way, which would be applauded by his predecessor. It begins with the countercultural affirmation that unless duties take precedence over rights, the latter can get out of control and become *"mere license"* (*CV*, no. 43). That is to say, some people in affluent countries, not guided by duties, now feel justified in defending a "'right to excess,' and even to transgression and vice" (*CV*, no. 43). When duties are the primary moral counter, they set limits to rights and ensure more respect for the basic and genuine rights of individuals and peoples. If enough people are guided by their duties, they will be moved to do something about "the lack of food, drinkable water, basic instruction and elementary health care in areas of the underdeveloped world and on the outskirts of large metropolitan centers" (*CV*, no. 43). Otherwise stated, when duties are primary in people's lives, the "elementary and basic rights" of everyone in the world have the best chance of being respected. The poor themselves, argues Pope Benedict, want help from the actors in the international community so that they are able to be "'artisans of their own destiny,' that is, to take up duties on their own" (*CV*, no. 43, quoting *PP*, no. 65). One of their primary duties is "to work for their own development. But they will not bring this about in isolation" (*CV,* no. 47, quoting *PP,* no. 77). Both popes observe that the young in the developing countries "ask to assume their active part in the construction of a better world" (*CV,* no. 49, quoting *PP,* no. 65).

Unfortunately, the priority of duties over rights is not widely accepted in liberal democracies and has not even been a prominent theme in Catholic social teaching, though it has been mentioned several times, most notably in Vatican II's *Gaudium et Spes (GS)* and in Pope John XXIII's *Pacem in Terris (PT).* Vatican II did place rights in a context where they could be integrated into the pre-modern virtue tradition where duties have priority over rights. *Gaudium et Spes* says:

> Therefore, by virtue of the gospel committed to her, the Church proclaims the rights of man. She acknowledges and greatly esteems the dynamic movements of today by which these rights are everywhere fostered. Yet these movements must be penetrated by the spirit of the gospel and protected against any kind of false autonomy. For we are tempted to think that our personal rights are fully insured only when we are exempt from every requirement of divine law. But in this way the dignity of the human person is by no means saved; on the contrary, it is lost. (*GS,* no. 41)[36]

This approach would put rights in the kind of framework — teleological, to be exact — that would enable Catholics to integrate rights doctrines with traditional teachings on duties and virtues. This passage clearly reveals the Church's awareness that people are tempted to invoke rights as a way to justify an autonomy independent of objective moral norms. This false autonomy would include the kind promoted by relativism and historicism.

In *Pacem in Terris* Pope John XXIII insists on grounding human rights in the natural law and keeping them linked to duties.

> For every fundamental human right draws its indestructible moral force from the natural law, which in granting it imposes a corresponding obligation. Those, therefore, who claim their own rights, yet altogether forget or neglect to carry out their respective duties, are people who build with one hand and destroy with the other. (*PT,* no. 30)[37]

---

36. Translation from the Vatican website, http://www.vatican.va/archive/hist_councils/ii_vatican_council/documents/vat-ii_cons_19651207_gaudium-et-spes_en.html.

37. Translation from the Vatican website, http://www.vatican.va/holy_father/john_xxiii/encyclicals/documents/hf_j-xxiii_enc_11041963_pacem_en.html.

By teaching that the foundation of human rights is natural law and that a person's duties remain in the age of rights, John XXIII reveals that his understanding of rights differs from that of Hobbes and Locke. Until these teachings of Vatican II and of Pope John XXIII find their way into local catechisms, Sunday homilies, and subsequent Church documents, most Catholics will most likely not understand their full import.

Another great theme in chapter four, building on *Populorum Progressio,* is that of the family's openness to life and population growth: *"Morally responsible openness to life represents a rich social and economic resource"* (*CV,* no. 44). Paul VI defends the right of the state to intervene in the area of population growth as long as it respects the moral law and the right of husband and wife to make their own decisions on how many children they will bring into the world. Because of the changed circumstances in the world, especially the population decline in Europe, Pope Benedict is compelled to go beyond Paul VI's defense of the family, with which he, of course, agrees. Pope Benedict says that families, which bring children into the world, are an economic resource since many countries need more workers and a larger "brain pool." The quantity and quality of the workforce is crucial for the prosperity of a country and the support of social welfare systems. Without sufficient workers, for example, there will not be enough money to support pensions and health care for retirees.

The last point in chapter four drawn from *Populorum Progressio* is "that the economy, in all its branches, constitutes a sector of human activity" (*CV,* no. 45, and *PP,* no. 14). What Pope Benedict means by calling the economy a human activity is that the whole economy, not just discrete sectors, should be governed by ethical norms.

Chapter five, "The Cooperation of the Human Family," contains only two references to *Populorum Progressio,* one on our tendency not to think carefully and the other on the importance of never abandoning the wisdom in our culture as a way of promoting development. Pope Paul VI concluded his encyclical arguing that thoughtful study and greater love on the part of individuals could lead to "a way of life marked by true brotherhood" in their country (*PP,* no. 85). In response to this observation Pope Benedict invited his readers to think philosophically about the category of relation in the lives of human beings. In so doing, individuals could discover, as Pope Paul VI hoped, that "the human creature is defined through interpersonal relations. The more authentically he or she lives these relations, the more his or her personal identity matures. It is not by isolation that man establishes his worth, but by placing himself in relation with others and with God" (*CV,* no. 53). In other words, the better one's relation with others and God, the more one's personal identity flourishes. This means the more individuals and peoples promote the development of their neighbors at home and abroad and form bonds with them, the more they perfect their own dignity. Pope Benedict comments, "the unity of the human family does not submerge the identities of individuals and cultures, but makes them more transparent to each other and links them more closely in their legitimate diversity" (*CV*, no. 53).

Pope Paul VI's other point is that individuals in developing nations should not sell their souls for the sake of development (see *PP*, nos. 10 and 41). They must hold on to the good things in their culture while taking advantage of modern technology. In reflecting on this point Pope Benedict invites technologically advanced societies to rediscover the traditions of wisdom and virtue that helped them to become more prosperous and urges the developing nations never to let go of what is good and true in their own cultures. Then, he calls everyone's attention to the existence of the natural law, the universal morality that can be grasped and lived by people in diverse cultures, thereby building bridges among the nations of the world.

Chapter six of *Caritas in Veritate*, "The Development of Peoples and Technology," has only two references to *Populorum Progressio*. The first is Paul VI's quotation of *Gaudium et Spes* on the worship of God: "The human spirit, 'increasingly free of its bondage to creatures, can be more easily drawn to the worship and contemplation of the Creator'" (*CV*, no. 69, quoting *PP*, no. 41, which is quoting *GS*, no. 57). Paul VI also mentions that having too many things can also be an obstacle to worship. Pope Benedict comments on the technology that lifts people out of poverty and disease. His basic point is that we should do an ethical evaluation of everything that technology makes possible. "Moving beyond the fascination that technology exerts, we must reappropriate the true meaning of freedom, which is not an intoxication with total autonomy, but a response to the call of being, beginning with our own personal being" (*CV*, no. 70).

The second point drawn by Pope Benedict from *Populorum Progressio* is that the social question is worldwide (*CV*, no. 75, and *PP*, no. 3), but has now become "a *radically anthropological question*" (*CV*, no. 75). Because of the technological advances that have made possible eugenic programming through in vitro fertilization and research on embryos, and that may soon allow the manufacturing of clones and human-animal hybrids, people's consciences are in danger of no longer being able to "distinguish what is human" (*CV*, no. 75). The worldwide practice of abortion and the growing pro-euthanasia mindset indicate that people have failed to grasp the meaning of human dignity. Because of the ignorance and confusion about the meaning of life and human dignity, Pope Benedict infers that the rich countries may not be able to see that justice and charity require them to respond to the pleas for help from the poor of the world. The pope is implying that the inadequate appreciation of human life and human dignity in the developed world blinds people to the plight of the poor living in degrading situations.

The "Conclusion" is a reflection on Paul VI's point that the practice of Christian humanism is the "greatest service to development" because it "enkindles charity and takes its lead from truth, accepting both as a gift from God" (*CV*, no. 78). This means that we cannot possibly succeed at bringing about the integral development of individuals and peoples unless we have a relationship with God, in which we are receptive to his gifts. Christian humanism only develops as a result of people's relation to God. "Openness to God makes us open towards our brothers and sisters and towards an understanding of life as a joyful task to be accomplished in a spirit of solidarity" (*CV*, no. 78). When you genuinely worship God, you want to love your neighbors so as to do good for them. Genuine love wants to take its bearings by truth. Being aware of God's immense love gives us patient endurance in our work for justice and development. "God gives us the strength to fight and suffer for love of the common good, because he is our All, our greatest hope" (*CV*, no. 78).

Conclusion: Going Beyond *Populorum Progressio*

It is truly remarkable how much Pope Benedict drew from *Populorum Progressio* and used it as a springboard for related thoughts. He shows that Paul VI was as prescient and wise in his elaboration of Catholic social teaching as he was in the encyclical *Humanae Vitae* (1968). In my judgment, it will take some time for Catholics to absorb the implications of all that Pope Paul VI and Pope Benedict XVI taught in *Populorum Progressio* and *Caritas in Veritate* on Catholic social teaching.

By way of conclusion, I briefly mention a few of Pope Benedict's points that go beyond the purview of Pope Paul VI's *PP.* In chapter two, Pope Benedict says that we have "to cultivate a public conscience that considers *food and access to water as universal rights of all human beings, without distinction or discrimination*" (*CV*, no. 27; emphasis added). The public conscience should also include openness to life because the "acceptance of life strengthens moral fiber and makes people capable of mutual help" (*CV*, no. 28). Without this openness a society will not generate "the motivation and energy" to attend to the needs of the poor. In addition, the public conscience needs to embrace religious freedom because *"God is the guarantor of man's true development"* (*CV*, no. 29).

In my mind, chapter three is remarkable because of Pope Benedict's thoughts on the effects of original sin and the desirability of "gratuitousness" in the economic realm. The pope first quotes the *Catechism of the Catholic Church,* no. 407: "Ignorance of the fact that man has a wounded nature inclined to evil gives rise to serious errors in the areas of education, politics, social action and morals" (*CV*, no. 34). Then, he mentions two errors that people are making today: thinking that evil can be eliminated by human effort alone and that "the economy must be shielded from 'influences' of a moral character" (*CV*, no. 34). The consequence of these errors has been the establishment of political, social, and economic systems that have been unable to deliver justice because they "trample upon personal and social freedom" (*CV*, no. 34). This failure, in turn, leads to a loss of hope, which is indispensable in the work for the high goal of integral development. "Hope encourages reason and gives it the strength to direct the will" (*CV*, no. 34). Recall Benedict's previous comment that a deficient will is one of the causes of underdevelopment in the world. Without hope, charity, which is a virtue of the will, cannot effectively sustain a commitment to achieve integral development.

Pope Benedict's emphasis on the necessity of practicing "gratuitousness" in civil society has left commentators on the encyclical wondering what this means in practice. We know that what is gratuitous is bestowed freely, not in response to any claim or merit. The pope tells us that "the human being is made for gift." Then, he adds that the *"principle of gratuitousness"* is "an expression of fraternity" (*CV*, no. 34). Gratuitousness connotes friendship, solidarity, and charity; it "fosters and disseminates solidarity and responsibility for justice and the common good among the different economic players" (*CV*, no. 38). Invoking gratuitousness, then, is just another way of saying that human beings cannot achieve the perfection of their dignity, imitate Jesus, and contribute to the common good, unless they freely give themselves in service to others in all areas of their life. The necessity of gratuitousness also means that no economy will ever function properly if the participants lack this quality. As Pope Benedict explains, "in *commercial relationships* the *principle of gratuitousness* and the logic of gift as an expression of fraternity can and must *find their place within normal economic activity.* This is a human demand at the present time, but is also demanded by economic logic. It is a demand both of charity and truth" (*CV*, no. 36). In other words, you do not have to accept Catholic teaching to realize at the present time that participants in the economy must avoid dishonesty and live in solidarity, brotherhood, and mutual trust. In the pope's mind, because that trust no longer exists, the economy is in grave difficulty.

Furthermore, I would like to highlight Pope Benedict's comments in chapter four on environmental and human ecology. Pope Benedict begins his discussion of environmental matters with an important observation about two extreme attitudes that people have toward the environment: either they consider it "more important than the human person," a kind of "untouchable taboo," a reflection of "neo-paganism or a new pantheism," or they abuse it with "total technical dominion over nature" (*CV,* no. 48). Both attitudes are serious obstacles to development, and, in my judgment, quite common today. The proper attitude is the desire to "exercise a *responsible stewardship over nature*" (*CV,* no. 50). This means using natural resources in such a way as to provide for everyone on the planet with attention to the needs of future generations and without doing harm to the environment. The pope stresses the need for a "world-wide redistribution of energy resources" (*CV,* no. 49). This kind of stewardship is the responsibility of individuals, groups, companies, and the various levels of government, including the international community. Companies and states exercise responsible stewardship when they do not hoard non-renewable energy resources and when individuals moderate their consumption of natural resources, avoiding hedonism and consumerism. Echoing Pope John Paul II's teaching, Pope Benedict says that what is really needed is the adoption of a way of living "in which the quest for truth, beauty, goodness and communion with others for the sake of common growth are the factors which determine consumer choices, savings and investments" (*CV,* no. 51).[38] Living this way is really an exercise in solidarity since moderation in the consumption of resources necessarily will redound to the benefit of others.

In order to protect nature, the decisive factor is the *"overall moral tenor of society"* (*CV,* no. 51). To preserve that moral tenor the protection of life is especially important. Otherwise stated, environmental ecology depends on "human ecology." Human life must be protected from conception until natural death. "If there is a lack of respect for the right to life and to a natural death, if human conception, gestation and birth are made artificial, if human embryos are sacrificed to research, the conscience of society ends up losing the concept of human ecology and, along with it, that of environmental ecology" (*CV,* no. 51). This is another point that is not on the screen of the world's liberal democracies, which keep talking about respect for the environment while maintaining the right to kill unborn children for research and for any other reason.

38. Pope Benedict is quoting *Centesimus Annus,* no. 36.

What is hardly understood today is that "our duties towards the environment are linked to our duties towards the human person considered in himself and in relation to others" (*CV*, no. 51). If there is a widespread lack of respect for the human person, born or unborn, there is really no hope of assuring respect for the environment or of encouraging lasting moderation in the use of resources.

Part of chapter five's reflections on the principles of subsidiarity and solidarity breaks new ground. Pope Benedict explains that the principle of subsidiarity is a "particular manifestation of charity and a guiding criterion for fraternal cooperation between believers and non-believers" (*CV*, no. 57). To affirm that respecting the principle of subsidiarity is a way of loving one's neighbor is a brilliant observation that I have not previously found in the body of Catholic social teaching (*CV*, no. 57). Intermediate associations and the state offer aid to human persons so that they can participate in the life of society and make their contribution to the common good, an eminent form of charity. In other words, people practice charity by observing the principle of subsidiarity since they show respect for the dignity of others by putting them in a better position to practice charity themselves. Since charity, or "reciprocity," is the "heart of what it is to be a human being" (*CV*, no. 57), subsidiarity is much more than a principle of government; helping people to love is an eminent contribution to their salvation and hence to integral development.

As a governing principle, subsidiarity does, however, make an important contribution. It facilitates the participation of all citizens in the life of society, protecting them from the "all-encompassing welfare state" (*CV*, no. 57), and guiding the governance of globalization so that political authority does not become overbearing. To work well subsidiarity must not be divorced from the principle of solidarity. As Pope Benedict says, "*The principle of subsidiarity must remain closely linked to the principle of solidarity and vice versa*, since the former without the latter gives way to social privatism, while the latter without the former gives way to paternalist social assistance that is demeaning to those in need" (*CV*, no. 58). When the two principles remain linked together, economic aid "must be distributed with the involvement not only of the governments of the receiving countries, but also local economic agents and the bearers of culture within civil society, including local Churches" (*CV*, no. 58). The yoked principles also require giving developing nations the opportunity both to sell their products in the international market and to help them improve and adapt their products, as is necessary to satisfy the demand. Subsidiarity ensures that those receiving aid are also helped to become agents of charity themselves.

Finally, in chapter six, Pope Benedict's most striking statement is the following: "*Development must include not just material growth but also spiritual growth,* since the human person is a 'unity of body and soul,' born of God's creative love and destined for eternal life" (*CV,* no. 76). This means that the nations of the world cannot adequately pursue the development of their peoples unless they understand the richness of human nature or what it really means to speak of the dignity of the human person. As St. Augustine argued, human beings are made for God and are restless until they rest in him. "When he is far away from God, man is unsettled and ill at ease. Social and psychological alienation and the many neuroses that afflict affluent societies are attributable in part to spiritual factors" (*CV,* no. 76). So the developing nations must be careful not to imitate the typical narrow understanding of development that prevails among affluent peoples. The spiritual and moral welfare of every individual in every nation must always be kept in mind in the work for development in the developing nations. This, of course, implies that the affluent nations must come to a deeper understanding of the spiritual needs of the human person. Unless this spiritual renewal takes place in Europe and the United States, then the developing nations, in my judgment, are likely to imitate the narrow understanding of development that prevails in Western societies.

Pope Paul VI would be quite pleased to see how Pope Benedict XVI explained *Populorum Progressio* and then went beyond his purview. There is nothing in *Populorum Progressio* (1967), *Humanae Vitae* (1968), *Octogesima Adveniens* (1971), or *Evangelii Nuntiandi* (1975) that would stand in opposition to anything in *Caritas in Veritate.* Au contraire, my text, I would argue, shows that Pope Benedict has made Pope Paul VI's social teaching more alive and effective by his third encyclical.[39]

---

39. See also my book, *Church, State, and Society: An Introduction to Catholic Social Doctrine* (Washington, D.C.: Catholic University of America Press, 2011).

"I Am with You Always": *Caritas in Veritate* and the Christological Foundations of Catholic Social Teaching

Roberto Goizueta

The most significant contribution of John Paul II and Benedict XVI to Catholic social teaching has been their systematic articulation of its theological and, specifically, Christological ground. Nowhere is this more evident than in Benedict's encyclical *Caritas in Veritate (CV)*. Though drawing on the tradition of natural law sources, these are framed by and rooted in Christ: ultimately, human freedom and social justice are the gift of a God who, in the person of Jesus Christ, loved us first and promises to be with us always (*CV*, no. 78). This encyclical is thus in a long line of Ratzinger/Benedict's writings in which the fundamental thesis, that which undergirds all the others, is that "Christian love, which seeks no reward and includes everyone, receives its nature from the love of Christ who gave His life for us."[1] More than a social encyclical, therefore, *Caritas in Veritate* is a spiritual treatise; like all of Benedict's encyclicals, it is fundamentally a call to conversion, a call to enter into relationship with the "God who has a human face" (*CV*, no. 55).[2] Benedict's claim is radical and unequivocal: the personal and ecclesial relationship with Christ *constitutes* Catholic social teaching.

Benedict's Christocentric approach has important implications for our understanding of the very character of Catholic social teaching. Indeed, the

---

1. Congregation for the Doctrine of the Faith, "Instruction on Certain Aspects of the 'Theology of Liberation' *(Libertatis Conscientia),*" no. 56. Translation from the Vatican website, http://www.vatican.va/roman_curia/congregations/cfaith/documents/rc_con_cfaith_doc _19840806_theology-liberation_en.html.

2. Translation at http://www.vatican.va/holy_father/benedict_xvi/encyclicals/documents/ hf_ben-xvi_enc_20090629_caritas-in-veritate_en.html.

Holy Father goes beyond even the 1971 Synod "Justice in the World," at which the bishops famously declared that "action on behalf of justice and participation in the transformation of the world fully appear to us as a constitutive dimension of the preaching of the Gospel, or, in other words, of the Church's mission for the redemption of the human race and its liberation from every oppressive situation."[3] Benedict suggests not only that the commitment to social justice is integral to the preaching of the gospel but that, even more fundamentally, such commitment is integral to the very *reception* of the gospel and a condition of the possibility of that reception. Conversely, this implies that: (1) the commitment to justice is itself dependent on such receptivity, (2) what is received is true, and (3) such receptivity to the *kerygma* as truth is itself inherently relational, which is to say, inherently practical. The act of faith is indeed an *act* or, more precisely, a response to God's own act in the person of the crucified and risen Christ.

In this essay, I examine these interrelated implications of Benedict's Christocentric reading of Catholic social teaching. The Holy Father begins his encyclical with an appeal to "charity in truth, to which Jesus Christ bore witness by his earthly life and especially by his death and resurrection" (*CV,* no. 1). Benedict's entire argument in the encyclical is encapsulated in these words. At the very outset, he emphasizes the centrality of Christ and, more specifically, of the crucified and risen Christ for the Christian understanding and practice of love. The crucified and risen Christ is *the* criterion of love. Citing his earlier encyclical, *Deus Caritas Est,* Benedict reiterates that "everything has its origin in God's love, everything is shaped by it, everything is directed towards it" (*CV,* no. 2). If the crucified and risen Christ is the embodiment of love, he is also its guarantor and safeguard. Benedict thus posits certain conditions of the possibility of the Christian commitment to social justice: (1) the crucified and risen Christ truly does bear witness to the God who loved us first; (2) that love — as freely given — is utterly gratuitous; (3) as gratuitous, God's love in Christ includes but goes beyond and frames the demands of justice; (4) as a gratuitous love that frames the demands of justice, God's love and truth can only be received as gift; and, therefore, (5) the truth embodied in the crucified and risen Christ can only be known in and through a human praxis that, as receptive to the divine love which is its origin, participates in God's own liberating activity in the world. Thus, our work for justice is an intrinsic dimension of and, indeed, our mode of receiving God's love as embodied in Christ.

---

3. Synod of Bishops, "Justice in the World," no. 6. English translation available in *The Synodal Document on the Justice in the World* (Boston: St. Paul Editions, 1971).

Christ, Love in Truth

In *Caritas in Veritate,* the foundational role of Christology also makes possible an integral approach to social teaching; the key principles of Catholic social teaching have common roots in the person of Christ. As "the Way, the Truth, and the Life," Jesus Christ is the hermeneutical criterion for understanding the statement "God is love":

> Without truth, charity degenerates into sentimentality. Love becomes an empty shell, to be filled in an arbitrary way. In a culture without truth, this is the fatal risk facing love. It falls prey to contingent subjective emotions and opinions, the word "love" is abused and distorted, to the point where it comes to mean the opposite. Truth frees charity from the constraints of an emotion-alism that deprives it of relational and social content, and of a fideism that deprives it of human and universal breathing-space. In the truth, charity reflects the personal yet public dimension of faith in the God of the Bible, who is both *Agápe* and *Lógos:* Charity and Truth, Love and Word. (*CV,* no. 3)

The love that God is, and which is expressed in the person of Christ, is the source of and the touchstone for authentic love. Not only does Christ reveal the Trinitarian God in whose image we are created, but through him God invites us to participate in that Trinitarian life: "The Trinity is absolute unity insofar as the three divine Persons are pure relationality. . . . God desires to incorporate us into this reality of communion as well: 'that they may be one even as we are one' (Jn 17:22)" (*CV,* no. 54). Far from submerging individuality within a totalitarian unity, the Trinitarian love of God is the source of person-hood, which is inherently relational. Inasmuch as human love participates in this Trinitarian love, so too does love give birth to an authentic autonomy and individual freedom, one rooted not in an illusory ego but in the inherent re-lationality of the person. Much more than an ethical injunction, the develop-ment of a just human community is a participation in the Trinitarian commu-nity. Social justice, therefore, is not simply the consequence of respect for human dignity, rights, and the common good (though it includes all these); social justice is the consequence of new relationships, beginning with our new relationship with the God who is "pure relationality."

Benedict's emphasis on relationality implies, moreover, that the truth that Christ is and expresses is not fundamentally a conceptual truth but a practical truth. This is, after all, what it means to proclaim that "God is love." In Christ, truth and charity are co-implicit: truth needs to be sought, found, and expressed within the "economy" of charity, but charity in its turn needs to be understood, confirmed, and practiced in the light of truth. In this way, not only do we do a service to charity enlightened by truth, but we also help give credibility to truth, demonstrating its persuasive and authenticating power in the practical setting of social living. This is a matter of no small account today, in a social and cultural context that relativizes truth, often paying little heed to it and showing increasing reluctance to acknowledge its existence (*CV*, no. 2).

The countercultural, transformative character of both truth and love depends precisely on their integral unity. Without truth, love is reduced to sentiment and emotion. Without love, truth is reduced to words and concepts. In either case, the result is idolatry since it reduces God to human experience, whether emotions or concepts.

The emphasis on charity in *truth* is crucial, for only if God's love in Christ is true, or real, can it transform, or liberate: "Truth preserves and expresses charity's power to liberate in the ever-changing events of history" (*CV*, no. 5). Here Benedict addresses his *bête noir*, the postmodern tendency to reduce "truth" and "reality" to social constructions, and to reduce human knowledge to its social location. If truth is merely a social construction, or if knowledge is always determined by its social location, then truth can only reflect human experience and cannot transform it, whether in the personal or social sphere. Thus charity and work for social justice presuppose access to a truth, a reality that does not merely emerge from and express human experience but irrupts into that experience. Here one is reminded of Simone Weil's assertion that one can no more save oneself than one can reach heaven by jumping a little higher every time; at some point, one must be pulled up. All Catholic social teaching stands or falls on the assertion that Jesus Christ is indeed who he says he is. *"The Gospel is fundamental for development,"* writes Benedict, "because in the Gospel, Christ, 'in the very revelation of the mystery of the Father and of his love, fully reveals humanity to itself'" (*CV*, no. 18). If this is the case, then a fortiori Christ fully reveals the meaning of a liberated humanity. Any reduction of this truth to a mere social construction, an expression of some generalizable human desire or value, thus undermines the very possibility of work for justice since the very possibility of charity and justice irreducible to human whim would be called into question.

Moreover, the truth of Christ, precisely as *charity* in truth, is a truth that, by definition, cannot be imposed on others. Of its very nature, truth cannot be imposed coercively: *"Truth,* in fact, is *lógos* which creates *diá-logos,* and hence communication and communion" (*CV*, no. 4). After all, the cross is the symbol of a truth that refuses to impose itself. By identifying Christ with charity in truth, therefore, Benedict is asserting the indispensability of truth but, equally, the indispensability of charity and justice as constitutive of truth. Indeed, the credibility of the truth depends on charity: "Truth needs to be sought, found and expressed within the 'economy' of charity, but charity in its turn needs to be understood, confirmed and practised in the light of truth. In this way, not only do we do a service to charity enlightened by truth, but we also help give credibility to truth, demonstrating its persuasive and authenticating power in the practical setting of social living" (*CV*, no. 2).

Beyond insisting on its intrinsic links to truth, Benedict specifies love even further, again in order to preclude distorted, sentimentalized interpretations of charity. The Holy Father thus notes the intrinsic connection between charity and justice:

> If we love others with charity, then first of all we are just towards them. Not only is justice not extraneous to charity, not only is it not an alternative or parallel path to charity: justice is inseparable from charity, and intrinsic to it. Justice is the primary way of charity or, in Paul VI's words, "the minimum measure" of it, an integral part of the love "in deed and in truth" (1 Jn 3:18), to which Saint John exhorts us. On the one hand, charity demands justice: recognition and respect for the legitimate rights of individuals and peoples. It strives to build the *earthly city* according to law and justice. On the other hand, charity transcends justice and completes it in the logic of giving and forgiving. . . . Charity always manifests God's love in human relationships as well, it gives theological and salvific value to all commitment for justice in the world. (*CV*, no. 6)

Benedict is concerned here not only with specifying the nature of charity but also with ensuring its effectiveness in society. While love goes beyond justice, this latter is the form that love takes in the human *polis*, through the promotion of the common good: to take a stand for the common good is on the one hand to be solicitous for, and on the other hand to avail oneself of, that complex of institutions that give structure to the life of society, juridically, civilly, politically, and culturally, making it the *polis*, or "city." The more we strive to secure a common good corresponding to the real needs of our neighbors, the more effectively we love them. Every Christian is called to practice this charity, in a manner corresponding to his vocation and according to the degree of influence he wields in the *polis*. This is the institutional path — we might also call it the political path — of charity, no less excellent and effective than the kind of charity that encounters the neighbor directly, outside the institutional mediation of the *polis* (*CV*, no. 7).

Thus, if love is to avoid becoming sentimentalized it must not only be grounded in truth but must incorporate the demands of social justice as intrinsic to the practice of charity. And all three — truth, love, and justice — are embodied in the person of Christ, for it is Christ who "fully reveals humanity to itself" (*CV,* no. 18).

Christ, the Gratuitous Love of God

If Christ fully reveals the God-who-is-love as the truth that grounds all human love, and if social justice is a dimension intrinsic to love, then work for justice is itself grounded in the radically gratuitous character of God's love in Christ. "The *earthly city,*" writes Benedict, "is promoted not merely by relationships of rights and duties, but to an even greater and more fundamental extent by relationships of gratuitousness, mercy and communion" (*CV,* no. 6). For Benedict, Jesus Christ is the Trinitarian God's own self-gift. Consequently, charity in truth can itself be only gift (*CV,* no. 34). Citing *Populorum Progressio (PP),* as he does throughout the encyclical, Benedict asserts that if "life in Christ is the first and principal factor of development," it is because "it is the primordial truth of God's love, grace bestowed upon us, that opens our lives to gift" (*CV,* no. 8).

Receptivity to the truth of God's love is a precondition for work on behalf of justice and for authentically human activity. Indeed, the act of receiving God's grace is itself the highest form of human activity, for "the human being is made for gift" (*CV,* no. 34). The act of receiving is that which grounds and makes possible all action on behalf of justice; this openness to gift constitutes the deepest dimension of all authentically human praxis. As opposed to distorted versions of love, the truth of God's love in Christ "bursts into our lives as something not due to us" and "imposes itself upon human beings" (*CV,* no. 34). For Benedict, this is the key to Christian faith, to life in Christ. This, therefore, is the key to social justice. At bottom, social justice is itself gift since it originates in God's own Trinitarian self-donation. In his encyclical *Laborem Exercens,* Pope John Paul II wrote that "human work is *a key,* probably *the essential key* to the whole social question."[4] In *Caritas in Veritate,* Pope Benedict XVI avers, in turn, that the essential key to human labor — precisely *qua* human — is receptivity to gift. "The highest things," wrote Benedict in *Jesus of Nazareth,* "the things that really matter, we cannot achieve on our own; we

---

4. Pope John Paul II, *Laborem Exercens,* no. 3. Translation at http://www.vatican.va/holy_father/john_paul_ii/encyclicals/documents/hf_jp-ii_enc_14091981_laborem-exercens_en.html.

have to accept them as gifts and enter into the dynamic of the gift, so to speak."[5] In a culture that presumes that human happiness, and therefore justice, can only be achieved or grasped at through human effort, this "dynamic of the gift" can only be perceived as naïve or even scandalous: "Now [God] descends into the depth of . . . human sufferings. Yet that very act prompts, and will continually prompt, his hearers — the hearers who nonetheless think of themselves as disciples — to say, 'This is a hard saying; who can listen to it?' (Jn 6:60). This new goodness of the Lord is no sugarplum. The scandal of the Cross is harder for many to bear than the thunder of Sinai had been for the Israelites."[6] The cross is absolute receptivity, for on the cross, Christ remains open to the Father's self-gift even as that gift takes the form of silence and absence. God's silent, unexpected nearness is scandalous precisely because in a world that idolizes invulnerability, it demands vulnerability; in a world obsessed with constant activity, it calls for receptivity; in a world that admires power, it privileges powerlessness. In such a world, the dynamic of gift will be derided and dismissed as a call to passivity and inaction rather than valued as the most liberating and most demanding form of action.

Yet the dynamic of gift is essential to social justice inasmuch as human dignity and the common good cannot ultimately have their source in a self-generated praxis; any praxis that has its source in the agency of a self-enclosed, autonomous ego can only give expression to that ego's own needs. By definition, social justice represents a response to the needs of the other, needs that can only be addressed if they are first received from the other. Before we can respond to the needs of victims we must be able to hear the victims' cries. Before we can work on behalf of justice for the victims we must be able to ask them, "What are you going through?" More important, we must listen to the answer. Only at that point dare we unite with the victims in their struggle for justice.

This is precisely the significance of the cross. On the cross, Christ asks all victims, "What are you going through?," hears their cries, and joins his own cry to theirs. As Benedict had written in his encyclical *Spe Salvi*, the very hope for a justice that vindicates the innocent victims of history presupposes a God who fully becomes one with the victims:

> Bernard of Clairvaux coined the marvellous expression: *Impassibilis est Deus, sed non incompassibilis* — God cannot suffer, but he can *suffer with*. Man is worth so much to God that he himself became man in order to *suffer*

---

5. Pope Benedict XVI, *Jesus of Nazareth*, vol. 1 (San Francisco: Ignatius, 2007), p. 268.
6. Pope Benedict XVI, *Jesus of Nazareth*, pp. 67-68.

with man in an utterly real way — in flesh and blood — as is revealed to us in the account of Jesus's Passion. Hence in all human suffering we are joined by one who experiences and carries that suffering *with* us; hence *con-solatio* is present in all suffering, the consolation of God's compassionate love — and so the star of hope rises.[7]

In the person of the crucified and risen Christ, God's "com-passion" becomes the source of a hope that will ultimately be vindicated in the resurrection. Here Benedict was also arguing for the decisiveness of Christ as the Victim who, by suffering with the human victims of history, reveals the hope of the resurrection, not merely as the hope of life after death but, even more, as the hope of justice for the innocent victims.

And it is God's very nearness, or "com-passion," that becomes the precondition for human community. Our receptivity to the gift of charity in truth, as embodied in the crucified and risen Christ, is what makes human community possible in all its dimensions. Confronting the apostles after his resurrection, the crucified and risen Christ had reconstituted the *communio* torn asunder on the way to Calvary, when his friends had deserted him. With Jesus' simple "Peace be with you," God's mercy irrupts in the Upper Room and transforms the despair of the apostles. The crucified Victim who had "suffered-with" forges a transformed community precisely out of the wounds he still bears in his body: "Put your finger here."

Earlier, in his encyclical *Deus Caritas Est,* Benedict had explicitly recalled the connection between God's "com-passion" and human communion:

> Love of God and love of neighbor are thus inseparable, they form a single commandment. But both live from the love of God who has loved us first. No longer is it a question, then, of a "commandment" imposed from without and calling for the impossible, but rather of a freely-bestowed experience of love from within, a love which by its very nature must then be shared with others. Love grows through love. Love is "divine" because it comes from God and unites us to God; through this unifying process it makes us a "we" which transcends our divisions and makes us one, until in the end God is "all in all" (1 Cor. 15:28).[8]

7. Pope Benedict XVI, *Spe Salvi,* no. 39. Translation at http://www.vatican.va/holy_father/benedict_xvi/encyclicals/documents/hf_ben-xvi_enc_20071130_spe-salvi_en.html.

8. Pope Benedict XVI, *Deus Caritas Est,* no. 18. Translation at http://www.vatican.va/holy_father/benedict_xvi/encyclicals/documents/hf_ben-xvi_enc_20051225_deus-caritas-est_en.html.

As the outgrowth of God's own love, work for justice thus involves much more than the balancing of abstract rights and duties (though it includes this); justice ultimately involves the reconstitution of relationships. In other words, social justice is less a "what" than a "who," less a set of principles than a network of reconstituted relationships.

These reconstituted relationships must characterize, above all, the ecclesial community. In *Deus Caritas Est,* Benedict emphasized the divine roots of the ecclesial *communio:*

> "All who believed were together and had all things in common; and they sold their possessions and goods and distributed them to all, as any had need" (*Acts* 2:44-5). In these words, Saint Luke provides a kind of definition of the Church, whose constitutive elements include fidelity to the "teaching of the Apostles," "communion" *(koinonia),* "the breaking of the bread" and "prayer" (cf. *Acts* 2:42). The element of "communion" *(koinonia)* is not initially defined, but appears concretely in the verses quoted above: it consists in the fact that believers hold all things in common and that among them, there is no longer any distinction between rich and poor (cf. also *Acts* 4:32-37). As the Church grew, this radical form of material communion could not in fact be preserved. But its essential core remained: within the community of believers there can never be room for a poverty that denies anyone what is needed for a dignified life.[9]

But Benedict also insisted that the communion that should characterize the Church cannot be limited to the Church, but should extend to the larger human community:

> The Church is God's family in the world. In this family no one ought to go without the necessities of life. Yet at the same time *caritas-agape* extends beyond the frontiers of the Church. The parable of the Good Samaritan remains as a standard which imposes universal love towards the needy whom we encounter "by chance" (cf. *Lk* 10:31), whoever they may be. Without in any way detracting from this commandment of universal love, the Church also has a specific responsibility: within the ecclesial family no member should suffer through being in need. The teaching of the *Letter to the Galatians* is emphatic: "So then, as we have opportunity, let us do good to all, and especially to those who are of the household of faith" (6:10).[10]

9. Pope Benedict XVI, *Deus Caritas Est,* no. 20.
10. Pope Benedict XVI, *Deus Caritas Est,* no. 25b.

Having thus established the intrinsic connection between love of God and human communion, and the roots of both in the God-who-is-love, Benedict goes further in *Caritas in Veritate*, where he specifies what it means to say that the love of neighbor has its source in divine love. Here he makes the extraordinary assertion that "economic, social and political development, if it is to be authentically human, needs to make room for *the principle of gratuitousness* as an expression of fraternity" (*CV*, no. 34). The economy of the market, the logic of commerce, must allow for the logic of the gift. "In *commercial relationships*," writes Benedict, "the *principle of gratuitousness* and the logic of gift as an expression of fraternity can and must *find their place within normal economic activity*" (*CV*, no. 36). While the law of contractual exchange is necessary for the functioning of the economy, this must be supplemented by the law of the unconditional gift as that which safeguards the proper relationship between labor and capital. Benedict thus reiterates the longstanding principle of Catholic social teaching that asserts the priority of labor over capital, but he grounds this principle in a theological anthropology of gratuitousness. If to be a human being is to be created for gift, then truly human social structures will make possible and facilitate expressions of unconditional gratuitousness, even within the commercial logic of the market.

Benedict's emphasis on the priority of Christ, and therefore on gratuitousness and receptivity, represents an important contribution — perhaps his most significant contribution — to Catholic social teaching. This is true even in relation to *Populorum Progressio*, on which Benedict's latest encyclical draws so explicitly. So, for instance, Benedict recalls that, in *Populorum Progressio*, Pope Paul VI

> taught that life in Christ is the first and principal factor of development and he entrusted us with the task of travelling the path of development with all our heart and all our intelligence, that is to say with the ardour of charity and the wisdom of truth. It is the primordial truth of God's love, grace bestowed upon us, that opens our lives to gift and makes it possible to hope for a "development of the whole man and of all men," to hope for progress "from less human conditions to those which are more human," obtained by overcoming the difficulties that are inevitably encountered along the way. (*CV*, no. 8)

Yet a close reading of the passages cited here from Paul VI's encyclical reveals a somewhat different emphasis in that 1967 text. Paul VI lays stress on creation's orientation toward God and the human responsibility to act in accord with that orientation:

Self-development, however, is not left up to man's option. Just as the whole of creation is ordered toward its Creator, so too the rational creature should of his own accord direct his life to God, the first truth and the highest good. Thus human self-fulfillment may be said to sum up our obligations. Moreover, this harmonious integration of our human nature, carried through by personal effort and responsible activity, is destined for a higher state of perfection. United with the life-giving Christ, man's life is newly enhanced; it acquires a transcendent humanism which surpasses its nature and bestows new fullness of life. This is the highest goal of human self-fulfillment. (*PP,* no. 16)[11]

While Benedict's Christian humanism takes grace and gift as its starting point, Paul VI's Christian humanism takes as its starting point the natural orientation of the person toward God. *Caritas in Veritate* begins with an affirmation of Jesus Christ as the source of all authentic human development (*CV,* no. 1). *Populorum Progressio* begins with an affirmation of the Church's concern for injustice in the world and the "demands imposed by Christ's Gospel in this area" (*PP,* nos. 1-2). For Paul, "true humanism points the way *toward* God" (*PP,* no. 42; emphasis added). For Benedict, "Christian humanism . . . enkindles charity and takes its lead *from* truth, accepting both as a lasting gift *from* God" (*CV,* no. 78; emphasis added). Needless to say, these are hardly mutually exclusive positions since Paul's understanding of nature includes grace and Benedict's understanding of grace and gift includes the human response. Nevertheless, we should not gainsay the significance of the differing emphases, for it reveals Benedict's contribution to Catholic social teaching.

Christ, *Factum Historicum*

To understand Benedict's Christocentric methodology in *Caritas in Veritate* (as well as in his other encyclicals), it is helpful to read the text in the light of the methodology explicitly set forth in the Holy Father's book *Jesus of Nazareth.* If *Caritas in Veritate* calls us to enter into relationship with the "God who has a human face," *Jesus of Nazareth* represents Benedict's own "personal search 'for the face of the Lord' (cf. Ps 27:8)."[12] The latter represents, in short, Benedict's own attempt to embrace the challenge set forth in his encyclicals. If the

11. Translation at http://www.vatican.va/holy_father/paul_vi/encyclicals/documents/hf
_p-vi_enc_26031967_populorum_en.html.

12. Pope Benedict XVI, *Jesus of Nazareth,* p. xxiii.

encyclicals look to Christ as the embodiment of charity in truth, Benedict's book traces the features of that historical embodiment.

In *Jesus of Nazareth,* Benedict outlines a methodological approach that presupposes the inseparability of the so-called Christ of faith and the Jesus of history: "But what can faith in Jesus as the Christ possibly mean, in Jesus as the Son of the living God, if the *man* Jesus was so completely different from the picture that the evangelists painted of him and that the Church, on the evidence of the Gospels, takes as the basis of her preaching?"[13] If Christ is the full expression of charity in truth, the Gospels are credible accounts of that expression as indeed a *factum historicum.* This is precisely what is most distinctive about the Christian understanding of the phrase "charity in truth":

> For it is of the very essence of biblical faith to be about real historical events. It does not tell stories symbolizing suprahistorical truths, but is based on history, history that took place here on this earth. The *factum historicum* (historical fact) is not an interchangeable symbolic cipher for biblical faith, but the foundation on which it stands: *Et incarnatus est* — when we say these words, we acknowledge God's actual entry into real history.[14]

The gift, which Christ is, is a historical fact, and so can only be received in history. The Gospels testify to this historicity, even if they do so through hermeneutical lenses. It is the very historicity of the gift, moreover, that demands an equally historical reception and response; because Jesus is a historical fact we are called to an equally historical social responsibility. So the historical facticity of Jesus of Nazareth, as depicted in the Gospels, is a crucial aspect of the truth he expresses. If the credibility of the truth of Christ depends on its embodiment in the lives of his followers, then that credibility ultimately depends on its full embodiment in Jesus of Nazareth himself.

At the same time, Christ's historical facticity is not a "mute" datum; as God's gratuitous self-expression it demands and calls forth our receptivity, which receptivity is itself integral to the reality of the gift precisely *qua* gift. Just as the truth, which Christ is, is understandable only in light of the incarnation as historical event, so is that historical event understandable only in light of the truth that Christ is. Just as, ultimately, Christian praxis is but a participation in God's own praxis in history, so, ultimately, is the human authorial voice in each biblical text a participation in the divine voice that "is at

---

13. Pope Benedict XVI, *Jesus of Nazareth,* p. xi.
14. Pope Benedict XVI, *Jesus of Nazareth,* p. xv.

the deepest level the one speaking."[15] In other words, "neither the individual books of Holy Scripture," writes Benedict, "nor the Scripture as a whole are simply a piece of literature."[16] All of this is presupposed in the encyclical *Caritas in Veritate.*

For Benedict, Catholic social teaching is nothing but the articulation of ethical demands implicit in the Christian's ongoing relationship with Christ. The fundamental presupposition, then, is that Jesus Christ does indeed accompany us as he promised he would, that the Gospels can indeed be trusted (*CV,* no. 78).[17] This is the message with which the Holy Father ends his latest encyclical: trust in the Gospels and trust in Christ. Inspired by that trust, we will undertake work on behalf of justice and human development not out of duty to abstract principles but out of gratitude for the gift of Christ's companionship. *"Development needs Christians with their arms raised towards God* in prayer," writes Benedict, "Christians moved by the knowledge that truth-filled love, *caritas in veritate,* from which authentic development proceeds, is not produced by us, but given to us" (*CV,* no. 79).

---

15. Pope Benedict XVI, *Jesus of Nazareth,* p. xxi.
16. Pope Benedict XVI, *Jesus of Nazareth,* p. xx.
17. See also Pope Benedict XVI, *Jesus of Nazareth,* p. xxi.

The Anthropological Vision of *Caritas in Veritate* and Its Implications for Economic and Cultural Life Today

David L. Schindler

"The truth of development consists in its completeness: if it does not involve the whole man and every man, it is not true development."[1] This, says Pope Benedict in his encyclical *Caritas in Veritate (CV)*, is "the central message of Paul VI's *Populorum Progressio (PP)*, valid for today and for all time" (*CV*, no. 18). Integral human development on the natural plane, as a response to a vocation from God the Creator, demands self-fulfillment in a " 'transcendent humanism which gives [to man] his greatest possible perfection: this is the highest goal of personal development.' The Christian vocation to this development therefore applies to both the natural plane and the supernatural plane" (*CV*, no. 18, citing *PP*, no. 16).

According to Benedict, God-centered charity in truth is the key to this "integral human development." "Everything has its origin in God's love, everything is shaped by it, everything is directed towards it" (*CV*, no. 1). Love is "the principle not only of micro-relationships (with friends, with family members, or within small groups) but also of macro-relationships (social, economic, and political ones)" (*CV*, no. 1).

The call to love, in other words, is not something imposed on man from

1. Pope Benedict XVI, *Caritas in Veritate*, no. 18. Translation at http://www.vatican.va/holy_father/benedict_xvi/encyclicals/documents/hf_ben-xvi_enc_20090629_caritas-in-veritate_en.html. This essay on Pope Benedict's *Caritas in Veritate* first appeared in *Communio* as "The Anthropological Vision of *Caritas in Veritate* in Light of Economic and Cultural Life in the United States," *Communio* 37, no. 4 (Winter 2010): 558-79.

This essay first appeared in *Communio* 37, no. 4 (Winter 2010): 558-79. Used by permission.

the outside, as an extrinsic addition to his being. "The interior impulse to love" is "the vocation planted by God in the heart and mind of every human person," even as this love is "purified and liberated by Jesus Christ," who reveals to us its fullness (*CV*, no. 1). "In Christ, *charity in truth* becomes the Face of his Person" (*CV*, no. 1). The Church's social teaching thus, in a word, is "*caritas in veritate in re sociali:* the proclamation of the truth of Christ's love in society" (*CV*, no. 5).

My purpose is to discuss the anthropological vision informing the Church's social teaching as summarized in this statement and articulated in the encyclical, in its meaning for economic and cultural life.

Part I

To get at the heart of what I wish to propose, let me begin by indicating some questions raised by four different commentators in America regarding the encyclical. The questions arise in relation to the anthropological emphasis of *Caritas in Veritate.*

(1) One author suggests that "the intellectual style and philosophical-theological underpinnings seem noticeably different from that of the preceding tradition of the Church. . . . Benedict XVI's repeated appeal to metaphysics, as important as it is to his own theology and to his social message, seems to return to an earlier deductive model of teaching on social questions."[2] This model, the author says, has been "abandoned by Vatican II's move to the symbolic rhetorical style of positive theology and reading the signs of the times in its social teaching." The author says further that the encyclical's metaphysical appeals also may make the terms of the encyclical "seem less accessible for many readers" because, as Benedict himself recognizes, "modern Western culture generally no longer articulates its fundamental convictions in metaphysical terms."[3]

(2) Not unrelated to these concerns, another author has suggested that, "where John Paul II or Paul VI cultivated an ecumenical voice when they wished to speak about global problems, Benedict cultivates a dogmatic one."[4] Consistent with his Regensburg address in 2007, Benedict invites dialogue,

---

2. Drew Christiansen, "Metaphysics and Society: A Commentary on *Caritas in veritate,*" *Theological Studies* 71 (2010): 3-28, p. 7. It should be noted that Christiansen affirms many positive features of *Caritas in Veritate.*

3. Christiansen, "Metaphysics and Society," p. 7.

4. David Nirenberg, "Love and Capitalism," *The New Republic,* September 23, 2009.

but then sets "the Catholic synthesis of faith and reason as a prerequisite for that dialogue." To be sure, says the author of this criticism, in "a de-secularizing age" such as our own, we should be free to draw on the wisdom of each of our traditions. Nevertheless, if such "teachings are to contribute to global 'unity and peace,' they will have to be taught in a way that seeks to transcend the boundaries of the traditions that produced them." The author says that Pius XI and John Paul II both understood this, and, although Benedict presents *Caritas in Veritate* as a continuation of their teaching, he does not follow their example. On the contrary, "Benedict's 'love' is narrowed by his 'truth.' "[5]

(3) Also pointing toward a discontinuity between *Caritas in Veritate* and earlier documents of the Church's social teaching, though in a different vein, a third author has said that Catholics must ask themselves whether there are now two social-teaching traditions, one reaching from Leo XIII's *Rerum Novarum* to *Centesimus Annus,* the other from *Populorum Progressio* through *Sollicitudo Rei Socialis* to *Caritas in Veritate.*[6] The author sees these two traditions stressing, respectively, freedom, virtue, human creativity, and the market economy, on the one hand, and such things as the benefits of "world political authority" and the redistribution of wealth over wealth creation, on the other. He emphasizes in this context that *Centesimus Annus (CA)* had "jettisoned the idea of a Catholic 'third way' that was somehow 'between' or 'beyond' or 'above' capitalism and socialism — a favorite dream of Catholics ranging from G. K. Chesterton to John A. Ryan and Ivan Illich," and implies that *Caritas in Veritate* weakens this claim. The author also points toward what he thinks is the incomprehensibility of such views expressed in *Caritas in Veritate* as that "defeating Third World poverty and underdevelopment requires a 'necessary openness, in a world context, to forms of economic activity marked by quotas of gratuitousness and communion.' "[7]

(4) Finally, there is the suggestion that the encyclical "reflects only the most limited insight into the practical moral problems of people" in business.[8] According to the author of this criticism, "Benedict reiterates recurring themes from Catholic social teaching on the rights of workers but offers no further counsel on how to resolve the difficult employment, sourcing, safety, and en-

5. Nirenberg, "Love and Capitalism."

6. George Weigel, "*Caritas in Veritate* in Gold and Red," *National Review* online, July 7, 2009.

7. Weigel, "*Caritas in Veritate* in Gold and Red."

8. Kirk O. Hansen, "What's the Business Plan?" in "Papal Correspondence," *America,* November 30, 2009.

vironmental challenges business executives face." In a word, he chooses to address moral decisions only at the "systemic level."[9]

Let me say that I find much that is interesting in each of these articles. I direct attention to their questions mainly to set a backdrop for the theme I wish to address. The questions all draw attention in different ways to the intended character of *Caritas in Veritate:* to what is perceived, not incorrectly, as the anthropological — metaphysical and theological, or again dogmatic — nature and emphasis of the encyclical. It is beyond my purpose to respond to the questions with the specificity that would be required in another forum. The burden of my argument, rather, is constructive: to demonstrate, against the background of the critical concerns briefly described, that the methodological role played by anthropology is just the point. The burden of the encyclical, in other words, lies decisively in its anthropological orientation, or reorientation — its development within continuity — of Catholic social teaching.

What I hope to show, in short, is that *Caritas in Veritate* conceives the Church's social teaching in a way that challenges the terms of that teaching as presupposed in the criticisms. My presentation thus has two main parts: to consider the basic anthropological terms of Catholic social teaching; and to indicate how these terms reconfigure in subtle but crucial ways the dominant approaches to socioeconomic life in today's increasingly global liberal order.

Part II

The "integral human development" introduced by Paul VI in *Populorum Progressio* and reaffirmed by Benedict in *Caritas in Veritate* is thus basic. This "integral human development" is entirely consistent with what *Centesimus Annus,* published shortly after the political events of 1989, affirms as "the positive value of an authentic theology of integral human liberation."[10] *Caritas in Veritate* recalls the teaching of John Paul II in this latter encyclical, which states that a comprehensive new plan of development is called for not only in the formerly communist countries of Eastern Europe but also in the West. Benedict emphasizes that this is "still a real duty that needs to be discharged" (*CV,*

9. Hansen, "What's the Business Plan?"
10. See Pope John Paul II, *Centesimus Annus,* no. 26. This statement references the Congregation for the Doctrine of the Faith's Instruction on Christian Freedom and Liberation, *Libertatis Conscientia* (March 1986): AAS 81 (1987), pp. 554-821.

no. 23). The Church, in other words, has a duty in relation to *both* the socialist economies that had prevailed in Eastern Europe *and* the liberal market economies of the West, even if this duty is not symmetrical in its respective implications for the one and the other.

On the one hand, then, the purpose of the Church is not to suggest a distinct economic system *as an economic system*. Catholic social teaching has no intention of providing technical solutions with respect to economics and development (*CV*, no. 9). At the same time, by virtue of her sacramental embodiment of the truth of Christ as Creator and Redeemer, the Church does become an "expert in humanity"[11] — to use the words spoken at the United Nations by Paul VI — in the sense that she has "a mission of truth to accomplish, in every time and circumstance, for a society that is attuned to man, to his dignity, to his vocation" (*CV*, no. 9).

The point is that the Church proposes principles that affect all human activities from the inside, including activities in politics and the public realm (*CV*, no. 56) and every phase of economic activity (*CV*, no. 37). This implies that the Church does not begin by simply accepting the terms of freedom and rights and liberation as conceived in the dominant forms of either socialism or the liberal market, while then *adding* a Christian intention. The Christian difference is one not merely of additional motivation but of inner transformation. The Church accepts what is true in the dominant forms of socioeconomic activity, but only as it dynamically reorders these in a way that reaches to their roots, in light of man's nature as destined for fulfillment in the love of Jesus Christ.

Part III

But if the Church's social teaching is not a set of technical solutions or simply an alternative economic system, even as it informs, or indeed dynamically transforms, all of such solutions and systems, then what is it?

What I take to be the answer of *Caritas in Veritate* is this: Catholic social teaching is a vision of reality — an understanding of being, man, and God — that unfolds an entire way of life at the heart of which is a moral-social practice. Catholic social teaching, in a word, is a social practice only as at once a matter of truth. Four brief comments will help clarify what this means.

11. Pope Paul VI, *Discourse to the General Assembly of the United Nations Organization*, October 4, 1965, no. 3.

(1) The foundation for such a claim lies in the encyclical's affirmation of the unity of truth and love in the person of Jesus Christ as the revelation of the Trinitarian God. Jesus Christ is the word, or Logos, of God as the *deed* of God's love. Christ embodies in his person the original unity of truth (hence "theory" or "dogma") and love (hence deed: *pragma, praxis*), the original unity of truth and social practice.[12]

(2) The unity of truth and love is also disclosed in the structure of the creaturely being as gift. Our being is a being-given meant itself to give. As St. Augustine says, citing the words of the apostle John: "We cannot love unless we are first loved."[13] "In this is love, that God has first loved us" (1 John 4:10).

(3) Love whom or what? We love God naturally above all things. As Augustine and Aquinas both say in their different ways, we naturally love God more than ourselves, because he is more interior to us than we are to ourselves.[14] And we cannot but naturally love all other creatures with whom we share a common relation to God: above all other persons, but also non-personal entities that share proportionately-analogically in the creaturely meaning of being as gift, and hence as good in itself, by virtue of its creation.

Our love, in other words, is in its roots *filial:* we are not the unoriginated origins of love but participants in a love that is always first given to us, by God. And this love is by nature radically *social:* it is at once God-centered and inclusive of the whole of creation, of all beings and each singular and unique being.

(4) This filial-social love that we participate in *by nature,* by virtue of creation, is destined for, and fulfilled in, our participation *by grace* in God's own love as revealed in Jesus Christ through his sacramental Church.

It is helpful, in light of these four comments, to recall the text that both John Paul II and Benedict XVI take to contain the central teaching of Vatican II: *Gaudium et Spes,* no. 22, which states that, in his revelation of the Trinitarian love of God, Jesus Christ discloses the meaning of man and, by implication, all of physical creation, to itself.

---

12. The theologian Ratzinger already developed this theme in a profound way in his early book, *Introduction to Christianity* (San Francisco: Ignatius, 1968), which shows that, according to Christian belief, at the origin of things lies the Creator who is characterized by the unity of reason and love or freedom. Ratzinger comments on the Trinity in this light, and then shows how Christological dogma, and in turn each of the articles of the Creed, articulate the concrete meaning of love: the *meaning* or *doctrine* of God in relation to the world, as *love* and thus already as *action* that is *social.*

13. Augustine, *Sermon* 34, 1-3.

14. See Augustine, *Confessions* 3, 6; Aquinas, *Summa Theologica,* I, 8, 1, and *De Veritate,* 22, ad 2.

In a word, truth is a *logos* of love, and love is the way of truth, as revealed by God in Jesus Christ and, naturally-analogically, in creation itself.

Part IV

Thus we have the fundamental principles in terms of which *Caritas in Veritate* is able to respond to the criticisms briefly noted above.

First, regarding the metaphysical character of the encyclical and its so-called deductive model of social teaching, it is crucial to see here that this criticism is mediated by its own notion of truth ("theory") and love (social practice) and of the relation between them, though this notion remains implicit and thus unaccounted for. The criticism (implicitly) disjoins truth from love in a way that *Caritas in Veritate* does not; and the criticism's different way of approaching the relation between truth and love is a function not of no metaphysics but of what is rather an alternative metaphysics, indeed, one that presupposes an alternative understanding of what it means for God to be author of, and present in, his creation, as well as an alternative Christology. It is true that Western culture today no longer articulates its vision of things in metaphysical terms, and that explicitly metaphysical language is not readily accessible to contemporary readers. However, metaphysics — some vision of reality inclusive of ideas about being, man, and God — does not cease to operate and to guide one's social practice, simply because it is ignored or left tacit. It is in this context that we see the burden of *Caritas in Veritate:* to recuperate the authentic meaning of social practice *as a vision of reality* whose most basic content is God-centered love, and in so doing to expose the inadequate alternative visions of reality that are implied in and give the basic form to the conventional economic models of socialism and the liberal market, even where these alternative visions remain unconscious as *metaphysical,* and at least by implication also *theological,* visions.[15]

Second, regarding dialogue and the recovery of an ecumenical voice, the key again is *Caritas in Veritate*'s unity of truth and love. Genuine dialogue need not, and should not, fracture this unity. In entering dialogue, the weight should be placed not on bracketing the truth in its fullness — though of course not everything needs to be made explicit on every occasion — but on demonstrat-

---

15. Pope John Paul II's publication of the encyclical *Fides et Ratio,* with its emphasis on the recovery of metaphysics in the articulation of faith, is not at all unrelated to the concern indicated here.

ing ever more fully the nature of truth as the *logos of love:* on giving integrated witness to truth as love. *Caritas in Veritate* presumes that the way of dialogue is given in Jesus himself, who testifies with his whole being, in a way that wholly respects and does not impose on others, even as he demonstrates that truth rightly understood tends toward witness, even unto the suffering of death. Benedict in other writings also offers the non-Christian Socrates as an example: one who testifies to the transcendent origin and reality of truth with his entire life — and martyred death — all the while imposing nothing on others, but inviting them when he is questioned to look at what has convinced him and why.

Caritas in Veritate thus finds the common ground necessary for dialogue in man's concrete nature as restless to be loved and to love, all the way to the ultimate source and end of this love. The author who criticizes *Caritas in Veritate's* lack of an ecumenical voice seeks instead a more abstract common ground, one that disposes the dialogue partners to leave implicit their own concrete search for meaning and to bracket what matters most to them, and indeed to separate their verbally articulated claims from the wholeness of their reality as embodied in deed and social practice. From the perspective of *Caritas in Veritate,* dialogue rooted in such an abstract common ground can give only fragmented witness. And in fact such a ground seems to be accepted as genuinely common — universally accessible and meaningful — only by those who already stand on the ground set by Western liberal assumptions. *Caritas in Veritate* thinks on the contrary that a truly common ground can be found for all persons only by starting from within the reality of each person in the concrete wholeness of his or her search for meaning or love in its ultimate source and end.

Regarding the question of a "third way," the difficulty is that those who criticize *Caritas in Veritate* for implying openness to a "third way" beyond socialism and the liberal market fail to grasp that what is at stake in Catholic social teaching is precisely the nature of God's relation to the world, as expressed in Christ and his Church. These critics invariably assume that there realistically exist today only two economic alternatives, socialist-liberationist on the one hand and liberal capitalist on the other; and that the task of the Church in this context is to add a distinct Christian intentionality or a morality that would provide support for, but without truly *informing,* either alternative. But this implies a reductive understanding of the rightful "worldly" implications of the reality of God, Christ, and the Church for socioeconomic institutions and practice. The critics thus leave intact in their different ways, from the left and from the right, the fragmentary vision of man that may be termed *homo economicus,* a vision that wrongly abstracts the economic meaning of man from the ontological and theological roots of his being.

Finally, regarding the objection that *Caritas in Veritate* neglects to provide counsel on how to resolve the practical moral problems in business, this objection fails to grasp that the Church rightly considers herself to be an "expert in humanity" in the sense indicated above, not an expert in the technical aspects of employment, sourcing, safety, environmental problems, and the like. This does not mean that the Church has no concrete interest in such problems. Rather, as *Caritas in Veritate* insists, the purpose of the Church, and the teaching expressed in her social encyclicals, is to demonstrate that God-centered love affects all human activities and makes a significant difference to every technical solution, ordering each from within toward the common good and toward an integrated view of human dignity.

But let me conclude this first part of my discussion by taking note of persons whose lives render concrete the unity of truth and love or social practice articulated by Benedict in *Caritas in Veritate,* and thereby provide concretely embodied responses to the above criticisms of Benedict. I have in mind, for example, Peter Maurin and Dorothy Day in America and Madeleine Delbrêl in France, the latter a contemporary of Day who lived and worked among the communists who were dominant in the economic and political institutions of Ivry, near Paris.[16] In their different ways, each of these persons recognized that "social work" takes place at the intersection of time and eternity, that God is a social good, and that meaninglessness is the deepest form of poverty. They understood that the question of the meaning and existence of God lies at the core of social practice, and that wealth consists most fundamentally in the quality of one's relationships to those with whom relation is given constitutively, in the act of creation: God, family, other persons, and all the creatures of nature.

These persons, in a word, all lived the truth articulated by Mother Teresa when she said that her social work involved at root "being a contemplative in the world."

We should note that the persons cited here are celibates, with the whole of their lives dedicated to living and working among the poor and dispossessed. But those who have families and whose lives are occupied with worldly professions, for all of the obvious and important differences in state of life, are not exempt from living the unity of truth and love in relation to God and

---

16. See Madeleine Delbrêl, *We, The Ordinary People of the Streets* (Grand Rapids: Eerdmans, 2000), with its fine introduction by Father Jacques Loew.

others, in all that they do. There is only one call to holiness, albeit with two distinct but intrinsically related forms in celibacy and marriage.

Finally, it is the case that the persons named are sometimes criticized for overemphasizing a personal approach to social justice that fails really to transform or liberate institutions. But these persons show us what is in fact the true meaning of such liberation as presupposed in *Caritas in Veritate* (and *Centesimus Annus*): that personal transformation of meaning in love is the inner condition of, and gives the anterior form to, any institutional change that would be genuinely human, and not just a rearrangement of external structural machinery.[17]

Part V

Let us turn to the second part of my argument. As indicated, the main presupposition undergirding the argument of *Caritas in Veritate* is the universality of the vocation to love. According to Pope Benedict, all of us know, even if only implicitly and thus not fully consciously, that we "are not self-generated" (*CV*, no. 68). An implicit sense of the Creator abides in each of us, which Cardinal Ratzinger/Pope Benedict describes in other writings in terms of *anamnesis*, the memory of God that is "identical with the foundations of our being."[18] This memory of God can be ignored or denied but it is never absent from any human consciousness. In a word, a dynamic tendency toward communion with God, and with other creatures who share relation to God, lies in the inmost depths of every human being and not only Christians, even as this tendency is fulfilled only in the grace of God's own love that is revealed in Jesus Christ.

The encyclical's call for a new trajectory of thinking informed by the principles of gratuitousness and relationality takes its starting point from this universal *anamnesis* of love and God (*CV*, nos. 53, 55). Let us now consider in four parts how this new way of thinking reorders some key aspects of the prevalent approaches to sociopolitical justice.

(1) Regarding tendencies expressed in Western socioeconomic institutions, *Caritas in Veritate* rejects the reading of *Centesimus Annus* that would

17. See the Pontifical Council for Justice and Peace, *Compendium of the Social Doctrine of the Church* (Washington, D.C.: United States Conference of Catholic Bishops, 2004), no. 42.

18. Cardinal Joseph Ratzinger, *Values in a Time of Upheaval*, trans. B. McNeil (San Francisco: Ignatius, 2006), p. 92.

understand the three "subjects" of the social system — the state, the economy, and civil society — each to have a logic of its own, only extrinsically related to the others (see *CV,* nos. 38-40). As Cardinal Bertone stated in an address to the Italian Senate: "This conceptualization, which [for example] confuses the market economy that is the genus with its own particular species which is the capitalist system, has led to identifying the economy with the place where wealth or income is generated, and society with the place of solidarity for its fair distribution."[19] *Caritas in Veritate* rejects this dichotomy between "subjects," which would undermine the call to love as integrative of every human activity and all development — of the whole man and every man. To paraphrase Cardinal Bertone, we must supersede the dominant view that expects the Church's social teaching, involving the centrality of the person — and in this light solidarity, subsidiarity, and the common good — to be confined, as it were, to sociocultural activities, while "experts in efficiency" would be charged with running the economy and, indeed, the order of politics.

Caritas in Veritate thus strongly reaffirms the idea of the common good. "To desire the *common good* and strive towards it," says Benedict, *is a requirement of justice and charity"* (*CV,* no. 7). Concern for the common good involves the "complex of institutions that give structure to the life of society, juridically, civilly, politically, and culturally, making it the *pólis,* or 'city'" (*CV,* no. 7). Commitment to the common good shapes "the *earthly city* in unity and peace, rendering it to some degree an anticipation and a prefiguration of the undivided *city of God"* (*CV,* no. 7). Regarding economic activity, the pope thus insists that it cannot resolve social problems simply through the application of *commercial logic,* but "needs to be *directed towards the pursuit of the common good,* for which the political community in particular must also take responsibility" (*CV,* no. 36). "The *principle of gratuitousness* and the logic of gift as an expression of fraternity can and must *find their place within normal economic activity,"* as expressed in *commercial relationships* (*CV,* no. 36).

Benedict's emphasis on the common good bears two especially important implications. On the one hand, it entails rejection of the dualism between temporal and eternal that is a hallmark of liberal societies. Contrary to the view of John Locke, for example, and countless of our contemporaries, Benedict holds that public-economic activity is not a matter exclusively of the temporal order, as though the eternal order, or the heavenly city, arrives only *after*

---

19. Address of Cardinal Tarcisio Bertone, Secretary of State, During His Visit to the Senate of the Italian Republic, July 28, 2009, http://www.vatican.va/roman_curia/secretariat_state/card-bertone/2009/documents/rc_seg-st?20090728_visita-senato_en.html.

life on earth, or in any case remains in this life something purely "private." Locke recognizes that religion is important for morality and thus useful for the functioning of the earthly city, but only as a *means* of maintaining *external public order,* and not as an intrinsic good for the civil community as such.[20]

Caritas in Veritate thus also makes clear that the Church affirms the notion of the *common good,* rather than that of *public order,* as the proper purpose of political-economic activity. The encyclical, in other words, rejects the "juridical" idea of political and economic institutions that has been a prevalent reading, not only of John Paul II's *Centesimus Annus (CA),* but also, for example, Vatican II's *Dignitatis Humanae.* According to the "juridical" idea, political and economic institutions do not have as their purpose the projection of any view of human nature or destiny, but on the contrary are limited simply to the securing of the procedural mechanisms necessary for the fair and equal exercise of freedom by citizens. Such a juridical idea of political or constitutional order is subject to the criticism that *Caritas in Veritate,* as noted above, makes regarding those who interpret *Centesimus Annus* to affirm an extrinsic relation between the end of civil society and the end of the market and the state.[21]

Regarding the institution of the academy, the integrated human development described in the encyclical involves a "broadening [of] our concept of reason and its application" (*CV,* no. 31). "Charity is not an added extra, like an appendix to work already concluded in each of the various disciplines: it engages them in dialogue from the very beginning" (*CV,* no. 30). This does not mean that one can legitimately bypass reason and its proper conclusions. The point is simply that "intelligence and love are not in separate compartments: *love is rich in intelligence and intelligence is full of love*" (*CV,* no. 30), and that love must animate the disciplines in a whole marked by unity and distinction

20. Thus Locke's view, from the perspective of *Caritas in Veritate,* is already the beginning, not of "legitimate secularity," but of secularism. The point here is important in connection with Benedict's call for a new reflection on the concept of "laïcité." See, for example, his statement in the opening address of his apostolic visit to France: "I am firmly convinced that a new reflection on the meaning and importance of 'laïcité' is now necessary" (September 12, 2008).

21. The juridical idea of political or constitutional order is advanced with respect to both *Dignitatis Humanae* and the U.S. Constitution by the American theologian John Courtney Murray, S.J. Indeed, Murray affirms an identity in the idea of the right to religious freedom in both documents: that this idea, rightly understood, is to be conceived as juridical in nature. For a defense of Murray, which contrasts Murray's view with that of John Paul II, see Herminio Rico, S.J., *John Paul II and the Legacy of* Dignitatis Humanae (Washington, D.C.: Georgetown University Press, 2002); for a critical study of Murray's juridical idea, see David L. Schindler, "Civil Community Inside the Liberal State: Truth, Freedom, and Human Dignity," in *Ordering Love: Liberal Societies and the Memory of God* (Grand Rapids: Eerdmans, 2011).

(*CV,* no. 31). The problem today is an "excessive segmentation of knowledge" that results in an inability to "see the integral good of man in its various dimensions" (*CV,* no. 31). Thus, recovery of the place of metaphysics and theology, especially in their integrative capacities in the realization of wisdom and as themselves integrated by love, "is indispensable if we are to succeed in adequately weighing all the elements involved in the question of development and in the solution of socio-economic problems" (*CV,* no. 31).[22]

In light of the foregoing comments, we should see that *Caritas in Veritate* carries a significant challenge with respect to the dominant logic of economic, political, and academic institutions as conceived in liberal societies. Economic and political institutions in liberal societies are understood primarily, *qua* institutions, as procedural mechanisms whose purpose is to create space for the exercise of freedom, and not to offer any pedagogy regarding the meaning — order and end — of man. This implies a contradiction with what *Caritas in Veritate* says about the common good and the interrelation of the three "subjects" — market, state, and civil society — in the "system" of the body politic. It is also inconsistent with the statement of the *Catechism of the Catholic Church* that "every institution is inspired, at least implicitly, by a vision of man and his destiny, from which it derives the point of reference for its judgment, its hierarchy of values, its line of conduct."[23]

In a similar vein, the academy in liberal societies typically conceives the disciplines as methods from which any implication of guiding metaphysical and theological notions has been eliminated. Benedict XVI in *Caritas in Veritate,* and earlier in his Regensburg address to university faculty, in contrast, clearly points toward a renewed sense of integration among the disciplines, in light of truth as an order of love ultimately centered in God.

Indeed, we may say, in sum, that the core task of an "authentic theology of integral human liberation" and "integral human development" with respect to the West lies in a dynamic transformation of the West's liberal economic, political, and academic institutions in light of a common good infused with the idea of truth as an order of love.

(2) The idea of humanity as a single family, and of marriage and family, as well as life issues, play an important role in providing a foundation for, and

22. The Abba School founded recently by the Focolare in Italy provides a good example of the kind of rethinking of the disciplinary methods of the academy implied by Benedict in *Caritas in Veritate* and in his Regensburg lecture. See Chiara Lubich et al., *An Introduction to the Abba School* (Hyde Park, N.Y.: New City, 2002).

23. *Catechism of the Catholic Church,* no. 2244. English translation available at http://www.vatican.va/archive/ENG0015/_INDEX.HTM.

in giving original form to, the principles of gratuitousness and relation and indeed the logic of freedom and rights that is implied by the common good, as outlined here.

Strikingly, Benedict says that *"the development of peoples depends, above all, on a recognition that the human race is a single family"* (*CV*, no. 53) and that "the Christian revelation of the unity of the human race presupposes a *metaphysical interpretation of the 'humanum' in which relationality is an essential element"* (*CV*, no. 55). The idea that all human beings make up a single family derives from the common origin of each in the Creator. "The unity of the human race is called into being by the Word of God-Who-is-love" (*CV*, no. 34).

This idea of a single unified family deriving from a common relation to the Creator invites further reflections drawn from the theological anthropology of Cardinal Ratzinger/Pope Benedict and Pope John Paul II — notably, regarding the idea of filiality, in the former, and regarding the "original solitude" of man, in the latter. *Caritas in Veritate* emphasizes the love that is first received by us, not generated by us. Already in his commentary on the anthropology of *Gaudium et Spes,* Ratzinger stresses the capacity for worship as the primary content of man's imaging of God. This is so because human beings are most basically sons and daughters in the Son: they are images of God in and through Jesus Christ who is God precisely as the Logos who is from-and-for the Father (Col. 1:15-18); or, as Ratzinger puts it succinctly elsewhere, "the center of the Person of Jesus is prayer."[24] Likewise, John Paul II affirms the primacy of man in his "original solitude," by which he means that man's relationality begins most radically in his "aloneness" before God. The point is not that man is originally without relation, but that man's relationality, his original being-with, is a being-with God before (ontologically not temporally) it is a being-with other human beings. Man's being-with God, as creaturely, is first a *being-from,* in the manner of a child who participates in being only as the fruit of the radical generosity of the One Who Is.

Here, in what we may call the filial relation associated with the family, we find the root meaning of the encyclical's central category of relation as *gift.* Indeed, once we see the radicality of this relation, which originates in God as the Creator, we see that it must include not only all human beings, though especially and most properly these, but all creatures and thus also all of the natural, physical-biological, entities of the cosmos. Thus Benedict says that

---

24. Cardinal Joseph Ratzinger, *Behold the Pierced One,* trans. G. Harrison (San Francisco: Ignatius, 1986), p. 25.

"*nature expresses a design of love and truth*. It is prior to us . . . and speaks to us of the Creator (see Rom. 1:20) and his love for humanity. It is destined to be 'recapitulated' in Christ at the end of time (see Eph. 1:9-10; Col. 1:19-20). Thus it too is a 'vocation.' Nature is given to us . . . as a gift of the Creator who has given it an inbuilt order, enabling man to draw from it the principles needed in order 'to till and keep it' " (Gen. 2:1) (*CV*, no. 48). Indeed, we could say that, in its own analogical way, and with the help of man, nature thus participates in the prayer constitutive of the creature in its inmost filial movement toward the Creator.

Further regarding the implications of filiality, we teach our children to say "please" and "thank you." But, rightly understood, this is not a matter merely of manners. On the contrary, it is a matter of teaching them who they are in their deepest reality: gifts from God who are thus meant to be grateful, to act in gratuitous wonder, in *response to* what is first *given*, as *gift*. Here is the origin of that recognition of being as true and good and indeed beautiful — *qua given* and not simply *quia factum* or as a function of human making — which must lie at the basis of any healthy human society. Here is the root of the encyclical's call for new lifestyles centered around the quest for truth, beauty, goodness, and communion with others (*CV*, no. 51).

Of course, children are sons and daughters of God only through a human father and mother, and the child is born as itself apt for either fatherhood or motherhood. Further, the fruitfulness of the union of the father and the mother is a continuing sign and expression of the creative generosity of God. Ratzinger in his commentary on *Gaudium et Spes* refers to this spousal communion between a man and a woman as the immediate consequence *(Folge)* of the content *(Inhalt)* of a person's imaging of God that lies first in the person's "unitary" being as child of God.[25] John Paul II refers to this constitutive aptness for spousal union-fruitfulness as the "original unity" of man and woman. This aptness for spousal union, established first in man's and woman's common filial relation to God, is constitutive of the human being.[26] Each human being is a member of the single family of creatures under God, in and through membership in a particular familial genealogy of his own. This is the ground for the encyclical's calling on the state to promote "the centrality and the integrity of the family founded on marriage between a man and a woman, the primary

25. Joseph Ratzinger, "Erster Hauptteil: Kommentar zum 1," in *Lexikon für Theologie und Kirche 14: Das Zweite Vatikanische Konzil,* vol. 3, ed. H. Vorgrimier (Fribourg: Herder and Herder, 1968), article 12.

26. *Compendium of the Social Doctrine of the Church,* nos. 37, 110, and 147.

cell of society, and to assume responsibility for its economic and fiscal needs, while respecting its essentially relational character" (*CV,* no. 44).

The implications of the constitutive relationality affirmed in *Caritas in Veritate* are radical: no relations taken up by human beings in the course of their lives are purely contractual, or simply the fruit of an originally indifferent act of choice (as in liberal "contractualism").[27] Man is never, at root, "lonely," which is to say, in the language of *Caritas in Veritate,* never poor in the sense of "isolated" (*CV,* no. 53). On the contrary, his being is always a being-with.

Hence, human freedom is an *act* of choice only as already embedded in an *order* of naturally given relations (*CV,* no. 68) to God, family, others, and nature. And *regarding human rights,* just as the juridical idea of rights presupposes a contractualist idea of freedom, so does a truthful order-bearing idea of rights presuppose a relational idea of the self. Just as the contractualist idea entails a priority of rights over duties, so does the relational idea entail a priority of duties over rights,[28] though of course rights remain unconditional coincident with this anterior responsibility (see *CV,* no. 43). Rights, in a word, are properly invested in every person, but no person is a solitary agent who can be abstracted from relations. On the contrary, the creaturely person as he or she exists, always and everywhere, is inwardly ordained to God and others, is a child born into a family, is sexually differentiated and apt for fatherhood or motherhood, and is intrinsically related to the whole of humanity and of nature. An adequate idea of rights must take into account this order of relations that is constitutive of each person. (The prevalent liberal idea of right and freedom in America presupposes a Cartesian human subject.)

(3) *Caritas in Veritate* says that Paul VI's encyclical, *Humanae Vitae,* is "highly important for delineating the *fully human meaning of the development the Church proposes*" (*CV,* no. 15). *Humanae Vitae* makes clear "the *strong links between life ethics and social ethics,* thus ushering in a new area of magisterial teaching that has gradually been articulated in a series of documents, most recently John Paul II's encyclical *Evangelium Vitae*" (*CV,* no. 15).

The pope notes in this connection *Humanae Vitae*'s emphasis on the unitive and procreative meaning of sexuality, thereby locating "at the foundation of society the married couple [who] are open to life" (*CV,* no. 15). He suggests

27. In the liberal societies of the West, the tendency is to conceive human relations most basically in contractual terms. And, when such relations appear rather to be natural or "constitutive," as, for example, in the case of the family, the tendency is then to conceive these relations as merely matters of physicalist biology.

28. Duties are not to be understood here as opposed or extrinsic to charity and the logic of gift; see *Caritate in Veritas,* nos. 6, 34, and 38.

that the tendency to make human conception and gestation artificial contributes to the loss of "the concept of human ecology and, along with it, that of environmental ecology" (*CV*, no. 51). The point here, though not explicitly developed in *Caritas in Veritate*, is that *Humanae Vitae*, in its affirmation of the unity of the personal and the procreative meaning of sexuality, implies a "new" understanding of the body as a bearer of the objective order of love, in a way consistent with and instructive for *Caritas in Veritate*'s view that the nature of the physical-biological cosmos as a whole "expresses a design of love" (*CV*, no. 48).

Regarding the relation between life ethics and social ethics, the pope notes the inconsistency of societies which, affirming the dignity of the person and justice and peace, tolerate the violation of human life when it is at its weakest and most marginalized (*CV*, no. 15). He thus insists that *"openness to life is at the center of true development"* (*CV*, no. 28), and that we need to broaden our concept of poverty and underdevelopment to take account of this question of openness to life. It is precisely in its increasing mastery over the origin of human life manifest, for example, in *in vitro* fertilization, the harvesting of human embryos for research, and the possibility of manufacturing clones and human hybrids, that we see "the clearest expression" of a supremacy of technology in contemporary society (*CV*, no. 75).

(4) *Caritas in Veritate* takes up the complicated question of technology in its final chapter. "Technology enables us to exercise dominion over matter" and "improve our conditions of life," and thus goes to "the heart of the vocation of human labor" (*CV*, no. 69). The relevant point, however, is that "technology is never merely technology" (*CV*, no. 69).[29] It always invokes some sense of the order of man's naturally given relations to God and others. Technology thus, rightly conceived, must be integrated into the call, indeed the covenant with God, implied in this order of relations (*CV*, no. 69): integrated into the idea of creation as something first *given* to man, as *gift*, "not something self-generated" (*CV*, no. 68) or *produced* by man.

Here again we see the importance of the family. It is inside the family that we first learn a "technology" that respects the dignity of the truly weak and vulnerable — for example, the just-conceived and the terminally ill — for their own sake. It is inside the family, indeed, the family as ordered to worship, that we first learn the habits of patient interiority necessary for genuine relation-

---

29. That is, technology is never "pre-moral," to use the language employed by *Veritatis Splendor*, no. 48, in its rejection of the idea that the body is neutral with respect to human-moral meaning.

ships: for the relations that enable us to see the truth, goodness, and beauty of others as given (and also to maintain awareness of "the human soul's ontological depths, as probed by the saints"; *CV,* no. 76). It is inside the family that we can thus learn the limits of the dominant social media of communication made available by technology, which promote surface movements of consciousness and gathering of technical information, and foster *inattention* to man in his depths and his transcendence as created by God. It is in the family that we first become open to the meaning of communication in its ultimate and deepest reality as a *dia-logos* of love that is fully revealed by God in the life, and thus including also the suffering, of Jesus Christ (*CV,* no. 4).

In light of the foregoing, we can see, in sum, why *Caritas in Veritate* insists that the social question today *"has become a radically anthropological question"* (*CV,* no. 75); that *"the question of development is closely bound up with our understanding of the human soul"* (*CV,* no. 75); and that "only a humanism open to the Absolute can guide us in the promotion and building of forms of social and civic life — structures, institutions, culture and *ethos"* (*CV,* no. 78).

Part II: Reimagining Social and Political Order

"Dispersed Political Authority": Subsidiarity and Globalization in *Caritas in Veritate*

William T. Cavanaugh

There is a brief sketch in an episode of *Monty Python's Flying Circus* called "How to Do It." It is a television show with three very enthusiastic presenters breathlessly explaining to the audience such things as how to play the flute, how to split an atom, and how to reconcile the Russians and the Chinese. Here is Jackie to explain how to rid the world of all known diseases: "Well, first of all become a doctor and discover a marvelous cure for something and then when the medical profession really starts to take notice of you, you can jolly well tell them what to do and make sure they get everything right so there'll never be any diseases ever again." I sometimes think of this sketch when reading papal social encyclicals because of the enormity of the problems addressed and the brevity and generality with which the solutions to such problems are treated. It is easy to fault papal social encyclicals for their generality, but it is good to remember that these encyclicals are not meant to be blueprints for the reconstruction of the world order. They are not really about "How to Do It," but rather open up different ways of imagining the world. It is helpful to think of them not as wishing to impose a preconceived model on society from the top down, but rather as seeking to imagine new spaces for a more human society to be enacted.

In this essay I want to explore how *Caritas in Veritate (CV)* seeks to open up such alternative social spaces. I first do an exegesis of the document and show how it attempts to get beyond the binary of state and market by imagining the possibility of other types of social space. I then show how the related theme of subsidiarity has been interpreted in two ways, one more state centered, the other more critical of the state. Finally, I argue that *Caritas in Veritate* fits into the latter trajectory, and show how it can be connected to a Christian tradition of advocacy for a more complex and decentralized social space in the late nineteenth and early twentieth centuries.

I. Beyond the State-Market Binary

Caritas in Veritate is marked by a profound sense that economic development cannot be left to market forces if the goal of integral human development is to be achieved. This is not because the market is an evil in and of itself. The market is simply an instrument that facilitates encounters and exchanges between persons. As I have argued elsewhere,[1] there is no point in blessing or damning "the free market" as such. The real question is "When is a market free?" In other words, under what conditions do exchanges happen that contribute to the flourishing and integral freedom of the parties involved? To answer this question requires a substantive account of the true ends of the human person, and Benedict XVI assumes such an account in *Caritas in Veritate*. As the first paragraph makes plain, it is only in truth that a person becomes free. This truth is not any generic truth, but Christ himself who is the Truth (John 14:6 is cited). Charity appears in the document as the driving, "erotic" force that unites us to God and to one another. In order that charity not degenerate into "sentimentality" and "emotionalism," it must always remain united with the truth.[2] True freedom is freedom in truth. It is truth that frees us from mere subjective opinions and cultural limitations to unite in an objectively valid understanding of the value of things (*CV*, no. 4). Truth is where true communion is made possible.

The fact that truth is bigger than subjective preferences at the same time liberates charity from being confined to a private realm of preferential giving to the less fortunate. Charity, as Pope Benedict makes clear, is "the principle not only of micro-relationships (with friends, with family members or within small groups) but also of macro-relationships (social, economic and political ones)" (*CV*, no. 2). This is one of the most significant emphases in the document. The key third chapter, on "Fraternity, Economic Development and Civil Society," begins with a reflection on the experience of gift. Charity in truth is

---

1. William T. Cavanaugh, *Being Consumed: Economics and Christian Desire* (Grand Rapids: Eerdmans, 2008), chapter 1.

2. Pope Benedict XVI, *Caritas in Veritate (CV)*, no. 3. Translation at http://www.vatican.va/holy_father/benedict_xvi/encyclicals/documents/hf_ben-xvi_enc_20090629_caritas-in-veritate _en.html.

"the absolutely gratuitous gift of God," and it also manifests the essence of gift itself. Gift by its nature is excessive and ecstatic; it goes beyond merit to super-abundance. Applying this kind of language to economics would seem to have a profoundly destabilizing effect on a discipline that treats scarcity as axiomatic and merit as crucial to the just distribution of goods. Benedict makes clear in the same paragraph, nevertheless, that any appeal to the autonomy of the economy, any attempt to shield economics from moral influences stemming from the language of gift, can only lead to abuses of the economic process. "In addressing this key question, we must make it clear, on the one hand, that the logic of gift does not exclude justice, nor does it merely sit alongside it as a second element added from without; on the other hand, economic, social, and political development, if it is to be authentically human, needs to make room for the *principle of gratuitousness* as an expression of fraternity" (*CV,* no. 34).

The relationship between justice, the rendering of *suum cuique* — to each his or her own — and gift, which calls into question the distinction between mine and thine, is spelled out more closely in paragraph 6. Charity goes beyond justice because it offers "what is 'mine' to the other," but it also demands first that justice be done, so that the other gets first what is rightfully his or hers. The earthly city should be built according to law and justice, but charity transcends and completes justice in giving and forgiving. Benedict seems to indicate that charity is not simply superadded to justice in the earthly city. "The *earthly city* is promoted not merely by relationships of rights and duties, but to an even greater and more fundamental extent by relationships of gratuitousness, mercy and communion" (*CV,* no. 6). In this way the earthly city can be "to some degree an anticipation and a prefiguration of the undivided *city of God*" (*CV,* no. 7).[3] What is remarkable about this formulation is the way in which it radically destabilizes the modern boundaries between "secular" and "religious" phenomena. Theology does not face economics and politics across a wide divide; to the contrary, economics and politics are radically incomplete without theology. And theology does not complete them merely by adding on to the foundation they establish; the grace of God of which theology speaks

3. Benedict here seems to be using "earthly city" in a different way than does St. Augustine, for whom the *civitas terrena* is an essentially negative phenomenon, marked by "self-love reaching the point of contempt for God"; Augustine, *The City of God,* trans. Henry Bettenson (Harmondsworth: Penguin, 1972), p. 593 [XIV.28]. For Augustine, it is usually the *civitas Dei* on earth, not the *civitas terrena,* which is the prefiguration of the undivided city of God in heaven, though in XV.2 he allows, in interpreting Old Testament figures like Hagar, that "one part of the earthly city has been made into an image of the Heavenly City, by symbolizing something other than itself, namely that other City."

transforms justice, transforms the economic and the political, into anticipations of the city of God.

Pope Benedict gives this destabilization more specificity by criticizing what he calls "the continuing hegemony of the binary model of market-plus-state" (*CV,* no. 41). Both market and state as they are currently envisioned exclude the kinds of gratuitousness and charity that make for a humane politics and economy. "The market of gratuitousness does not exist, and attitudes of gratuitousness cannot be established by law" (*CV,* no. 39). Benedict acknowledges that *Rerum Novarum* was ahead of its time by advocating for state intervention in the market for the purposes of redistribution. In a mild gesture of discontinuity with his papal predecessor, however, Benedict writes, "Not only is this vision threatened today by the way in which markets and societies are opening up, but it is evidently insufficient to satisfy the demands of a fully humane economy" (*CV,* no. 39).[4] We can no longer trust the economy to create wealth and the state to distribute it because economic activity has overrun all territorial boundaries, while state authority remains within national borders (*CV,* no. 37).

Neither the market nor the state is able to accommodate the kinds of charity in truth that Benedict envisions as fundamental to a truly human social order. Furthermore, and crucially, Benedict comes close to grasping the way in which the choice we commonly face between the state and the market is not really a choice at all because the state and the market work together. In the United States, political party lines are most commonly drawn between the party of the market — Republicans — and the party of the state — Democrats. What is becoming increasingly apparent, however, and may be behind the general disgust with both parties and cynicism about the political elites, is that the state and the market are not opposed forces but collaborate much more often than they contradict one another. In the recent economic crisis, government bailouts of financial institutions that were "too big to fail" bring this reality home. Free market ideology protects corporations from state curbs on corporate power while corporations simultaneously avail themselves of massive state subsidies and state protection from having to face the discipline of the market for reckless behavior. Benedict hints at the collaboration of state and market in terms of their mutual agreement to exclude true conditions of charity and gratuitousness.

---

4. Benedict very quickly returns to a hermeneutic of continuity. The next sentence reads: "What the Church's social doctrine has always sustained, on the basis of its vision of man and society, is corroborated today by the dynamics of globalization" (*CV,* no. 39).

When both the logic of the market and the logic of the state come to an agreement that each will continue to exercise a monopoly over its respective area of influence, in the long term much is lost: solidarity in relations between citizens, participation and adherence, actions of gratuitousness, all of which stand in contrast with *giving in order to acquire* (the logic of exchange) and *giving through duty* (the logic of public obligation, imposed by state law). In order to defeat underdevelopment, action is required not only on improving exchange-based transactions and implanting public welfare structures, but above all on gradually *increasing openness, in a world context, to forms of economic activity marked by quotas of gratuitousness and communion.* The exclusively binary model of market-plus-state is corrosive of society, while economic forms based on solidarity, which find their natural home in civil society without being restricted to it, build up society. (*CV,* no. 39)

As this passage indicates, Benedict's preferred solution to the state-market binary is to encourage the formation of alternative spaces that outwit the logic of both market and state. A key role here is played by "intermediate groups" which, together with individuals and families, make up society (*CV,* no. 7). "To take a stand for the common good is on the one hand to be solicitous for, and on the other hand to avail oneself of, that complex of institutions that give structure to the life of society, juridically, civilly, politically and culturally, making it the *pólis,* or 'city' " (*CV,* no. 7). The pope urges us to think beyond the "private business leader of a capitalistic bent on the one hand, and the state director on the other," and develop both business and political institutions in a complexly "articulated way" (*CV,* no. 41). Business should overcome the "simple distinction between 'private' and 'public' " and between nonprofit and for-profit enterprise (*CV,* no. 41). In the realm of politics, we should "promote a dispersed political authority" (*CV,* no. 41). This does not mean the elimination of the state, and the pope acknowledges the existence of weak states where the rule of law needs to be strengthened. However, "the support aimed at strengthening weak constitutional systems can easily be accompanied by the development of other political players, of a cultural, social, territorial or religious nature, alongside the State. The articulation of political authority at the local, national and international levels is one of the best ways of giving direction to the process of economic globalization. It is also the way to ensure that it does not actually undermine the foundations of democracy" (*CV,* no. 41). It is this emphasis on a "dispersed political authority" and "other political players" beside the state that I find intriguing about the encyclical.

The encyclical has more to say about creating economic spaces that are neither state-run enterprises nor obey market logic. The market tends to bifurcate businesses into for-profit and not-for-profit enterprises. *Caritas in Veritate*, however, encourages the emergence of "hybrid forms of commercial behavior" (*CV*, no. 38) that are neither ruled by the acquisitive logic of market exchange nor confined to the merely private realm of what is commonly considered "charity." "Space also needs to be created within the market for economic activity carried out by subjects who freely choose to act according to principles other than those of pure profit, without sacrificing the production of economic value in the process. The many economic entities that draw their origin from religious and lay initiatives demonstrate that this is concretely possible" (*CV*, no. 37). Here the pope presumably has in mind businesses like Spain's Mondragón Cooperative, founded by the Basque priest José Maria Arizmendiarrieta, a multibillion-dollar company that is entirely worker owned and worker governed, and the Focolare movement's Economy of Communion, whose founder Chiara Lubich describes it as "an economy of giving."[5] It would be possible to write such businesses — along with Fair Trade and other kinds of socially oriented enterprises — into the larger market narrative as niches that appeal to certain persons' preferences. The pope might seem to be doing so by simply juxtaposing them with other, more typical enterprises of market and state. "Alongside profit-oriented private enterprise and the various types of public enterprise, there must be room for commercial entities based on mutualist principles and pursuing social ends to take root and express themselves" (*CV*, no. 38). However, Pope Benedict continues on to indicate that such entities are not meant to remain confined to niches, but are rather meant to evangelize the economy as a whole: "It is from their reciprocal encounter in the marketplace that one may expect hybrid forms of commercial behaviour to emerge, and hence an attentiveness to ways of *civilizing the economy*" (*CV*, no. 38). Clearly the effect of such enterprises is not meant to be limited.

To say this, however, is not therefore to say that scale is unimportant, or that such enterprises are meant to grow large. There are many indications in *Caritas in Veritate* that scale is important and, while not wistfully wishing to ignore or turn back the clock on globalization, the pope indicates that local enterprises must be considered afresh as offering important advantages for the civilization of the economy. For example, in paragraph 27 the pope discusses food insecurity and points to the necessity of local communities being involved in any decisions having to do with the use of the land. In this vein, Pope

---

5. Chiara Lubich, quoted at www.edc-online.org/uk/_idea.htm. For more information on the Mondragón Cooperative, see www.mondragon.mcc.es.

Benedict also recommends the proper use of traditional farming techniques, alongside innovation, as an apparent contrast to the ways in which globalized agribusiness has imposed its solutions on local economies. The encyclical similarly warns in paragraph 40 that the "growth in scale" of business has made it increasingly rare that businesses remain loyal to any particular territory or remain in the hands of a "stable director who feels responsible in the long term, not just the short term." Thus has emerged a "new cosmopolitan class of managers" (*CV*, no. 40) that are beholden only to the shareholders of anonymous funds. Forgotten in this cosmopolitan atmosphere are the other stakeholders, in particular geographical areas that have to live with the consequences of corporate behavior. "The so-called outsourcing of production can weaken the company's sense of responsibility towards the stakeholders — namely the workers, the suppliers, the consumers, the natural environment and broader society — in favour of the shareholders, who are not tied to a specific geographical area and who therefore enjoy extraordinary mobility" (*CV*, no. 40). The pope does not wish to shut down all international investment, but thinks that it must be undertaken only while considering the "real contribution to local society" (*CV*, no. 40) that such investments can make. When discussing development projects, he also emphasizes that "the people who benefit from them ought to be directly involved in their planning and implementation," and recommends "micro-projects" alongside "macro-projects" (*CV*, no. 47).

While it cannot be said that Pope Benedict is simply adopting a "small is beautiful" approach to the economy, it is clear that an approach that seeks to prioritize charity must also give priority to face-to-face encounters between human beings. As the pope writes, "In a climate of mutual trust, the *market* is the economic institution that permits encounter between persons. . . . And today it is this trust which has ceased to exist, and the loss of trust is a grave loss" (*CV*, no. 35). The larger the scale of the state and corporation becomes, the more difficult trust becomes because it is difficult to trust people that you cannot see. The anonymous nature of global finance, to which the pope refers, is one symptom of the magnification of scale that has attended globalization. In response, Pope Benedict recommends in particular micro-credit and micro-finance more generally (*CV*, nos. 45, 65). Again, however, micro-finance is not meant to create niches: "Efforts are needed — and it is essential to say this — not only to create 'ethical' sectors or segments of the economy or the world of finance, but to ensure that the whole economy — the whole of finance — is ethical, not merely by virtue of an external label, but by its respect for requirements intrinsic to its very nature" (*CV*, no. 45).

Pope Benedict's emphasis on the local is clearly indebted to the principle of subsidiarity articulated by his predecessors. According to *Caritas in Veritate*, "subsidiarity is first and foremost a form of assistance to the human person via the autonomy of intermediate bodies" (*CV*, no. 57). The word "autonomy" is interesting here, because it indicates something more than intermediate bodies as a simple stepping stone between the individual and the state, something more than the way individuals present themselves in groups before the state, or the way that the state's will is mediated to individuals. Intermediate bodies have their own life and proper autonomy. In them, subsidiarity "fosters freedom and participation through assumption of responsibility," something that a large, bureaucratic state cannot foster. "By considering reciprocity as the heart of what it is to be a human being, subsidiarity is the most effective antidote against any form of all-encompassing welfare state" (*CV*, no. 57). It is worth noting that here the main target of subsidiarity is not, as it was in previous papal encyclicals, the totalitarian state, less a threat since the fall of the Berlin Wall. The welfare state is a first world, not second world, phenomenon. Subsidiarity should be used, according to *Caritas in Veritate*, to create better welfare systems, eliminating waste and fraudulent claims (*CV*, no. 60), by including individuals and intermediate groups. "A more devolved and organic system of social solidarity, less bureaucratic but no less coordinated, would make it possible to harness much dormant energy, for the benefit of solidarity between peoples" (*CV*, no. 60). Although the prescriptions here are vague, Pope Benedict does recommend, in the sentence immediately following this one, the possibility of "allowing citizens to decide how to allocate a portion of their taxes they pay to the State" (*CV*, no. 60).

This devolution of political authority to individuals and groups seems hard to square with Pope Benedict's call in paragraph 67 for "a true world political authority." What exactly the pope has in mind is hard to say, but he envisions a regulatory body with more power than the United Nations. "Such an authority would need to be universally recognized and to be vested with the effective power to ensure security for all, regard for justice, and respect for rights. Obviously it would have to have the authority to ensure compliance with its decisions from all parties, and also with the coordinated measures adopted in various international forums" (*CV*, no. 67). At the same time, Pope Benedict recognizes that such an authority would need to be "organized in a subsidiary and stratified way" in order that it not produce "a dangerous universal power of a tyrannical nature" (*CV*, no. 57). How exactly this balancing act is to work is not spelled out. What is clear, however, is that the pope is pointing to models both below the state — intermediate associations and cooperative forms of business — and above the state — transnational political authorities — in advocating a more dispersed and articulated political authority.

II. Interpreting Subsidiarity

How one reads *Caritas in Veritate* will have a lot to do with how one interprets the principle of subsidiarity more generally. It can be viewed as a procedural principle that takes current political and social structures for granted, but states that social problems should be addressed at the lowest level at which they can be addressed effectively. Applying the principle would then be a matter of empirical tests of effectiveness at the various levels of social authority. We might disagree over the results of those tests and how to conduct them, but who could disagree that families, neighborhoods, businesses, and social groups should be allowed to resolve their problems themselves, insofar as they can, and the state should only step in when needed? If both the European Union and the George W. Bush administration embraced the principle of subsidiarity, who could be against it?[6] On the other hand, the principle of subsidiarity can be read as more than a procedural principle, as rooted in a theological anthropology that is deeply subversive of the modern state's tendency to reduce social relations to an oscillation between the state and the individual.

Bryan Hehir can serve as an example of the first type of approach. In an essay on subsidiarity in a volume on religion and the welfare state in America, Hehir argues that subsidiarity is a "second-order principle" that only makes sense within a broader framework that moves from interpersonal relations, to citizen-state relations, to state-state relations, then to the international system.[7] Subsidiarity is a "procedural guideline not an independent substantive concept" that helps determine at which level problems should be addressed.[8] According to Hehir, subsidiarity does not begin with a defensive posture against the size or intrusiveness or expansion of the state, but with a consideration of the normative responsibilities of the state for the common good. In this respect, says Hehir, we should not overemphasize the differences between Catholic and liberal views of the state.[9]

According to Hehir, the story of subsidiarity belongs within the shift from papal support under Gregory XVI and Leo XII for an organic "ethical state"

6. Robert K. Vischer, "Subsidiarity as Subversion: Local Power, Legal Norms, and the Liberal State," *Journal of Catholic Social Thought* 2, no. 2 (Summer 2005): 277-78.

7. J. Bryan Hehir, "Religious Ideas and Social Policy: Subsidiarity and Catholic Style of Ministry," in *Who Will Provide? The Changing Role of Religion in American Social Welfare,* ed. Mary Jo Bane, Brent Coffin, and Ronald Thiemann (Boulder, Colo.: Westview, 2000), p. 101.

8. Hehir, "Religious Ideas and Social Policy," p. 101.

9. Hehir, "Religious Ideas and Social Policy," pp. 101-2.

that monitored moral and religious activity in society to the post–Vatican II acceptance of a "constitutional state" that recognized religious liberty and pluralism within civil society. Hehir adopts John Courtney Murray's telling of this shift, and fits the rise of the principle of subsidiarity, first articulated by Pius XI, within it.[10] According to Hehir, subsidiarity is part of the process of "shrinking the state" in Catholic social thought insofar as Catholic social thought assumes that the state will no longer be in charge of religious and moral hygiene. While Leo XIII assumed that the state was responsible for the whole of the common good, his successors would limit that role and recognize other actors such as unions and professional groups as contributing to the common good.[11] At the same time, however, Hehir claims that the fundamentally positive view of the state carries over into subsidiarity from the older conception of the state.

Murray specifies the socioeconomic teaching of Leo XIII and Pius XI as the initial point of divergence from the ethical to the constitutional notion of the state's role in society. Subsidiarity fits into this process of development. It does set limits to the state's role, but it does so from a starting point of a conception of state power that gave it *primary* responsibility for the achievement of the common good. Contemporary conservative discourse *begins* with a highly restricted conception of the state's social role and then seeks to use subsidiarity to maintain or even tighten these restrictions. But the background from which the principle emerged began with a quite positive conception of the state's role, and then sought to assess how that conception should function vis-à-vis socioeconomic policy.[12]

Hehir manages to situate subsidiarity both within a narrative of "shrinking the state" and within a narrative of a fundamentally positive view of the state that looks benignly on the state's expansion. According to Hehir, the key figure in the "evolution" of subsidiarity toward a greater role for the state is John XXIII, whose 1961 encyclical *Mater et Magistra* recognized subsidiarity but treated it within the context of a recognition of increasing "socialization." Socialization, says Hehir, is a "descriptive term identifying growing levels of complexity in modern society which have moral consequences."[13] Socialization justifies state intervention in social and economic life to guarantee basic human rights and fulfill human needs. In fact, it provides the warrant for John XXIII and his successors to reinterpret and even override subsidiarity. "The reinterpretation

10. Hehir, "Religious Ideas and Social Policy," p. 102.
11. Hehir, "Religious Ideas and Social Policy," p. 105.
12. Hehir, "Religious Ideas and Social Policy," pp. 102-3.
13. Hehir, "Religious Ideas and Social Policy," p. 106. The word "socialization" does not actually appear in the text of *Mater et Magistra,* nor does "socialize" or "socialized."

maintains subsidiarity as a key functional principle in Catholic social teaching and continues to give it primacy as a norm for assessing the appropriate role of the state and its relationships to other social institutions. But the character of socialization and its impact on the rights and duties of individuals provides a rationale for overriding the limit subsidiarity places on the state."[14] Hehir does not ignore the role of intermediate associations in this scheme, but he locates them within a story of how Catholic institutions, such as hospitals, evolved in the United States from a parallel presence with regard to existing social institutions to a collaborative presence fully engaged with the federal government at all levels. Though acknowledging problems of identity and integrity of mission, Hehir thinks the collaborative model best exemplifies the positive Catholic view of the expansive state.[15]

In contrast to Hehir, a second type of reading of subsidiarity emphasizes its critical edge with regard to state power. Robert Vischer's article "Subsidiarity as Subversion: Local Power, Legal Norms, and the Liberal State" is one example of this type of reading. Vischer begins not with an abstract ideal of the "role of the state" as such. He begins instead with an empirical analysis of the way liberal states actually function to weaken intermediate forms of human association. He cites Bernard de Jouvenel's work *On Power* to argue that, despite our normal assumption that individual rights act as a check on state power, the opposite is the case. The democratic state grows ever larger and more powerful in an attempt to liberate the individual from the tyranny of social ties, that is, from forms of norm-setting for common life other than those of the state.[16] Legal decisions in the liberal state tend to view not social groups but only the individual and his or her consumer preferences as the subject of rights. As an example, Vischer cites a recent case in which the California Supreme Court compelled Catholic Charities to subsidize contraception to its employees despite the fact that to do so would violate Catholic teaching. As Vischer points out, in refusing to exempt Catholic Charities from a state law mandating the coverage of contraception under employer prescription drug plans, the court recognized not only a negative liberty of the individual to practice contraception regardless of his or her employer, but a positive liberty

14. Hehir, "Religious Ideas and Social Policy," p. 106.

15. Hehir, "Religious Ideas and Social Policy," pp. 106-13.

16. Vischer, "Subsidiarity as Subversion," pp. 279-81. Robert Nisbet's work is excellent in making the same point. Nisbet shows, from a sociological point of view, that "the real conflict in modern political history has not been, as is so often stated, between State and individual, but between State and social group"; Robert Nisbet, *The Quest for Community* (London: Oxford University Press, 1953), p. 109.

to compel the employer to pay for that practice.[17] Vischer is consequently much less sanguine than Hehir about the "collaboration" of the Catholic health system with the state. Vischer sees "conscience clauses" as a necessary but desperate rearguard action against a wider trend toward state enforcement of the availability of morally controversial procedures such as abortion in all health care facilities that receive state funding.[18]

The principle of subsidiarity for Vischer is much more than a procedural guideline for governments, but is rather deeply rooted in a Christian anthropology of the person as essentially in relationship with others. Subsidiarity works against both individualism and collectivism by establishing the priority of deep forms of face-to-face community. The person is only a person in communion with others, and this cannot be replaced by either more abstract forms of collectivity like the nation-state or more isolating forms of individualism based on consumer preference. Subsidiarity is therefore subversive of the reigning paradigm of the state. When the state in actual practice seeks "either to marginalize intermediate associations or remake them in the state's own image," subsidiarity's support for the integrity and autonomy of such associations can serve as a "subversive wrench in the collective enthronement of individualism."[19] Vischer does not wish to do away with all centralized authority. "Subsidiarity does, however, reframe our image of the modern state, envisioning it as a resource for localized empowerment and coordination, rather than as the arbiter and provider of the social good."[20] The goal should be carving out a plurality of public spaces where different visions of the good can flourish. According to Vischer, this does not at all mean the abandonment of the notion of truly objective common goods; it only means a reluctance to impose them through state coercion.[21]

III. Alternative Social Spaces

My intention here is not to do a thorough exposition of Hehir's and Vischer's own views, but to use them to show two distinct trajectories in the interpre-

17. Vischer, "Subsidiarity as Subversion," p. 281.
18. Vischer, "Subsidiarity as Subversion," p. 282.
19. Vischer, "Subsidiarity as Subversion," p. 288.
20. Vischer, "Subsidiarity as Subversion," p. 288.
21. Vischer, "Subsidiarity as Subversion," pp. 305-11. Vischer thinks that state coercion is justifiable in a case like abortion, where the matter to be decided is the unavoidably collective matter of who is to be included as a person. He thinks, on the other hand, that legally discouraging the use of contraception would not be a legitimate use of state coercion.

tation of subsidiarity, one with a fundamentally positive view of the modern state, and one with a more critical view of state power. To which trajectory does *Caritas in Veritate* belong? Though not without ambiguity, the document I think belongs in the latter camp. In it, subsidiarity seems to be more than a procedural guideline for political leaders but fits within Benedict's attempt to promote charity, gratuitousness, and obedience to truth in social relations. Benedict sees that state coercion cannot enforce love and the market cannot leave truth to the individual's consumer preferences. *Caritas in Veritate* thus gropes for a way to move beyond the state-market binary by encouraging the proliferation of alternative political and economic spaces, intermediate associations and hybrid forms of business, a dispersed political authority, and economies infused with charity. It is primarily in those kinds of spaces that true human encounters can take place, and charity in truth can flourish. The point, however, is decidedly not to restrict charity in truth to enclaves, but to disperse such gifts throughout the whole precisely by dispersing the state-market binary that would confine and marginalize them.

Caritas in Veritate can be connected to a tradition of Catholic social thought and practice in the early twentieth century that emphasized the importance of decentralized forms of social life. The *Compendium of the Social Doctrine of the Church* traces the principle of subsidiarity back to *Rerum Novarum*.[22] Though it is not explicitly articulated there, Leo XIII does write of state interference in lesser associations, the "principle being that the law must not undertake more, nor proceed further, than is required for the remedy of the evil or the removal of the mischief."[23] The state has a negative duty to prevent such associations from spreading evil, but the state is not prior to such associations and is not responsible for their genesis. Society, for Leo XIII, is not an aggregate of individuals but a society of societies that, at least in the case of families and religious confraternities and societies, spring directly from the law of nature.[24] Though he does not question the designation of intermediate societies as "private,"[25] as Benedict XVI perhaps would, Leo XIII nevertheless emphasizes that such associations are "real societies."[26] His vision of the social order is based on the proliferation of organisms like the "artificers'

22. Pontifical Council for Justice and Peace, *Compendium of the Social Doctrine of the Church* (Washington, D.C.: United States Conference of Catholic Bishops, 2004), no. 185, p. 81.

23. Pope Leo XIII, *Rerum Novarum*, no. 36. Translation at http://www.vatican.va/holy_father/leo_xiii/encyclicals/documents/hf_l-xiii_enc_15051891_rerum-novarum_en.html.

24. Pope Leo XIII, *Rerum Novarum*, nos. 13-14, 53.

25. Pope Leo XIII, *Rerum Novarum*, no. 51.

26. Pope Leo XIII, *Rerum Novarum*, no. 50.

guilds of olden times,"[27] unions, mutual aid societies, confraternities, and a host of other, organically related forms of social life.[28] Leo XIII expresses his concern that, since the final destruction of guilds in the eighteenth century, workers have remained isolated and defenseless.[29]

The origin of an explicit principle of subsidiarity is commonly traced to paragraph 79 of *Quadragesimo Anno:* "Still, that most weighty principle, which cannot be set aside or changed, remains fixed and unshaken in social philosophy: Just as it is gravely wrong to take from individuals what they can accomplish by their own initiative and industry and give it to the community, so also it is an injustice and at the same time a grave evil and disturbance of right order to assign to a greater and higher association what lesser and subordinate organizations can do."[30] Subsidiarity was articulated by Pius XI as part of his vaguely corporatist scheme to revitalize guild-like associations to break the monotonous relationship of state and individual. As he says in paragraph 78 of *Quadragesimo Anno:* "When we speak of the reform of institutions, the State comes chiefly to mind, not as if universal well-being were to be expected from its activity, but because things have come to such a pass through the evil of what we have termed 'individualism' that, following upon the overthrow and near extinction of that rich social life which was once highly developed through associations of various kinds, there remain virtually only individuals and the State."[31] Bryan Hehir is right that Pius XI came out of a Thomist tradition that had a positive view of the state in the abstract, but Pius was clearly alarmed by the actual form of the modern state that had absorbed the authority that "the wrecked associations once bore."[32]

Pius XI was concerned that economic life not be left to the competition of the market or directed by an all-embracing state.[33] The remedy was largely entrusted to self-governing guilds and associations that would bring workers and owners of industry together, and in which the interests of the whole industry or profession would hold first place.[34] Even more explicitly than

---

27. Pope Leo XIII, *Rerum Novarum,* no. 49.

28. Pope Leo XIII, *Rerum Novarum,* nos. 48-54. In paragraph 30, Leo XIII makes clear, as does Benedict XVI, that state welfare is not an adequate substitute for Christian charity.

29. Pope Leo XIII, *Rerum Novarum,* no. 3.

30. Pope Pius XI, *Quadragesimo Anno,* no. 79. Translation at http://www.vatican.va/holy_father/pius_xi/encyclicals/documents/hf_p-xi_enc_19310515_quadragesimo-anno_en.html.

31. Pope Pius XI, *Quadragesimo Anno,* no. 78.

32. Pope Pius XI, *Quadragesimo Anno,* no. 78.

33. Pope Pius XI, *Quadragesimo Anno,* no. 88.

34. Pope Pius XI, *Quadragesimo Anno,* no. 85.

Leo XIII, Pius XI emphasized that all such social organisms were not dependent on the state for recognition, but were derived from a "natural right to form associations" by "those who needed it most to defend themselves from ill treatment at the hands of the powerful."[35]

As the language of guilds makes clear, both Leo XIII and Pius XI looked to the medieval past for models of a proper social order. "For there was a social order once," writes Pius XI, "which, although indeed not perfect or in all respects ideal, nevertheless, met in a certain measure the requirements of right reason."[36] If it has perished, he goes on to say, it is not because it could not have been adapted to changing conditions, but because modernity has been too much tainted by love of self. Both popes were heavily influenced by the corporatist romanticization of the Middle Ages so popular in Catholic circles in the late nineteenth and early twentieth centuries. Figures such as Karl von Vogelsang in Austria, Friedrich von Schlegel and Adam Müller in Germany, and René de la Tour du Pin in France advocated replacing the current capitalist system with guilds that would include both workers and employers. These guilds or corporations would be semi-autonomous with regard to the state and would exercise the right to set prices, wages, and working conditions based on principles of justice and charity.[37] Leo XIII did not adopt the corporatist position in its extreme form, but was more directly influenced by Bishop Wilhelm von Ketteler of Mainz, who did not wish to abolish capitalism but to reform it piecemeal with corporatist ideas and structures.[38] Pius XI's posture was similar, though the advent of totalitarianism gave him even more reason to be wary of centralized state control.

Corporatism in Europe was ultimately a failure. The term was adopted by right-wing regimes in Catholic countries such as Austria, Italy, Portugal, and Spain. In these countries corporatism was little more than a façade for bringing workers to heel under associations dominated by capitalists and totalitarian regimes. Corporatism was recruited into the very kind of state centralization that the original corporatists had tried to counteract.[39] Despite this hijacking

---

35. Pope Pius XI, *Quadragesimo Anno,* no. 30. See also nos. 37 and 87.

36. Pope Pius XI, *Quadragesimo Anno,* no. 97.

37. Richard L. Camp, *The Papal Ideology of Social Reform* (Leiden: E. J. Brill, 1969), pp. 26-27.

38. Camp, *The Papal Ideology of Social Reform,* pp. 27-29. See also John E. Kelly, "The Influence of Aquinas' Natural Law Theory on the Principle of 'Corporatism' in the Thought of Leo XIII and Pius XI," in *Things Old and New: Catholic Social Thought Revisited,* ed. Francis P. McHugh and Samuel M. Natale (Lanham: University Press of America, 1993), pp. 104-43.

39. Camp, *The Papal Ideology of Social Reform,* p. 37.

of corporatist language, I want to argue, nevertheless, that there was something valuable in the emphasis of the earlier tradition on the dispersal of political and economic authority through the proliferation of semi-autonomous associations. I think such ways of resisting the centralizing tendencies of state and market are very relevant today, and have affinities with the vision of *Caritas in Veritate.*

In addition to the continental Catholic corporatist tradition that the popes drew on, there was an English tradition of pluralist social thought in the same period that, in some ways, has better stood the test of time. Although some of it was steeped in a romanticized and nostalgic view of the medieval period,[40] interesting work was being done in legal and political theory that attempted to resist the growth of the sovereign state in modernity by calling on an earlier tradition of dispersed political authority. The publication of Otto von Gierke's *Political Theories of the Middle Age* in English in 1900[41] gave impetus to Anglo-Catholic pluralists like John Neville Figgis and to English Catholic distributists like G. K. Chesterton and Hilaire Belloc. Gierke shows how, with the growing hegemony of Roman law in the High Middle Ages, the idea that associations or "corporations" were organic and natural entities — as they clearly are in modern papal social tradition — was replaced by the idea that a corporation is a *persona ficta,* that is, a person by fiction only. And this fiction is a creation of the sovereign power; "fiction theory" leads to "concession theory." As F. W. Maitland put it in his introduction to the English version of Gierke's work, for modernity, "the corporation is, and must be, the creature of the State. Into its nostrils the State must breathe the breath of a fictitious life, for otherwise it would be no animated body but individualistic dust."[42] No body exists naturally between the state and individual unless the state recognizes its existence. A corollary of this concentration of power in the state is, as Gierke says, the "tendency to emancipate the Individual from all bonds that are not of the State's making."[43]

In the medieval view, by contrast, the whole was not simply a collection of individuals, but each part was a microcosm of the whole and possessed its

---

40. For an overview of Catholic medievalism in the late nineteenth and early twentieth centuries, see Philip Gleason, "Mass and Maypole Revisited: American Catholics and the Middle Ages," *Catholic Historical Review* 57, no. 2 (July 1971): 249-74.

41. The book in English was a translation of just one section of a much larger work, *Das deutsche Genossenschaftsrecht (The German Law of Associations).*

42. Frederick William Maitland, "Translator's Introduction," in Otto Gierke, *Political Theories of the Middle Ages* (Boston: Beacon, 1958), p. xxx.

43. Gierke, *Political Theories of the Middle Ages,* p. 94.

own intrinsic value. Each part reflected the order of God's rule of the whole within it.[44] Furthermore, the image of the commonwealth as the body of Christ facilitated what Gierke calls a "Mediate Articulation"[45] whereby each member is not joined directly to the head: "otherwise there would be a monstrosity; finger must be directly joined, not to head but to hand; then hand to arm, arm to shoulder, shoulder to neck, neck to head."[46] In other words, to call the organic associations of human social life "intermediate associations" is inadequate because it assumes that such associations merely stand directly between the individual and the state and mediate power between those two poles.

The English pluralists active in the early decades of the twentieth century drew on Gierke and others to put forward a vision of society not as a monolithic aggregate of individuals, but as a complexly articulated association of associations. Unlike the American pluralism of Robert A. Dahl, English pluralism did not see intermediate associations as conflicting competitors for influence over the state. Associations were seen rather as public spaces in their own right, bodies in which people pursued truly common purposes and to which people owed loyalties that were not simply trumped by allegiance to a sovereign state. In a way similar to Pius XI, the English pluralists advocated a conception of society based on self-governing associations of producers and workers. The specific problems of the railways would be dealt with by a governing body of the railway industry, outside the government's active control, but still under its formal legal power to intervene. The state would still be necessary to coordinate, but it would be a minimal state whose primary task would be the creation of the conditions necessary for associations to flourish.[47]

I cannot begin to unpack the full proposals of the English pluralists here, nor is it my intention to do so. I only mean to suggest that *Caritas in Veritate*'s call for a "dispersed political authority" can be located within a longer trajectory of Christian social thought for whom subsidiarity meant more than simply delegating tasks to the lowest part of the social pyramid that stretches from individuals through intermediate associations to the sovereign state. I am not arguing that Benedict XVI necessarily consciously locates himself within this trajectory. I do think, however, that reading this encyclical within that trajec-

---

44. Gierke, *Political Theories of the Middle Ages*, pp. 7-8.

45. Gierke, *Political Theories of the Middle Ages*, p. 28.

46. Gierke, *Political Theories of the Middle Ages*, p. 135n89.

47. Paul Q. Hirst provides an excellent introduction to the English pluralists in *The Pluralist Theory of the State: Selected Writings of G. D. H. Cole, J. N. Figgis, and H. J. Laski* (London: Routledge, 1989), pp. 1-41.

tory can not only connect *Caritas in Veritate* to an earlier tradition in Catholic thought, but it can also connect Catholic social thought to some of the interesting work being done by "radical democrats" like Sheldon Wolin and Romand Coles in the United States. *Caritas in Veritate* puts forth a breathtakingly ambitious vision of a political economy that is based in love and truth. This vision cannot be realized within a larger resignation to the state-market binary, but requires a more radical reconfiguration of social space.

Practicing Gratuity: A Vision for Families and the Social Order

Julie Hanlon Rubio

By way of introduction, I offer an anecdote from my family. My mother taught me to shop. From her I learned that when I enter a store, I am playing to win. I should come armed with knowledge of food prices in my area, store sales, and coupons. Though I would never fail to pay or use coupons dishonestly, my aim is to leave having bought only "loss leaders" and sale items, leaving behind more expensive merchandise the store managers hoped would lure me. Because my mother is such a good shopper, my father rarely enters a store. On those occasions when he does, we always ask how much he has paid for his merchandise. Inevitably, it is too much. My mother expresses her disbelief that he has paid four dollars for a protein bar or twenty-five dollars for a hat. My father always says, "Now, Fran, I'm sure the people who run that store are real nice people." My mother rolls her eyes. This may be true, but it is beside the point. While in our family, neighborhood, or church community, my brothers and I were taught by word and example to be charitable, in public life we were expected to be competitive in order to get the better of those playing against us.

In private life we extol those who give more than they receive, but selfless giving in public life is considered weak or even irresponsible. Pope Benedict XVI's radical message in *Caritas in Veritate (CV)* is that for Christians there is one ethic for family and society, and it is an ethic of solidarity, participation, and, most important, gratuity, "all of which stand in contrast with *giving in order to acquire* (the logic of exchange) and *giving through duty* (the logic of public obligation, imposed by State law)."[1] For Benedict, domination

---

1. Pope Benedict XVI, *Caritas in Veritate* (Washington, D.C.: United States Conference of Catholic Bishops, 2009), no. 39.

of the ethos of market and state "is corrosive of society, while economic forms based on solidarity . . . build up society" (*CV,* no. 39). In this essay, I hope to illuminate and defend Benedict's prophetic contention that gratuity is to be the animating principle not only of family ethics but also of social ethics and describe what this might mean for ordinary believers. I begin by situating *Caritas in Veritate* in the context of Catholic social teaching where, I argue, love holds a central place. In the rest of the essay, I sketch the implications of this claim for individuals, for marriage, and for families.

I. Love at the Heart of Catholic Social Teaching

Catholic social teaching is celebrated for bringing the attention of Catholics and men and women of good will to the reality of injustice and calling them to work for a better world. On issues as diverse as war, economics, health care, the environment, human rights, capital punishment, racism, sexism, and the rights of families, popes and bishops exhort readers to take their place in a tradition that, from the prophets of the Hebrew Bible to Jesus of Nazareth, links belief in God to action for justice. Under the rubric of justice, Catholic social teaching is noted for bringing forward principles of human dignity, respect for life, association, participation, the option for the poor, solidarity, stewardship of creation, subsidiarity, equality, and the common good.[2]

While all of these principles affirm connections among human beings, they can seem distant from principles of love that stand at the center of Catholic family ethics. Consider the late John Paul II's teaching in *Familiaris Consortio:* "Creating the human race in his own image and continually keeping it in being, God inscribed in the humanity of man and woman the vocation, and thus the capacity and responsibility, of love and communion. Love is therefore the fundamental vocation of every human being."[3] According to the pope, the vocation of total self-giving is lived out primarily in marriage or religious life.[4] Most who hear these words understand their meaning at an intuitive level and

2. See William J. Byron, "Ten Building Blocks of Catholic Social Teaching," *America,* October 31, 1998 (http://www.americamagazine.org/content/article.cfm?article_id=11729 &s=1).

3. Pope John Paul II, *Familiaris Consortio* (Washington, D.C.: United States Conference of Catholic Bishops, 1981), no. 11. Translation at http://www.vatican.va/holy_father/john_paul _ii/apost_exhortations/documents/hf_jp-ii_exh_19811122_familiaris-consortio_en.html.

4. Pope John Paul II, *Familiaris Consortio,* no. 11.

would agree that giving themselves in love to another person ought to be a central priority in their lives.

However, in *Caritas in Veritate,* Pope Benedict XVI makes the radical move of naming love as central to Christian social ethics. "Charity," he says, "is at the heart of the Church's social doctrine," the key principle for both micro- and macro-relationships (*CV,* no. 2). Benedict knows how counter-cultural this will sound. Presumably, he is moved to speak about charity in response to the isolation or alienation that is becoming more and more the human experience, especially in the developed world. Most of our interactions are functional rather than reciprocal because we are not consciously aware of being in relationship with those who, for example, make our clothes, grow our food, repair our homes, live on our street, or sell us protein bars. Time with other people is increasingly shared online and even personal encounters typically include TV, movies, the Internet, texting, or gaming, especially, but not exclusively, for children and teens.[5] Aware of the growing pervasiveness of the market and technology, the pope is asking what that does to us. What happens when so many of our interactions are founded on utility and not mutuality? He calls alienation "one of the deepest forms of poverty" and challenges us to live more of our lives in a relational mode that is truer to our essence, saying that the more authentically a person lives in relationship, the better. The more relationally we live, the more human we become because to be human is to be in relation (*CV,* no. 53). Because this is the truth of who we are as human beings, "the earthly city is promoted not merely by relationships of rights and duties, but to an even greater and more fundamental extent by relationships of gratuitousness, mercy and communion" (*CV,* no. 6).

Caritas in Veritate's emphasis on charity is consistent with traditional Catholic social teaching. Modern popes have been critical of the excesses of capitalism and national government, and have mourned the loss of community in the post–Industrial Revolution world. Again and again, they have emphasized the principle of subsidiarity, which prioritizes smaller groupings, as an anecdote to alienation. Documents in the earlier part of the twentieth century, such as *Rerum Novarum* and *Quadragesimo Anno,* offered a vision of family, craft guilds, and smaller communities as an alternative to modern urban life. Later popes like John XXIII and John Paul II embraced the market, business and industry, and national and international government. They exhorted

---

5. See "Daily Media Use among Children and Teens Up Dramatically from Five Years Ago," http://www.kff.org/entmedia/entmedia012010nr.cfm.

Christians to enter and transform the world instead of withdrawing from it. Still, though the earlier visions of a simpler society are now seen by most readers of Catholic social teaching as nostalgic and unrealistic, they remain powerful reminders of a way of life that seems more human, even though it is inevitably more limited.[6]

In the face of growing loss of relationality, a newer generation of Catholic theologians and activists has shown a greater interest in Catholic affirmations of local community. Theologian Kelly Johnson has looked closely at the personalism of the Catholic Worker co-founder Peter Maurin, suggesting it is worthy of imitation today.[7] Catholic Workers in St. Louis are promoting reflection on the economic theory of distributism, which is "rediscovering the small — the local economy, family farms, and cooperation" — so that the economy can better serve local needs, workers can be paid just wages for worthwhile labor, and people can live in greater harmony with their environment.[8] Localism is seen as a way to be authentically human or to live in right relation with people and the earth. It requires creating an alternative space within the larger (dysfunctional) economy.

Others in the new generation offer less radical alternatives that prioritize the local while not absolutizing it. William Cavanaugh suggests that a desire to live in communion (born of the experience of "being consumed" into the body of Christ) should push Christians to seek alternatives to regular market exchanges, such as buying fair trade coffee, humanely raised meat from local farms, and products from worker-owned cooperatives, but he does not make these the only moral options.[9] Similarly, David Matzko McCarthy responds to the loss of community by offering a celebration of the working-class urban neighborhood, where a system of open gift exchange prevails over the strict reciprocity of the market and the suburban enclave. In local networks, McCarthy claims, there is "a pattern of reciprocity" in which "a series of overlapping non-identical gifts take on value and balance in an intricate constellation of wedding showers, baptisms, and first communions, three-bean casseroles for

6. See Christine Firer Hinze, "Commentary on *Quadragesimo anno*," in *Modern Catholic Social Teaching: Commentaries & Interpretations*, ed. Kenneth R. Himes, O.F.M. (Washington, D.C.: Georgetown University Press, 2005), pp. 151-75, especially pp. 168-72.

7. Kelly Johnson, *The Fear of Beggars: Stewardship and Poverty in Christian Ethics* (Grand Rapids: Eerdmans, 2007).

8. Jenny Truax, "Distributism Made Ridiculously Simple," *The Roundtable* (Winter 2010): 3-7, p. 4 http://karenhousecw.org/RTDistributism2010.htm.

9. William Cavanaugh, *Being Consumed: Economics and Christian Desire* (Grand Rapids: Eerdmans, 2008).

grieving families, rides to work, babysitting, informal childcare, and hand-me-down clothes."[10]

Pope Benedict's newest encyclical emerges from this same cultural moment in which many experience less gratuity and communion than they would like. Though he acknowledges that the global market is here to stay, he argues for making space in the economy for alternative ways of being that are more hospitable to gift-giving. He hopes for some transformation of what he realizes will be the more dominant profit-driven industries. Above all, he asks Christians not to lose sight of the charity that should be at the heart of all parts of their life. *Caritas in Veritate* can be read as "one long call to conversion" requiring "new eyes and a new heart."[11] It can justly be called radical and yet, in view of the truth of its social analysis, deserving of close consideration of all Christians. However, Catholic social teaching has often offered prophetic calls to conversion that have had little effect on the everyday lives of Catholics, perhaps because the statements are general enough to allow most to believe their lives are in harmony with the Church's vision. It is necessary to flesh out implications of this call to conversion in social and personal life, so that more people are able to see what a life marked by gratuity would look like.

II. All Called to Concern for the Social Order

According to *Caritas in Veritate,* love of neighbor means working for the common good so that each person can effectively pursue what is good on his or her own terms. "To love someone," the pope argues, is not simply to have good will toward another but rather "to desire that person's good and to take effective steps to secure it" (*CV,* no. 7). In families, parental love for children involves a commitment to provide education, bring them into a religious community, help them avoid destructive influences, and establish practices in the home that contribute to their moral formation.[12] Spouses, too, give evidence of their love not only by showing affection to each other but also by supporting each other's public work and personal growth. Few would dispute this contention, but the pope makes a significant move when he claims that love of those neighbors who live outside one's home entails involving oneself in "the life of

---

10. David Matzko McCarthy, *Sex and Love in the Home,* 2nd ed. (London: SCM, 2004), pp. 103-4.

11. Douglas Farrow, "Charity and Unity," *First Things* (October 2009): 38.

12. Pope John Paul II, *Familiaris Consortio,* nos. 36-41.

society, juridically, civilly, politically and culturally, making it the *pólis,* or city" (*CV,* no. 7). No one who claims to love others can avoid social or political responsibility for creating and sustaining a society wherein people can pursue the good.

However, the ways in which Christians will take up this responsibility will vary. Some have vocations to work directly tied to political or social reform, while others may work more at the neighborhood or community level (*CV,* no. 7). Some have more power, money, or influence than others. Still, the insistence on work for social justice as a manifestation of neighbor love is clear. It stands as a challenge to U.S. Catholics. Ninety percent agree that concern for the poor is essential to Christian life and a slightly smaller percentage claim to believe that an option for the poor is also essential. However, 40 percent also believe that one can be a good Christian without actually doing anything for people who are poor.[13] Even if a majority rejects this idea, there is only limited evidence that concern for the poor is central to the lives of most Catholics. Moreover, though most Catholic parishes collect food or clothes for the poor at various times of the year, very few have strong social ministry organizations that involve parishioners in ongoing service to their poorer neighbors.[14] *Caritas in Veritate* rejects this separation between feeling and action, love and justice, faith and life.

Benedict further challenges Catholics by applying the concept of gratuitousness not only to charity but also to economics. Rather than limiting the public sphere to competition and lifting up the private sphere, the pope puts forward the idealistic view that "social relationships of friendship, solidarity and reciprocity can also be conducted within economic activity, and not only outside it or 'after' it" (*CV,* no. 36). Because the economic sphere is human, it must be ethical. The "logic of the gift" must have a *"place within normal economic activity"* (*CV,* no. 36). We have to think about how larger economic systems and policies serve the true needs of human beings and make space for alternative economic initiatives that go beyond the ordinary moral demands of the public sphere in order to prioritize the needs of vulnerable populations (*CV,* nos. 37-38). In an age of great cynicism about business and government,

13. For data on Catholics and the poor, see *American Catholics Today: New Realities of Their Faith and Church,* ed. William V. D'Antonio et al. (Lanham: Rowman & Littlefield, 2007), p. 37.

14. Mary Beth Celio, *Celebrating Catholic Parishes: A Study Done in Conjunction with the Cooperative Congregational Studies Project, Faith Communities Today (FACT) — A Preliminary Report on Roman Catholic Parishes* (Seattle: Catholic Archdiocese of Seattle, March 2001), pp. 10-11.

Benedict nonetheless asserts, "both the market and politics needs individuals who are open to the reciprocal gift" (*CV,* no. 39).

This call to social action should allay concerns that Benedict, in *Deus Caritas Est,* was trying to move the Church away from work for social or institutional change to charity personally defined. The elevation of Pope Paul VI's *Populorum Progressio,* which Benedict calls "the *Rerum Novarum* of the present age," and the emphasis on development in our times makes isolationism at the national level or parochialism at the local level untenable (*CV,* no. 8). It calls Christians to think more deeply about how economic structures and institutions they support contribute to the common good and in particular to the good of the neediest among us.

Most Christians, however, do not have vocations linked to international economic development. Aside from voting, writing letters, and making contributions to politicians (all valid paths), they do not have much ability to influence policy in the direction of the common good. We can justly hope that *Caritas in Veritate* will inspire more Catholic universities to encourage students to study in developing countries and major in political science or environmental studies, that it will move more Catholic business schools to rethink their understanding of good business practices and become forces for the common good, and that it will encourage more Catholic politicians to prioritize the sort of education and job creation initiatives that enable people to seek their own good. But most of us will encourage good development less from above than from below. That is, our best opportunities for influencing how society is structured will come from our ordinary, day-to-day choices about what to buy and what not to buy, and how to raise our children, take care of our parents, and spend time with our spouses and friends. This is why Benedict's call for new lifestyles where the quest for "truth, beauty, goodness and communion with others" drives economic choices of consumption, investment, and savings is so significant (*CV,* no. 51). What might this mean concretely?

The pope's focus on changes that need to be made by those in the developed world suggests that "we're going to have to look at our lifestyle [and ask]. . . . What do I need? What don't I need?"[15] Although these choices may seem small in the context of the large issues the pope is addressing, they will determine the viability of just economic enterprises. This is why Benedict raises the issue of the ethical responsibilities of consumers, encouraging them to form buying co-ops with their neighbors and choose products

---

15. "Advocates See Encyclical as Opportunity," *America,* August 31, 2009, p. 9.

from the developing world (*CV,* no. 66). Both the local economy and the global economy are recognized and valued. The simple act of shopping is transformed into a moral act, giving us the power to cooperate with good instead of evil. We are encouraged to ask, "How do my choices contribute to creation of a civilization of love? Am I supporting institutions that pay workers justly, value sustainability, and create useful products that enhance human life, or do my choices sustain industries that continue to pay sub-standard wages and produce things that nobody really needs?" It is simply not enough to know that buying a product supports jobs creation in a com-munity. We must ask, "What kinds of jobs? What kind of products? What kind of community?"[16] In so asking, we manifest concern for the social order in our everyday lives.

However, few ordinary middle-class Christians make their economic choices using this kind of calculus. Among those who do are Catholic Workers who live in poor neighborhoods, offer hospitality to needy people, homeschool their children, cultivate substantial gardens, buy local food, wear secondhand clothes, and forgo most of the rest of what their middle-class friends think is necessary. One says, "I want to be in right relationship with everyone I'm in relation with,"[17] and for her this means obtaining almost everything from people she knows personally. She is aware of all of the relationships in her life, wants them all to be personal and loving, and is willing to live very simply in order to make this more possible than it would be for most. Her lifestyle choices are a practical illustration of gratuity and they stand as a challenge to all U.S. Christians. Ironically, it is marriage that leads many to the judgment that gratuity is impractical and compromise is necessary. Yet marriage ought to be the core of a life of gratuity rather than a step away from countercultural choices based on love.

III. Marriage and Family as the Core of Gratuity

Many commentators note *Caritas in Veritate*'s affirmation of "strong links be-tween life ethics and social ethics" (*CV,* no. 15).[18] Pope Benedict refers to the indivisible nature of "life, sexuality, marriage, the family, [and] social relations"

16. See also Wendell Berry, *What Matters? Economics for a Renewed Commonwealth* (Berkeley: Counterpoint, 2010), pp. 1-30.

17. Carolyn Griffeth, personal interview, December 10, 2009.

18. Here the pope is noting this connection in Paul VI's documents, *Humanae Vitae* and *Populorum Progressio.*

(*CV,* no. 51). Among social problems that impede growth in the developing world, he cites in particular "immoral behavior," and he notes that the mobility of labor can stimulate wealth but can also complicate life plans, making marriage more difficult to sustain (*CV,* no. 25). In sum, the document asserts the connection between family and society without much explanation. It may be somewhat overstating things to name this connection between family and social ethics as a central theme, and it is difficult to know what Benedict wanted to convey in the brief statements he does make. However, by placing his assertions in the context of the larger document and Catholic social teaching as a whole, we can begin to understand the connections to which the pope alludes, and see how concern for the social order is intimately connected with the mission of the family.

If isolation is one of the deepest forms of poverty, family is, according to Catholic teaching, the location where human beings most often experience the richness of human relationships. Benedict promotes family as the best place for human flourishing (*CV,* no. 44). It is not an artificially imposed structure but a form of life that corresponds to "the deepest needs and dignity of the person," who has an "essentially relational character" (*CV,* no. 44). As *Gaudium et Spes* puts it, family is "a school of deeper humanity," a place where most of us have our profoundest experiences of community, give most deeply of ourselves, and learn by uneven practice how to become better than we are.[19]

Although this may sound overly idealistic, there is a sense in which this teaching is not so far from mainstream thinking. Even though most in the U.S. have known imperfection and failure in their own families, they are still idealistic about marriage in theory. They value it more than people in other countries, are smitten by romance on the screen and in fiction, spend precious resources on weddings, choose marriage over lifelong cohabitation in large numbers, name divorce as tragic and adultery as immoral in significant numbers, and continue to hope that their own marriages will last a lifetime.[20] Although this idealism is not as strong everywhere in the world, it is common for

19. Vatican II, *Gaudium et Spes,* no. 52 (www.vatican.va/archive/hist_councils/ii_vatican_council/documents/vat-ii_cons_19651207_gaudium-et-spes_en.html).

20. Andrew Cherlin, *The Marriage-Go-Round: The State of Marriage and Family in America Today* (New York: Alfred Knopf, 2009). Eighty-four percent of American women marry by age 40, in contrast to 70 percent in Sweden and 68 percent in France (p. 19). Ninety percent marry eventually (p. 136). Ninety-four percent believe you should marry your soul-mate (p. 139). Most Americans still believe in marriage as a permanent, loving, sexually exclusive relationship and see divorce as a last resort (p. 26). In contrast, Europeans cohabitate more frequently, marry less, and have more liberal views about infidelity.

sociologists to say that marriage is not dying but changing.[21] Still, it is not difficult to see an eroding belief in marriage both here and in the developing world. In many countries in Latin America, for instance, a majority of couples do not marry legally or in the church. Many give their marital status as "en junto," or in union, which means more than cohabitation here, but does not necessarily imply fidelity or prevent men from entering into secondary relationships. In 2008, for instance, 29 percent of Salvadorans said they were single, 25 percent said married, and 29 percent chose "en junto."[22] However, in rural communities the percentage of married people is likely much lower, perhaps just 10 percent. In interviews, most do not attest to a belief in marriage as an "intimate partnership of life and love." They value fidelity to children (though women are more faithful to children in practice than most men), but a lifelong commitment to a spouse involving both sexual fidelity and a practice of gratuity that would allow a relationship to grow and flourish is noticeably absent.[23]

In the United States, the infidelities of David Letterman, John Gosselin (of "John and Kate plus 8" fame), Senator Mark Sanford, Senator John Edwards, Governor Eliot Spitzer, Representative Jon Ensign, and Tiger Woods have been in the news. Adultery seems to be everywhere. Despite Americans' strong disapproval of extramarital sex, about 25 percent of married men and 15 percent of married women admit to at least one act of infidelity.[24] Though nearly all married persons expect marital fidelity of themselves and their partners, fidelity is a promise that a substantial number are unable to keep.

21. Paul R. Amato et al., *Alone Together: How Marriage in America Is Changing* (Cambridge: Harvard University Press, 2007), pp. 262-63.

22. The data come from National Reproductive Health Surveys: http://www.cdc.gov/reproductivehealth/surveys/SurveyCountries.htm#Latin%20America%20&%20Caribbean%20(y%20en%20Español. See also Jennifer S. Hirsch, *A Courtship after Marriage: Sexuality and Love in Mexican Transnational Families* (Berkeley: University of California Press, 2003).

23. Hirsch, *A Courtship after Marriage,* shows that traditionally, marriage in Mexico was more about children than intimacy, and infidelity and abuse were common. Recently, on both sides of the border, exposure to modern values has begun to transform that vision.

24. Adrian J. Blow and Kelley Hartnett, "Infidelity in Committed Relationships II: A Substantive Review," *Journal of Marriage and Family Therapy* 31, no. 2 (2005): 221. The United States is unusually intolerant of infidelity in principle. Ninety-nine percent of married individuals expect fidelity of their spouses and say that their spouses expect the same of them, and 80 percent say extramarital sex is always wrong. However, in other countries, the percentage of those disapproving of adultery is far lower (67 percent in Britain and Italy, 36 percent in Russia, 58 percent in Japan). Men's affairs are also viewed as more acceptable in some African, Latin American, and Asian countries. See Judith Treas, "Infidelity," in *International Encyclopedia of Marriage and Family Relationships,* vol. 4, 2nd ed., ed. James J. Ponzetti (New York: Macmillan Reference, 2000), pp. 299-308.

In a *Time* cover story in the summer of 2009, Caitlin Flanagan spoke for many who bemoan this current trend, saying that marriage has become "an increasingly fragile construct depending less and less on notions of sacrifice and obligation than on the ephemera of romance and happiness as defined by and for its adult principals."[25] Flanagan argues that while lifelong marriage is still the dream of most Americans, most are unwilling to work at it or sacrifice for it. Just look at "Jon & Kate" — a show that portrayed a marriage dedicated to kids, but ended when Jon moved on, saying, "I have a new chapter in my life. I'm only 32 years old. I really don't know what's going to happen." Contrast this behavior with that of Jenny Sanford, who is "willing to sacrifice the thrill of a love letter for the betterment of their children." "His career is not a concern of mine," says Mrs. Sanford. "He'll be worrying about that, and I'll be worrying about my family and the character of my children." Sanford, according to Flanagan, knows that marriage is about bringing up the next generation. Unburdened by unrealistic expectations for marriage and clear about the consequences of walking away from it, she exemplifies the commitment that prevents so many of us from having the marriages we say we want.

In another significant article of the summer of 2009 in the *Atlantic Monthly*, "Let's Call the Whole Thing Off," Sandra Tsing Loh goes to the opposite extreme, telling readers why she is ending her marriage and encouraging them to do the same.[26] Loh portrays marriage as platonic partnership dedicated to preparing children for college, maintaining a beautiful home, and providing support for two important careers. She recounts how, when she shared her thoughts of divorce with friends, they admitted to nonexistent sex lives and boredom with husbands obsessed with hobbies and Internet pornography. They, too, have thoughts of divorce. After having an affair with someone more exciting than her husband, Loh says she is willing to continue to work and parent, but "cannot take on yet another arduous home- and self-improvement project, that of rekindling our romance." Though not opposed to all sacrifice, she finds the work of being in a lifelong relationship particularly unappealing. She admits that children need parental care, but calls romance unnecessary. She advises readers to accept marriage as a mortgage-sharing/child-rearing arrangement and "pleasantly agree to be friends, to set the bedroom aglow at night by the mute opening of separate laptops and just be done with it."

25. Caitlin Flanagan, "Is There Hope for the American Marriage?" *Time,* July 2, 2009, http://www.time.com/time/nation/article/0,8599,1908243,00.html.

26. Sandra Tsing Loh, "Let's Call the Whole Thing Off," *The Atlantic Monthly,* July–August 2009, http://www.theatlantic.com/magazine/archive/2009/07/lets-call-the-whole-thing-off/307488/.

To those horrified by her proposal, she asks, "Why do we still insist on marriage?" She gives the usual answers. We are optimists, convinced of our power to succeed at marriage even when others fail. That's why 90 percent of us continue to marry. Yet, we are also restless individualists, always seeking the next best thing. So we celebrate marriage more than anyone else in the world and marry more, but we also divorce more, leaving us with what the sociologist Andrew Cherlin recently called *The Marriage-Go-Round*.[27] Rather than continue the hypocrisy, Loh asks, why not aim to provide domestic stability for children with a stable partner and avoid making vows we cannot keep? Children will be happy as long as they have two parents who love them, if not each other. Their parents, however, will be better off finding their bliss with a series of passionate partners. Though some stay married to give their children the gift of a stable home, such marriages come at a high cost for adults, so they must be reconsidered.

Unlike Flanagan, who decries adultery and counsels staying together for the kids, Loh refuses to apologize for her affair and wants to maintain a commitment to parent while ending her marriage and wondering if we all should give up the charade. Yet, ironically, her understanding of marriage is not all that different from Flanagan's. Loh prizes worldly success while Flanagan emphasizes character, but both agree that parents have a duty to focus on their children's welfare. In this sense, both affirm family values but have low expectations for marriage. Flanagan sits on one side of the culture war while Loh sits on the other, yet neither holds out much hope for marital friendship and neither believes that marriage has anything to do with the world outside the home.

The Catholic tradition offers something richer: a vision of marriage that is both "for itself" and "for others." The "for others" piece is crucial, but in order to be "for others" you have to be yourself. Marriage is not simply an institution directed to the service of some other good — even a fundamentally important good like raising children. Being married is a fundamentally good thing in itself and a necessary foundation for all that married couples are called to do in the world.[28] This is wisdom Catholics have to offer.

All Christians look back to the creation stories of Genesis and understand them to mean that marriage is part of God's hope for human beings who find fulfillment in relationship. Because God *is* self-giving love, God created human beings to love and to find themselves in loving. Pope John Paul II read Genesis

---

27. Cherlin, *Marriage-Go-Round*, p. 17.
28. Pope John Paul II, *Familiaris Consortio*, no. 18.

as a story of how God created male and female to give themselves in love to each other or to become "one flesh."[29] As Pope Benedict has more recently pointed out, the vision of Genesis is the assumed norm of the Old Testament (despite the many stories of people who disobey this norm).[30] The Old Testament also includes the metaphorical use of married love to describe God's relationship to the Hebrew people. In the book of Hosea, God is faithful as a husband is faithful, even to an adulterous spouse. The Song of Songs portrays the beauty and longing of one beloved for another in glorious detail. Jesus reaffirms marriage in the New Testament and points back to the origins of marriage in Genesis (Matt. 10:35-38). Paul's Letter to the Ephesians compares marriage between a man and a woman to the relationship between Christ and the Church, saying that a husband is to love his wife as Christ loved all of humanity (Eph. 5:21-26).

Today, contemporary theologians celebrate marriage as a sacrament of human friendship, a communion of love, and a covenant of intimate partnership in which both spouses can *be Christ* for one another.[31] They insist that it is through our most intimate relationships that we taste something of divine love. The theology of John Paul II in *Familiaris Consortio* calls spouses to loving attention to each other.[32] In contrast to those who advocate a simplistic, sacrificial focus on the family, the pope holds out hope that though it involves sacrifice, home is the place where we can fulfill our deepest longings to love and be loved. He calls this commitment to belonging to another person "forming a communion of persons."[33] John Paul II distinguishes himself from earlier popes who were more suspicious about the goodness of marriage by the inspired way in which he describes married love and in his hope that it will rise to the heights for which it is destined.[34] He calls Christians not just to honor

---

29. Pope John Paul II, *Familiaris Consortio,* no. 11.

30. Congregation for the Doctrine of the Faith, *Letter to the Bishops of the Catholic Church on the Collaboration of Men and Women in the Church and in the World,* http://www.vatican.va/roman_curia/congregations/cfaith/documents/rc_con_cfaith_doc_20040731_collaboration_en.html.

31. See especially Richard Gaillardetz, *A Daring Promise: A Spirituality of Christian Marriage* (New York: Crossroad, 2002), and McCarthy, *Sex and Love in the Home.* The contemporary tradition improves on the patriarchal assumptions of the biblical texts cited above.

32. Pope John Paul II, *Familiaris Consortio,* nos. 18-20.

33. Pope John Paul II, *Familiaris Consortio,* no. 15.

34. For an overview of this movement in Catholic teaching before Pope John Paul II, see John Gallagher, "Marriage and Sexuality: Magisterial Teaching from 1918 to the Present," reprinted in *Moral Theology No. 13: Change in Official Catholic Moral Teachings,* ed. Charles E. Curran (New York: Paulist, 2003), pp. 227-47.

their commitment to stay married, but to grow in love.[35] He asks for far more than a functional partnership of two parents who value being left alone at the end of the day, free to engage in outside sexual relationships.

The Catholic vision of marriage as a communion is rarely celebrated in popular cultural contexts, though a thinner version is. If one looks at the movies or *telenovelas,* for instance, the story of marriage is about two people who are irresistibly drawn to each other. Their journey to couplehood is interesting but once they get together, the story is over, unless it involves infidelity. Marriage is not portrayed because, as David McCarthy points out, we seem to believe that it deadens relationships by providing them with stability, routine, place, and responsibility.[36] Though this is supposedly what people seek, there is something unsettling about home, something not worth writing about. Satisfied with romantic beginnings, we lack narratives of marriage in its reality and its fullness. The Catholic vision is one of a communion of two called to live in love through time. This vision is far richer and far more complex than the first weeks or months of romance.

But the tradition does not argue that staying committed is the right thing to do even though it will make us miserable. This is Flanagan's call to honor our obligations — to endure even when things are difficult. It is what Loh is fleeing — the boring work of reviving a sexless marriage. It is what men and women in the developing world have traditionally seen as loyalty to children expressed through financial support for men and nurture for women. The tradition aspires to something more by calling men and women to be in relationship with each other for a lifetime and by claiming that it is in the arms of a beloved spouse that we will know what it truly means to be loved. This does not mean that we will not also know the dark nights of marriage when we will feel alone and misunderstood.[37] But there is hope that if we stay faithful for long enough, marriage will carry us through the darkness to light. Fidelity is not meant to bind us against our nature but to hold us fast so that we have the time and freedom to develop the deep relationships for which we were created.

To be married, then, is first of all to *be* something together. It is to be best friends who belong to each other, to be lovers with an abiding commitment to the good of each other along with a willingness to stretch and be changed.

---

35. Pope John Paul II, *Familiaris Consortio,* no. 17, reads in part, "the family has the mission to become more and more what it is, that is to say, a community of life and love."

36. McCarthy, *Sex and Love in the Home,* pp. 34-42.

37. Gaillardetz, *A Daring Promise,* p. 50.

Through what Gaillardetz calls "the crucible of marriage," we become what we are meant to be: people who can love with our whole beings, people who practice gratuity in the home.[38]

IV. A Special Role for Women?

Does gratuity sound like a feminine virtue? It is hard not to notice that most public infidelity cases involve famous men, that men cheat at higher rates than women, that Latin American machismo culture seems to grant women less power to get men to the altar, that mothers are routinely celebrated for their selflessness, especially on Mother's Day, or "El Dia de los Madres." In fact, gratuity sounds very much like what John Paul II and Benedict XVI have called the "genius of women," which raises the question of whether women have a special role in bringing an ethic of gratuity to family and the social order.[39] This question becomes even more salient when we realize that the economy of communion model upheld by Pope Benedict in *Caritas in Veritate* was brought to life by women (*CV,* no. 46). As we know from Amelia Uelman's recent work, the Focolare movement was founded by Chiara Lubich in Trent, Italy, during World War II when a small group of women decided to share an apartment and form a community.[40] The group eventually expanded and diversified, but it was women who had the vision to create a movement that still exists today in the forms of a network of "concrete practices that sustain ongoing efforts to build relationships of love and unity within smaller and larger communities; ongoing programs of formation toward a culture of unity within smaller and larger communities; and quite a few specific projects for social, economic and cultural development."[41]

It is not only women in the two-thirds world who are identified with community and giving of themselves to others. In economic literature on women and development, women are often identified as the targets of development efforts like micro-finance. Banks and nongovernmental organizations

---

38. Gaillardetz, *A Daring Promise*, pp. 51-54.

39. Pope John Paul II, *Letter to Women*, http://www.vatican.va/holy_father/john_paul_ii/letters/documents/hf_jp-ii_let_29061995_women_en.html. See also Congregation for the Doctrine of the Faith, *Letter to the Bishops of the Catholic Church on the Collaboration of Men and Women in the Church and in the World.*

40. Amelia Uelman, "*Caritas in Veritate* and Chiara Lubich," *Theological Studies* 71, no. 1 (March 2010): 29-45, especially pp. 33-34.

41. Uelman, "*Caritas in Veritate* and Chiara Lubich," p. 35.

(NGOs) know that women are more likely to invest the fruits of their labor in their children and communities. World Bank officials affirm "the empowerment of women is smart economics. . . . Studies show that investments in women yield large social and economic returns."[42]

Is self-giving or gratuity something women are simply more equipped to adopt? John Paul II spoke of how motherhood prepared women to love, saying, "The woman is called to offer the best of herself to the baby growing within her. It is precisely by making herself 'gift,' that she comes to know herself better and is fulfilled in her femininity."[43]

While their role in the home is primary, women, according to John Paul II, are needed in public life because "a greater presence of women in society will prove most valuable for it will help to manifest the contradictions present when society is organized solely according to the criteria of efficiency and productivity, and it will force systems to be redesigned in a way which favors the processes of humanization which mark the 'civilization of love.'"[44] John Paul II not only identified women with self-giving or gratuity, but also believed their presence would bring love to a society dominated by market values. He expressed gratitude both to women who are mothers and to women who work, and called for policies in the workplace to make possible the harmonious combination of work and motherhood for those who chose it.[45] He celebrated the feminine genius of "ordinary women who reveal the gift of their womanhood by placing themselves at the service of others in their everyday lives," and said that women "acknowledge the person, because they see persons with their hearts," and "try to go out to [others] and help them."[46]

In his former role as prefect of the Congregation for the Doctrine of the Faith, Pope Benedict issued a letter in which he seemed to agree with John Paul II's view that "woman in her deepest and most original being, exists 'for the other'" and reaffirmed that women's genius is their "capacity for the other."[47]

42. Quoted in Rosalind Eyben and Rebecca Napier-Moore, "Choosing Words with Care? Shifting Meanings of Women's Empowerment in International Development," *Third World Quarterly* 30, no. 2 (2009): 285-300, p. 295. The authors are critical of this focus on women as agents of wealth creation, and advocate women's empowerment for its own sake.

43. Pope John Paul II, "The Vocation to Motherhood," no. 1, Angelus reflection, July 16, 1995, in *John Paul II on the Genius of Women* (Washington, D.C.: United States Conference of Catholic Bishops, 1997).

44. Pope John Paul II, *Letter to Women*, no. 4.

45. Pope John Paul II, *Letter to Women*, nos. 2, 4.

46. Pope John Paul II, *Letter to Women*, no. 12.

47. Congregation for the Doctrine of the Faith, *Collaboration of Men and Women in the Church and in the World*, nos. 6, 13.

However, he also makes it clear that both men and women are called to exist for the other, and though women may be "more immediately attuned to these values," they are human values not feminine values.[48] All human beings are called to be for the other. So while the letter affirms essential differences between men and women, it ultimately calls all persons to lives of self-giving in family, church, and society.

However, *Caritas in Veritate* makes little mention of gender differences. Pope Benedict does not suggest that women excel at gratuity or claim that their capacity to "be for the other" should render their work outside the home less important. He does not suggest that women tutor men in gratuity. He does not defend a gender split in which women practice gratuity at home and men bring it to the world. Nor does he suggest that since women excel at gratuity they can lead the social revolution toward the civilization of love he so wants to inspire. Instead, all people of good will are directed to take up what might be called a feminine ethic of gratuity at home and in the world.[49]

In my judgment, this is a good thing. Identifying gratuity with women would excuse men and burden women. Catholic theology should not compound problems in the family by justifying the ways in which some men limit their self-giving in the home as evidenced in high rates of adultery and declining rates of marriage. Already, social acceptance of male infidelity, avoidance of marriage, and limited involvement in family care are too widespread. In addition, we should be aware that encouraging some women to integrate more gratuity into their lives could be problematic as they are already, as Valerie Saiving saw back in 1960, more susceptible to falling into the sin of putting everyone's needs before their own.[50] The practice of gratuity in per-

---

48. Congregation for the Doctrine of the Faith, *Collaboration of Men and Women in the Church and in the World,* nos. 6, 14.

49. One might wish for more attention to how women might take up public roles and how men might own more responsibility in the home. See Agbonkhianmeghe Orobator, S.J., "*Caritas in veritate* and Africa's Burden of (Under)Development," *Theological Studies* 71, no. 2 (June 2010): 320-34, p. 330. Orobator speaks to the need to address women's role in development, and Maura A. Ryan, "A New Shade of Green? Nature, Freedom, and Sexual Difference in *Caritas in veritate,*" *Theological Studies* 71, no. 2 (June 2010): 335-49, calls for more attention to gender equity in the home and in public life. However, I would disagree with Ryan's contention that *Caritas in Veritate* "affirms a view of women and men as possessing different inborn essences that issue in distinct roles within marriage and distinct contributions to society" (p. 346). While one can read *Caritas in Veritate* through the lens of previous teaching, I contend that the absence of gendered language is significant.

50. Valerie Saiving, "The Human Situation: A Feminine View," *Journal of Religion* 40, no. 2 (April 1960): 100-112.

sonal and social realms is too important to leave to either sex alone. Self-giving must be shared to be just. Striving to create families that are rich in gratuity and communion should be the common project of all Christian men and women.

V. Beyond Focus on the Family

It is important to remember that as much as Catholic social documents like *Caritas in Veritate* call for attention to families, they do not advocate a narrow focus on the family. In fact, *Caritas in Veritate* most often uses the word "family" to remind readers that though "many people today would claim that they owe nothing to anyone, except to themselves," "*the human race is a single family* working together in true communion, not simply a group of subjects who happen to live side by side" (*CV,* nos. 43, 53).[51] This vision of the interrelatedness of all human beings is thought to be essential to generating the motivation and energy for placing gratuity at the center of one's life. Benedict believes that if we will only see how connected we all are, we will want to give to others just as we want to give to our own families.

Globalization may enable us to see the truth about ourselves, that we are brothers (and sisters) existing in "authentic fraternity" or sorority (*CV,* no. 20).[52] Thus Benedict affirms globalization as good, insofar as it aims at increasing communion among people, though caution is warranted (*CV,* no. 43). To be human is to be in relation, and this does not just mean committed to relatives and friends. The more a person sees connections to and responsibility for other human beings both near and far, "the more authentically he or she lives these relations, the more his or her personal identity matures" (*CV,* no. 53). The more human we are, the more human our families are, the more our concern for others expands, and the more we know that, in the prophetic words of John Paul II, "we are all really responsible for all."[53] Which means, I think, that those

---

51. See also *Caritas in Veritate,* no. 54, where the pope refers to "the one community of the human family" and compares it to the three Persons of the Trinity.

52. This is not to overlook the very real evils that globalization also brings, including increasing sexual exploitation of women and economic exploitation as women are often the cheapest labor sought out by corporations seeking only profit. See Orobator, "*Caritas in Veritate* and Africa's Burden of (Under)Development," p. 330.

53. Pope John Paul II, *Sollicitudo Rei Socialis,* no. 41. (http://www.vatican.va/holy_father/john_paul_ii/encyclicals/documents/hf_jp-ii_enc_30121987_sollicitudo-rei-socialis_en.html).

families in the developed world who have more need to think much harder about giving more money and time to those who have the least.

However, Benedict rightly calls us to remember that gratuity is an ethic for both "peoples in hunger" and "peoples blessed with abundance" (*CV,* no. 17). It applies to people in both worlds because "every life is a vocation" and all people deserve the chance to use their freedom to create their own lives (*CV,* nos. 16-17). This welcome emphasis on participation should direct readers to support development policies and projects that involve those who will benefit from them, solicit the wisdom of their experience, and offer them a role to play.

"Reciprocity," the pope says, is "the heart of what it is to be a human being" (*CV,* no. 57). At the personal level, this means that the best relationships are oriented to mutual love, and at the social level, it means finding good work for everyone. Gratuity in both realms is not meant to flow one way, but to be loosely reciprocal. People in the developing world want to own their duty to shape their destiny. Thus the "sharing of reciprocal duties" is a better framework for authentic development than either an adversarial rights model or a model of charity from above (*CV,* no. 43). Development with a priority on participation should be the norm at the macro- and micro-levels (*CV,* no. 47). The Catholic social teaching insistence on subsidiarity stands as an important check on paternalistic social assistance and should push Christians to prioritize grassroots participation in economic development (*CV,* no. 58). By participating in development from below, Christians in the developing world practice gratuity on the way to transforming their social order. They are models of gratuity.

In conclusion, I offer an alternative vision of public life to the one with which I began for those in the developed world. When students at my university spend time in the two-thirds world, they return having been converted. It begins in the homes of their families, where they call their hosts "hermana," "mama," and "papa"; where they feel total acceptance in spite of their poor language skills and the sins of their country; where they are given so much — cooked for, waited on, cleaned up after, nursed when they fall sick. They come back with a deep appreciation for the ways in which families and neighborhoods freely give their time, their attention, and their love. They want to live like that, in a community where instead of trying to get the best deal among strangers, they are working for the common good among friends. But it does not stop there. Because they know people who live without enough food, water, and education, because they feel connected to them *as* family, they want to change the social structures that privilege us and make life so difficult for others. The lines separating countries no longer make much difference to them. They want a more human life for everyone, so they seek community and work that will enable them to contribute to social change.

This is the sort of conversion to which *Caritas in Veritate* calls all Christians. Its message is very much in keeping with the wisdom of *Gaudium et Spes* in which the bishops told us that "a man can fully discover his true self only in a sincere giving of himself," and called all men and women of good will to commit to this both personally and politically.[54] Practicing gratuity begins for many with committing to spousal and parental love. It continues with fidelity to living in an intimate partnership of life and love through time. Loving marriage at its best gives spouses energy for moving from the home to the neighborhood to the community and the world. *Caritas in Veritate* affirms this but calls us to go further, to extend gratuity in our families by embracing lifestyles marked by practices of simplicity, charity, and work directed to the common good. If love is at the heart of Catholic social teaching, we cannot leave the application of *Caritas in Veritate* to politicians and economists. Rather, men and women must own their place as practitioners of gratuity in the social order.

54. Vatican II, *Gaudium et Spes*, no. 24.

Global Order in Catholic Social Teaching: From Benedict XV to Benedict XVI

Patrick Callahan

I want to examine Pope Benedict XVI's teaching on global order in the context of papal teaching since Pope Benedict XV at the time of World War I. Within papal teaching are two distinct visions of international political authority. The first was developed by the popes of the first eighty years of the twentieth century and was articulated most emphatically by Pope John XXIII; the second was articulated by Pope John Paul II. In honor of John XXIII, I refer to the first as the Johannine vision. I refer to the second as the Wojtylan vision, based on John Paul's family name. The Johannine vision advocates stronger international institutions not only by making them more effective but also by transferring authority from nation-states and thus making them to some degree supranational. The Wojtylan vision, on the other hand, favors stronger international institutions only in the sense of enhancing their effectiveness; it does not advocate any transference of political authority to a supranational body.

My basic thesis is threefold. First, Benedict's view shares traits with each of the two visions. Second, his thinking overall is more consistent with the Wojtylan vision than with the Johannine. Third, one can derive or infer from his statements the shape of a possible synthesis of the two.

Strains of Papal Teaching on Global Order

Although there are points of divergence between the two strains of papal teaching on global order, the divergences reflect their shared foundation on certain fundamental points. Appropriately, Benedict emphasizes each. Four deserve mention here:

(1) We live in a world of marked international interdependence.
(2) The human community is global; therefore, moral obligations extend beyond national boundaries.
(3) Catholic social teaching, which originally emphasized justice within countries, has been internationalized. The society whose common good is to be attained is a global society.
(4) Consequently, political authority, which is necessary for the realization of the common good, must be global, in some way and to some extent.

The two strains of papal teaching diverge on this point: the how and the extent of international political authority, especially as it regards the status and authority of states.

The Johannine vision calls for some transference of political authority from nation-states to supranational institutions. It requires that the transfer be peaceful and consensual; it recognizes that the transference will happen only gradually, but insists that must happen eventually. For the popes of the era of world wars, the world urgently needed an organization strong enough to prevent the outbreak of war among nation-states. Beginning with John XXIII, economic and social interdependencies are identified as needs calling for strong international institutions. In his encyclical *Pacem in Terris*, John made the point with characteristic strength:

> Today the universal common good presents us with problems that are world-wide in their dimensions; problems, therefore, which cannot be solved except by a public authority with power, organization and means co-extensive with these problems, and with a world-wide sphere of activity. Consequently the moral order itself demands the establishment of some general form of public authority.[1]

For John, the public authority must be competent to address the full range of problems affecting the common good and must rest on having higher authority than existing states. The status of nation-states is starkly diminished. State sovereignty is endorsed only as a safeguard against domination by the powerful.[2]

---

1. *Pacem in Terris*, nos. 134-37. Translation at http://www.vatican.va/holy_father/john_xxiii/encyclicals/documents/hf_j-xxiii_enc_11041963_pacem_en.html.
2. See, for example, Pope John XXIII, *Mater et Magistra*, no. 174 in the context of no. 170;

The Wojtylan vision supports enhancing the effectiveness of international organizations but not granting them supranational authority. In this vision, nations continue to have distinctive value. Indeed, in places John Paul gave them equivalence with the society and even the family. For John Paul, nations transmit and protect cultures. Cultures in turn have value because they facilitate the search for truth and God; they represent a people's effort to come to grips with the transcendent. The protection of cultures, and of the nations who carry them, is not just permissible, as it is in the Johannine vision; it is obligatory. Moreover, nations are valued for another reason: they represent a deep human impulse to form bonds with other people, from the family up to, in John Paul's words, "the whole of their ethnic and cultural group, which is called, not by accident, a 'nation', from the Latin word 'nasci': to be born."[3]

The Wojtylan vision de-emphasizes central political authority for yet another reason. It holds a different perspective on the relationship between political authority and the economy. More so than his predecessors, John Paul saw virtue in free markets. While acknowledging that the state has a substantial role in correcting defects in markets, or mitigating the harms of those defects, he attributed to it a more restrictive role than did earlier popes, even warning against the creation of the "social assistance state." As the role of the state internal to nations is lessened in the Wojtylan position, so too is the regulatory role of international authority.

For John Paul, international organizations need not have more authority in order to be more effective. Rather, their increased effectiveness will follow from a transformation of human hearts and minds — a conversion, actually — to a more thorough love for all of humankind. Solidarity will lead states to use existing international organizations to promote the global common good. Moreover, solidarity would be a prerequisite for the peaceful emergence of supranational organization, anyway. With solidarity, supranational organization is not an urgent need; without it, supranational organization is unattainable on morally acceptable terms.

Pacem in Terris, no. 92; Pope Paul VI, *Populorum Progressio*, no. 54; and *Octagesimo Adveniens*, no. 43.

3. Address to the United Nations General Assembly, October 5, 1995, no. 7, http://www .vatican .va/holy _father/john _paul _ii/speeches/1995/october/documents/hf _jp-ii _spe _05101995_address-to-uno_en.html.

Charity in Truth in Context

How does Benedict XVI's teaching fit in this tradition? He clearly favors a substantial increase in the effectiveness of international organizations and uses language that suggests a transference of authority from states to supranational organizations. To that extent, he shares the Johannine vision. In other ways, however, his teaching falls closer to the Wojtylan vision and overall he seems to be more Wojtylan than Johannine. (Benedict himself would object to the drawing of these distinctions, emphasizing instead the continuity of the papal magisterium.)

The Johannine Benedict

In his encyclical *Caritas in Veritate (CV)*, Pope Benedict called for a "true world political authority." The controversy is over just what he meant by that. The hypothesis that he endorsed some degree of transference of authority is supported by the scope of its activities and the degree of its authority. The pope uses strong verbs that imply decisive action: the authority would "*manage* the global economy," "*revive* economies," "*bring about* integral development" and "disarmament, food security, and peace," "*guarantee* the protection of the environment," and "*regulate* migration" (*CV*, no. 67; emphasis added).[4] Moreover, the body must have sufficient power "*to ensure compliance* with its decisions from all parties" (*CV*, no. 67; emphasis added).

This is not the language of decentralized political processes with power distributed pluralistically across multiple centers of power with no point of final or effective decision-making authority. It appropriates responsibility to the global political authority and, unless one assumes that moral suasion would suffice, it grants it the capacity to compel. The clear connotation is that it would be, to some degree, supranational.

The Wojtylan Benedict

The Johannine vision takes Catholic teaching on political authority and projects it from the state level to the international level. It is important to note that Catholic teaching limits the authority of government at any level. The limits

4. Translation at http://www.vatican.va/holy_father/benedict_xvi/encyclicals/documents/hf_ben-xvi_enc_20090629_caritas-in-veritate_en.html.

concern processes and means: government must be democratic, protect the freedoms of people, and be consistent with the principle of subsidiarity, that is, that higher-level bodies must not usurp the functions of lower-level ones. The limits also concern ends or purposes: government must promote justice and the common good. Those same limits would apply as well to any international political authority. These limits bring us to the two main points on which Benedict's teaching converges with John Paul's: (1) regarding the limits on processes and means, the continuing value of national states and diverse cultures; (2) regarding the limits on ends or purposes, the highly contingent value of international organization.

States and Cultures

Pope John Paul insisted on the continuing value of national states as protectors of diverse cultures. This is one point of convergence between the Wojtylan vision and Benedict's teaching. Consistent with the principle of subsidiarity, Benedict advocates the continued prominence of states. To some extent, his position accommodates practical realities. "Both wisdom and prudence," he writes, "suggest not being too precipitous in declaring the demise of the State." He not only expects the role of the state to increase, he even advocates the strengthening of the state in places where state weakness hinders development. That globalization circumscribes the effectiveness of national political authorities does not warrant their being supplanted by a higher authority; rather, it requires that the state's role and powers "be prudently reviewed and remodelled so as to enable them, perhaps through new forms of engagement, to address the challenges of today's world" (*CV*, no. 24).

To be clear, the pope does not favor strengthening states at the expense of necessary international political action. Rather, states must be strengthened in such a way as to enable all levels of government to function most effectively. Doing so will safeguard against the erosion of democratic rule and even enhance popular rule and civic engagement:

> Once the role of public authorities has been more clearly defined, one could foresee an increase in the new forms of political participation, nationally and internationally, that have come about through the activity of organizations operating in civil society; in this way it is to be hoped that the citizens' interest and participation in the *res publica* will become more deeply rooted. (*CV*, no. 24)

Like John Paul, Benedict also values the diversity of cultures. He writes of "the profound significance of the culture of different nations, of the traditions of the various peoples, by which the individual defines himself in relation to life's fundamental questions" (*CV*, no. 26). The diversity of cultures gives humanity a resource for dialogue, for collectively searching for a fuller understanding of the truth. His esteem for diversity of cultures is especially shown in his critique of the globalized "commercialization of cultural exchange." He names two threats: cultural eclecticism and relativism, on the one hand, and cultural leveling, on the other. Both cultural eclecticism and cultural leveling obscure "the profound significance of the culture of different nations, of the traditions of the various peoples, by which the individual defines himself in relation to life's fundamental questions" (*CV*, no. 62).

Benedict is aware that cultural differences can be abused. In his 2006 World Day of Peace address, he warned against "an extreme exaltation of differences" that contradicts the fundamental truth that *"all people are members of one and the same family."*[5] That cultural differences can be turned toward clashes of civilizations does not negate the value of different cultures, however. He declared: "We need to regain an awareness that *we share a common destiny which is ultimately transcendent,* so as to *maximize our historical and cultural differences, not in opposition to, but in cooperation with, people belonging to other cultures."*[6] This statement is subtle to the point of risking obscurity. I take it, nonetheless, to mean that there are real, natural differences among cultures and those differences must not be submerged; instead, they must be embraced as a basis for cooperation across cultures in the shared quest for transcendent truth. At the same time, our common familiarity and fate requires that cultural differences not be exaggerated in pursuit of a divisive political program.

While Benedict shares John Paul's valuing of both states and cultures, he does not explicitly make John Paul's argument that national states are necessary for the promotion of cultures. In that sense, his attachment to this element of the Wojtylan vision is incomplete. His sharing of the second element, that strengthening of international political authority must follow from prior conversion of hearts and minds, is much stronger. Indeed, it is the main emphasis of Benedict's teaching on the political dimension of global order.

5. Pope Benedict XVI, World Day of Peace Address, January 1, 2006, no. 6, http://www.vatican.va/holy_father/benedict_xvi/messages/peace/documents/hf_ben-xvi_mes_20051213_xxxix-world-day-peace_en.html.

6. Pope Benedict XVI, World Day of Peace Address, January 1, 2006, no. 6.

Proper Functioning

Any global political authority must be assessed not as an end but as a means toward attaining morally required ends. Reforming or replacing the United Nations to create a supranational entity would be permissible if and only if it better promoted justice, integral development, and the common good. While stronger institutions might be necessary for those ends, they would not necessarily be sufficient. Strong institutions that obstructed justice and the common good would be corrupt.

The insufficiency of stronger institutions is implied by Benedict's critique of what he calls a "technical mindset" and "technological applications in the fields of development and peace" (*CV,* no. 71). (I think it safe to infer from the encyclical that changes in organizational structure in and of themselves would qualify as technological thinking.) His examples emphasize economics but implicate the realm of politics, too. He counsels:

> Development will never be fully guaranteed through automatic or impersonal forces, whether they derive from the market or from international politics. *Development is impossible without upright men and women, without financiers and politicians whose consciences are finely attuned to the requirements of the common good.* Both professional competence and moral consistency are necessary. When technology is allowed to take over, the result is confusion between ends and means, such that the sole criterion for action in business is thought to be the maximization of profit, in politics the consolidation of power, and in science the findings of research. (*CV,* no. 71)

What matters, then, is not the power or authority vested in a global political institution. Rather, the critical issue is how the institution is run by the people who run it. A reformed and strengthened United Nations or a new world government could be good, but it could also be bad and ugly.

A properly functioning political authority would be marked in part by the ends it promoted. Benedict stresses that *"progress of a merely economic and technological kind is insufficient"* (*CV,* no. 23). Rather, it must promote authentic or integral development, "that is, it has to promote the good of every man and of the whole man' " (*CV,* no. 18). And joining all his predecessors in the papacy, he insists that the foundation of integral development is spiritual and moral development. This is so for individuals; it is so for humanity as a whole. If man were merely the fruit of either chance or necessity, or if he had to lower his aspirations to the limited horizon of the world in which he lives, if all reality were merely history and culture, and man did not possess a nature destined to transcend itself in a supernatural life, then one could speak of growth, or evolution, but not development. This has consequences for public policy. Benedict continues:

> When the State promotes, teaches, or actually imposes forms of practical atheism, it deprives its citizens of the moral and spiritual strength that is indispensable for attaining integral human development. (*CV*, no. 29)

This also affects how we evaluate globalization. He writes:

> In the context of cultural, commercial or political relations, it also sometimes happens that economically developed or emerging countries export this reductive vision of the person and his destiny to poor countries. This is the damage that "superdevelopment" causes to authentic development when it is accompanied by "moral underdevelopment." (*CV*, no. 29)

A political authority that promoted a flawed form of development in place of integral development would be self-defeating. Its immediate effect would be isolation; people would succumb to "man's basic and tragic tendency to close in on himself, thinking himself to be self-sufficient or merely an insignificant and ephemeral fact, a 'stranger' in a random universe." Isolation in turn prevents the formation of fraternal solidarity and keeps human relationships from being infused with charity. Mere interdependence is not enough. As Benedict elegantly phrased it: "As society becomes ever more globalized, it makes us neighbours but does not make us brothers" (*CV*, no. 19).

So, a flawed conception of development spawns isolation and isolation precludes fraternity. And fraternity is a *sine qua non* of the proper functioning of institutions. "In the course of history," he writes, "it was often maintained that the creation of institutions was sufficient to guarantee the fulfillment of humanity's right to development. Unfortunately, too much confidence was placed in those institutions. . . . In reality, institutions by themselves are not enough, because integral human development is primarily a vocation, and therefore it involves a free assumption of responsibility in solidarity on the part of everyone. Moreover, such development requires a transcendent vision of the person, it needs God: without him, development is either denied, or entrusted exclusively to man, who falls into the trap of thinking he can bring about his own salvation, and ends up promoting a dehumanized form of development" (*CV*, no. 11).

Toward a Synthesis

Let us step back, then, and ask, "What is the pope's overall vision for global order? Do the two strains of papal teaching meld into a coherent vision, or do they leave us managing a perpetual tension?" I would like to conclude this essay by proposing a synthesis. In doing so, I am assuming, out of respect for Benedict's intellect, that a synthesis is possible, that he is not guilty of gross inconsistencies in his thinking. I suggest that the Johannine and Wojtylan visions can be reconciled by factoring in time frame. The development of global order occurs in stages, perhaps, and looks different at different stages.

In the near term, global order is characterized primarily by more effective use of existing networks of international organizations, which already are making important contributions in preventing conflicts and promoting conflict resolution and humanitarian law. Capability exists; it needs to be used more effectively. Also in the short run, though, there would be some enhancement of the authority of international organizations for two ends. First, and always consistent with the principle of subsidiarity, there would be better facilitation of cooperation among states and other international actors. Second, there would be new capability created for effective collective action in emergency or crisis situations, as, for instance, with the establishment of the principle of "Responsibility to Protect," which authorizes military intervention in clearly delineated and hopefully rare occasions,[7] or the granting to the United Nations Economic and Social Council the capacity to make binding decisions to protect nations from financial aggression.[8] Such modest enhancement would not create, to quote the papal consultant Stefano Zamagni, "a United Nations on steroids"[9] or "a kind of a superstate."[10]

Sometime in the future, after the necessary moral development of humankind, would come a second stage. Then there would be the transference of sufficient authority to supranational institutions, capping the creation of the

---

7. Address by Archbishop Celestino Migliore, Apostolic Nuncio, Permanent Observer of the Holy See, General Debate of the 64th session of the General Assembly of the United Nations, New York, September 29, 2009, http://www.un.org/ga/64/generaldebate/pdf/VA_en.pdf.

8. Archbishop Celestino Migliore, "Opening Plenary Address," Tradition and Liberation Conference, DePaul University, April 21, 2010.

9. John L. Allen Jr., "Pope Greets Obama. Encyclical Precedes Historic Visit. Deft Timing for 'Caritas in Veritate,'" *National Catholic Reporter,* July 27, 2009, pp. 1, 6.

10. Cindy Wooden, "United Nations could create economic body with 'real teeth,' economist says," *Catholic News Service,* July 14, 2009, http://thecatholicspirit.com/index.php?option=com_content&task=view&id=2165&Itemid=397.

global polis to attain the global common good. It would work because the sense of fraternity and solidarity would make the transfer of authority voluntary and would ease the marshaling of cooperation necessary for effective government. Then and only then would the Johannine vision be fulfilled.

The Alice's Restaurant of Catholic Social Teaching: Global Order in *Caritas in Veritate*

Michael Budde

> *You can get anything you want at Alice's Restaurant.*
>
> Arlo Guthrie, 1967

When it comes to discussions of global order, you can get anything you want in *Caritas in Veritate (CV)* — a critique of global capitalism and an endorsement of global capitalism, concerns about state power and calls for more powerful states, support for more powerful multilateral state actors in politics and economics, and support for more powerful nongovernmental organizations and movements. You can get metaphysical discussions and technical policy statements; you can get broad statements about the common good, the universal nature of human reason, and natural law; and you can get religious encouragement and affirmation in working to solve human problems.

Hopes ran high in anticipation of this document — it had been years in the drafting, postponed several times to include new developments (including the 2008 financial crisis), and timed in its release to coincide with a meeting of the G-8 summit and Pope Benedict XVI's first meeting with U.S. President Barack Obama.

Since its release, the encyclical has stimulated considerable commentary and analysis — in the secular media worldwide, among scholars and civic leaders, and with attention to its contributions to discussions on theology, social ethics, public policy, and pastoral life. Its complexity confounded some analysts, its size impressed others, and its breadth drew comment from many, and for many people this ambitious document seems well on its way toward making contributions to the modern conversation on Catholicism and social concerns.

Several people have noted the extent to which the encyclical broadens and deepens papal teaching on so-called global order. Like earlier Vatican documents, it endorses world political institutions like the United Nations. It also notes the important and positive roles of multilateral financial and economic organizations, corporations, nonprofit groups, regional associations, and more. It endorses subsidiarity and solidarity, by which it signals commitment to a proper if flexible interplay of local actors and supranational actors, up to and including world authority and responsibilities.

Instead of discussing all the particulars of *Caritas in Veritate* on global order, I would like to focus on a handful of considerations that stand prior to the encyclical's ideas on global order. Doing so, I suggest, might help in assessing the particulars of the document's pronouncements on global order — including its call for greater enforcement powers of various sorts for transnational institutions.

1. The Common Good

Several commentators have praised *Caritas in Veritate* for its discussion of the common good in our time of transnational capitalism, global flows, and worldwide problems and opportunities. Vincent Miller claims that the pope "offers one of the most extended discussions of the common good in a magisterial text,"[1] while for Drew Christiansen its treatment of the common good provides strong and welcome evidence of Benedict's commitment to a structural (rather than apolitical) approach to social justice.[2]

The literature on the common good is extensive in Catholic theological, philosophical, and political circles. Affirming the existence of a common good is meant to signal a conception of justice and society that exceeds individualism, contractarianism, or radical notions of ethical constructivism or positivism; the common good is distinguishable from goods to be pursued at lower levels of social organization or by individuals, and is something other than the sum of individual goods. It can be accessed by human reason, and knowledge

1. Vincent Miller, "Encyclical Signals Church Not Pulling out of Politics," *National Catholic Reporter,* July 24, 2009, p. 8.

2. Drew Christiansen, S.J., "Metaphysics and Society: A Commentary on *Caritas in veritate,*" *Theological Studies* 71, no. 1 (March 2010): 3-28, p. 13.

of it is not contingent on a particular religious or theological vision, even a Christian one.

Caritas in Veritate offers an extended section on the common good and how the pope sees it in our time:

> To love someone is to desire that person's good and to take effective steps to secure it. Besides the good of the individual, there is a good that is linked to living in society: the common good. It is the good of "all of us," made up of individuals, families and intermediate groups who together constitute society. It is a good that is sought not for its own sake, but for the people who belong to the social community and who can only really and effectively pursue their good within it. To desire the *common good* and strive towards it *is a requirement of justice and charity.* To take a stand for the common good is on the one hand to be solicitous for, and on the other hand to avail oneself of, that complex of institutions that give structure to the life of society, juridically, civilly, politically and culturally, making it the *pólis,* or "city." The more we strive to secure a common good corresponding to the real needs of our neighbours, the more effectively we love them. Every Christian is called to practice this charity, in a manner corresponding to his vocation and according to the degree of influence he wields in the *pólis.* This is the institutional path — we might also call it the political path — of charity, no less excellent and effective than the kind of charity which encounters the neighbour directly, outside the institutional mediation of the *pólis.* When animated by charity, commitment to the common good has greater worth than a merely secular and political stand would have. Like all commitment to justice, it has a place within the testimony of divine charity that paves the way for eternity through temporal action. Man's earthly activity, when inspired and sustained by charity, contributes to the building of the universal *city of God,* which is the goal of the history of the human family. In an increasingly globalized society, the common good and the effort to obtain it cannot fail to assume the dimensions of the whole human family, that is to say, the community of peoples and nations, in such a way as to shape the *earthly city* in unity and peace, rendering it to some degree an anticipation and a prefiguration of the undivided *city of God.* (*CV,* no. 7)[3]

This is a dense and meaning-laden section, the unpacking of which is necessary to understanding the strengths and weaknesses of the pope's document.

---

3. Translation at http://www.vatican.va/holy_father/benedict_xvi/encyclicals/documents/hf_ben-xvi_enc_20090629_caritas-in-veritate_en.html.

And while a single encyclical does not stand as a comprehensive treatment of the common good in Catholic ethics, *Caritas in Veritate* does provide windows through which most of the important questions and reservations may be raised regarding common good thinking.

The core of my reservations of the use of common good language flows from what in social theory is described as units/levels of analysis questions. What are the units of analysis in question: individuals, families, voluntary organizations, national governments, ethnic communities, economic entities, regional or supra/subnational bodies, intergovernmental organizations, or some other sort of actor, singly or in combination? What level or levels does one examine to study relations, processes of causality, or interactive effects: the level of individual interaction, relations among states, transnational flows of commodities or ideas, local micro-level ecosystems, or the planetary ecosystem itself? And how do these units and levels interact with one another, constitute one another, or confound one another?

Caritas in Veritate notes that "besides the good of the individual, there is a good that is linked to living in society" (*CV*, no. 7). In asserting that there exists a common good that is other than a summary of individually constituted goods (the position of classical liberalism), the encyclical suggests that there is a hierarchy of goods to be sought by human beings in social life.

But who or what defines the parameters of a "society"? Who is the "all of us" the encyclical claims must be served by the common good? If "all of us" is constituted by "individuals, families and intermediate groups," then who or what is excluded? *Caritas in Veritate* asserts that the common good exists at multiple levels, between the goods of individuals and the universal good of the human family: it claims that this good affects "the people who belong to the social community and who can only really effectively pursue their good within it" (*CV*, no. 7). This presumes a multiplicity of social communities, each of which with goods in common to be pursued, each of which constituting something of the common good.

Given that "society" is undefined, or defined in a circular fashion, the encyclical's use of "common good" language cannot provide a workable understanding for how to proceed with conflicts in conceptions of the good, nor of different sorts of societies — at different, intermixed, or overlapping levels of social organization — pursuing their legitimate rights and ends. To say that the common good requires clean air for all is to make a broad and general statement; to say the right of Chinese peasants to warm their children by burning coal, a proximate means of pursuing the good of family life, is to make a specific statement. To say these conflicting goals are not in conflict is to engage in definitional evasion; to say that conflicts between different units or levels of "society" in how they understand the common good (how broadly common? what of goods that are in competition with one another?) can be resolved by the use of reason is to ignore the imbalances of power that structure discourse in the contemporary world. In either case, it is hard to know how to proceed.

Despite the document's acknowledgment of globalization across every part of life — economic, cultural, political, biophysical, and more — the pope's treatment of the common good still seems to imagine something of a micro-to-macro spatial organization, of relatively discrete units (individuals, families) being integrated into ever-larger clusters of regions, areas, or countries. It seems that the boundaries of societies largely correspond with the territorial borders of national states; the global common good itself is discerned, defined, and debated at the level of interstate interaction, with non-state actors of various sorts joining in.

The levels of analysis question plagues discussions of the common good: pursuing the common good of "America" might mean acting in ways contrary to the goods defined by subnational groups, movements, or individuals; it might also conflict with a more broadly defined sense of the common good of the planet, or of the global community of nations (defined how? by what authority?). One or another society or group exercising those rights the encyclical identifies as essential (to food, to water; *CV*, no. 27) routinely seems to contradict the common good defined elsewhere (e.g., slash-and-burn agriculture in tropical zones versus ecological stability). Is there a single world society in which all are members, which defines the level at which a truly common good can be defined? Or does the proliferation of societies and communities (whether defined by cultural affinities, economic interactions, ideological dispositions, religious affiliations, political obligations, etc.) within all but the most primitive communities confound efforts to assert a common good at anything but a most generalized level of platitude or cliché? The very boundaries of what constitutes society seem to be a moving target in our time, as the extensity and intensity of relations change over time due to various sociological dynamics (global commodity chains, transnational and intra-national communications networks, migratory and ideological affinity networks, etc.), such that persons who live contiguous to one another may be diversely connected in more fundamental ways to those geographically removed from them. To what communities, and to what societies, a given collection of persons belongs most fundamentally — and which conception of the good and with what notion of ranking should other conceptions of the good be encountered

— none of these questions seem to have complicated the picture of the common good in this or other papal documents.

The document claims that "the more we strive to secure a common good corresponding to the real needs of our neighbours, the more effectively we love them" (*CV*, no. 7). But the pope does not tell me, for purposes of moral reasoning, whom I should consider as my neighbor in considering the common good. Residents of the affluent suburb nearby — should their conceptions of the good be given more weight than the poor people who live across the border in northern Mexico? What sort of particularisms are justified or necessary, given the realities that Catholic social teaching accepts and endorses (nations, peoples, states, families, ethnic groups, religious communities), when trying to discern the specifics of the common good? Particularity and specificity are needed if one aims to describe "real needs" (as does the quotation above), and if a healthy notion of the common good places "real needs" as superior or more determinative than lesser needs or desires held by another society or group. Can the common good as advocated by Catholic social teaching speak to this beyond the level of generalities?

Commentators have seized on one section of the common good discussion to mark the pope's commitment to political action as an essential part of Catholic social engagement; in some earlier work, notably *Deus Caritas Est* (2005), Benedict was thought to signal a higher value for direct service to persons in need compared to institutional or social transformation.[4] So in *Caritas in Veritate,* the pope ties the common good to "the institutional path — we might also call it the political path — of charity, no less excellent and effective than the kind of charity which encounters the neighbour directly, outside the institutional mediation of the *pólis*" (*CV*, no. 7).

For all of his alleged Augustinian pessimism regarding the sinfulness of the world, after becoming pope Joseph Ratzinger showed a decidedly idealized view of the *pólis* and political authority. Already in *Deus Caritas Est,* his description of political authority sounds as if it were taken from a civics book — virtuous, bloodless, and self-evidently good (*Deus Caritas Est,* nos. 26, 28). When he extols the excellence of state action as the instantiation of justice in the world, he similarly paints a picture in which the dark side of "political order" remains ever obscured or denied.

In some sense, is this the crux of the matter? Can states love? Can the *pólis* love? Can the irremovably violent nature of the *pólis* and the state be an "excellent" means by which Christians may love their neighbor, their enemy, and

4. Christiansen, "Metaphysics and Society," p. 6.

those who would persecute them? It seems such a love would be out of bounds for the secular state, or indeed for any political authority that constructs "order" on exclusion, coercion, and the right to kill. But if the state can only love its own members, to what credit is that? Even pagan tax collectors do that (see Matt. 5:46-47). Of course, the call to Christians to love their enemies seems like an unreasonable standard for measuring the practice of love by the *pólis* or the modern state — but maybe that is the point. Perhaps this encyclical needs a reminder that the *pólis* and the modern state can only be pagan since they depend fundamentally on the right to kill in pursuit of order (global, national, or local); and they remain pagan in their understanding of order, despite whatever sort of Christian gloss might be laid over them.

2. An Invisible Church in a Global World?

Caritas in Veritate has a great deal of metaphysics — on truth, on love, and on reason. Curiously, it has relatively little on the Church as a material, institutional reality — as a body of believers united in discipleship as a new people from all parts of the world and across all divides. This is even more curious given Joseph Ratzinger's longtime concern to preserve the distinctiveness and visibility of the Church as an essential element in the economy of salvation for the entire world.

The Church in *Caritas in Veritate* is a searcher for, and a proclaimer of, truth (*CV*, no. 9); it promotes integral human development in its own educational and charity work and in the public political arena (*CV*, no. 11); it offers the "values of Christianity" as a useful contribution to the world (*CV*, no. 4); and it calls on Christians to pursue integral human development in their various individual roles and positions (*CV*, no. 7).

In all of this, the Church might as well be a think tank, or a cheerleader for upright living, or a chaplain to independently constituted structures, communities, or vocations. Its reliance on natural law categories, almost to the point of being boilerplate language (*CV*, no. 59), seems to minimize the degree to which creation needs Christianity to proclaim "the whole man and all men" as the criterion for evaluating cultures and religions (*CV*, no. 55). Being a Christian, in the overall sense intimated by *Caritas in Veritate,* is an add-on to those roles and responsibilities that human societies already form and infuse, drawing them to their best selves, to be sure, but not posing any fundamental challenges to them or positing any significant differences between being a good person and being a disciple of the risen Lord.

The disappearance, or at least the disembodying, of the Church as a real-world community is facilitated by the sense in which Benedict connects political action to the eschatological consummation and recapitulation of creation by God.

When animated by charity, commitment to the common good has greater worth than a merely secular and political stand would have. Like all commitments to justice, it has a place within the testimony of divine charity that paves the way for eternity through temporal action. Man's earthly activity, when inspired and sustained by charity, contributes to the building of the universal *city of God,* which is the goal of the history of the human family. In an increasingly globalized society, the common good and the effort to obtain it cannot fail to assume the dimensions of the whole human family, that is to say, the community of peoples and nations, in such a way as to shape the *earthly city* in unity and peace, rendering it to some degree an anticipation and prefiguration of the undivided *city of God.* (*CV,* no. 7)

Several commentators have noted the sense in which Benedict has altered the traditional Augustinian notions of the earthly and heavenly cities in this passage. Douglas Farrow laments Benedict's joining of human efforts in the earthly city to the realization of the city of God, a move that obscures in Augustine the important distinction between the Church and the world.[5] David Nirenberg similarly notes that Augustine would likely not have approved of this papal construct:

[In the *City of God,* Augustine] frowned on claims that a sphere of human activity such as politics or economics, which "has its good in this world, and rejoices in [the material world] with such joy as such things can afford," could ever prefigure the city of God.[6]

In contrast, Drew Christiansen notes the same change in usage and emphasis, but welcomes it as a beneficial evolution in Pope Benedict's thinking. The pope's view of temporal action, to Christiansen, sets Benedict "in the line of the social teaching of Paul VI, but embraces as well the optimistic, immanent, Teilhardian eschatology of Vatican II."[7] In two footnotes, Christiansen describes this as Augustine's *City of God* language as modified by a Thomistic

5. Douglas Farrow, "Charity & Unity," *First Things* 196 (October 2009): 39.
6. David Nirenberg, "Love and Capitalism," *The New Republic* 240, no. 17 (September 2009): 40.
7. Christiansen, "Metaphysics and Society," p. 7.

and Vatican II view; as a result, the pope's "common good" language adapts Augustinian "earthly city" ideas to "the immanent eschatology of *Gaudium et Spes* and the love-transforming-culture approach of Paul VI. . . . Theologically, this set of moves is of major significance, showing the profound influence of Paul VI and Vatican II on Benedict's thought. In turn, they prepare the way for the transformative social policy proposals that follow."[8]

One consequence of this increasingly irenic vision of church and world is that *Caritas in Veritate* seems to imagine the world as inhabited by all varieties of human institutions, systems, and structures which — for all their diversity — are empty shells of moral purpose just waiting to be filled by whoever controls them at any given time. There seem to be few or no structural constraints, limitations, or tendencies in the global world Benedict sees — merely neutral instrumentalities whose practices and imperatives are entirely determined by the actions chosen by their agents. Institutions like governments, corporations, and social groupings, however much they differ among themselves, are all like automobiles — no direction or purpose unless and until willed by the agent behind the wheel. Cars can go in good directions or bad directions, but cars in themselves are neutral matters that are driven by, but are in no way able to "drive," those in the driver's seat.

Such is an appealing notion at first, to be sure, but it is almost altogether too simplistic to be helpful beyond a certain very limited point. No "car" exists in isolation from the systems that make cars, tax for roads, advertise them as status goods, go to war to secure oil for them, structure spatial patterns of living in ways that require their possession and privileging, fabricate myths and ideas about progress (and development) that give them pride of place, and much more. A car is not an isolated, politically and morally inert piece of instrumentality that can always be assumed to conform to the will of the driver — in many ways, and for some specific purposes, cars create and "form" their drivers, including the driver's sense of moral decision-making, priorities, and commitments.

How all of this relates to the encyclical's treatment of global order is that the pope offers something like a neo-Christendom picture of institutional dynamics — be they states or global hedge funds, all global institutions are capable of loving Christianly, if only the right people with the right dispositions get into positions of power. These non-Christian institutions and systems do not form Christian affections, loyalties, or practices, but instead Christians can bend these institutions and systems to good effect without compromising

8. Christiansen, "Metaphysics and Society," p. 12.

the evangelical purposes for which God constitutes the Church — to give a taste, however imperfect, of order built on forgiveness and mutuality rather than coercion, of human sociability built on something other than race or tribe or ideology or ethnic peoplehood or greed or self-interest or the other so-called natural categories on which institutions of power are built.

3. Global Order and Processes of Formation

Processes of formation are important in understanding the encyclical's discussion of global order because of a semi-schizophrenia on display in the document. On the one hand, it recognizes the importance of formation in human cultures:

> The term "education" refers not only to classroom teaching and vocational training — both of which are important factors in development — but to the complete formation of the person. In this regard, there is a problem that should be highlighted: in order to educate, it is necessary to know the nature of the human person, to know who he or she is. The increasing prominence of a relativistic understanding of that nature presents serious problems for education, especially moral education. (*CV,* no. 61)

The pope recognizes that "automatic or impersonal forces," in either economic or political processes, are insufficient; formation is required for the creation of "upright men and women" (*CV,* no. 71). But there is no discussion whatsoever that global markets form people, that states form people, that institutions of global power form cadres and functionaries in specific ways that may or may not correspond with the formation of disciples. The prospect of competitive formation — Christian and other types — is neither contemplated nor raised. The exception to this sense that institutions and systems form people comes in an unusual discussion on the power of communications media.

> For better or for worse, [the means of social communication] are so integral a part of life today that it seems quite absurd to maintain that they are neutral — and hence unaffected by any moral considerations concerning people. Often such views, stressing the strictly technical nature of the media, effectively support their subordination to economic interests intent on dominating the market and, not least, to attempt to impose cultural models that serve ideological and political agendas. Given the media's fundamental importance in engineering changes in attitude toward reality and the human

person, we must reflect carefully on their influence, especially in regard to the ethical-cultural dimension of globalization and the development of peoples in solidarity. (*CV,* no. 73)

It is a curiosity here that, while communications media are seen as having formative effects that shape human persons, such seems not to be the case for capitalism, which in itself is largely inseparable from the sort of media formation the pope observes but is treated as a neutral and more innocent force.

Admittedly, the market can be a negative force, not because it is so by nature, but because a certain ideology can make it so. . . . Economy and finance, as instruments, can be used badly when those at the helm are motivated by purely selfish ends. Instruments that are good in themselves can thereby be transformed into harmful ones. (*CV,* no. 36)

Those sections of the encyclical that address global economic institutions, and the nature of "development" under conditions of global capitalism, are burdened by a defective theory of capitalism inherited from *Centesimus Annus.*[9] Much of what constitutes economic and ethical analysis in that encyclical, and in *Caritas in Veritate,* goes not much further than making a list of "good things" one wants from capitalism and a list of all the "bad things" to be avoided. Right action means choosing all the good things and avoiding all the bad things; that there are structural relations between the two, that one cannot often get the good things — profitability, innovation, efficiency, wealth, and more — without the bad (unemployment, unregulated economic processes, unequal political and social power relationships) seems to be an unthinkable prospect. So much of *Caritas in Veritate*'s discussion of capitalism and development seems to be of a piece with this — a right to food and a right to water, stronger unions and welfare systems, strong governance of markets and protection of the weak, all while stressing the beneficial aspects of capital mobility, transnational corporations, and market-centered dynamics at all levels of social organization. The pope's calls for greater enthusiasm for stakeholder notions of capitalism, for the social obligations to be fulfilled by businesspersons of good will, of ideas of friendship and gift-giving within capitalism — all of these seem to presuppose situations of social surplus, of costs voluntarily assumed by business leaders who are not in highly competitive situations. In such situations, as Milton Friedman has reminded generations of would-be

9. For one discussion, see Michael Budde and Robert Brimlow, *Christianity Incorporated: How Big Business Is Buying the Church* (Grand Rapids: Brazos, 2002).

capitalist altruists, pursuing costly goals other than profits puts their enterprises at a competitive disadvantage and eventually out of business. The encyclical's pious generalizations about social responsibility and contributions to the common good minimize the structural constraints and power of capitalism while giving an unrealistic picture of what can be done within competitive markets and political institutions which themselves compete for corporate investment, tax bases, and employment. All of this becomes relevant when considering one of the document's central sections on global governance and order.

> There is a strong felt need, even in the midst of a global recession, for a reform of the *United Nations Organization,* and likewise of *economic institutions and international finance,* so that the concept of the family of nations can acquire real teeth. One also senses the urgent need to find innovative ways of implementing the principle of the *responsibility to protect and of giving poorer nations an effective voice in shared decision-making. This seems necessary in order to arrive at a political, juridical and economic order which can increase and give direction to international cooperation for the development of all peoples in solidarity. To manage the global economy; to revive economies hit by the crisis; to avoid any deterioration of the present crisis and the greater imbalances that would result; to bring about integral and timely disarmament, food security and peace; to guarantee the protection of the environment and to regulate migration: for all of this, there is urgent need of a true world political authority. . . .* Such an authority would need to be universally recognized and to be vested with the effective power to ensure security for all, regard for justice, and respect for rights. Obviously it would have to have the authority to ensure compliance with its decisions from all parties, and also with the coordinated measures adopted in various international forums. . . . [It] also require[s] the construction of a social order that at last conforms to the moral order, to the interconnection between moral and social spheres, and to the link between politics and the economic and civil spheres, as envisioned by the Charter of the United Nations. (*CV,* no. 67)

In this long explanation of what world order should be, two things come to mind based on our earlier discussion. (1) There is no hint of where, if at all, the Church as an international organization, or transnational community of belief and belonging, or of the body of Christ, might fit in. The Church is invisible, subordinated to more powerful loyalties, roles, and allegiances that form the lifeworlds of the faithful. (2) These political and economic authorities

— existing and enhanced, or new and powerful — will themselves make moral claims on the allegiances, affections, and loyalties of Christians and other people worldwide. Will Christians now be called on to kill for international institutions and structures in addition to the hundreds of national governments that have divided Christian loyalties and turned the baptized against one another? I am not among those whose suspicion of "world government" is rooted in a preference for nationalist allegiances and patriotism; still, I worry about what will be required for Benedict's world governance to have "real teeth" to enforce its directives and decrees. Christians will be called on to kill for order yet again, on the world level instead of the national or local level, and the Christian call to love enemies will be buried still further beneath the necessities of wielding and supporting the power of the sword.

It is not clear to what extent we are here bumping up against the tensions in Ratzinger's thought, or the limits of the encyclical genre itself. This document continues the encyclical tradition of addressing itself to all people, believers and unbelievers alike, seeking a common standard of reason not strictly dependent on the revealed truths of Christianity (even as it argues that reason and truth are best considered in terms of Christian theological categories). To that extent it sees itself as talking "ad extra" to those outside the Christian community, in terms general and accessible enough to be compelling to them as well as to members of the body of Christ. As a result, and because they attempt to address issues of complexity and broad implications, encyclicals tend to be abstract, generic, and minimalist in what they require in terms of their audiences.[10]

And yet Ratzinger is not a typical papal author of encyclicals. He is, after all, the doctrinal officer who has described the Church as something of a contrast society in the world, one whose fidelity to the gospel may make it smaller in the years ahead as it experiences an "evangelical pruning" via trials and opposition. He has criticized the sort of transmutation of Christianity into "values" that all can support, even if such is couched in the generally Christian language of the kingdom of God:

> The centrality of the Kingdom [to some people] is supposed to mean that everyone, reaching beyond the boundaries of religions and ideologies, can now work together for the values of the Kingdom, which are, to wit: peace, justice, and the conservation of creation. This trio of values has nowadays

10. For one discussion of the limits of the encyclical tradition, see Michael Budde, *The Two Churches: Catholicism and Capitalism in the World-System* (Durham, N.C.: Duke University Press, 1992).

emerged as a substitute for the lost concept of God and, at the same time, as the unifying formula that could be the basis, beyond all distractions and differences, for the worldwide communion of men of goodwill (and who is not one of them) and thus might really be able to lead to that better world. This sounds tempting. Who is there who does not feel bound to support the great aim of peace on earth?[11]

This is the Ratzinger who asserted that contemporary relativism includes the "dissolution of Christology and of the ecclesiology that is subordinate to it yet indissolubly associated with it."[12] The encyclical critiques relativism but seems bashful, ironically enough, about the Church itself.

The place of the Church in the global order is curiously unspecified. Is the Church simply part of civil society like Greenpeace or the Red Cross? Does it form real peoples and real communities, with material and affective ties across borders and cultures, or is it a loose affiliation whose members are and should forever be submerged in allegiances, roles, and functions derived from powers and ends divorced from the gospel?

One ends up here, not with the Ratzinger for whom the Church is supposed to be something of a contrast society relative to worldly institutions, but one desperate to prove its instrumental utility to global order as constituted by those same worldly institutions of capital, politics, and society. Ironically enough, *Caritas in Veritate* seeks to argue that the "values of Christianity" (*CV*, no. 4) are useful and essential to a proper sort of globalization, and that if you follow Church teachings on sexuality and family you get good social outcomes in terms of population growth and economic prosperity (*CV*, no. 44).

Curiously, we get in *Caritas in Veritate* a document that obscures the real-world Church on one hand, but is too explicitly Christian for some secular commentators. One of them, David Nirenberg, complains that the encyclical argues that "only 'love in truth,' true love, Christian love, can bring about authentic 'social, juridical, political and economic development.'"[13]

Unlike those previous [encyclicals by John Paul II and earlier popes], Benedict's *Caritas in Veritate* foregrounds the argument that only Catholicism contains the "Love in Truth" that is necessary to address our global problems. . . . Only Catholicism provides the synthesis of faith and reason, of

---

11. Joseph Ratzinger, *Pilgrim Fellowship of Faith: The Church as Communion* (San Francisco: Ignatius, 2005), pp. 288-89.

12. Ratzinger, *Pilgrim Fellowship of Faith*, p. 212.

13. Nirenberg, "Love and Capitalism," p. 39.

spirit and flesh, necessary to produce an "authentic economic development."
. . . And only Catholicism, Benedict tells us, can achieve the universal fraternity necessary for authentic community.[14]

All of this may do nothing more than highlight the weaknesses inherent
in the encyclical genre itself — so broad and generic (even with the metaphysical supplement provided by this pope) to be of dubious value to the Christian
movement in the world. Such was the position argued several decades ago by
the late Peter Hebblethwaite, one with which I find myself increasingly in
agreement.

There is more to be said, but I conclude here by wondering how much
different this encyclical might have been if it started with a non-encyclical
thought of Ratzinger, as well as the closing paragraph of *Caritas in Veritate*.
Together, these remind us that a more explicitly Christocentric, and even ec-
clesiocentric, approach to matters of love and truth might make crucial contributions to global order even if such do not prove the instrumental utility of
Christian "values" to secular institutions and powers.

> Fellowship in the body of Christ and in receiving the body of Christ means
> fellowship with one another. This of its very nature includes mutual accep-
> tance, giving and receiving on both sides, and readiness to share one's goods.
> The fact that some people are indulging themselves while others are in want
> cannot be reconciled with Church fellowship. This is always "table fellow-
> ship" in the most demanding sense of the word, and its members always
> have to give each other "life" — physical and spiritual, but especially physi-
> cal, too. In this sense, the social question is given a quite central place in the
> Christian concept of communion.[15]

> *Development needs Christians with their arms raised towards God* in prayer,
> Christians moved by the knowledge that truth-filled love, *caritas in veritate*,
> from which authentic development proceeds, is not produced by us, but given
> to us. . . . Development requires attention to the spiritual life, a serious con-
> sideration of the experiences of trust in God, spiritual fellowship in Christ,
> reliance upon God's providence and mercy, love and forgiveness, self-denial,
> acceptance of others, justice and peace. All of this is essential if "hearts of
> stone" are to be transformed into "hearts of flesh" (Ezek. 36:26), rendering life
> on earth "divine" and thus more worthy of humanity. (*CV*, no. 79)

14. Nirenberg, "Love and Capitalism," p. 42.
15. Ratzinger, *Pilgrim Fellowship of Faith*, p. 69.

Institutional Pluralism, Global Governance, and Nigerian Emails: Benedict's Call for Truth and Trust

Maryann Cusimano Love

Daily I receive emails, often from Nigeria, offering financial partnerships and lots of easy money. You likely receive them too. The themes vary, from estates left unclaimed to widows needing assistance from corrupt government bureaucrats, but usually they boil down to a pledge that huge sums will be deposited in my bank account if I merely divulge my account numbers. Why do we delete these emails? Because we do not believe the information is true and we do not trust the "business partners."

What do we do when the entire economy becomes a Nigerian email scam? This is essentially what happened to us in the global economic crisis. People, investors, and banks lost trust because they did not believe economic players were telling the truth, and so they were unwilling to do business with them. Banks stopped lending, individuals stopped buying investments, due to a loss of trust and truth across the global market.

The market meltdown was not national. Thanks to globalization, problems that began in the United States and British financial and real estate markets did not stay there, but ripped across borders in tsunami-like fashion, wrecking havoc to economies around the world. The people hurt most, the world's poor, were those who had the least to do with causing the crisis.

For most of us, our eyes glaze over at talk of the causes of the economic crisis. Complex derivatives, subprime mortgages, overleveraging of corporations, inflated rating systems, dark markets — the terms and practices are convoluted and opaque. Pope Benedict XVI's summary of the problem is not. The pope's 2009 encyclical, *Caritas in Veritate (CV)*, offers ethical standards for the global economy. Economies need truth and trust to work. Absent those, they do not work. We have to put people before profits. When we do not, the whole enterprise comes tumbling down. As the pope notes, "Without truth, without trust and love for what is true, there is no social conscience and re-sponsibility, and social action ends up serving private interests and the logic of power, resulting in social fragmentation, especially in a globalized society at difficult times like the present. . . . I would like to remind everyone, especially governments engaged in boosting the world's economic and social assets, that *the primary capital to be safeguarded and valued is man, the human person in his or her integrity*" (*CV,* no. 72).[1]

We cannot blame only Bernie Madoff, Nigerian scam artists, or a few unscrupulous individuals for the recession. The lying, lack of full transparency, and insufficient attention to love of neighbor, the common good, and justice were widespread. Individuals, banks, investment companies, insurance com-panies, and major corporations lied (even to themselves) or were not fully transparent or were misled about how much income and debt they had, what their assets and liabilities were worth, how much risk they were exposed to and were exposing others to, and how much risk and debt they could afford. When the deceptions (and lack of full transparency) became apparent, trust disappeared and so did the market. Credit froze and people pulled their money out of banks and investments because they did not know who was telling the truth and whom to trust anymore; good businesses and business people suf-fered along with the unscrupulous ones. When the markets died so did people; the poor and most vulnerable around the world suffer the most as they lose jobs, food, homes, and health. One hundred million more people now go hun-gry than when this crisis began. Charities lost their investments and donations dried up precisely when more people need their services.

Benedict's encyclical cuts to the heart of the matter, literally, to the lack of heart, of love and care for others. The current global economic meltdown is not primarily an economic or a technical failure but a moral failure, an absence of truth, trust, love, justice, and the common good. No one is left off the hook in Benedict's analysis: individuals, companies, civil society, governments, and international institutions all have important roles to play in restoring ethical behavior. Ethical failures to prioritize human life lead to a host of linked and preventable tragedies, including abortion, food scarcity, unemployment, nu-clear arms races, poverty, and environmental damage.

Benedict thus calls for individual and institutional renewal and reform at

---

1. Translation at http://www.vatican.va/holy_father/benedict_xvi/encyclicals/documents/ hf_ben-xvi_enc_20090629_caritas-in-veritate_en.html.

all levels. When challenges are this dire, "all hands on deck" are needed to protect the world's most vulnerable and build more just and effective institutions.

The Need for Global Governance

Some criticize the encyclical for its "something for everyone" lists of pressing social problems and ethical responsibilities. But these lists illustrate the nature and challenges of pursuing social justice in an era of globalization: these issues are intricately connected, and so must be our solutions. We do not have political and institutional structures capable of resolving, managing, or preventing these problems. So we must build them. But in building institutional structures we do not start from scratch. We start with what we have, strengthen, reform, and extend existing institutions, "mind the gaps" between institutions, and work to fill those gaps.

The encyclical shines a light on a global deficiency: the world has a governance problem.[2] We need more of it, at a time when we have less of it. Globalization has created gaps between the problems we face and our abilities to respond. The problems move quickly, but our institutions do not. Problems such as the meltdown of the global financial system and global climate change cross borders and require urgent and coordinated action across countries. But governance stops at the borders of our primary institutions, sovereign states.

New forms of governance are emerging to fill the gaps, especially in the private sector, sometimes in public-private partnerships, sometimes alone. Civil society combines in transnational networks to change corporate and government behavior on issues from debt relief to land mines. Nongovernmental organizations (NGOs) and private companies provide services previously deemed to be the purview of states — from building roads to providing security. Civil society and companies develop and hold businesses accountable to corporate social responsibility codes. A private regulatory body governs the Internet, to the extent that anyone does. The public sector also attempts to increase capacity and collaboration across borders. We create new international institutions (the United Nations Peacebuilding Commission, the World Trade Organization) and adapt old ones (the North Atlantic Treaty Organization [NATO] and the United Nations). Religious actors are part of the mix because religion is resurgent while states are challenged around the world.

2. Maryann Cusimano Love, "Filling the Gaps," *America,* August 3, 2009, p. 9.

Religious actors provide direct services to people in need, and sometimes work to strengthen state and international institutions (as when the church in Rwanda trains people in transitional justice, or the church in Nigeria helps monitor elections).

All these efforts are still not enough. People are dying, but states cannot save us.[3] The United States and other strong states cannot solve these problems alone; their institutions are not wired for it. Nearly one-third of the people on the planet live in the weakest states in the system, detailed by a new report by the Fund for Peace, "The Failed State Index."[4] These failed and failing states cannot provide roads and drinking water, basic law, order, and governance. Their citizens are the most vulnerable, yet these states are the least able to respond to the challenges of globalization.

Archbishop Mauro in the Congo understands this. Nearly six million people have died, most in his diocese, as many Jews as died in the Holocaust, in a conflict driven by failed sovereignty, bloodshed over natural resources to sell to the lucrative global market that powers cell phones, and problems spilling over Central Africa's leaky borders. Congo has a governance problem. Even if the Democratic Republic of Congo had a strong and capable government (which it does not), Congo's problems do not start or stop at its borders. The United Nations has issued a devastating report implicating the government of Rwanda in Congo's horrific violence, noting the Rwandan regime may be complicit in genocide, war crimes, and crimes against humanity. The U.S. Congress passed and President Barack Obama signed the Conflict Minerals Transparency Act, requiring transparency about companies' mineral supply chains. Companies listed on the Securities Exchange Commission (SEC) must report and publish on their websites the origins of their minerals. This will allow consumers to exercise the power of their purchases to pressure companies not to buy coltan or other minerals from conflict areas, the profits of which enrich the warlords and fuel the Congo's resource wars. NGOs and religious organizations work in the Congo, helping refugees, internally displaced persons (IDPs), and victims of rape and violence to survive and rebuild their lives. These are examples of institutional pluralism in the face of a severe governance problem: efforts to pressure governments, international institutions like the United Nations and other intergovernmental organizations (IGOs), NGOs,

3. Maryann Cusimano Love, *Beyond Sovereignty: Issues for a Global Agenda*, 4th ed. (New York: Wadsworth/Cengage, 2010).
4. Fund for Peace, "The Failed State Index 2010," http://www.fundforpeace.org/web/index.php?option=com_content&task=view&id=99&Itemid=140.

churches, and individuals to change the structures that foster violence and instead build peace.

Congo is not the only failed state or place with a governance problem. The worst of these states are what I call "kleptocracies"; their kleptomaniacal leaders treat their governments as ATM machines, to be used for personal enrichment. Check out Transparency International's list of the world's most corrupt governments for the top ten list of the world's worst kleptocracies. Half the people on the planet live without basic freedoms (in both "strong" and "weak" states); their governments deny them the abilities to participate in or hold their governments accountable for the activities undertaken in their name. The worst of these states are predatory, deliberately killing the very citizens they are supposed to protect.

Sovereignty — the idea that governance aligns with territory, and that those outside the geographic boundaries have no authority to meddle in internal affairs — is problematic for most of the people on the planet. But our ideas about how the world works have not caught up with these realities. Most leaders and scholars "whistle past the graveyard" of sovereignty in world politics, focusing on government action even as states are less able to resolve global problems alone.

Pragmatic Institutional Pluralism

I am not a neutral observer of these issues. I finished the fourth edition of my book on globalization, *Beyond Sovereignty: Issues for a Global Agenda,*[5] when the pope released the encyclical *Caritas in Veritate.* Pope Benedict XVI reveals himself to be an institutional pragmatist. When the challenges are this urgent, we have to use all available tools, and work through, reform, strengthen, expand, and improve many institutions: states, existing and new international institutions, civil society partnerships, more ethically oriented businesses, churches, and individuals — all have a role, and no one is off the hook. Media controversy focused on *Caritas in Veritate,* no. 67. "*There is urgent need of a true world political authority* . . . to seek to establish the common good . . . [in] charity and truth. Such an authority would need to be universally recognized and to be vested with the effective power to ensure . . . compliance with its decisions from all parties. . . . [And this] require[s] the establishment of a greater degree of international ordering, marked by subsidiarity, for the management of globalization."

5. Love, *Beyond Sovereignty.*

But focusing on 7 lines out of a 144-page document may distort the point: Benedict calls for effective international institutions, as did his predecessors, but he calls for updating and making more ethical and effective *all our institutions* as well.

Few noted paragraph 41, which urges us "to promote a dispersed political authority, effective on different levels," and paragraph 57, noting that *"the governance of globalization must be marked by subsidiarity, articulated into several layers and involving different levels that can work together.* Globalization certainly requires authority, insofar as it poses the problem of a global common good that needs to be pursued. This authority, however, must be organized in a subsidiary and stratified way."

This is not a new sentiment. In the United States Conference of Catholic Bishops' 1983 pastoral letter, "The Challenge of Peace," the bishops urged new efforts to prevent the spread of nuclear weapons in the world and to control the conventional arms race.[6] They also stated, "We call for the establishment of some form of global authority adequate to the needs of the international common good."[7] This is very similar to Benedict's wording in *Caritas in Veritate*. Benedict notes that we all have moral responsibilities to build a more just international economy and more just individuals, communities, companies, governments, and international institutions. The United States Conference of Catholic bishops made the same claim regarding peace. While "The Challenge of Peace" was most remembered for the bishops' reflections on nuclear war and deterrence, the bishops also spoke eloquently on our *moral obligations to build peace,* at the international, national, church, community, and individual levels. The bishops noted that building peace is not the work of governments alone, but that all citizens have more responsibilities to build a more peaceful world free of the dangers of nuclear weapons.

There are other similarities as well. Benedict's encyclical was criticized by many in the media for being idealistic and impractical, calling for a new, more just world economic order with for-profit companies and new international institutions more concerned with the common good. Similarly, many criticized the United States Conference of Catholic Bishops at the time for being naïve, for writing an overly idealistic letter that was hopelessly out of touch with international political realities. Instead, the bishops were prescient. In consultation with a Polish pope, the bishops saw that another world was both possible

6. Maryann Cusimano Love, "The Challenge of Peace," keynote address to St. John's Seminary, Los Angeles, California, November 10, 2009.

7. See http://old.usccb.org/sdwp/international/TheChallengeofPeace.pdf.

and necessary. Just a few years after their letter, the Berlin Wall came tumbling down, and all the Cold War precepts have been tumbling ever since. In the arms control, disarmament, and nonproliferation arenas, today the world is catching up to what the bishops have been urging all along, including the need to develop new international institutions.

What the critics of both miss is that states and international institutions are not mutually exclusive nor are they the only tools at our disposal; we need them all, public and private sector, local and international, if we are to face urgent problems and save lives. The pope neither calls for one world government nor untrammeled sovereign autonomy, but for effective global governance. This is consistent with Catholic views of sovereignty, the sanctity of life, subsidiarity, and the preferential option for the poor.

Sovereignty and Responsibility

The Catholic Church today has a nuanced view of sovereignty.[8] The Catholic Church preceded the sovereign state system by sixteen centuries, then was a sovereign state, and now while it no longer has armies, it operates both within and outside the sovereign state system. The Holy See is recognized as a micro-state, has a foreign service that exchanges diplomats with 177 sovereign states, and has a permanent observer seat at the United Nations. These trappings of sovereignty afford the Catholic Church a unique position among religious organizations and NGOs, with a foot in both camps, able to readily work with and negotiate with sovereign states, while maintaining extensive operations and networks as a trans-state actor, operating across sovereign state borders in all countries. The Catholic Church believes the sovereign state exists to serve the human person and human communities, not the other way around. Thus the Church works with sovereign states where state institutions are able and interested in protecting the human person. The work of the Church continues even where the state is predatory, antagonistic, or failing.

For many of the world's most vulnerable, sovereign control is either absent or predatory. Nearly one-third of the world's population, two billion out of the more than six billion people on the planet today, live in failed or failing states, absent the conditions of law and order, *tranquillitas ordinis,* which make hu-

---

8. Maryann Cusimano Love, "What Kind of Peace Do We Seek?" in *Peacebuilding: Catholic Theology, Ethics, and Praxis,* ed. Scott Appleby et al. (New York: Orbis, 2010).

man development possible.[9] According to Freedom House, an overlapping two billion people live in forty-three countries where the state deprives them of basic human rights and freedoms.[10] The worst of these states, like Sudan today or Rwanda in 1994, are predatory, killing their own people in genocides. The Catholic Church does not stand on the sidelines where sovereign states are unable or unwilling to protect human life and dignity and the common good. In NGO parlance, the Church is more like Doctors Without Borders than the International Red Cross, ready to act wherever people are in need whether or not it has the prior permission of the sovereign state. A key difference with the international NGO comparison is that the Church is already in countries around the world, and thus is not only an external actor.

As Vatican II's document, *The Church in the Modern World (Gaudium et Spes)* noted: "The social order and its development must constantly yield to the good of the person, since the order of things must be subordinate to the order of persons and not the other way around, as the Lord suggested when he said that the Sabbath was made for man and not man for the Sabbath."[11] The Catholic Church begins with the protection of human life and dignity over deference to sovereignty.[12]

The United Nations and the U.S. government have moved toward this position in adopting the Principle of a Responsibility to Protect, but putting that principle into practice has been limited by state interests and concerns of state sovereignty. The International Commission on Intervention and State Sovereignty in 2001 made a recommendation to the United Nations secretary general in a report entitled "The Responsibility to Protect." In it, the commission affirmed "the idea that sovereign states have a responsibility to protect their own citizens from avoidable catastrophe," but also urged that "when they are unwill-

---

9. Maryann Cusimano Love, "Sovereignty: Who Cares?" in *Beyond Sovereignty*, pp. 355-76.

10. There is overlap among these populations; some live in failing states that are also repressive. See *Freedom in the World 2008*, January 18, 2008, http://www.freedomhouse.org/uploads/fiwo8launch/FIWo8Overview.pdf.

11. Vatican II, *Gaudium et Spes, Pastoral Constitution on the Church in the Modern World*, no. 26, http://www.newadvent.org/library/docs_ec21gs.htm.

12. This is not an exclusionary or triumphalist position. Other non-state actors, both religious and secular institutions, privilege attention to human persons and communities over the interests of sovereign states, in both principles and practices. Because the Catholic Church is so large and has United Nations observer status and diplomatic missions, the higher levels of the Church (the Vatican and the various Bishops' Conferences) have sustained relations with states. But the dominant focus of the Church's work is not at the state level but at the community level.

ing or unable to do so, that responsibility must be borne by the broader community of *states*."[13] More than 150 countries agreed to the "Responsibility to Protect" (R2P) principle during the 2005 World Summit. The development of the R2P principle was influenced by Francis Deng, a diplomat, scholar, and Catholic originally from southern Sudan, where more than two million people died in Africa's longest civil war. Deng emphasized sovereignty as responsibility.[14] The idea is that sovereignty entails a positive responsibility to protect human life, not merely a negative right to noninterference from external actors. States retain the primary responsibilities of protecting their populations from genocide, war crimes, crimes against humanity, and ethnic cleansing. But when states are unable or unwilling to protect life in the most egregious cases of abuses, the international community has responsibilities to protect life. Paragraphs 138 and 139 of the World Summit Outcome Document state:

> That each individual state has the primary responsibility to protect its populations from genocide, war crimes, crimes against humanity and ethnic cleansing. And it is also a responsibility for prevention of these crimes.

> That the international community should encourage or assist states to exercise this responsibility.

> The international community has the responsibility to use appropriate diplomatic, humanitarian and other peaceful means to help protect populations threatened by these crimes. When a state manifestly fails in its protection responsibilities, and peaceful means are inadequate, the international community must take stronger measures, including collective use of force authorized by the Security Council under Chapter VII.[15]

This R2P principle was further established in United Nations Security Council 1674, adopted April 28, 2006, accepting "the responsibility to protect populations from genocide, war crimes, ethnic cleansing, and crimes against humanity."[16]

---

13. The International Commission on Intervention and State Sovereignty, "The Responsibility to Protect," 2001, http://www.iciss.ca/report-en.asp. Emphasis added.

14. Francis M. Deng, *Sovereignty as Responsibility* (Washington, D.C.: Brookings Institution, 1996).

15. United Nations General Assembly, Responsibility to Protect, World Summit Outcome Document, September 15, 2005, A/60/L.1, www.unep.org/greenroom/documents/outcome.pdf.

16. United Nations Security Council Resolution 1674, April 28, 2006, http://daccessdds.un.org/doc/UNDOC/GEN/N06/331/99/PDF/N0633199.

In his speech accepting the Nobel Prize, the then United Nations Secretary General Kofi Annan said, "In the twenty-first century I believe the mission of the United Nations will be defined by a new, more profound awareness of the sanctity and dignity of every human life. . . . This will require us to look beyond the framework of sovereign states. . . . The sovereignty of States must no longer be used as a shield for gross violations of human rights."[17]

The current United Nations Secretary General Ban Ki-moon echoes the same theme. In his January 12, 2009, report, "Implementing the Responsibility to Protect," he noted the responsibilities of the international community "for the vulnerable and the threatened when their Governments become their persecutors instead of their protectors or can no longer shield them from marauding armed groups."[18]

Building new international norms and institutions is not an idle academic or political discussion, but an urgent need for the millions whose lives are on the line in genocides and conflicts, who lack effective structures to protect them, and whose states are predatory or incompetent or both. In a July 21, 2009, report to the General Assembly, Ban Ki-moon noted the need for institutional change. "We can save lives. We can uphold the principles on which this house is built. We can demonstrate that sovereignty and responsibility are mutually reinforcing principles. And we can assert the moral authority of this institution. . . . Never forget the victims of atrocities and crimes. They number in the millions. Those losses have permanently stained the history of the twentieth century. Together, the United Nations can chart a different course in this century. We must never give in to the complacency and cynicism that have kept this organization from acting in the past . . . [this debate] is about the character of this institution and the future of humankind. Join me in the search for a better way."[19]

This moves the United Nations and the United States a step closer to the position of the Church, and to other non-state actors, who maintain that deference to state sovereignty should not trump the protection of human persons.

17. United Nations Secretary General Kofi Annan, Nobel Peace Prize acceptance speech, December 10, 2001.

18. United Nations Secretary General Ban Ki-moon, "Report on Implementing the Responsibility to Protect," January 12, 2009, www.un.org/preventgenocide/adviser/pdf/SG%20Report%20R2P.pdf.

19. United Nations Secretary General Ban Ki-moon, "Remarks to the General Assembly on the Responsibility to Protect," July 21, 2009, http://www.un.org/apps/sg/sgstats.asp?nid=3982.

Pope Benedict mentioned R2P specifically in *Caritas in Veritate* in his discussion of creating more robust international institutions.

Conclusions: Expanding Our Moral Imaginations

What Benedict and the Church are trying to do is to expand our moral imaginations. It is easier to imagine building peace, prosperity, and justice in our families, parishes, and universities. It is harder to imagine bringing peace, justice, and prosperity into our world. But this is our job, and the job of many of our intermediate institutions of NGOs, communities, and companies, not merely the responsibility of distant presidents or United Nations agencies.

Benedict urges us to construct "a social order that at last conforms to the moral order, to the interconnection between moral and social spheres, and the link between politics and the economic and civil spheres, as envisioned by the Charter of the United Nations" (*CV*, no. 67).

Institutional pluralism carries costs, including overlapping jurisdictions and coordination difficulties. But these institutions already exist, and so can be more quickly reformed to better serve the needs of the world's most vulnerable.

Pragmatic pluralism is not neat, but it is necessary. Benedict teaches that profit should not be the only goal of commerce. Love, truth, trust, the common good, and justice apply to the market and to corporate behavior, just as they do to our personal behavior. Critics and commentators question this position as unrealistic. What corporations will ever subscribe to that? Can corporate culture and capitalism ever be weaned from short-term profits that carry long-term costs for others?

But current global problems, including the economic meltdown, focus these questions in a new way. How realistic is it to continue the status quo? Unregulated capitalism and sovereignty without responsibility, without attention to the common good, is not working. Ask the unemployed all over the world, or the many countries that have experienced violent food riots. Benedict notes that while globalization has increased wealth for many, it has also dramatically increased "the scandal of glaring inequalities" and our sad indifference to the plight of the poor among us and around the world.

As Benedict notes, our institutions need "people-centered ethics" to function correctly (*CV*, no. 45). Without moral norms, the global economy ground to a halt; to restore it, ethics must be restored first, for people to more easily discern the difference between honest businesses and the economic equivalents of Nigerian email scams.

Precisely because our world is more closely connected than ever before, so we must love each other better than ever before, or face grave consequences. Global problems from the economic meltdown, to genocide, nuclear security, and environmental problems, are all discussed in *Caritas in Veritate*. But none of these issues are captured by the traditional view of international relations as the activities of states.

This is why Pope Benedict urges us to consider strengthening existing and creating new and more effective forms of international institutions. Existing institutional structures are not working to protect human life and dignity in the turbocharged challenges of globalization. The challenge before us is to do better.

If globalization presents challenges, it also presents opportunities. Throughout history Catholic and religious norms and institutions have often led, pressured, and informed the development of secular institutions. Non-state, voluntary norms and ideas ("soft law") over time have ways of becoming "hard law," adopted and enforced by states. The encyclical notes numerous successful examples of institutional creativity in protecting human life and dignity, from the Focolare movement's Economy of Communion, to fair trade, to the R2P.

"Globalization, *a priori,* is neither good nor bad. It will be what people make of it" (*CV,* no. 42). Benedict urges us to make a more just and sustainable world. Failure to do so is not just immoral, it is impractical, causing resource wars, food riots, and violence against current institutions seen as unjust or incapable of addressing basic human needs. As Benedict notes, "The crisis thus becomes *an opportunity for discernment, in which to shape a new vision for the future*" (*CV,* no. 21).

PART III: RETHINKING THE ECONOMY AS GRATUITOUS

Profit Maximization and the Death of God: Theology and Economics in Benedict XVI's *Charity in Truth*

D. Stephen Long

Responses to Benedict XVI's encyclical on the economy came fast and furious, initiated by George Weigel's controversial editorial in the *National Review*.[1] He found parts of the encyclical capitulating to the Peace and Justice Pontifical Commission established by Pope Paul VI in his 1967 encyclical *Populorum Progressio*. In response, Weigel attempted a quest for the historically authentic Benedict by dividing the encyclical between the "gold" written by Benedict himself and the "red" sponsored by the Peace and Justice Pontifical Commission. For Weigel, the latter was a capitulation by Benedict not to be taken seriously.

All the usual suspects then rose up to claim either that this posed no significant challenge to the capitalist economic order or called it decisively into question. Those on the left emphasized Benedict's "economy of communion," his advocacy for government interference, his critique of globalization, and his challenge to letting the free market alone determine wages. They often neglected the sexual and reproductive issues. Those on the right neglected or dismissed the language of gift, the "economy of communion," and the call for government interference, but emphasized the sexual and reproductive issues, reminding those on the left of Benedict's affirmation of the 1968 encyclical *Humanae Vitae*. But perhaps what both sides missed in this give and take is the profound and *particular* theological convictions that inform this encyclical. Instead, we were regularly told that behind this letter is a doctrine of person-

---

1. George Weigel, *"Caritas in Veritate* in Gold and Red," *National Review* online, July 7, 2009.

alism, or a doctrine that notes the significance of the human person. And this is true, but what is even more important is the Christological foundation for this anthropology. Unlike other encyclicals on the economy, beginning with *Rerum Novarum* in 1891 and following, Benedict's encyclical is the most thorough *theological* approach to economic matters in that grand tradition. He does not prescind from essential Christian teachings in an attempt to make common cause between those in and outside the Church. He unapologetically establishes a Christological and Trinitarian context for how we should think about economic exchange.

What makes Benedict XVI such a fascinating pope and theologian is that his exercise of the Church's teaching office is, in many ways, the fruit of some profound shifts in Catholic theology in the mid-twentieth century, particularly in understanding the relation between nature and grace. Benedict, following in the footsteps of theologians like Henri de Lubac and Hans Urs von Balthasar, is not enamored with the rigid distinction between nature and grace fostered by nineteenth-century neoscholasticism and often still shared by neoconservatives and progressives, both of whom seek to engage in the broader so-called culture wars by thinking of politics and economics fundamentally in terms of the natural law. That approach emerges from the neoscholastic distinction that assumed the human person had a twofold end, one found in nature and the other in supernature. Politics and economics were understood primarily in terms of that natural end. For this reason, the natural law sufficed to direct all people to the natural end that could make them happy. It allowed the Church to speak to all people of good will without necessarily proclaiming more particularist Christian convictions, especially the doctrines of the Trinity and the incarnation and the necessary mediating role of the Church. Indeed, true happiness was found in the supernatural end, and for that one needed the Church with its mediation of Word and sacrament, and its teachings about Jesus and the Triune God, but these were not necessary for the natural end, and therefore only tangentially related to economics and politics. For that the law of nature gives us what we need. This could easily be translated into an affirmation of the autonomy of reason via the social sciences, whether that meant Hayek on the right or Marx on the left. But Benedict XVI has repeatedly stated that the natural law has become nothing but a "blunt instrument," and that this division rendered Jesus too tangential for Catholic social ethics. He seldom uses the natural law when he addresses political and economic matters. Instead, he is unabashedly Christological and Trinitarian in his counsel to Catholics, Protestants, Muslims, Jews, secularists, and others.

Benedict does not deny that nature has a "law" or "grammar," that is to say, an order that God gives to it and that we can discover.[2] This order is what makes "truth" possible, and such an order, as he has repeatedly stated, requires both truth and charity to be rightly discerned. But truth is for him personal because, following the Gospel of John, Truth is a Person. I hope to show first how the connection between charity and truth is an inextricably Christological claim. Christology provides the theological foundations of creaturely existence. I then want to show how this makes Christianity a factor in economic life — a factor that gets lost in the modern era and must be retrieved. Finally, I contrast Benedict's "Christocentric anthropology" (the term comes from Tracey Rowland's work) with some contemporary ethicists and economists and discuss what it might demand of us.

1. Truth and Charity: The Theological Foundation of Existence

Benedict XVI unapologetically claims that Christ's life establishes the foundation for human existence. It is basic to his argument in *Caritas in Veritate (CV)*. He writes, "Charity in truth, to which Jesus Christ bore witness by his earthly life and especially by his death and resurrection, is the principal driving force behind the authentic development of every person and of all humanity" (*CV*, no. 1). Read in comparison to *Populorum Progressio (PP)*, on which *Caritas in Veritate* comments, this is a startling claim. It stated, "To be authentic, [development] must be well rounded; it must foster the development of each man and of the whole man" (*PP*, no. 14).[3] *Populorum Progressio* tended to explain this development primarily in terms of the human creature's natural end. All that was necessary was a doctrine of creation. Therefore, Paul VI wrote, "Just as the whole of creation is ordered toward its Creator, so too the rational creature should of his own accord direct his life to God, the first truth and the highest good. Thus human self-fulfillment may be said to sum up our obligations" (*PP*, no. 16). Note how the "rational creature" here directs himself to God and the good "of his own accord." Our obligation is "human self-fulfillment," and the call for "development" makes no explicit reference to Jesus, God's gifts,

2. He writes that nature is "a wondrous work of the creator containing a 'grammar' which sets forth ends and criteria for its wise use, not its reckless exploitation" (*CV*, no. 48). Translation follows Pope Benedict XVI, *Caritas in Veritate* (Washington, D.C.: United States Conference of Catholic Bishops, 2009).

3. Translation at http://www.vatican.va/holy_father/paul_vi/encyclicals/documents/hf
_p-vi_enc_26031967_populorum_en.html.

or even the Triune God. This is not to argue that Paul VI did not think they mattered; of course he did, but they remained implicit.

Benedict, on the other hand, states explicitly that the "principal driving force behind authentic development" is Jesus. That, I think, provides the intelligibility to language such as "gift" and "communion" in this letter. It is not some capitulation to leftist thought, but the *theological* affirmation that creation takes place in, through, and for Christ. Benedict's explicit reference to particular Christian dogmas in comparison to Paul VI's appeal to a more generic anthropology also shows the post-Christian and post-secular reality of Western politics and economics in the twenty-first century. It reflects a post-Christian reality in that basic Christian teachings must now be explicitly heralded. We no longer assume a stable Christian civilization or culture, a patrimony tacitly or otherwise acknowledged, within which something like an appeal to the "natural law" might be intelligible. It is post-secular in that supposed common universals within secularism that seemed to make common cause with the natural law, such as Habermas did in his "Dialogue" with Cardinal Ratzinger, also no longer provide a compelling patrimony.[4] The Church's role in the world has changed markedly since 1967, which in some sense reflects a failure of Catholic social teaching. No one has been listening. The arguments were set forth in such a way that they actually contributed to secularization. Benedict takes the Church back to its roots while at the same time reminding us of the Christian patrimony that we neglect to our peril.

Those claiming Benedict speaks for their side in the culture wars too often neglect his "Christocentric anthropology." But this has been a consistent emphasis throughout his work.[5] It is important for understanding the place of "development" in *Caritas in Veritate,* for "development" can quickly underwrite a secular program where the "dignity of the human person," another of the supposed secular universals, suffices for an anthropology. The 1967 *Populorum Progressio* lent itself to such an interpretation as did the Vatican II document *Gaudium et Spes.* For all of the good it has accomplished, the sharp distinction

---

4. See Joseph Ratzinger and Jürgen Habermas, *Dialectics of Secularization: On Reason and Religion,* trans. Brian McNeil (San Francisco: Ignatius, 2006). In this dialogue, Habermas suggested that the Roman Catholic natural law tradition "has no problem in principle with an autonomous justification of morality and law (that is, a justification independent of the truths of revelation)" (p. 25). Ratzinger found less help in the "natural law" for addressing this question than did Habermas. He wrote, "Unfortunately, this instrument [natural law] has become blunt. Accordingly I do not intend to appeal to it for support in this conversation" (p. 69).

5. Tracey Rowland, *Ratzinger's Faith: The Theology of Pope Benedict XVI* (Oxford: Oxford University Press, 2008), p. 34.

between nature and supernature in some Catholic social teaching contributed to the secular marginalization of Christian teaching. Without losing that good, Benedict charts a different course.

As early as 1969, Joseph Ratzinger wrote an essay critiquing some implications of the kind of language arising from Vatican II that marginalized Christology. For instance, he found *Gaudium et Spes* "still based on a schematic representation of nature and the supernatural viewed far too much as merely juxtaposed."[6] This fostered an anthropology that still "divided" the doctrine of the human person too much between "philosophy and theology." He then asked, "why exactly the reasonable and perfectly free human being described in [*Gaudium et Spes*] first article should suddenly be burdened with the story of Christ."[7] He recognized that the way of arguing for Catholic social ethics marginalized Christology. "Burdening" anthropology with Christ best characterizes Benedict's approach to politics and economics. A clear example of this is his undelivered address, "The Truth Makes Us Good and Goodness Is True." In 2007 Benedict XVI was invited to present a lecture at La Sapienza University in Rome. Because of student protests against the pope's visit in the name of free speech, the lecture was not given, which is more than ironic. Benedict's lecture was about the need for universities to have a requisite freedom to seek truth. But a genuine freedom to seek truth should not police against revelation, against receiving something more than what an immanent philosophical approach alone could provide. To explain this, Benedict drew on the doctrine of the incarnation to describe how nature and grace, or philosophy and theology, should relate.

> I would say that St. Thomas's idea of the relationship between philosophy and theology could be expressed in the Council of Chalcedon's formula for Christology: Philosophy and theology must relate to each other "without confusion and without separation." "Without confusion" means that both of them preserve their proper identity. Philosophy must truly remain an undertaking of reason in its proper freedom and proper responsibility; it must recognize its limits, and precisely in this way also its grandeur and vastness. Theology must continue to draw from the treasury of knowledge that it did not invent itself, that always surpasses it and that, never being totally exhaustible through reflection, and precisely because of this, launches thinking. Together with the "without confusion," the "without separation" is also in force: Philosophy does not begin again from zero with the subject

6. Rowland, *Ratzinger's Faith*, p. 34.
7. Rowland, *Ratzinger's Faith*, p. 34.

thinking in isolation, but rather stands in the great dialogue of historical wisdom, that again and again it both critically and docilely receives and develops; but it must not close itself off from that which the religions, and the Christian faith in particular, have received and bequeathed on humanity as an indication of the way. Various things said by theologians in the course of history and also things handed down in the practice of ecclesial authorities, have been shown to be false by history and today they confuse us. But at the same time it is true that the history of the saints, the history of the humanism that grew up on the basis of the Christian faith, demonstrates the truth of this faith in its essential nucleus, thereby making it an example for public reason.[8]

Philosophy has an independence from theology. It is an "undertaking" of reason. But it is never "pure." It does not begin anew in each generation. Its grandeur arises both from what it can accomplish and from a humble recognition of its limits. Such limits make it open to receive wisdom both from a historical patrimony and from faith. True reason need not fear the gift of faith any more than faith spurns reason. The grandeur of reason is found in both what it can accomplish and in a humble acknowledgment of its limits that makes it open to both "historical wisdom" and "faith." This theme of gift, that Weigel appears to have colored in red, is actually a longstanding commitment of Benedict.[9]

---

8. Translation available at http://www.zenit.org/article-21526?l=english.

9. Weigel wrote, "Now comes *Caritas in Veritate* (Charity in Truth), Benedict XVI's long-awaited and much-delayed social encyclical. It seems to be a hybrid, blending the pope's own insightful thinking on the social order with elements of the Justice and Peace approach to Catholic social doctrine, which imagines that doctrine beginning anew at *Populorum Progressio.* Indeed, those with advanced degrees in Vaticanology could easily go through the text of *Caritas in Veritate,* highlighting those passages that are obviously Benedictine with a gold marker and those that reflect current Justice and Peace default positions with a red marker. The net result is, with respect, an encyclical that resembles a duck-billed platypus. . . . But then there are those passages to be marked in red — the passages that reflect Justice and Peace ideas and approaches that Benedict evidently believed he had to try and accommodate. Some of these are simply incomprehensible, as when the encyclical states that defeating Third World poverty and underdevelopment requires a 'necessary openness, in a world context, to forms of economic activity marked by quotas of gratuitousness and communion.' This may mean something interesting; it may mean something naïve or dumb. But, on its face, it is virtually impossible to know *what* it means. The encyclical includes a lengthy discussion of 'gift' (hence 'gratuitousness'), which, again, might be an interesting attempt to apply to economic activity certain facets of John Paul II's Christian personalism and the teaching of Vatican II, in *Gaudium et Spes* 24, on the moral imperative of making our lives the gift to others that life itself is

We see this Christological reading of the relation between philosophy and theology, and nature and grace, repeated, incorporated, and developed in *Caritas in Veritate*. Benedict writes, "Reason also stands in need of being purified by faith . . . religion always needs to be purified by reason" (*CV*, no. 56). Faith and reason, grace and nature, should no longer be relegated to separate realms. There is a "porosity" between them that will inevitably entail "border-crossing" despite the academic policing that takes place on the left and the right.[10] Faith needs reason. It must engage the best that philosophy and the sciences offer. But reason also needs faith. It needs that openness to something beyond its own immanent borders. For this reason, economics cannot proceed as an insular discipline cordoned off from faith, theology, and metaphysics. The latter represent a necessary openness to history and being that will always be something more than "human self-fulfillment" through its own natural resources, albeit those natural resources are necessary for the ongoing "purification" of faith. For this reason Benedict calls for a "new humanistic synthesis" with regard to the economy that requires "faith, theology, metaphysics and science to come together in a collaborative effort in service to humanity" (*CV*, no. 31). Economics must do its work as a "philosophical discipline." But if it is to do this well, it will need to be open to something more than rational choice theory, profit maximization, utilitarian calculation, marginalism, and the like. Faith, theology, and metaphysics must also play a role. This is a profound challenge

---

to us. But the language in these sections of *Caritas in Veritate* is so clotted and muddled as to suggest the possibility that what may be intended as a new conceptual starting point for Catholic social doctrine is, in fact, a confused sentimentality of precisely the sort the encyclical deplores among those who detach charity from truth. There is also rather more in the encyclical about the redistribution of wealth than about wealth-creation — a sure sign of Justice and Peace default positions at work. . . . Those with eyes to see and ears to hear will concentrate their attention, in reading *Caritas in Veritate,* on those parts of the encyclical that are clearly Benedictine, including the Pope's trademark defense of the necessary conjunction of faith and reason and his extension of John Paul II's signature theme — that all social issues, including political and economic questions, are ultimately questions of the nature of the human person." Weigel, "*Caritas in Veritate* in Gold and Red."

10. The language here is that of William Desmond. He writes, "We can plot a border between territories and insist that faith and reason only travel to the other's country under proper visa. Then they will enter illegally, without certification or passport. There are no univocal borders in mind and spirit which bar trespass or illegal entry; there is a porosity more elemental than all passports and academic policing. . . . Where is the pure faith relative to which thought is excluded? Where is there pure reason that entirely excludes all trust?" *Is There a Sabbatical for Thought? Between Religion and Philosophy* (New York: Fordham University Press, 2005), pp. 98-99.

to the study and practice of economics that would require an interdisciplinary approach that few secular universities would permit.

If we are to take Benedict's teaching seriously, then the goal of economic life would be seen primarily as arising from and returning to the Eucharist. Its goal is, as he puts it, "true communion." Notice how when he explains what this is, he relates grace and nature, faith and reason, in an interesting way: "Today humanity appears much more interactive than in the past: this shared sense of being close to one another must be transformed into true communion. *The development of peoples depends, above all, on a recognition that the human race is a single family* working together in true communion, not simply a group of subjects who live side by side" (*CV*, no. 53).[11] We have the natural reality of our close proximity and dependence on each other. But this proximity requires "true communion" if we are to have the kind of development that suits us as the human race. The natural reality of close proximity requires the grace of "true communion," if that globalized proximity is to achieve its true end. This requires transformation. What is this "transformation" into "true communion"?

Again, this language has precedence in Benedict's earlier work. It is found in his book *Jesus of Nazareth,* where he argues that the politics of Christianity is of a "different order of reality." That work addresses the question of a Christian politics, which Benedict claims, is found in "every Eucharistic assembly" for it is "a place where the King of peace reigns in this sense."[12] If we do not have this politics, we cannot offer to the world "charity in truth." For this reason Benedict argues, "The Christological (theological) argument and the social argument are inextricably entwined."[13] Christology defines the social, even the place of the nations. This does not mean God wishes "to abandon the nations to themselves" for Jesus "has brought the God of Israel to the nations . . . brought the gift of universality." This could easily be misunderstood in a Kantian trajectory if we lose sight of the claim that for Benedict, this universality is intimately linked to "communion with Jesus."[14] Communion is the key here. This universality is a *theological* catholicity — a common life that exists transnationally, found primarily in the Catholic Church existing across space and time. Its task is to bring this "communion" to all the nations, and all nations into this communion.

11. Our global proximity is not necessarily good. Globalization, Benedict writes, "makes us neighbors but does not make us brothers" (*CV,* no. 19).

12. Pope Benedict XVI, *Jesus of Nazareth,* vol. 1 (New York: Doubleday, 2007), p. 84.

13. Pope Benedict XVI, *Jesus of Nazareth,* p. 115.

14. Pope Benedict XVI, *Jesus of Nazareth,* p. 116.

In *Caritas in Veritate,* Benedict states that for this "communion" we need "new thinking" that is not just concerned with the "social sciences" but also draws on "metaphysics and theology" for the development of an adequate "category of relation" (*CV,* no. 53). In order to do so, he first draws on the doctrine of the Trinity (*CV,* no. 54) and then on marriage (*CV,* no. 55). These specific Christian teachings do not mean wisdom is not found elsewhere. Benedict recognizes that "other cultures and religions" also "teach brotherhood and peace." Those teachings also provide a direction for an "integral human development" (*CV,* no. 55) that has as its end "true communion."

Why then is Benedict's theological engagement with *Populorum Progressio* called "Charity in Truth"? Because the latter is Christ, and creation is in, through, and for him. What then is truth? "Truth is the light that gives meaning and value to charity. That light is both the light of reason and the light of faith through which the intellect attains to the natural and supernatural truth of charity: it grasps its meaning as gift, acceptance and communion" (*CV,* no. 3).

2. The Loss and Retrieval of the "Christian Factor" and Its Concomitant Economic Practices

We lose the central role of truth and charity in economics when "the sole criterion of truth is efficiency and utility." Once reason or nature is construed solely in their terms, then "development is automatically denied" (*CV,* no. 70). This is no small challenge to economics. On the whole, "pure" economic reason only uses "efficiency and utility" as the criterion for truth. It has no place for theology, metaphysics, and the goal of true communion. Take, for instance, the Acton Institute's Jay Richards. He explains how we are to think about the relation between a business owner and his or her employees solely in terms of a purely economic reason. He writes, "To a business, employee wages are costs. . . . A wage is a price on a commodity — labor."[15] Richards then argues that it must not be understood as anything more than that. If it is, the system will not work. For this reason, we must not have any minimum wage let alone a just wage. This is of course classic liberalism, which only knows "efficiency and utility" and polices out any theological or metaphysical uses of reason. As much as the left adopted a secular social science alone in Marxism to explain economics, so the right adopts Hayek's or Weber's analysis without any "transformation"

---

15. Jay Richards, *Money, Greed, and God: Why Capitalism Is the Solution and Not the Problem* (New York: HarperCollins, 2009), p. 38.

of that rationality by faith and the goal of "true communion." How did this secular reasoning cordon off the "Christian factor" from economic analysis? How can it be retrieved? Benedict's work gives insight into both.

We can begin to see this with an important claim made in *Caritas in Veritate*. A properly theological development gets thwarted when life gets fragmented. This occurs when business gets defined solely by "maximization of profit," politics by "consolidation of power," and science by "findings of research" (*CV*, no. 71).[16] Then life gets trapped in an immanence that is not open to anything beyond itself. Managers find their only constituency to be shareholders. We lose theology and metaphysics, and especially the importance of "gift" in our economic analysis. Of course, this poses a significant challenge to contemporary capitalist arrangements. At least in the United States, corporate law enshrines profit maximization. The 1919 Supreme Court ruling *Dodge v. Ford Motor Co.* stated the legal obligation a CEO has is only to his or her shareholders to maximize profits. Economists and ethicists are in ready supply who defend this principle. As Elaine Sternberg put it, "business organizations which seek anything but long-term owner value are guilty not of socialism, but of theft."[17] Life gets fragmented because managers, owners, shareholders, and others are trained only to respond to the question of profit. We no longer find economic exchange also to be a response to the transcendental predicates of being such as beauty, the true, and the good. Nor do we think it is a matter of a response to God. The natural and theological orders, as well as their mutual relation, get ignored solely for a materialism that finds that the "real powers" that shape history are "politics and economics" devoid of metaphysics or theology.[18]

The latter is a reference to Ratzinger's 1968 *Introduction to Christianity*, where he took on the privatization of Christianity and its catastrophic effects for our understanding of the human person. Ratzinger then asked the question whether God's irrelevance for everyday life was not something already present in the

16. Benedict writes, "Once profit becomes the exclusive goal, if it is produced by improper means and without the common good as its ultimate end, it risks destroying wealth and creating poverty" (*CV*, no. 21). He then challenges a basic premise in contemporary corporate law by arguing that "grave risks" occur when businesses are "exclusively answerable to their investors" (*CV*, no. 40). He states that a significant problem in the present economy is a "new class of managers" who are "often only answerable to shareholders generally consisting of anonymous funds" (*CV*, no. 40).

17. Elaine Sternberg, *Just Business: Business Ethics in Actions* (London: Little, Brown, 1994), quoted in Andrew Hartopp, *What Is Economic Justice?* (Colorado Springs: Paternoster, 2007), p. 168n23.

18. Joseph Ratzinger, *Introduction to Christianity*, 2nd ed., trans. J. R. Foster (San Francisco: Ignatius, 2004 [1968]), pp. 14-15.

Christian West. "We all have to behave now *etsi Deus non daretur* (as if there were no God)."[19] Ratzinger then wrote, "But as Nietzsche describes it, once the news really reaches people that 'God is dead' and they take it to heart, then everything changes. This is demonstrated today on the one hand, in the way that science treats human life: man is becoming a technological object while vanishing to an ever greater degree as a human subject, and he has only himself to blame."[20] The science that treats the human subject this way includes economics.

In *Introduction to Christianity,* Ratzinger traced this dominance of the technological approach to our understanding of the human person through a variety of stages, but he primarily traced it through Vico's variation on an Aristotelian metaphysical theme. He wrote, "Following formally in Aristotle's footsteps, [Vico] asserts that real knowledge is the knowledge of causes. I am familiar with a thing if I know the cause of it; I understand something that has been proved if I know the proof. But from this old thought something completely new is deduced: If part of real knowledge is the knowledge of causes, then we can truly know only what we have made ourselves, for it is only ourselves that we are familiar with."[21] This notion of truth is what traps us in an immanent world of our own making. Vico turns away from the scholastic "verum est ens" to "verum qui factum" — a move away from truth as a "transcendental predicate of being" to the true as the made. Truth is what we make. This introduces the "scientific" age, and the dominance of the *factum,* or the fact. The result is a materialism that assumes that the "real powers" that shape history are "politics and economics."[22] Ratzinger found Latin American liberation theology adopting this materialist assumption through its primacy of "praxis." This did allow for some positive movements: Marx's claim that the point is not to interpret the world but to change it was a positive influence, but this primacy of praxis meant "God had nothing to do."[23] That is to say, even the theologians who were attempting to overcome the privatization of theology did it in such a way that God did not matter.

If this 1968 book recognized and challenged any immanent, secular basis for Latin American liberation theology's social analysis, the 2009 *Caritas in Veritate* recognizes and combats a similar problem in capitalist economic analysis. Both materialist analyses should be ruptured by the "gift" of faith. Ratzinger differentiates this understanding of the relation between theology

---

19. Ratzinger, *Introduction to Christianity,* p. 16.
20. Ratzinger, *Introduction to Christianity,* p. 17.
21. Ratzinger, *Introduction to Christianity,* p. 61.
22. Ratzinger, *Introduction to Christianity,* pp. 14-15.
23. Ratzinger, *Introduction to Christianity,* p. 17.

and philosophy from a philosophy informed by the modern version of "the true is the made." He writes, "faith is not something thought up by me but something that comes to me from outside; its words cannot be treated and exchanged as I please; it is always foreordained, always ahead of my thinking. The positivity of what comes toward me from outside myself, opening up to me what I cannot give myself, typifies the process of belief or faith. Therefore, here the foregiven word takes precedence over the thought, so that it is not the thought that creates its own words but the given word that points the way to the thinking that understands. With this primacy of the word and the 'positivity' of belief apparent in it goes the social character of belief, which signifies a second difference from the essentially individualistic structure of philosophical thinking."[24] Benedict makes a similar argument in *Caritas in Veritate*. The "ultimate source" for "truth and love" is not humanity but God. He writes, "This principle is extremely important for society and for development, since neither can be a purely human product; the vocation to development on the part of individuals and peoples is not based simply on human choice but is an intrinsic part of a plan that is prior to us and constitutes for all of us a duty to be freely accepted. That which is prior to us and constitutes us — subsistent Love and Truth — shows us what goodness is and in what our true happiness consists. *It shows us the road to true development*" (*CV*, no. 52).

3. Economic Consequences

So what would Benedict's theological economics require of us? First, it requires that we acknowledge that economics is never an independent, autonomous exercise. It is always situated in a larger, political, metaphysical, and theological context. The political context is ruled by the requirements of justice. For this reason, Benedict argues, "The market is subject to the principles of so-called *commutative justice*, which regulates the relations of giving and receiving between parties to a transaction. But the social doctrine of the Church has unceasingly highlighted the importance of *distributive justice* and *social justice* for the market economy, not only because the market belongs within a broader social and political context, but also because of the wider network of relations within which it operates" (*CV*, no. 35). That larger context also includes a natural and metaphysical order — truth, beauty, goodness. Citing John Paul II, Benedict writes, "What is needed is an effective shift in mentality which can

24. Ratzinger, *Introduction to Christianity*, p. 92.

lead to the adoption of *new lifestyles* 'in which the quest for truth, beauty, goodness and communion with others for the sake of common growth are the factors which determine consumer choices, savings and investments'" (*CV*, no. 51, citing *Centesimus Annus*, no. 36). Finally, it includes a theological order, one already alluded to in this metaphysical order; it is an order that acknowledges that our being comes as gift and has its true purpose in communion.

Let me conclude by attempting to place economic analysis in terms of this larger natural, metaphysical, and theological structure. Think of the natural, metaphysical, and theological not as three discrete, autonomous circles, but as a single layered reality. We can begin with the "natural" — with our basic animality, its needs and desires. But that "natural" always opens up to a yet greater reality, a metaphysical one where the unavoidability of goodness, beauty, and truth gives the natural its shape. Without that metaphysical quest, the natural loses its own basic reality and becomes nothing but a materialist order defined by technological calculations. But that natural and metaphysical reality is not the only reality for we are by nature oriented to something yet even greater — to a desire for God. This is a desire that cannot be satisfied naturally, but seeks something more — the gift of charity and true communion. In order to explain this I return to the theme of work and ask what is required of us if we think of economic relations in terms of this larger structure.

Any relation to workers exists first within a natural structure. We have biological needs and desires that must be fulfilled for "authentic human development," needs for food, rest, clothing, shelter, health care, security, play, and the like. We cannot survive without the satisfaction of these basic needs and desires. But what regulates them? Commutative justice might suggest that legal contracts alone provide proper regulation. If I enter freely into an economic arrangement and agree to provide or purchase goods and services at market prices, then that is the only "natural" context that should determine "value." Catholic social teaching never accepted this. Since Leo XIII's *Rerum Novarum* it has claimed that market forces alone cannot determine just wages. As Leo XIII put it, "there underlies a requirement of natural justice higher and older than any bargain voluntarily struck: the wage ought not to be in any way insufficient for the bodily needs of a temperate and well-behaved worker. If having no alternative and fearing a worse evil, a workman is forced to accept harder conditions imposed by an employer or contractor, he is the victim of violence against which justice cries out."[25] Benedict XVI continues this long-

---

25. Pope Leo XIII, *Rerum Novarum*, no. 45. Translation at http://www.vatican.va/holy _father/leo_xiii/encyclicals/documents/hf_l-xiii_enc_15051891_rerum-novarum_en.html.

standing Catholic teaching when he says that foreign workers "cannot be considered as a commodity or a mere workforce" (*CV*, no. 62). The natural order alone cannot be truly represented by claiming that market value alone constitutes what is "natural," let alone that the market, as a "natural" reality, identifies or responds properly to the metaphysical and theological ordering of our basic animality.

I already mentioned Jay Richards's argument that a purely natural economic reason would treat wages as nothing but a commodity. But this overlooks the layered reality within which economics takes place. For some reason, theological voices that defend the "free" market overlook this basic teaching. Take, for instance, the work of William McGurn. He questions the role of government to legislate against child labor based on the real possibilities afforded an Asian child who works in a garment factory sewing clothes for Wal-Mart. He by no means defends child labor, but he wants to make his "American" audience aware of the market realities this child faces. He writes, "An Asian audience would immediately recognize that the real alternative for that Bangladesh girl would not be trundling off to class but scavenging through garbage heaps or prostituting herself."[26] And he concludes, "To our sensibilities, this is not an attractive trade-off. But in real life poor people typically do not have the choices we wish them to have, and the market sometimes brings better choices even when that is not its intention. While it might soothe Western consciences to 'eliminate' child labor through regulations, in reality we may — if successful — be forcing children into something worse."[27] What is troubling about this statement is that McGurn claims it is "our sensibilities" that make the option between child labor and child prostitution an "unattractive trade-off." But this has nothing to do with "western consciences"; it is a matter of what justice demands based on the natural human desires that well up in us, pointing us to their proper ordering that can only be known once we examine metaphysics and theology. To be outraged by such a reality is to begin to have one's basic desires properly ordered. To be told that it is a false sensibility is to disorder desire. If the unregulated free market is recommended because it gives an Asian child a choice between prostitution and child labor, then it does not have much to recommend it. It is not "natural," but an unnatural situation that calls for remedy.

For Benedict, natural justice demands not just commutative justice, but

26. William McGurn and Rebecca M. Blank, *Is the Market Moral? A Dialogue on Religion, Economics & Justice* (Washington, D.C.: Brookings Institution, 2004), p. 131.

27. McGurn, *Is the Market Moral?* p. 132.

also distributive and social. He writes, "In fact, if the market is governed solely by the principle of the equivalence in value of exchanged good, it cannot produce the social cohesion that it requires in order to function well" (*CV*, no. 35). What would it mean to function well? Not only distributive and social justice, but also metaphysics and theology will be determinative factors that must be taken into account if it is to function well. What would this entail? It requires God to be considered in economic exchanges, for they are always forms of communion that implicate our lives in those of others. Economic exchange is not a bare act of will two people perform when they trade with each other. It is an act that always presumes something that came prior, which Benedict identifies as "subsistent Love and Truth" (*CV*, no. 52). Perhaps the English version capitalizes these terms for a reason. Subsistent relations are relations among the Triune Persons. The Father shares his essence with the Son, who is Truth. The Son only is the Son because of his relation to the Father. He "subsists" in the Father. Likewise, the Father and Son share their common essence with the Spirit, who is Love. The Spirit "subsists" in them. This means that the Persons are not individual substances who have some autonomous "I" that constitutes their being. They are who they are because they subsist in another, and they do so immediately.

We are made in and for this "image." We are not God so our relations do not have the same immediacy as the Triune Persons, but we are nonetheless implicated in each other's lives such that without acknowledging that implication we will fail truly to develop as we should. This order comes before us and we neglect it at our peril. Oliver O'Donovan nicely explains this when he encourages us not to think in terms of "economic exchange" at all, but to think of these relations in terms of "communication." He finds the term "exchange" to be inappropriate as a reference to God's relations with creation. He writes, "'Exchange' imports the idea of closure to a transaction, restoring the parties to the independence of the status quo ante, each strengthened by the return of value in a different form."[28] He rightly cautions against any such contractual use of exchange in theology. "The concept of exchange is not fundamental to community. It is a device, abstract and formal, created together with the institution of trade, the market. To trade is to effect an exchange of goods between two otherwise equal and unrelated agents."[29] Instead, "communication" (from *koinonia*) is a more basic theological term. He quotes Althusius, who defines

---

28. Oliver O'Donovan, *The Ways of Judgment: The Bampton Lectures, 2003* (Grand Rapids: Eerdmans, 2005), p. 246.

29. O'Donovan, *The Ways of Judgment*, p. 246.

communication as goods held in common such as "things, services, and common rights *(iura)*, by which the numerous and various needs of each and every symbioate are supplied, the self-sufficiency and mutuality of life and human society are achieved, and social life is established and conserved." Communication is, then, to give anything "meaning" and thus has as its "paradigm object" the word.[30]

So let us not even use the term "economic exchange." When I purchase goods and services I am "communicating"; my life becomes a mediated subsistent relation intertwined with others. Purchasing and consuming are more like language, sharing a meal together, or engaging in sexual intercourse than they are isolated discrete acts that are nothing but a bare "exchange." This is why economics, language, and sex are always related, why it is right to be obsessed with sex — if we are always at the same time obsessed with economics and language. Stanley Hauerwas tells of a Jewish friend who states, "Any God who will not tell you what to do with your pots and pans and genitals isn't worth worshipping." Sex, language, and economics are all forms of communication that cannot be reduced to bare forms of exchange without thwarting our humanity. They must all be open to something beyond them if we are to be truly human. Sex should be open to life, to the gift that comes through procreation. Language makes us open to the gift of community, for none of us has a private language. Economics opens us to the metaphysical and theological order that antedates our existence, an existence founded on a generous act of *creatio ex nihilo* where God creates solely out of the Love and Truth that defines God's being. This theory of relations must be present whenever economic calculations are made.

---

30. O'Donovan, *The Ways of Judgment*, p. 250.

Christianity and the Challenges of the Contemporary Economy and Culture

Paulo Fernando Carneiro de Andrade

1. The Malaise in the Contemporary Situation

One of the core characteristics of our time is the expansion of the market, which has become both omnicomprehensive and omnipresent. The market has advanced, offering the means to satisfy a number of demands that were previously outside its sphere of influence. New markets for services have been created by different means, including the privatization of state-owned companies and the curbing of the welfare state. This means that health, education, and social welfare needs have started to be met by the market (such as private health insurance and private pension schemes). With the creation of new specific services, even caregiving and finding new friends and partners can today be satisfied by the market (such as relationship and social networking websites). Meanwhile, trade and tax barriers have been toppled, leading to the formation of global markets with unlimited coverage, reaching everywhere from the farthest-flung village to the largest urban center. Not only is the market omnicomprehensive, but it is also omnipresent. As a result of this unprecedented expansion of the market, (almost) all human relations are being turned into market relations, or at least relationships ruled (or colonized) by the market logic.[1]

The phenomenon of neoliberal globalization and the vertiginous expansion of the market are linked to a profound crisis of the culture that is hegemonically associated with the Fordist industrial economy. Enlightenment-

---

1. See P. Hirst and G. Thompson, *Globalização em questão* (Petropolis: Vozes, 1998).

based modernity, or the first modernity, meaning a culture centered on the driving idea of an ever brighter future, allowed men and women to be guided by self-enlightened reason, which is basically identified with scientific reason. When the Fordist-industrial society ran its course, this culture, which was at once its driving force and its outcome, also ran out of steam.[2]

The crisis of the first modernity was a crisis of its paradigms and the historical projects associated with it. In it, a historically determined discourse about God, man and woman, and the world became mistaken for and identified with reality and the whole truth. The exclusive access to truth claimed by modern reason ultimately emerged from an impoverishing, reductionist perspective that has engendered a contradiction at the heart of modernity. On the one hand, Enlightened modernity breaks away from a culture based on authority and tradition, introducing methodical criticism and thus giving space for liberty and demands for equality. On the other, in the Enlightenment-based modernist culture, instrumental reason precludes any truths that do not suit it and negates all differences by claiming universal status and generating new mechanisms of domination.[3]

In this way, while enlightened modernity may have taken great strides toward a libertarian project, it has failed to realize it fully.[4] Some issues that are today perceived as being crucial could not be adequately resolved by it, or rather, were often not even understood as being issues. Such is the case of ecology-related questions and the issue of gender and subjectivity.

The act of the individual reducing himself or herself to the rational dimension led in practice to a negation of subjectivity. Affections, passions, mysticism, and spirituality all became subjugated to reason in the name of human happiness. When all truth is reduced to instrumental rationality, those things that cannot be rationalized or controlled by modern reason are deemed false or at the very least inferior. The process of civilization then started to be understood as a process of progressive rationalization, where men and women became increasingly human as they polished themselves through the prism of reason and control of their passions.[5] This control was also needed to make men and women fit for the demands of industrial production, whose

2. See D. Havey, *Condição Pós-Moderna* (Sao Paulo: Loyola, 1994); S. Connor, *Postmodernist Culture: An Introduction to Theories of the Contemporary* (Cambridge: Blackwell, 1997).

3. See S. Best and D. Kellner, *Postmodern Theory: Critical Interrogations* (London: Macmillan, 1994).

4. See A. Badiou, *Il século* (Milan: Feltrinelli, 2006).

5. See R. Bodei, *Geometria delle passioni. Paura, speranza, felicita: filosofia e uso politico* (Milan: Feltrinelli, 1992).

hallmark was the mechanical pace of the assembly line and its underlying rationale. This new industrial man or woman was also often invited to sacrifice his or her own aspirations in the name of the future, the accumulation of capital.[6]

Interestingly, this demand for sobriety and self-discipline set by the Symbolic Order of the industrial society (the Big Other that Lacan speaks of), aptly represented by the figure of the ideal worker presented in nineteenth- and twentieth-century culture as one of the figures of the ideal ego, is set in stark contrast to the mounting enticements to consume seen increasingly in advertising and in the postwar imaginary. This process occurs within the structure of the welfare state, ultimately clashing with the new demands placed on individuals by a market that was increasingly omnicomprehensive. The new Symbolic Order heralded by the market enticed the subject toward unlimited enjoyment, breaking with the social imaginary of the first modernity. Another noteworthy point is that market relations are fundamentally instrumental. The neoliberal market reduces subjects who produce to the status of competitors, who supply their products to other subjects who are correspondingly reduced to the status of consumers. From this perspective, the fetishistic nature of market relations can also be seen, which are assumed to be ruled by a blind, mechanical, automaton-like law (the invisible hand of the market), where every person must first and foremost look out for herself or himself, thereby achieving a balance that leads to the greater good of all. As the market becomes omnicomprehensive and all social relationships start to fall under the pattern of market relations, there is a weakening of social ties and consequently we have the increasing prevalence of perverse relations linking subjects.[7] In this sense, the contemporary subject heralded by the market, under the superego's injunction and the symbolic mandate to have unlimited enjoyment, finds himself or herself in the place of the perverse subject, less able to form ties that are not instrumental and capable of sustaining a society.[8] Societies tend to become increasingly fragmented, desegregated, and violent.[9]

The crisis of the first modernity has given rise to several new phenomena,

6. See Z. Bauman, *O mal estar na pós-modernidade* (Rio de Janeiro: Jorge Zahar Editor, 1998); *Modernidade e ambivalência* (Rio de Janeiro: Jorge Zahar Editor, 1999).

7. See S. Zizek, *The Ticklish Subject* (New York: Verso, 2000).

8. See M. Fleig, *O desejo perverso* (Porto Alegre: CMC editora, 2008); E. Pulcini, *L'individuo senza passione. Individualismo moderno e perdita del legame sociale* (Turin: Bollati Boringhieri, 2005).

9. See S. Zizek, *Violence* (New York: Picador, 2008).

including the formation of a new subjectivity, where the Cartesian driving idea,[10] "I think, therefore I am" has shifted into "I feel, therefore I am," with reason being replaced by feeling. This movement is a negation of the belief that modern reason has the capacity to lead men and women to happiness. The act of denying the value of reason could set up a radical relativization of values and ideas. If nothing makes sense, then anything could make sense too, but this transfer of meaning is but a short route from tolerance to an indifference in which there is no point debating anything and no idea worth discussing because all arguments are worthless. The only things of any value are feelings and emotions, which are mixed up and identified with sensations. Alongside the discrediting of reason has come a discrediting of knowledge and scientific learning, the loss of the social function of intellectuals, and the loss of prestige of formal education and traditional seats of learning. We are on the road toward the most extreme form of individualism, where people turn in on themselves in the belief that nothing outside them is safe, objective, or quite as it seems. In some cases, the raising up of subjectivity to the detriment of objectivity leads to a total schism between public and private spheres, with only the latter being considered worthwhile, while politics and the notion of representativeness are dismissed.[11]

The most tragic thing in all this is that indifference and the refusal to seek out any sense or meaning for experience and human life ultimately produces an existential degradation, associated with an impoverishment of the imaginary and a retraction of desire. This sets up a contradiction, where the superego's injunction to enjoy is absorbed by subjects who, on trying to fulfill it, actually alienate their own desire and paradoxically lose their capacity for wonder and enthusiasm, their capacity to organize life around an ideal, and their capacity to love. In other words, the subject becomes numbed and consequently incapable of feeling enjoyment. If modern civilization's malaise was caused by the restrictions imposed by the superego on enjoyment, in our contemporary situation it is caused by a superego's injunction that imposes an enjoyment that cannot be fulfilled.[12]

---

10. We use the concept of the *driving idea* here to mean a signifier that serves as a structuring principle and cornerstone for a particular formation of social imaginaries. See C. Taylor, *Modern Social Imaginaries* (Durham: Duke University Press, 2004). See also C. Taylor, *A Secular Age* (Cambridge: Belknap Press of Harvard University Press, 2007).

11. See R. Sennett, *O declínio do homem público. As tiranias da intimidade* (Sao Paulo: Companhia das Letras, 1999).

12. See C. Melman, *O homem sem gravidade. Gozar a qualquer preço* (Rio de Janeiro: Companhia de Freud, 2008).

2. A Risk to Christianity

Within this context lies a risk facing all religions, and particularly Christianity. This risk consists of succumbing to the temptation of being caught up by the market, making religion just one more good available for consumption. It is a real risk that is manifested in two apparently opposing ways, but which are actually two sides of the same coin.

(1) First, there is the emergence of the neo-Pentecostal Christian churches, which promise their followers economic prosperity as long as they are willing to make generous donations to their respective churches. A market relationship is established between the faithful and God, through the mediation of these churches. Religion becomes just one instance that amplifies and retransmits the superego's injunction to enjoy and provides a means for it to be attained.[13] Indeed, the Catholic Church also harbors some forms of spirituality experienced by certain groups and movements that occupy this same field in a similar manner. In these cases, religion is reduced to pure emotion: a supply of enjoyment placed at the disposal of the faithful.[14]

(2) Second, there is the emergence of fundamentalist movements which, if they might initially seem like a reaction against modernity or the loss of identity in contemporary times, can also be understood as deriving from the same trend that perpetuates the forging of perverse bonds established by the omnicomprehensive market and the crisis of modernity in contemporary times.[15] Although in their discourse fundamentalists would seem to condemn the modern world and curtail enjoyment, in practice they invite the faithful to place themselves at the service of the enjoyment of the Big Other, that is, the Symbolic Order. The faithful are expected to adopt a position whereby they renounce their autonomy in responding to the demands put on them by the religious leaders that embody the Symbolic Order. Once again, it is a summons to take an instrumental stance, and in this sense, the same submission to the superego's injunction to have unlimited enjoyment, this time offering up religion as the ultimate route toward attaining this enjoyment. Adherence to fundamentalism is engendered by the same hegemonic rationale that prevails in the institution of perverse desire. An instance that appears only as an injunc-

13. See A. Pedro Oro, A. Corten, and J.-P. Dozon, eds., *Igreja Universal do Reino de Deus. Os novos conquistadores da fé* (Sao Paulo: Paulinas, 2003).

14. See J. B. Libanio, *As religiões no início do novo milênio* (Sao Paulo: Loyola, 2002), pp. 234-46.

15. See H. Hadsell and C. Stückelberger, eds., *Overcoming Fundamentalism* (Geneva: Globethics.net, 2009).

tion to curtail enjoyment will always be bound to the apparently inverse position of the injunction to have unlimited enjoyment. This is the cruelty of the superego of which Freud speaks.[16]

3. Christianity and Criticism of the Contemporary Situation

The neoliberal market, with its symbolic demand and promise of enjoyment, is not self-sustaining. The multitude of people excluded by the new economy is the most blatant sign of its failure. It is precisely from the viewpoint of these excluded people that Christianity can and should prophetically denounce the perverse nature of the omnicomprehensive market and establish practices that can lead beyond the neoliberal economy and its associated culture. Concerning the relationship in the Church's mission between consciousness-building and action in the social sphere, Pope Paul VI stated in his apostolic letter, *Octogesima Adveniens (OA):*

> In the social sphere, the Church has always wished to assume a double function: first to enlighten minds in order to assist them to discover the truth and to find the right path to follow amid the different teachings that call for their attention; and secondly to take part in action and to spread, with a real care for service and effectiveness, the energies of the Gospel. (*OA*, no. 48)[17]

In his encyclical *Pacem in Terris,* Pope John XXIII presented the Catholic reception of the philosophical/legal doctrine of human rights and set forth a number of social and economic rights which, from a Christian perspective, cannot be dissociated from the right to life. Fulfilling these rights is a requirement of justice. According to the concept of the state in the Church's social doctrine, it is the state's responsibility to ensure that justice is accomplished and to ensure that everyone, without exception, has access to these rights.[18] As a result, the Church's social doctrine, from *Rerum Novarum* to *Caritas in Ver-*

16. See a more detailed discussion on this topic in my article, P. Andrade, *"Reflexões teológicas sobre a relação Fé e Política,"* *Atualidade Teológica,* PUC-Rio, Ano 8 (2004): 358-77, especially pp. 368-71. See also the approach to fundamentalism taken by psychoanalysis applied to large groups in V. Volkan, *Blind Trust: Large Groups and Their Leaders in Time of Crises and Terror* (Charlottesville, Va.: Pitchstone Publishing, 2004).

17. Translation at http://www.vatican.va/holy_father/paul_vi/apost_letters/documents/hf_p-vi_apl_19710514_octogesima-adveniens_en.html.

18. See Pope Benedict XVI, *Deus Caritas Est,* no. 28.

itate, has always rejected the liberal thesis that would grant the market absolute independence. It was this liberal course, which was strengthened after the fall of the Berlin Wall, which ultimately led to the institution of an omnicomprehensive market, whose cultural consequences we are in the process of analyzing. About the need to subordinate the market to politics and, through it, to values, Pope Paul VI stated: *"This is why the need is felt to pass from economics to politics. It is true that in the term 'politics' many confusions are possible and must be clarified, but each man feels that in the social and economic field, both national and international, the ultimate decision rests with political power"* (*OA,* no. 46). As for the restrictions that should be imposed on the market, it is important to recall the focus given to this by Pope John Paul II in his encyclical, *Centesimus Annus (CA):* "It would appear that, on the level of individual nations and of international relations, the free market is the most efficient instrument for utilizing resources and effectively responding to needs. But this is true only for those needs which are 'solvent,' insofar as they are endowed with purchasing power, and for those resources which are 'marketable,' insofar as they are capable of obtaining a satisfactory price. But there are many human needs which find no place on the market. It is a strict duty of justice and truth not to allow fundamental human needs to remain unsatisfied, and not to allow those burdened by such needs to perish" (*CA,* no. 34).[19] In his three social encyclicals, Pope John Paul II clearly established a correlation between an absolutist market, consumerism, and individualism.[20]

4. The Encyclical *Caritas in Veritate* and a Criticism of the Contemporary Economy

Continuing directly from the great tradition of the Church's social doctrine developed by his predecessors, Pope Benedict XVI, in his encyclical letter *Caritas in Veritate,* clearly states the need for the economy to be subordinated to morals and justice: "Then, the conviction that the economy must be autonomous, that it must be shielded from 'influences' of a moral character, has led man to abuse the economic process in a thoroughly destructive way" (*CV,* no. 34). As such, the pope explains:

19. Translation at http://www.vatican.va/holy_father/john_paul_ii/encyclicals/documents/hf_jp-ii_enc_01051991_centesimus-annus_en.html.

20. See Pope John Paul II, *Sollicitudo Rei Socialis,* nos. 28-29, translation at http://www.vatican.va/holy_father/john_paul_ii/encyclicals/documents/hf_jp-ii_enc_30121987_sollicitudo-rei-socialis_en.html.

The Church's social doctrine has always maintained that *justice must be applied to every phase of economic activity,* because this is always concerned with man and his needs. Locating resources, financing, production, consumption and all the other phases in the economic cycle inevitably have moral implications. *Thus every economic decision has a moral consequence.* The social sciences and the direction taken by the contemporary economy point to the same conclusion. Perhaps at one time it was conceivable that first the creation of wealth could be entrusted to the economy, and then the task of distributing it could be assigned to politics. Today that would be more difficult, given that economic activity is no longer circumscribed within territorial limits, while the authority of governments continues to be principally local. Hence the canons of justice must be respected from the outset, as the economic process unfolds, and not just afterwards or incidentally. Space also needs to be created within the market for economic activity carried out by subjects who freely choose to act according to principles other than those of pure profit, without sacrificing the production of economic value in the process. The many economic entities that draw their origin from religious and lay initiatives demonstrate that this is concretely possible. (*CV,* no. 37)

The market cannot be regarded as bad of itself, although it is clear to the pontiff that "economic activity cannot solve all social problems through the simple application of *commercial logic*" (*CV,* no. 36). The pressing issue being raised today is how social controls can be imposed on the market, which would ensure the continued existence of the positive aspects it has to offer for the development of peoples, while subordinating it to ethics and justice. In the face of the neoliberal market, which as it expands reduces all relationships to instrumental relationships, it is necessary to reconstruct spaces for gratuitousness and communion. While the state's function as regulator of the economy and executor of justice must not be disregarded, if an alternative to the current market form is to be found, something more than the dual elements of market and state must be brought into play. As Pope Benedict XVI states:

My predecessor John Paul II drew attention to this question in *Centesimus Annus,* when he spoke of the need for a system with three subjects: the *market,* the *State* and *civil society* [*CA,* no. 35]. He saw civil society as the most natural setting for an *economy of gratuitousness* and fraternity, but did not mean to deny it a place in the other two settings. Today we can say that economic life must be understood as a multi-layered phenomenon: in every one of these layers, to varying degrees and in ways specifically suited to each, the aspect of fraternal reciprocity must be present. In the global era, economic activity cannot prescind from gratuitousness, which fosters and disseminates solidarity and responsibility for justice and the common good among the different economic players. (*CV,* no. 38)

5. The Church in Latin America and the Perspective of the Poorest

In *Octogesima Adveniens,* Pope Paul VI said that the Church's social doctrine "develops through reflection applied to the changing situations of this world, under the driving force of the Gospel as the source of renewal when its message is accepted in its totality and with all its demands. It also develops with the sensitivity proper to the Church which is characterized by a disinterested will to serve and by attention to the poorest" (*OA,* no. 42). In light of that, we must now bring the issue of poverty back to center stage in discussions about the Church in Latin America, and the relevance of the perspective of poor people to any criticism of the malaise in the contemporary situation.

In the Medellín document, the bishops of CELAM pay special attention to poor people, and this reality is reaffirmed in Puebla, Santo Domingos, and Aparecida. This new perspective, now known as "the option for the poor," is a non-exclusive, preferential, evangelical option with two dimensions. The first dimension consists of a change of social place expressed in the ideal of "seeing the world through the eyes of the poor," meaning to be identified with their needs, sufferings, demands, and fears. The second dimension, which is inseparable from the first, is one that would make poor people historical and ecclesial subjects, that is, the subjects of their own destiny and their struggle for justice, citizenship, and rights, and becoming the protagonists of evangelization. This second dimension means that the Church's pastoral action does not make poor people its object, meaning it is not something to be done *for* poor people, but something by which poor people can transform themselves and become the protagonists of evangelization and transformations in history.

The social position of poor people and their exclusion from the market in and of itself lays bare the fact that the superego's injunction to have unlimited enjoyment is quite impossible to achieve, not just by the individual subject, but above all by humanity as a whole. As John Paul II noted, many must be excluded for a few to have ample and assured access to goods.[21]

The Church understands that its commitment to the poor and to justice

---

21. Pope John Paul II, *Sollicitudo Rei Socialis,* no. 14.

is neither supplementary nor secondary, but part of the essence of its evangelical mission. Pastoral action that strives to transform the economy and culture should do so on different dimensions, including prophetic denunciation, consciousness-building, the fostering of leadership, and effective support for grassroots organizations, always with the awareness that the aim of this support is to strengthen the leadership capacity of the social agents in transforming their own reality, and not to replace them as historical subjects. The issue of the malaise in our contemporary situation, especially when seen from the perspective of the poor, is intimately bound to justice and the very future of humanity. From the perspective of the Gospels, there can be no doubt of the need for spaces for gratuitousness to be won back and for the market to be subordinated to justice, superseding a Symbolic Order that produces perverse desires through its demand for unlimited enjoyment. The confirmation of the primacy of acts of charity and the need to promote integral human development made by Pope Benedict XVI in his encyclical *Caritas in Veritate* are an invitation for us all to reaffirm this commitment.

From Spirituality of Communion to "Economy of Communion": The Evolution of a New Economic Culture

Lorna Gold

> *Human beings, made in the image of God, who is Love, find their ful-*
> *fillment in loving, in giving. This is a need which is at the center of their*
> *being, whether believer or not.*

> Chiara Lubich, speaking on the Economy of Communion, 2001

> *All people feel the interior impulse to love authentically: love and truth*
> *never abandon them completely, because these are the vocation planted*
> *by God in the heart and mind of every human person.*[1]

> *Caritas in Veritate,* no. 1

Introduction

It could be argued that the most important message of *Caritas in Veritate (CV)* relates to the intrinsic nature of ethics in all forms of economic activity. According to Pope Benedict XVI, ethics, and the morality that underpins ethical evaluations, cannot be separated from the economic sphere as that

1. Translation at http://www.vatican.va/holy_father/benedict_xvi/encyclicals/documents/hf_ben-xvi_enc_20090629_caritas-in-veritate_en.html.

Portions of this essay first appeared in Lorna Gold, *The Sharing Economy: Solidarity Networks Transforming Globalization* (Burlington: Ashgate, 2004).

sphere of activity is part and parcel of human life. Commercial transactions, the cornerstone of market economic life, cannot happen within a vacuum of ethics. Rather, they presuppose the existence of values such as gratuitousness, solidarity, and fraternity: *"Without internal forms of solidarity and mutual trust, the market cannot completely fulfill its proper economic function"* (*CV*, no. 35). Nonetheless, the assumption remains that somehow these two spheres are separate and that commercial transactions can operate in isolation from the cultural and ethical norms that apply to other spheres of life, such as family and community. Exposing the fallacy of this separation and the truth of the integral nature of the human person is a critical challenge for humanity as it seeks to address multiple global crises, not least in the financial sector.

In *Caritas in Veritate,* Pope Benedict draws attention to the fact that within the market economy there is already existing a "plurality of institutionalized forms of business" — diversified forms of economic activity, many of which adhere to ethical norms and standards through their "willingness to view profit as a means of achieving the goal of a more humane market and society" (*CV*, no. 46). Such experiences demonstrate that "authentic human social relationships of friendship, solidarity and reciprocity can also be conducted within economic activity and not only outside or 'after' it" (*CV*, no. 36). In essence, such ethical values become part of "normal" economic activity rather than an addendum. Much can be learned from a closer examination of these economic entities, "which draw their origin from religious and lay initiatives [and] demonstrate that this is concretely possible" (*CV*, no. 37).

Among the economic entities referred to in *Caritas in Veritate* is the "Economy of Communion" (*CV*, no. 46), the primary expression of which is found within the Focolare movement. The aim of this essay is to examine the origins and evolution of the Economy of Communion (EOC) in the spirituality of the Focolare movement and to delineate the core characteristics of this innovative form of economic activity.

Spiritual Roots

The origins of the EOC can be traced back to the experience that Chiara Lubich and her companions had during World War II in the city of Trent in northern Italy. It was an experience that altered their deepest perceptions of who they were in relation to God, to other people, and to their place in the cosmos.[2] During the war, Chiara Lubich understood in a new way, through a series of personal experiences that have since been confirmed by several theologians as "mystical insights," the immanence of God's presence in human existence.[3] She began to perceive the infinite God as being within the realm of human experience. Perhaps Chiara Lubich's experience is most striking in that it generated a new understanding of God's personal love for her and for other people. It was an experience that also gave rise to powerful socioeconomic insights that form the spiritual foundation of the EOC.

Amid the destruction of war, Chiara began to see God "present everywhere with his love" in the minute details of life.[4] Above all, she understood that the core of the gospel message did not relate primarily to a series of moral directives, but to the revelation of God's love as a father who is very near to his children. In wartime, when God was being blamed for causing or not preventing atrocities, she seemed to discover a different God present in every circumstance, even in suffering. She called this profound experience/belief in the love of God the "inspiring spark."[5] It challenged her perspective on every aspect of human life, including economic and social realities. Every circumstance, every meeting, every happy and painful event, was willed or permitted by God. The other people to whom she communicated this new understanding were so convinced by her personal experience that they too began to change how they viewed reality and to follow her.[6] It was this inspiring spark that gave rise to the new ecclesial movement, the Work of Mary, or the Focolare, which is now present in almost all countries of the world.[7]

Trust in Providence

Unbounded trust in God's love and providence, a defining feature of the early experience of the Focolare movement, had practical implications for its emerging economic and social vision. The roots of the term "providence" can be

2. Franca Zambonini, *Chiara Lubich: L'avventura dell'unità* (Turin: Paoline, 1991), p. 45.

3. Marisa Cerini, *God Who Is Love in the Experience and Thought of Chiara Lubich* (New York: New City Press, 1992).

4. Chiara Lubich, *May They All Be One* (New York: New City, 1984).

5. Cerini, *God Who Is Love*, p. 11.

6. Zambonini, *Chiara Lubich*, pp. 161-62.

7. This essay does not go into detail on the various aspects of the Focolare movement. Detailed accounts of the Focolare can be found in numerous books and websites. See www.focolare.org for more information.

traced back to classical Greek and Latin thought. In the Bible, particularly in the Old Testament,[8] it signifies that God, the Creator, did not merely decree what should be, and then "retire to heaven" to watch what inevitably must come to pass in the created universe. Rather, in infinite wisdom and power, God mysteriously governs all circumstances, making all things work together to accomplish the divine will. Whereas the Old Testament emphasizes providence as God's blessing of the good and punishment of the wicked, the New Testament emphasizes the mercy of God who makes the sun rise and set on everyone. Many texts from the early days of the Focolare movement underline the revival of a profound belief in providence.[9]

The war forced the initial group associated with Chiara to give up their ordinary occupations and to earn their living in temporary jobs. Their rediscovery of the gospel led them to give away all of their possessions to the poor, keeping only the essentials for survival. When they did this, they started to receive items of all sorts from other people who had heard about how they were trying to help the poor in the city. People arrived at their flat with bags of food, clothing, firewood, and other items, a pattern of donation and distribution that continued throughout the war. This help, which seemed to always arrive at the right time, was seen as providence: a visible sign of God's blessing on the work being done. Several stories about providence form the oral history of the early days of the Focolare. The first story is about a pair of size 42 (European size) shoes:

> Jesus assured us: "Ask and you will receive" (Mt 7:7; Lk 11:9). We asked for the poor and we were filled with every good from God: bread, powdered milk, jam, firewood, clothing . . . which we took to those who were in need. One day — and this is a fact that is always told — a poor man asked me for a pair of shoes size 42. Knowing that Jesus identified himself with the poor, I asked the Lord this prayer in church: "Give me a pair of size 42 shoes for you in that poor person." I came out and a lady gave me a packet. I opened it: there was a pair of shoes, size 42. Millions of similar episodes have occurred like this through the years.[10]

8. See, for example, Daniel 4:32, 35; Psalm 139:7-18; Isaiah 41:21-31.

9. Many of the original sources such as personal letters have since been lost or destroyed. Edited versions of the remaining original sources from 1943 to 1954 have been published in Chiara Lubich, *Essential Writings: Spirituality, Dialogue, Culture* (New York: New City, 2006).

10. See Chiara Lubich, "Lezione per la Laurea Honoris Causa," in *Economia di Comunione: verso un agire a misura di persona* (Milan: Edizioni Vita e Pensiero, 2000).

This episode demonstrates how, from the very beginning of the Focolare, the spiritual and economic dimensions of life became *intrinsically bound together* in Chiara Lubich's understanding. Economic facts were interpreted as concrete signs of God's intervention in human life. They viewed their action to help the poor not as an optional appendage to the "religious" act of praying, but as an expression of spiritual life into social and economic life. They believed that if they did their part through living evangelical poverty and giving themselves to their neighbors, God would fulfill the gospel promise that whatever is necessary to help the poor would be provided. God himself would be present through their love for each other. Their part was to trust in providence and to create the underlying "conditions" of mutual love so that gospel promises could be fulfilled. In this way, through the various experiences in the war, they began to understand that the gospel contains a unique "economic logic." The amount given away to the poor corresponded with what they received in providence. They understood this to be as a consequence of Jesus' promises, not simply coincidence:

> There were eight of us Focolarine and every afternoon we went with lots of suitcases to take things to the poor. Someone could wonder: but where did so many things come from? I had nothing and my companions, the first Focolarine, were more or less like me. But providence kept arriving and in such quantities! The corridor of my house was always full of sacks of flour and potatoes. And there we were, distributing the goods to one or other of the poor people, according to their needs.[11]

Such belief in God's providence continued throughout the history of the Focolare and still remains a key point in understanding the relationship between economic affairs and spirituality. Within the movement as a whole and in the individual Focolare houses, providence (in the form of unexpected gifts and donations) is even calculated formally as a part of the overall budget. Calculations and decisions regarding future developments are made on the basis of such providence arriving. Necessary resources not arriving signify that a given development is not in God's will. In this way, Focolare institutions have evolved without accumulating debt.

Such a belief in providence sits in stark contrast with a modern rational, materialistic mindset. It raises some important issues and profound questions that lie at the heart of the relationship between faith and social action. In

11. See Lubich, "Lezione per la Laurea Honoris Causa."

particular, how does such a deep-rooted belief avoid association with superstition, magical tendencies, luck, or fantasy? How does it avoid association with an Old Testament mindset that sees riches as a blessing and poverty as a curse? A strong belief in providence carries the risk of reductionism, accompanied by positive reinforcement of a selective reading of historical facts. In particular, analyzing the relationship between economic action and spirituality carries the risk of seeing providence as a magic formula, a mechanism for guaranteeing success. The risk of such a mindset within the Focolare, particularly in the EOC as will be seen further on, has not escaped the attention of those studying this phenomenon. The dominant vision underlying the Focolare spirituality, however, considers providence a sign of God accompanying his people.

The "Communion of Goods"

Another key phenomenon from the early history of the Focolare which has informed the development of its economic vision is the "communion of goods." The active living of the gospel generated a community from a disparate group of persons. The unity of heart and soul produced by reciprocal love among the community generated a profound sharing, or communion, of material and spiritual goods. The first Focolare community, fascinated by events in Jerusalem just after the death and resurrection of Christ, mirrored their life on the passage from the Acts of the Apostles that describes the nature of that first Christian community.[12] In a commentary on this passage, Chiara Lubich highlighted a connection between material giving and living the gospel. She also outlined many of the key ideas on which the movement is based:

> While reading these words, we might begin to think that everything worked perfectly in the community. In fact, it is Luke himself who points out that there are incidents in which members of the Church of Jerusalem failed to live up to this standard (see Acts 6). However, despite these failures, the tone of the community was set by this effort, which animated everyone, to achieve the Christian community. It is this effort that Luke wants to emphasize. The examples of those who sold their property show the revolutionary power of the Gospel, i.e. its capacity for creating totally new social relationships with concrete effects on an economic level.
>
> Nobody was forced to dispose of his or her goods. Luke wanted to show

12. Acts 4:32, 34-35.

how the Gospel, while respecting each person's individual freedom, is able to make us overcome all the barriers that divide us, and of these barriers, the selfish use of private property is one of the most serious causes of division. Naturally, the social revolution starts from an inner power, from faith in and love for Jesus. For Luke, this practical sharing is the unit of measurement for meaningful authentic Christian love. No matter what economic system the Christian finds himself in, with the power of this love he will be called first and foremost to overcome every form of attachment to earthly goods, in which fear, greed and selfishness continually tend to imprison him.

The examination of conscience, which these words invite us to, covers a very wide field of values. We need to review our relations with the political community as a sign of solidarity by paying taxes. We need to review our relations with the social community by committing ourselves in a responsible way to building a more just society. We need to review our relationship with our church community, by giving our spare time, energy and material goods in order to help our brothers and sisters who are in need. We need to review our relations with our neighbors whose difficulties are perhaps known to us alone. In the first Christian community in Jerusalem, no one said that any of the things that he possessed was his own. This is the heart of the problem. What we must ascertain is whether we feel we are absolute owners or we feel we are children of God and brothers and sisters in Christ who act as administrators of the goods they receive and keep others always in mind. In the first centuries love for Jesus, by inspiring consciences, transformed pagan society, opening up the progressive liberation of long-standing situations of institutional injustice (slavery, the exclusion of women from society, poverty, the position of the defenseless and children in society, etc.). Why should our love for Jesus not do as much again today in the face of serious situations of injustice in the world?[13]

The radical vision of gospel living that emerges is not only a form of spiritual edification, but also a means of emancipation for the poor. Living the gospel had far-reaching social and political implications that led individuals to "review" their relationship with the various institutions and to make concrete changes in how they live.

The "heart of the problem," in Chiara Lubich's view, was the desire to claim possessions for one's self as opposed to feeling connected to others as a family. The distribution of wealth is perceived as an economic matter, but the question

---

13. Quoted in Edwin Robertson, *Catching Fire* (Guilford: IPS, 1993), p. 57.

of being brothers and sisters is regarded as a spiritual one.[14] The gospel offered a means of bridging this divide and bringing about a peaceful social revolution that would achieve greater equality through the charity that imbued people's hearts. In this way the "evangelical poverty" that traditional spiritualities considered a form of asceticism took on a new function within the Focolare. It was not an end in itself but a means of serving other people and creating greater equality. Reaching this equality became the main aim of the first Focolare community in Trent.

Redistribution in the Trent Community

So how did the first Focolare community live out this vision? Not long after the start of the movement, Chiara Lubich explained in detail how this redistribution took place in the community of Trent:

> The spirit of unity in charity was the ever living flame which kept this fraternity alive. . . . In some ways it was similar, in others dissimilar, to that first Christian community. In fact, while having the same aim, it did not require everyone to sell all that they had and to bring it to unity, but rather, that everyone gave what they possessed, depriving themselves of what they could without causing themselves harm. . . . This was possible among us who are already trained at living out in a radical way the first great principle "You shall love the Lord your God with all your heart" (Lk 10:27). Everyone brought the extra that they had, above all in money, and committed themselves to giving a monthly sum. The donor and the amount promised remained secret. With the money received, the Committee would help, month by month and in secret, those families in the community in need, carrying out this delicate task with the greatest charity and discretion. This was our aim: to reach the point where there would be no more people in need, and that everyone would have enough to live on.[15]

This article reveals how even at that stage the community of the Focolare was structured so as to help those in need while protecting the identity, and hence the dignity, of those who were helped and those who gave. People were primarily helped via the Focolare house itself, through a central fund, since those dedicated to the community were arguably in the best position to know

---

14. Chiara Lubich, "Letter to the Focolare Communities in Italy," *Gen* 6 (1968 [1944]): 1.
15. Chiara Lubich, "Erano un cuor solo e un anima sola," *Amico Serafico* (1948): 236-37.

the needs of people in the community as a whole. Even at this early stage of the Focolare, the key was *trust* in the people who were carrying out the redistribution based on their total commitment to the community and their understanding of the needs of the various members. This "communion of goods," as it was called, became a prominent feature of the life of the early Focolare community. It was not limited to the people who were part of the Focolare community itself. Right from the start, the first group was aware that the problems of inequality could not be solved unless the rich could be made to realize in some way the injustice of the situation. In the Focolare's guidelines on economy and work, Giosi Guella recalls their ideas of a social revolution at the beginnings of the movement:

> We wanted to solve the social problem of Trent . . . our reasoning was simple: we have more and they have less; we will raise their standard of living so as to reach a certain equality. We even thought of ousting the rich, not through violence, but through our ideal that would burn the hearts of those who have more and the communion of goods would be spontaneous.[16]

What is striking about this passage is how the group of the Focolare recognized creating greater equality in society required the active participation of all people — not just the poor. It was not enough that they themselves give away all that they had to the poor: they had to "oust" the rich through winning them over to the gospel ideals of the movement.

The strong parallels between this way of thinking and the communist doctrine so prevalent in the city of Trent at the time led to several brushes with the fascist regime, which was suspicious of their activities. Chiara Lubich's brother was an active member of the Communist Party, on the editorial team of *Il Popolo,* and a partisan.[17] Both were advocating a radical redistribution of wealth. Although the ultimate aim of greater equality was the same, the means suggested and employed in order to carry out this goal could not have differed more. For the communists, the end of equality justified the means — even violent repression of those in control of the means of production, resulting in revolution.

For Chiara Lubich and her companions, the rich could be ousted mainly by "burning their hearts" with the ideal that they themselves had discovered

---

16. Giosi Guella and Oreste Basso, *The Communion of Goods and Work Guidelines: Part 1,* Internal Focolare document, Focolare Center, Rome, 1984.

17. See Jim Gallagher, *Chiara Lubich: A Woman's Work* (New York: New City, 1997).

and begun to put into practice through giving away all of their possessions.[18] By seeing and learning from their example the rich themselves would be moved and become personally involved in the redistribution of wealth since they too would feel that the poor were their brothers and sisters and that they had a duty to share their possessions with them. Rather than alienating the rich, their way would create greater participation of all, fostering greater social integration and narrowing of the gap between rich and poor.

This strategy of overcoming the rich through engaging them is arguably more effective in the long term than using force since it is a personal practice that touches individuals in a real way. It does not replace the law or the role of the state, but provides "a more solid foundation of all other good and lawful means of guaranteeing an honest and dignified livelihood for all."[19] Perhaps for this reason, two communist activists who had noticed the effectiveness of what the group was doing in the city of Trent approached them:

> One day in May 1945, two communists came into our little Focolare and said to me "Look, we've been watching you. We've seen the way you girls share everything and how you give it away to those in need."
>
> Chiara remembers the meeting very clearly because the two communists asked her, "What's going on? Why on earth are you doing this? Tell us the secret of your success."
>
> She says, "I pointed to the crucifix on the wall, because he is the one who is love and who taught us to love. They lowered their eyes."
>
> One of them said to her, "What you're doing on a small scale, we will do all over the world."
>
> Chiara challenged them: "We are few, we're young, we're poor. But God is with us. Let's see who gets there first, shall we?"[20]

The fall of communist regimes in the early 1990s and the start of the EOC within the Focolare seemed to be a response to this question. In the 1950s and 1960s, however, the radical approach to wealth redistribution that they were advocating and the parallels between their message and that of the communists (and Protestants) led to lengthy investigations by the Holy See.[21] The Vatican could find no evidence of infiltration of ideas not in keeping with the

18. See Lubich, *May They All Be One*.

19. See Conference proceedings, *Movimento Umanitá Nuova: Il lavoro e l'economia oggi nella visione Cristiana* (Rome: Città Nuova, 1984), p. 31.

20. Gallagher, *Chiara Lubich*, pp. 43-44.

21. See Zambonini, *Chiara Lubich*, p. 63; Gallagher, *Chiara Lubich*, pp. 78-89.

message of the gospel, though, and approved the Focolare in 1963 for the first time. Final approval in 1990 provided an opportunity for the Focolare to expand further.

A Lifestyle Based on Giving

This economic and social vision, which is deeply rooted in the early origins of the Focolare, generated specific practices that continue today. The wartime practice of giving everything away to the poor is no longer literally applied to the range of circumstances in which people within the movement find themselves. Several thousand people still feel called to take on the commitment to sell all that they have and live a celibate life in community. Others prefer to remain in close contact with the movement but cannot actually leave everything behind, because of either their commitments as married people or their responsibilities in society. Instead, such people, who now make up the vast majority of the Focolare movement, change their lifestyle so that it reflects their commitment to put the fundamental Focolare principles into practice.

The first practice, present right from the start, is that of sharing material goods. As the movement has developed, this practice has evolved, enabling people from different social categories to participate in some form. Some give all their possessions to the poor via the Focolare and adopt the community based on the first Focolare community in Trent (the focolarini). Each month their salaries are deposited in a central account from which the individual community houses receive an allowance, with the rest being used to fund Focolare communities in developing countries and to help fund the international center of the Focolare in Rocca di Papa, near Rome. The focolarini bequeath all of their present and future possessions to the Focolare. Over the years, these bequests have enabled the Focolare to grow and to develop at a substantial rate. Many of its pieces of land were bequeathed by focolarini or well-wishers. For example, the land in the Chianti hills near Florence on which the town of "Loppiano" has been built was inherited by the Folonari children (a famous Milanese family of winemakers), three of whom joined the Focolare.

One practice that dates back to the origins of the Focolare in Trent, still carried out in many Focolare groups, particularly among young people, is known as the "bundle." It recalls how the first group of focolarini piled up all of their possessions in a room so as to give them to the poor.[22] At least once a

22. Zambonini, *Chiara Lubich*, p. 43.

year, members of the movement from the oldest to the youngest reassess their personal possessions and make a "bundle" of everything that they no longer consider necessary. This bundle is then shared with the local community. If all of the needs in the community are met, the remaining articles are sorted out — some sent to charity shops, others given to the Focolare house in case they need them or know of others who do. Occasionally, items are sent abroad to the center of the Focolare in Rome, to victims of disaster or war. Focolare communities also share money on a local scale. This takes place through donations by individuals who wish to contribute to the Focolare's activities. Within the smaller groups, the usual practice is to keep a common fund administered by one of the group to meet any immediate or future needs. A portion of this money is also given to the international center of the Focolare to fund the infrastructure of the movement across the world and to support community members in other countries.

Sharing within the Focolare is not limited to material possessions, but includes the material, social, and spiritual. In many cases sharing may take the form of an offer of help that involves time, skills, and energy. In other cases sharing may involve offering advice or a listening ear. Material sharing reflects the spiritual communion between people — their awareness of being brothers and sisters — and not simply a charitable action. The kind of giving advocated by the Focolare cannot easily be reduced to philanthropy, although elements of philanthropic giving are in it. In an article on the different kinds of giving, Aráujo highlights what is called "evangelical" giving, which the Focolare aims to promote:

> The "culture of giving" qualifies the human person as a being that is open to communion, to a relationship with the Absolute — God, with others, and with creation. Individuality and sociality converge in the gift of self, the gift of one's being and in the circulation of material goods, which are needed for the development and growth of everyone.
>
> Not every kind of giving therefore results in the culture of giving. There is a kind of giving which is contaminated by a desire for power over the other, a search for dominion and even the oppression of other peoples. It only has the appearance of giving. There is a kind of giving which seeks satisfaction and pleasure in the act of giving itself. Deep down, it is an egoistic expression of the self and, in general, this is perceived by the person who is on the receiving end as a humiliation or offence. There is also a kind of utilitarian giving which has an ulterior interest. This is present in the current forms of neo-liberalism, in which there is a search for a payoff in terms of profit. This kind of giving does not create a new mentality.

Last of all there is the giving which we Christians call "evangelical" because it is an integral part of the personal attitudes of those that welcome and commit themselves in the construction of the kingdom that Jesus brings. . . . This giving is open to the other — individual or people — and seeks out the other in respect for their dignity, which includes traditions, customs, culture, etc. It is an expression of our deepest being. The word "to give" is synonymous with loving in a practical way.[23]

Within the Focolare, the person in need is accorded a high position. Since possessions hold secondary importance, individuals are valued not for their capacity to have or give materially but for their capacity to give of themselves to others. In this respect, even someone with no possessions has something to give. Need is not something inherently negative, something of which to be ashamed, but rather a situation that allows sharing to be put into practice among the community. Offering a need to the community is therefore a positive action; people are encouraged to "offer" their need in order to give others the opportunity to help. This in turn empowers the community, creating greater solidarity among the members. The act of receiving is therefore transformed into an act of giving.

A New Economic Ethic

The root and the first consequence of this economic vision, a renewed awareness of the ethical content of the Christian message and its relevance to economic action, has led to tens of thousands of people across the world adopting a spirituality rooted in communitarian values, especially the value of trust. Such an application resembles strongly the Weberian idea of the "economic ethic of a religion." According to Max Weber, individuals attach to economic action meanings bound up with their religious beliefs, making it possible to discern different economic rationalities deriving from religious belief systems.[24] Weber, for example, distinguished between the rationalities in operation within Catholicism and Protestantism by the premium each tradition placed on an ascetic lifestyle at a given time. In his view, the Catholic emphasis on "absolution" deterred engagement in economic activities. The premium Calvinism placed on asceticism legitimized the "philosophy of avarice" that underpins

23. V. Aráujo, "The Challenge of Giving," *New City* (April 1994): 72-74.
24. Max Weber, *The Protestant Ethic and the Spirit of Capitalism,* trans. Talcott Parsons (New York: Scribners, 1958).

capitalism. Weber's approach has been criticized, particularly its logic in relation to the rise of capitalism.[25]

Despite its limitations, however, Weber's concept allows much scope for development, especially the way he relates economic rationalities to specific religious beliefs. In some ways, the strength of Weber's thesis lies not so much in his attempt to connect the rise of capitalism with religious traditions as his development of intermediate concepts that link culture and economic action. They provide a useful framework for understanding how the deep structures of spiritual understanding and symbolism alter perceptions, and ultimately choices of economic life.

Economic Ethic of the Focolare

This framework makes it possible to discern certain principles that appear to have governed the Focolare vision since the movement's founding and that form the cultural matrix against which all other dimensions of human life, including the economic, have to be measured. An instrumental economic rationale, in a sense, is displaced by the communitarian ethic in practice. This gives rise to new concepts and principles that shape economic choices. It is interesting that, unlike certain fundamentalist forms of Christianity, the Focolare's vision does not negate the capitalist system per se. It represents both a radical critique of the unsustainable dimensions of the current capitalist system and a positive vision of the place of wealth and business. Rather than basing itself on a puritan vision that rejects money, it is directed out toward the world in a highly positive vision of the redemptive power of Christ working in the community. In a way similar to Weber's analysis, the Focolare movement conveys powerful signs of an economic rationality framed by important religious principles that drives a new form of capitalism. At the same time, the Focolare's economic vision brings to the fore certain elements and concepts not so obvious in Weber's original thesis:

(1) *Work*. Because people are *co-creators* with God, their creative capacity has to be advanced. Work is a source of personal fulfillment and service, and plays an important function in building the community. It also entails sacrifice, which can be united to the abandonment of Christ. Work represents the principal will of God.

(2) *Trade, finance, and industry*. Christians and people of good will ought

25. G. Marshall, *In Search of the Spirit of Capitalism* (London: Hutchinson, 1982).

to actively seek to appropriate the means of production to be used to good ends, such as the redistribution of wealth to the poor. Debt is generally avoided within the institutional structures of the Focolare movement, and is strongly discouraged for all members of the movement. Abandonment to God's will also means trusting his ability to intervene in the practical circumstances of life, as well as in having the material resources to carry out that will. Nevertheless, certain forms of low-interest micro-finance are valued and alternative financing structures have been promoted.

(3) *Wealth and possessions.* In general there is a positive view toward wealth, with people expected to maintain a living standard and level of security appropriate to their function in society. Possessions, however, are generally put at the disposal of the common good. Poverty has value, both positive and negative. On the one hand, the involuntary deprivation of essential basic needs is an injustice that must be addressed. At the same time, it is a virtue, an essential prerequisite to spiritual fulfillment. Material attachments can form an obstacle to one's relationship with God and neighbor. The voluntary deprivation of surplus resources is encouraged through the communion of goods. This promotes simple living and the avoidance of clutter, with important environmental implications. Trusting in providence means that God will accompany people on their journey, using circumstances to reveal the divine will.

(4) *Relations with other economic actors.* The market retains its basic function as the most efficient form of exchange in an open economy. This, however, is set within the wider framework of the market as a "meeting place" between two or more ethical subjects — a place of fraternal relationships. The highest function of economic interaction is social, the normative aim of every economic encounter being communion. Within the Focolare, economic activity serves to build up the human community.

(5) *Economic change and technological development.* As stewards of God's creation, protection of the environment is an essential part of personal and corporate economic activity. Progress and technology derive from the innate creativity of the human person, made in God's image.

(6) *Relation to those without economic resources.* Those without economic resources are *brothers and sisters*. The redistribution of wealth ought to occur from the grass roots upward, as well as from the top down, emphasizing the importance of subsidiarity. Sharing is a practical sign of love for Christ and for neighbor. Revived through the EOC, the practice of *tithing* is an essential component of building God's kingdom in a world envisaged as a community of love. The practice of a communion of goods, drawing inspiration from the first Christians, is a key part of building the mystical body.

Consideration of the ideas that emerged at the historical origins of the Focolare and tracing their development reveals the interrelationship between the "spiritual" and the "economic" within the context of the movement and the practices that have derived from it. Such practices and ideas represent a radical departure from orthodox economic thinking about the mechanisms that operate within the market economy and to some extent mirror the more recent literature emphasizing the sociocultural dimensions of economic action. The Focolare, however, adds to this literature the spiritual dimension of human life, raising new questions about the place of religious concepts such as "communion" within the context of economic life. There are strands of thinking that can be drawn on when talking about the economic vision of the Focolare, such as the literature of Catholic social teaching based on the theory of human rights and the promotion of peace.

The Evolution of the "Economy of Communion"

One of the critical questions raised by social commentators is whether or not such alternative visions of the economy based on community and sharing can be extended from the local to the global and from private to the public sphere. Indeed, in *Caritas in Veritate* Pope Benedict asserts that charity in truth "is the principle not only of micro-relationships (with friends, with family members or within small groups) but also of macro-relationships (social, economic and political ones)" (*CV,* no. 2).

The distinctive vision of economic life within the Focolare has emerged like an ever widening circle as the movement has grown and developed. Initially, it remained more internally focused within the *personal economy* of individual people, families, and local communities. In the early days of the Focolare, the circulation of personal possessions among the various members of the community was based on the common bond of the shared Focolare spirituality. Over time, it began to be supposed that these larger "spaces" could also become "hearths" of sharing where the "culture of giving" might be lived out among small groups of people who share everything that they own. Such economies emphasize the values of cooperation, caring, and sharing, which are normally assumed to reside within a more personal sphere, based principally on face-to-face communication. Moreover, could the "hearth" of the Focolare be effectively operationalized at the scale of the institutions of the *global economy?*

Globalization and the "Communion of Goods"

As outlined above, from the very beginning of the Focolare, the economic vision of the Focolare revealed a strong emphasis on a certain kind of equality based on the communion of goods. The foundation of this equality, however, is radically different from dominant forms of egalitarianism that have emerged in the past several decades, based on the idea of "rights." To talk of "rights" in relation to the first Focolare community during the war clouds the central point of what was happening within that community. The absurd violations of war, in which there was an endemic climate of violence, stripped everyone of what could be called their basic rights. At the same time, this absence made the restoration of those rights an urgent necessity. One could say that in certain ways, the emergence of the Focolare in Trent led to the restoration of rights for some people, but that the way in which this happened had nothing to do with the discourse of rights itself.

Rather, the equality of the Focolare derived substantially from the understanding that human dignity derives first and foremost from the belief that all people are children of the one God, who loves each one with infinite love.[26] This renewed awareness of the oneness of the human family was the fundamental point that transformed their particular "communitarian" spirituality into economic and social action. This intimate relationship between spirituality and economic action, epitomized in the model of the first Christian community in Jerusalem, was the powerful force activating a sense of family within the emerging movement. Within this "family," equality was based on an "ethic of care" in which each one recognized his or her responsibility to care for the others. In a way similar to Simone Weil's emphasis on attending to the needs of others,[27] the Focolare's spirituality opened people's hearts to recognize and to attend to the needs of others, regardless of who these others might be. Reaching greater equality was bound up in the ability to hear the cry of those who were hurting and to say "Why are you hurting?" not "That's terrible — your rights have been violated." Through attending to the needs of those who were hurting, they could offer care in a personal and direct way.

This mutual attending also gave rise to the acceptance of a degree of natural inequality within the Focolare. Since equality within the community was not so much based on the possession of rights, but on the growth of ever greater mutual attending and therefore of spiritual communion, there was also the recognition

---

26. Chiara Lubich, *La dottrina spirituale* (Milan: Mondadori, 2001), pp. 95-106.
27. Simone Weil, *Waiting for God* (New York: Harper Colophon, 1951).

that different people have different material needs. What mattered was not so much inequalities on some arithmetic scale by which individuals were measured against each other, but the extent to which the communion among the members of the community was able to fulfill specific needs as they arose. Things were privately owned by individuals or families, but there was a strong sense that private ownership did not exclude the possibility of others having access to goods, whenever necessary. Ownership, therefore, was regarded as "stewardship" on behalf of the community rather than as an end in itself. At the same time, the sense of responsibility toward those who were in material need — lacking food, clothing, work, and shelter — remained the strongest sign of the active life of the community and the greatest witness of Christian love.[28]

"No Poor among Us"

The EOC emerged in 1991 as a consequence of the desire to make this ideal of communion within the Focolare work on an increasingly global scale. As the Focolare grew and developed, it became an international movement. Since the late 1970s, the number of members of the Focolare grew disproportionately within the poorest communities of Latin America, Asia, and Africa, as did many other radical religious groups.[29] For many of these groups, such as the Christian base communities of Brazil, religious affiliation was also seen as a means of emancipation from poverty.[30] During this same period, Pope Paul VI launched his encyclical on the "Development of Peoples," in which he drew attention to the desperate inequalities throughout the world and the Christian challenge of responding to these. While this internationalization gave rise to many initiatives to attend to the needs of people linked to the Focolare throughout the world, by the early 1990s there were increasing strains on the capacity of the movement to create equality on a global scale.[31] In particular,

28. L. T. Johnston, *Sharing Possessions: Mandate and Symbol of Faith* (Philadelphia: Fortress, 1981).

29. G. Gutierrez, *We Drink From Our Own Wells: The Spiritual Journey of a People* (London: SCM, 1984); D. Slater, *New Social Movements and the State in Latin America* (Amsterdam: Centro de Estudios y documentacion, 1985).

30. J. D. Wirth, ed., *State and Society in Brazil: Continuity and Change 1970-1984* (Boulder, Colo.: Westview, 1987).

31. This concern for the poor within the movement is clear in the inaugural talk that Chiara Lubich gave on May 29, 1991, in Araceli, Brazil, in which she launched the idea of the Economy of Communion.

the fall of the communist bloc in 1989 revealed entire Focolare communities numbering several thousand behind the Iron Curtain who were in desperate need of basic food and shelter.

This situation came to a head in May 1991, when Chiara Lubich visited the Focolare communities in Brazil. While she was there, she saw for herself the extent of the inequality that is so apparent in the city of Sao Paulo and its surrounding areas. The scale of the poverty caused her to reflect on what action the Focolare was taking in order to alleviate the problem. In a sense, her visit was an opportunity for everyone in the Focolare community in Brazil to reflect on how they were attending to the needs of the poor. She was moved by the commitment that the Focolare people had in starting and running a range of projects to improve the living conditions of people in the poorest areas. She visited some of the projects to see for herself the work being done. She became all too aware that the efforts of the Focolare were just one drop in the ocean considering the scale of the poverty in a city like Sao Paulo. She asked herself whether the Focolare, as a group, could make a greater contribution to resolving this entrenched social and economic inequality.

The launch of the EOC can also be interpreted as recognition that the "communion of goods," as a strategy to overcome the inequalities on a global scale, was no longer sufficient. Thus, although the communion of goods works as a powerful strategy of wealth redistribution at a local scale, it had obvious limitations in the context of the inequalities seemingly endemic within a globalized economy. The communion of goods said nothing about the nature of work and how value is created and distributed within an industrial (or post-industrial) society. In a sense, the practice of communion of goods is a kind of post hoc redistribution that may have a profound spiritual meaning, but does not have a direct impact on the public economy. It emerged during the war, at a time when there was no alternative to sharing since the normal patterns of work had been suspended. In the context of the economic imbalances within countries such as Brazil, the communion of goods did little to address the root causes of inequality: economic rationalization, low wages, and unemployment. In a sense, the Focolare, like other civil society organizations in Latin America, was picking up the pieces left by both an economic system that thrived on inequality and a government that was unable to cope with the rising social "fall out" from economic crisis.[32]

In Chiara Lubich's view, it was no longer enough to sit back and watch as

32. D. Green, "Latin America: Neo-liberal Failure and the Search for Alternatives," *Third World Quarterly* 17 no. 1 (1996): 109-22.

the economy created ever-greater inequalities. The principles of the Focolare spirituality had to be extended into the realm of business and industry. The communion of goods, which the Brazilian members of the Focolare practiced with great generosity, was certainly one part of the solution — this had to continue. But the scope of this communion had to be recognized and the root causes of the inequality on a structural level had to be addressed. Chiara Lubich suggested that the Focolare in Brazil was perhaps being called to start to live the communion of goods in a "superior way," which would later be called the EOC. The thinking behind the EOC is clear in a speech that she gave in Araceli on May 30, 1991:

> This is the novelty: in the Movement we have always practiced the communion of goods; the focolarini do it in a complete way, because they give everything; volunteers give what is superfluous, families also share out their surplus among themselves. Now we would like to propose a communion of goods which is at a superior level, that is, to give rise to businesses and industries here around the Mariapolis, which would be run by our people, who would put all the profits in common for the poor, having kept what is necessary to keep the business running. With these profits we will live the reality of the first Christians in the twentieth century: they brought all that they had to the feet of the apostles and distributed it to the poor, so that there was no one in need, there were no poor.[33]

What was new about this communion of goods, therefore, was that it would involve the participation of legally constituted commercial enterprises and not just individuals, who would choose to share what they regarded as superfluous or to proceed with social projects aimed at providing welfare for the poor. People were encouraged to start enterprises that would generate profits to be shared for predetermined aims. The EOC hence aimed to make the communion of goods productive, generating new wealth from the existing communion between the people of the movement.

At the same time, the businesses themselves would create a new space in which the "hearth" of the Focolare could be extended out into the realm of the public economy. Through creating businesses run by people who lived out the Focolare ideals of caring and sharing, the actual causes of inequality would be addressed in a radical way. It was a simple, but extremely challenging proposal. The principles of caring and sharing can arguably be easily applied to the realm of the *personal economy*, where there is a high degree of clarity and choice on

33. Chiara Lubich, Araceli, Brazil, May 30, 1991, p. 13.

how goods can be distributed due to the rights of ownership of private property. Within the sphere of the more *public economy,* however, the application of such ideas is not so straightforward, as will be seen from the case studies on the emergence of the EOC. Nevertheless, the members of the Focolare in Brazil grasped the challenge wholeheartedly.

The Challenge of *Centesimus Annus*

The texts relating to the launch of the EOC also reveal another strand of reasoning. In 1991 the aftermath of the fall of the communist regimes was reaching a critical point. There was euphoria over the triumph of capitalism, but also a profound and growing sense of disillusionment over the collapse of the communist states and socialist ideals. Many social critics were beginning to discuss the possibility of a "third way" and some even pointed to the new social and religious movements, including the Focolare, as the protagonists of economic alternatives.[34] In the spring of 1991, moreover, Pope John Paul II had published *Centesimus Annus,* celebrating a century of Catholic social teaching. The focus of this letter, in the aftermath of the fall of the Iron Curtain, was an in-depth critique of communism and also of the free market. While restating the Catholic principle of the right to own private property and individual freedom, in this letter he stressed the need to highlight the universal ownership of all goods and social responsibility. Although not explicitly advocating a "third way," the letter threw down the challenge to all people (and Catholics in particular) to engage with the capitalist system and use the freedom of the market to serve the common good.

Within the Focolare, the proposal of a radical alternative to the capitalist and communist models had never been far away. Right from the beginnings of the movement Focolare leaders had advocated the Christian principles on which the movement rests as an alternative that had far-reaching implications in the social and economic field. Yet this alternative had always been seen as a matter of personal choice, and until this point had not been advocated as an institutional alternative set apart from either capitalism or communism. But in 1991 Chiara Lubich seemed to recognize that the Focolare could perhaps point to a "third way," also in the public sphere, which would address the inequalities that she herself had seen.

34. B. Secondin, *I nuovi protagonisti* (Rome: Pauline, 1991).

New Businesses

The idea was extremely simple and the immediate response to it was one of excitement.[35] News of it spread through the existing local Brazilian and global networks of the Focolare rapidly.[36] Within hours of the launch of the idea, there were offers of participation pouring into Araceli from Focolare communities all over Brazil. Within a matter of days, the idea had spread to people all over the world and there were numerous offers of participation. From reading the documentation on the launch of the project and from watching footage of the meetings, the feeling one gets is that the EOC was viewed as a response, perhaps *the* response, to the urgent need for greater equality in Brazil and beyond. The following are extracts from letters from communities in different parts of Brazil that arrived at the Focolare Centers in Rome and Araceli, following the launch of the EOC. The first extract comes from a family who lived in the city of Sao Paulo, offering their participation in the project:

> 1 June, 1991, Sao Paulo . . . We have a small business which makes office furniture and we would like to offer to equip the office which will be used for the secretariat that will administer this new reality [the EOC]. This is what we have available: an Olivetti typewriter, Olympia calculator, 2 desks, 3 seats, 1 computer table, 1 stamping machine, 1 cupboard. We are also able to buy in objects from the factories that work with us at factory prices.

The most striking thing in this letter is the practical nature of the help offered. There was nothing abstract about the idea of the EOC, and the response to it reflected this clarity through concrete offers of help. At the same time many people readily grasped the potential of the idea to transform the economy. In another letter, from the Focolare community in Manaus, the writers reflected on the spiritual significance of the idea and how it had changed their own attitudes toward the economy:

> Manaus, 2 June, 1991. We have contemplated the project [EOC] for building of a new society based on Trinitarian relationships! . . . In their desire to give life to the EOC, simple and poor people have offered the little money they had saved for their vital needs with extraordinary generosity, in order to

35. Gallagher, *Chiara Lubich,* p. 160.
36. The Economy of Communion office in Araceli, Brazil, holds a documentary and audiovisual archive on the development of the EOC. The material in this section is based on primary materials from this archive.

participate in this great project in an unconditional way. Several communal and personal enterprises have already come about. These include: the opening of a bank account where the money for the capital will be deposited, jewelry, objects, availability of people to move house, offers of sales points for the produce of Araceli here in Manaus.

The first reaction of those who heard about it, therefore, was to intensify the communion of goods that they were already putting into practice in their communities. People offered whatever they could — even wedding rings — so as to make a contribution toward building up the EOC. People began to talk of a "third way" between capitalism and communism,[37] and many people who had little or no experience of business felt "called" to leave everything and to dedicate their lives to building up the project. People began to offer their services to assist the project in Sao Paulo and declared their availability to move to Araceli to start up businesses. The news of the EOC was not confined to Brazil. Responses to the idea soon began to arrive from around the world. In particular, a group of businesspeople belonging to the Focolare were participating in a meeting on the social and economic implications of the Focolare vision in Rome when news of the developments in Brazil reached them. Such was the enthusiasm for the proposal that several decided immediately to start businesses or to "convert" the businesses that they had for the EOC. Within a matter of weeks, the EOC had emerged all over the world through the Focolare networks.

"Creating" a New Economy

The basic principles of the EOC were laid out in a series of talks that Chiara Lubich gave during her trip to Brazil in 1991. Subsequently, these principles have been deepened, elaborated, and discussed by other leading members of the Focolare, as well as by economists and other professionals working within or alongside the Focolare movement.[38] This body of literature now forms a growing reference point for those engaged in the development of the EOC.[39] From this work, several key ideas relating to the nature of the EOC emerge.

37. T. Sorgi, "Un modello diverso," *Città Nuova*, nos. 15-16 (1991): 36-39.

38. L. Bruni, ed., *Economia di Comunione: per una nuova dimensione nell'economia* (Rome: Città Nuova, 1999); L. Bruni and V. Pelligra, eds., *Economia come impegno civile: relazionalitá, ben-essere ed Economia di Comunione* (Rome: Città Nuova, 2002).

39. A key reference tool for the EOC is the official website www.edc-online.org.

Profit Sharing

The main principle that underpins the EOC is that of increasing equality through making the communion of goods productive. People linked to the Focolare were encouraged to set up businesses as a means of increasing the overall amount of resources available to help those in the community who were in desperate need of food, clothing, and shelter. The novelty of the project was initially seen as the division of the profits of the businesses into three parts. One part was to be given to the poor, one kept for reinvestment in the firm, and the third part for creation of educational structures to promote the "culture of giving," as shown in Figure 1.

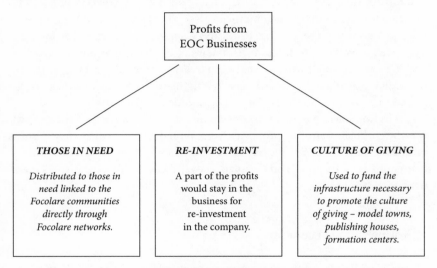

Figure 1. Sub-division of EOC Business Profits
Source: Adapted from L. Gold[40]

There are some similarities between this method of profit sharing and the tradition of "tithing" in some churches. Within the EOC, however, this desire to generate profits to share became one of the chief motivations behind starting up new businesses. Within the EOC, donations of profits were not seen as a benevolent afterthought — what to do when excess wealth has been accumulated — but as an integral part of the business mission. The administration of the project would take place through the Focolare Centers, which were the

---

40. L. Gold, *The EOS in Brazil*, M.A. thesis, University of Glasgow, 1996.

focus of the communion of goods, and the same structures that were in place for the communion of goods would be able to fulfill the functions of the EOC. The idea seemed simple, yet it had the potential to redirect wealth in a way that was much more productive than the communion of goods alone.

Based on the underlying vision of the human person within the Focolare spirituality, a key element of the project from the start was that participation in the EOC and sharing had to be entirely *voluntary*. If the sharing was not voluntary, but the result of pressure or coercion, it would result in the person who was giving being denied the possibility of granting consent. Without consent, the possibility of reaching "communion" between people is taken away, given that the freedom to say "no" is what makes authentic communion possible.[41] The act of giving within the EOC has to be the result of recognizing the needs of others and freely choosing to attend to those needs through practical assistance.[42]

The logical extension of this freedom is the fact that the businesses wishing to participate in the EOC remained in the direct management of the people who owned them. The Focolare did not create some kind of overarching communal ownership: the statutes of the Focolare state that, as an organization with charitable status, it cannot own or directly manage commercial activities except for where they directly relate to the more spiritual and educational functions of the movement. Such centralized ownership of the businesses, apart from not being in keeping with the statutes of the movement, could arguably lead to the development of a communistic mentality of central planning and could be highly bureaucratic. According to the EOC principles, the businesses should be managed and owned by private individuals who participate in the Focolare and live the culture of giving, not by the Focolare as an institution. Private ownership of the businesses, therefore, and all of the legal responsibilities that ownership brings, was seen as a prerequisite to the donation of profits.

The business owners/shareholders have no legal obligation to give profits to the EOC. The choice to share profits (and the proportion) comes primarily from the people within the business itself, based on their professional assessment of the needs of the business. Nevertheless, the businesspeople are encouraged to bear in mind their responsibility to others in the context of living out the "culture of giving." On the one hand, this affords the businesses the freedom to participate in the EOC to whatever degree they feel they can without having to fit into some rigid scheme. It also makes it possible for the range

41. D. Catapan, "A cultura do dar," *Cadernos Escola Social* 5(6) (Sao Paulo: Cidade Nova, 1994).

42. V. Aráujo, "The Challenge of Giving," *New City* (April 1994): 72-74.

of businesses wishing to participate to be as wide as possible. On the other hand, as will be seen, the interpretation of this freedom has led to difficulties that were perhaps unforeseen at the beginnings of the EOC. For example, if the businesses are granted the freedom to give as they please, how can one set criteria for those wishing to participate broad enough to include many kinds of businesses, yet tight enough to avoid possible misuses of the name "EOC"?

Widespread Ownership

Another key principle that emerged at the beginning of the EOC is the idea that ownership of the businesses should be widespread, giving as many people as possible the chance to participate in the project in some form. This idea of diffused ownership raises the question of the responsibility and rights of shareholders, and places it at the heart of the EOC. If the business involved aims to redistribute its profits outside the company, the shareholders must receive less. Such a decision cannot be forced on shareholders, but has to be based on a conscious choice. As a result, one of the initial objectives of the EOC had to be that of making sure that the majority of the shareholders in any company shared in the ideals of the Focolare and were prepared to forgo their dividends in order to help build up the EOC.

Business Parks

One of the key points that emerged right from the beginning of the EOC was the importance that special business parks linked to the Focolare little towns would have in the promotion of the project. The idea of the "model towns" was at the forefront of Chiara Lubich's mind when she launched the EOC in Brazil. While visiting Brazil in 1991, she recalled how she had always imagined these places as industrial places with full integration in the local economy. She recalled an event that had taken place in the 1960s, in which she had the impression that the Focolare was being called not only to put into practice a spirituality of unity, but also to create social structures and institutions that reflected this vision of the world. While she was on holiday in Switzerland, she came across the Benedictine Abbey of Einsiedeln and was struck by how the spiritual vision of St. Benedict's *"Ora et Laborem"* (prayer and work) was reflected in the buildings of the abbey and the surrounding village that had grown up around it. She had the impression that the vision of the Benedictines "lived on" in that place and was inspired to think that, in a similar way, the characteristic spatial structures of the Focolare would entail model towns wherein the ethos of the movement could be developed and put into practice. These towns would also act as models of how society would be if all people were to live out the ideal of mutual love.

Part of the vision of the towns, therefore, would be an economic dimension that would also reflect the Focolare movement's spirituality and culture. The towns of the movement could not remain spiritual enclaves, but had to exhibit the features of a modern town. As a result, the businesspeople in Araceli, in response to this vision, decided to start up an industrial park near the model town of Araceli, in which all the businesses would share the vision of the EOC.

The creation of business parks would serve several purposes. First, since the businesses would be located within the same area, this would facilitate the growth of linkages between the businesses. Second, the creation of an actual physical space in which the idea was being applied, not only by an isolated business but also by a group of diverse businesses, would offer a credible example to others who were more skeptical about the viability of the project. It would therefore have a demonstration effect that could be imitated by others, as an economic parallel to the social exemplar set by the model towns.

Global Networks

Although the EOC began in Sao Paulo, Brazil, in 1991, the project spread rapidly throughout the world and permeated a wide range of sectors of the economy through the Focolare networks. In the first four years following the launch of the project, there was a rapid increase in the number of businesses participating. This early exponential growth rate of the numbers of businesses across the world participating in the EOC reflected an initial phase of enthusiasm within the Focolare and among others who heard about the EOC and wished to participate in it.

The second phase of development of the EOC could be termed one of consolidation. The growth rate began to slow down in 1996 and since then the number of businesses participating in the project seems to have leveled off around the 753 mark. The rate of growth thus appears to have slowed down, suggesting that the EOC is entering a new phase of development.

The geographical distribution of the businesses throughout the world correlates closely with the diffusion of the Focolare movement. The first concentration is in Brazil, with 84 businesses. The second such concentration is in Western Europe, and in particular Italy, with 242 businesses, and Germany, with 53 businesses. There are also relatively high concentrations of EOC ventures in Argentina, the former Yugoslavia, and the United States.

There are several regions with few or no EOC ventures. The most noticeable absence is in Africa, north and south of the Sahara. In North Africa there is only one EOC business in Egypt. In the whole of Africa south of the Sahara there are eleven businesses in total. In part, this absence could be the result of lack of communication between the Focolare communities in African countries and the Focolare Center. The more likely explanation, however, relates to the inability of those who would like to participate in the EOC to generate adequate funds to start businesses. Likewise, there are few EOC ventures in former Soviet countries. In this case, the main reason is the limited presence of the Focolare movement within the former Soviet countries.

How EOC Profits Are Shared

One of the main aims of EOC ventures is to help create greater equality among all those linked to the Focolare across the world. An important element of this is the redistribution of profits, which are shared in three ways, as outlined above. The portion of profit for reinvestment is kept within the business itself. The amount is at the discretion of the business owner. The other two parts are divided equally between assistance to those in need and formation activities for a culture of giving, and are channeled through the central Focolare Center in Italy. Since 1994, the business profits given to those in need have been supplemented by personal donations from people within the Focolare movement. The redistribution of these profits and donations is carried out in two ways. First, direct community assistance, as described below, is provided through the community network structures of the Focolare movement. Second, a portion of the profits is directed toward more structured development projects via Azione Mondo Unito, which has been running projects based on the Focolare's principles since the 1980s.

Local-Global Distribution Networks

The data presented above highlight the global scope of the EOC. Through the EOC it is clear that a small-scale global "communion of goods" is already occurring within and through the Focolare movement. At first glance the Focolare decision-making processes seem rather centralized: there is one main fund based in Rome and decisions on the needs of remote communities across the world are taken there. On the surface, there are strong similarities between the EOC and other international NGOs that are continually faced with the problem of how to distribute funds worldwide.

When the decision-making processes of the EOC are examined within the context of the wider Focolare structures, however, a different picture emerges. Although the EOC results in one central fund, decisions on the amount of money required from the central EOC fund and on how it will be used remain with the local Focolare communities. This process of decentralized decision-making is operationalized through each local Focolare community working out in real terms what its particular needs are on a regular basis. Each year in June a "census" (commissioned by the Global Center) is carried out in order to establish the needs of all those linked to the local Focolare communities. The emphasis that the Focolare's spirituality places on attending to the needs of others makes this task relatively straightforward. In order to avoid such needs being overlooked, everyone is invited to present them directly to the Focolare houses, which act as central coordination points in the process. Thus, this primary stage of decision-making in the EOC is at the most decentralized, local level and is based on a kind of community self-assessment. Although this system is based almost entirely on trust, since those who are being helped actively participate in the life of the community, verification of circumstances would be relatively straightforward due to the high level of face-to-face relationships.

Once established, every attempt is made to cover the needs of the community, first using resources available on a local level through living the "culture of giving," which is the basis of the Focolare spirituality. In many cases, especially in Western nations, this communion of goods is enough to cover all of the needs of the immediate community and to generate an additional surplus that can be shared with other communities. If the needs of the local community cannot be met through this local communion of goods, they are put forward to the regional Focolare and the same process occurs. If the regional Focolare centers are still unable to cover the requests, the needs are then communicated to the International EOC Commission. In this way, requests that reach the International EOC Commission have already been verified by means of the communion of goods.

The responsibility for verifying the needs of the community on a regional level lies with the regional delegates of Focolare communities.[43] In a sense, the

---

43. Each regional community is represented within the Focolare at an international level by two regional delegates (one man and one woman) who are both single focolarini.

task of discerning who needs what lies with them more than with the International Commission. Delegates from Latin America, Italy, and the Philippines explained how they reached decisions regarding whom to help, and whether there were general guidelines on what help could be given. They revealed a range of interpretations of "basic needs" and diverse ways of attending to those needs in different countries. One delegate described how the Focolare in his region reached decisions on whom to help and how:

> We don't define it [help] by the amount he or she receives. It could be, for example, that you receive 100 and I receive 100 . . . but you have five children and I only have one, your father is sick and you have to care for him, or you have to pay for your house. . . . So we define this in a personal relationship, so that the person can reach the end of the month . . . we define it personally, in a personal relationship.

The decision on how to help, therefore, is based on a personal relationship between the person in need and a responsible member of the Focolare community. It is not based on some predetermined criteria of need on a global scale, but on the actual needs that are brought to the community and in particular to the attention of the delegates. The help, when it arrives, goes through the same channels of personal relationships. It is a result of attending to the particular needs of the individual or family. The census means that how much each one will receive is decided prior to receipt of the money. One delegate said: "This is all carried out before hand. First we find out what the needs are in a personalized way, with great discretion and charity. Then, after we have this list, we give it to the Center." This takes away any possibility of disagreement within the community when the help arrives. Hence, the task of the Center is more that of administering the distribution of funds that have been already allocated than deciding how money should be spent.

Direct Assistance to Those in Need

Given the highly personalized nature of these EOC networks, it is possible that there could be discrepancies in what constitutes a "basic need" within the project as a whole. The global scope of the EOC could give rise to questions regarding the nature of poverty in different parts of the world. Poverty can be both "relative" and "absolute" and is closely associated with cultural settings and geographical locations. For these reasons the Focolare Center was reluctant to set fixed standards at the start of the EOC, as it was thought that establishing needs was best left to those closest to the individuals who required help.

As the EOC has developed, however, it recognized that discrepancies did exist in what different countries defined as poverty. In order to avoid disagreements and misunderstandings, a working definition of what constitutes a "basic need" within the context of the EOC was established.

Once needs have been established, the total amount of money required to satisfy them in the local communities is added to the totals from the other regions each year in October, when the three hundred regional Focolare delegates hold their annual meeting in Rome. In the course of the month, each pair of regional delegates meets with the International EOC Commission to resolve any discrepancies arising from the information that they had provided and to discuss the progress of the EOC in their region.

How to share the money is then determined by means of a simple calculation based on the total funds received in the year. If the sum received for the year is the same or exceeds the amount requested by the various communities, then everyone receives exactly the amount requested. If the amount received is less than the amount requested (as has been the case since the start of the EOC), then each region receives a proportional amount based on this overall sum. For example, in 1997 the amount of EOC funds available fulfilled around 80 percent of total requests. In that year, each region received 80 percent of what they had requested.

This method of calculating each region's share has only been in effect since 1995; prior to 1994 the EOC contributions from businesses were allocated on a regional basis without passing through the Focolare Center. Those countries that had the highest level of EOC profits distributed them within that particular country. In 1994, however, the system was globalized. This decision came partly from the realization that the businesses were still not managing to produce enough profit to cover the needs of the Focolare communities throughout the world. A global structure, it was thought, would enable a more comprehensive distribution of the profits and therefore a more widespread communion of goods among countries and not just within the countries themselves.

In order to do this, in 1994 the Focolare adopted a calculation based on the cost of living in different parts of the world in order to bring about a fair distribution. In a sense, this can be seen as an attempt to acknowledge the pattern of global inequalities in an objective fashion. The different regions received help in proportion to the cost of living in that particular region, based on the number of people within the Focolare in need. This calculation, however, proved laborious as it did not relate directly to the needs of the individual communities in the countries that had requested help. As a result, the proportional calculation was adopted, which proved much quicker and more effective in achieving the aims of the EOC.

The greatest benefit of this procedure of profit distribution is the clarity of the system on a global scale. As a result of globalizing the EOC, the Focolare Center has achieved a system through which it can oversee distribution of EOC profits without assuming responsibility for deciding precisely how the funds are spent in the different regions. The regional delegates and local communities make those determinations according to the needs within their communities. This relieves the EOC of time-consuming bureaucracy. At the same time, the EOC's use of established networks within the Focolare and established meetings means that the EOC per se has almost zero administration costs. The profits collected specifically for the EOC can be given directly without any percentage being siphoned off to satisfy overhead expenses.

Since 2006 the EOC has been in a partnership with the NGO *Azione Mondo Unito* (Action for a United World). AMU, started by members of the Focolare movement and operated according to the same principles, has been running development projects throughout the developing world since the mid-1980s. When the EOC started in the early 1990s, AMU and the EOC were regarded as separate entities and operated in parallel. As the EOC has evolved, the necessity of expertise in development assistance management has become clearer because of requirements that the use of funds be transparent and that they be used not only to meet immediate needs but also for long-term development work. Partnership with AMU provided a workable solution.

In 2009 AMU administered €202,000 of EOC funds on behalf of the project. The role of AMU has consisted in vetting and providing support to those in the developing world seeking EOC funds. A distinctive contribution of the projects supported via AMU has been in the provision of sustainable livelihoods through small productive activities. In 2009 projects funded through this scheme were carried out in Argentina, Brazil, Chile, Colombia, Mexico, Paraguay, Peru, Uruguay, Cameroon, Ivory Coast, Kenya, Ethiopia, Uganda, Bosnia, Bulgaria, Croatia, Macedonia, Romania, and Serbia. This partnership with AMU looks set to become a growing element of the EOC in the coming years.

Centrality of Trust

The system of profit sharing within the EOC on a global scale depends on high levels of trust within the Focolare at every level. Such trust is normally assumed only in face-to-face, everyday community relationships at a local level. There is limited internal scrutiny of documents from the delegates on the part of the Center and profits are shared in the total trust that all the money will be well spent. In this way, the process is quick and efficient with paperwork kept to a minimum. Such a system could seem inappropriate within the dominant market economy, where everything spent or requested has to be justified through a laborious system of accountability. The EOC appears open to corruption, fraud, and misuse of funds. The nature of the Focolare spirituality that underpins the system, however, makes it difficult to abuse the trust on which it is founded. At the same time, it discourages questioning others' trustworthiness. Those in roles of responsibility, for example, have given up all their possessions to live in the Focolare houses and do not have access to personal bank accounts. Nevertheless, given that the EOC is working at the intersection between the normal public economy and the distinctive economic vision within the Focolare, this reliance on trust could present difficulties.

Conclusion

In this essay I have sought to provide an overview of the evolution of the EOC and its development on a global scale, highlighting the evolution of various local-global networks. I showed how the EOC emerged from the practices of sharing already present within the Focolare and gave these practices a more institutional presence within the context of the global economy. Structures within the Focolare, which grew out of the "communion of goods," proved an efficient and highly adaptable means of fostering solidarity through sharing.

At the same time, the analysis of the EOC data in its first nine years demonstrates several important features. First, although steady, the amount of profits redistributed by the businesses participating in the EOC project is not growing at the rate initially expected. Since 2000, partly as a consequence of new procedures adopted to guarantee transparency and accountability, the number has begun to rise slightly. Given the high levels of mortality among small and medium-sized entities (SMEs) in developing countries, this rise demonstrates a high degree of resilience among the EOC companies as a whole. Nevertheless, the question of how to support new businesses has to be considered. Second, the number of new businesses joining the project has slowed in recent years, especially in European countries. The initial burst of enthusiasm in the early years of the project seems to have given way to a slower but arguably more solid rate of growth, as it is based on thoughtful decisions rather than euphoria. Nevertheless, this slowdown of the number of businesses casts doubt over the universal applicability of the EOC on a wider scale.

Caritas in Veritate: A Challenge to "Dualistic" Economic Thinking

Simona Beretta

Introduction: Globalization and Development

The issue of globalization is a divisive one. This is somewhat curious, given that globalization is all about unity: the human family inhabits one globe, sharing one destiny. In our diversity, we realize the same desires: we are fascinated by the humanity of others as our personal experience of being human deepens and broadens, and we recognize in other persons the quest for beauty, meaning, and happiness that drives our own life. We want freedom, we cry for liberation; we want to "do more, know more and have more in order to be more" (*Caritas in Veritate* [*CV*], no. 18, citing *Populorum Progressio* [*PP*], no. 6).[1]

Caritas in Veritate speaks to this profound desire, sending one clear message to "all people of good will" (*CV*, title): the good news that Christ is "the driving force behind authentic development" (*CV*, no. 1). This message is incisively spelled out in this long and articulate letter: from its beginning, which states that charity and truth, inner aspirations that move the human heart, are indeed the "Face of one Person" (*CV*, no. 1); to its conclusion, where the human cry for liberation finds realistic hope: "'I am with you always, to the close of the age' (Mt 28:20)" (*CV*, no. 78).

This encyclical is essentially about "being," inviting each person of good will to personally adhere, in an élan of freedom, to the vocation to "integral human development" (*CV*, title). We find no moralism in the text; rather, this letter ex-

---

1. Translation at http://www.vatican.va/holy_father/benedict_xvi/encyclicals/documents/hf_ben-xvi_enc_20090629_caritas-in-veritate_en.html.

plicitly distances itself from conventional calls to ethics (most clearly in *CV,* no. 45) and from unqualified support of self-defined ethical agents or ethical behaviors (*CV,* no. 47). This is no surprise:[2] Christian life does not primarily consist in abiding by a set of religious rules or by some ethical etiquette; it is the actual life, in the concreteness of time and space, of a new people reborn in Christ and remaining in him, in "dynamic faithfulness to a light received" (*CV,* no. 12).

Pope Benedict XVI teaches that ethics are a consequence of being, and that the fullness of being (integral, or well-rounded, human development)[3] depends on knowing Christ's face. "Christianity is not moralism, it is not we who must do all that God expects of the world but we must first of all enter this ontological mystery: God gives himself. His being, his loving, precedes our action. . . . Ethics are a consequence of being. . . . Unfortunately, today too many people live far from Christ, they do not know his face and thus the eternal temptation of dualism . . . is constantly renewed."[4] Moralism is dualistic, oppressing, and boring; this is not what we truly desire: we want life, abundant life, a "whole" life.

This is why I was really intrigued by the announcement of the Conference that inspired this volume, which said that "Catholics and others interested in the new face of social progress touted by Pope Benedict must learn to read the encyclical as whole. . . . Catholicism overcomes bifurcations not just between liberalism and conservatism but between intellectual inquiry and social commitment, between the social gospel of North America and the cry for liberation of the South, and between confronting the person of Jesus Christ and calling for global assessment of economic structures."[5]

---

2. As a Father, Pope Benedict XVI revives the family traditions, sharing with us old and new riches along with "the Gospel image of . . . 'a householder who brings out of his treasure what is new and what is old' (Mt 13:52). The treasure is the great outpouring of the Church's Tradition, which contains 'what is old' — received and passed on from the very beginning — and which enables us to interpret the 'new things.' . . . Among the things which become 'old' as a result of being incorporated into Tradition . . . there is the fruitful activity of many millions of people. . . . Acting either as individuals or joined together in various groups, associations and organizations, these people represent *a great movement for the defence of the human person* and the safeguarding of human dignity" (Pope John Paul II, *Centesimus Annus,* no. 3). Translation at http://www.vatican.va/holy_father/john_paul_ii/encyclicals/documents/hf_jp-ii_enc _01051991_centesimus-annus_en.html.

3. The English version of *Populorum Progressio,* no. 14, uses the plastic and intuitive expression "well-rounded" for "integral" development. Translation at http://www.vatican.va/holy _father/paul_vi/encyclicals/documents/hf_p-vi_enc_26031967_populorum_en.html.

4. *Lectio divina,* Pontifical Roman Major Seminary, February 12, 2010.

5. Conference convened by the Center for World Catholicism and Intercultural Theology, DePaul University, April 20-21, 2010.

Practical bifurcations follow from dualistic thinking. This encyclical, read as a whole, offers a wealth of mind-opening invitations to overcome dualisms in many articulations of personal and social life. It challenges us to question the dualistic thinking that tends to be standard in public debates and some-times even in academic inquiry, which is especially worrying, if we recall the meaning of the word "uni-versity"! We risk spoiling this wealth of suggestions if we shop across *Caritas in Veritate* and pick only those parts that confirm our prejudgments.

These are the basic aims of this essay: highlighting some of the encyclical's challenges to deep-seated dualisms in economic thinking about human and global development; taking the challenge as seriously as I can; tentatively showing that it is reasonable to accept the challenge, on the basis of elementary human experience[6] that — with all our differences — makes us one de facto family, living on one globe.

Along this trajectory, the two words that comprise the title of the encyc-lical, love and truth, stand out as the basic language of elementary human experience and the possible common grammar for both human and interdis-ciplinary dialogue in the global society — one and plural.[7]

The first chapter is a rhapsodic, non-exhaustive list of passages in which *Caritas in Veritate* challenges dualisms in economic thinking, pointing to the need for an "orderly interdisciplinary exchange" (*CV,* no. 30), facilitated by the social doctrine of the Church, "expert in humanity" (*PP,* no. 13; *Sollicitudo Rei Socialis,* no. 41). Chapter two discusses the conditions that make it possible to realize a non-fragmented, truly interdisciplinary work: essentially, disciplines need a robust, common generative point allowing their cross-fertilization. The third chapter elaborates on the idea that elementary human experience can provide a solid basis for framing economic analysis around the notions of actions and relations, providing a more adequate account of what economic development is about and dismantling the all too common bifurcation be-tween scientific inquiry and ethical considerations. The subsequent chapters exemplify why it can be reasonable to accept two of the many challenges to

---

6. This simple and exigent method of inquiry applies to all that is human. See Luigi Giussani, *The Religious Sense,* trans. John Zucchi (Montreal: McGill-Queen's University Press, 1997), pp. 7-9.

7. "*Truth,* in fact, is *lógos* which creates *diá-logos,* and hence communication and com-munion. Truth, by enabling men and women to let go of their subjective opinions and impres-sions, allows them to move beyond cultural and historical limitations and to come together in the assessment of the value and substance of things. Truth opens and unites our minds in the *lógos* of love" (*CV,* no. 5).

dualistic thinking this encyclical offers, related to human and global development. One challenge consists in overcoming the dualism between a strictly economic account of wealth creation and the value-laden, political account of wealth distribution (chapter four). The second challenge concerns overcoming the separation between life ethics and social ethics (chapter five), using generation as a metaphor for development; in fact, both can be recognized because something new, ultimately *gratuitous,* happens. Chapter six looks at innovations and their practical need for gratuitousness as an example of the vital connection between social and anthropological questions.

I. Challenging Dualism

Hell is the place where nothing connects to nothing.

T. S. Eliot

Caritas in Veritate repeatedly makes it clear that dualisms are to be avoided: at times, as *en passant* suggestions; at times, as solid, path-breaking analytical statements. Why should dualisms be challenged? There is one reasonable answer: because it is convenient. It is unreasonable to artificially dissect what is in fact a "round" issue, taking splinters as if they where whole; fragmentation is bound to produce undesirable theoretical and practical consequences that human reason can recognize. Hence, human reason can assess whether challenging dualism gives a more realistic account of reality, or not.

Dualisms are deeply seated in current conventional wisdom about economic development: efficiency is juxtaposed to justice, population growth to environment protection, foreign aid to national policy space, and so on. The subtle and dangerous dualism underlying all of the above consists in conceiving ethical issues as *ex post* additions to the results of scientific inquiry and technological application — which, on their side, are presumed to be ethically neutral. In the economic field, a significant application of the above statement concerns the notion of efficiency: "The notion of 'efficiency' is not value-free" (*CV*, no. 50). There is no such thing as *the* economic solution to problems; non-neutral alternatives are there, and acknowledging their moral dimension adds realism in facing and solving problems.

Take the case of labor market institutions (labor remains the "key to the social question,"[8] also in times of globalization): "Economic science tells us

8. See Pope John Paul II, *Laborem Exercens,* no. 3. Translation at http://www.vatican.va/

that structural insecurity generates anti-productive attitudes wasteful of human resources, inasmuch as workers tend to adapt passively to automatic mechanisms, rather than to release creativity. On this point too, there is a convergence between economic science and moral evaluation. *Human costs always include economic costs,* and economic dysfunctions always involve human costs" (*CV,* no. 32).[9] Confirming a long tradition in the Church's social doctrine,[10] *Caritas in Veritate* challenges the dichotomy between entrepreneurial work and work for a wage: they share the common nature of response to the vocation to full personal development: "Business activity has a human significance, prior to its professional one. It is present in all work, understood as a personal action, an *"actus personae,"* which is why every worker should have the chance to make his contribution knowing that in some way "he is working 'for himself'" (*CV,* no. 41).[11]

Possibly, the most striking message of this encyclical consists in challenging the separation between gratuitous actions and normal economic activity. We could say that the term "gratuitousness" constitutes an innovation in the language of Catholic social teaching; it is indeed, in dynamic faithfulness to the Catholic tradition.[12] "The great challenge before us, accentuated by the

---

holy_father/john_paul_ii/encyclicals/documents/hf_jp-ii_enc_14091981_laborem-exercens _en.html.

9. In all quotes, italics are in the original text.

10. Consider how original was Leo XIII's message about the "social question" of his times, trying to convince the readers of *Rerum Novarum* that it was reasonable to broaden their view: fully understanding the actual, complex struggle of power of that period required more than just taking sides with one of two, opposed and dichotomized, social classes.

11. The quote from *Caritas in Veritate,* no. 41, continues: "With good reason, Paul VI taught that 'everyone who works is a creator.'" In *Populorum Progressio,* in a paragraph entitled "Nobility of Work," Paul VI writes: "God gave man intelligence, sensitivity and the power of thought — tools with which to finish and perfect the work He began. Every worker is, to some extent, a creator — be he artist, craftsman, executive, laborer or farmer. Bent over a material that resists his efforts, the worker leaves his imprint on it, at the same time developing his own powers of persistence, inventiveness and concentration" (*PP,* no. 27). *Laborem Exercens,* no. 24, highlights work in the subjective sense, and explicitly uses the expression *actus personae.* John Paul II, in *Laborem Exercens,* gave the Church an illuminating account of what it is to work, and what "priority of labour over capital" means.

12. The dynamics of gift, received and circulated, permeates the "story" of development in Catholic social teaching, a story woven by relations of gift. This is the basic structure of the story, as you can get it in the *Compendium of the Social Doctrine of the Church,* by the Pontifical Council for Justice and Peace: the goods of the earth are a gift of God to the human family; the human being is called to participate in creation through labor, which is a free response to God's initial gift. Labor is a transitive (relational) action: we work for and with someone; we

problems of development in this global era and made even more urgent by the economic and financial crisis, is to demonstrate, in thinking and behaviour, not only that traditional principles of social ethics like transparency, honesty and responsibility cannot be ignored or attenuated, but also that in *commercial relationships* the *principle of gratuitousness* and the logic of gift as an expression of fraternity can and must *find their place within normal economic activity.* This is a human demand at the present time, but it is also demanded by economic logic. It is a demand both of charity and of truth" (*CV,* no. 36).

Notice that the appropriate understanding of gratuitousness is a challenge to thinking and behavior — thinking comes first! Economic logic is fully valorized in the encyclical;[13] each discipline plays an important role in understanding reality, within an appropriate, well-rounded horizon. For example, if normal economic activities "can and must" include gratuitous actions, researchers should be able to analytically detect that gratuitousness makes a difference in the functioning of the economic system. This is economic reason in action, open to the roundness of reality.

Caritas in Veritate also challenges the commonplace ethical contraposition between the real economy (supposed to be "good") and the financial economy (which is "bad," having delivered us one of the worst crises in recent history). The encyclical clearly states that "efforts are needed . . . to ensure that the whole economy — the whole of finance — is ethical, not merely by virtue of an external label, but by its respect for requirements intrinsic to its very nature" (*CV,* no. 45). Notice, again, that the effort to realize a "good" economic and financial system is mostly about understanding its "very nature." We could say, fulfilling its ends, responding to its vocation; good science and good ethics go hand in hand.

---

use the real things — resources, capital, knowledge, technology — that have been actually handed down to us. Through our labor, we circulate what we have received. This circulation of gifts through labor drives wealth creation; in fact, alienation is defined as the sterile refusal to take part in the dynamic of gift (*Centesimus Annus,* no. 41). See also S. Beretta, "Wealth Creation in the Global Economy: Human Labor and Development," in *Rediscovering Abundance: Interdisciplinary Essays on Wealth, Income and Their Distribution in the Catholic Social Tradition,* ed. H. Alford et al. (Notre Dame: University of Notre Dame Press, 2005), pp. 175-201.

13. Here is another quote: "The dignity of the individual and the demands of justice require, particularly today, that economic choices do not cause disparities in wealth to increase in an excessive and morally unacceptable manner, and that we continue to *prioritize the goal of access to steady employment* for everyone. All things considered, this is also required by 'economic logic.' Through the systemic increase of social inequality, both within a single country and between the populations of different countries . . . not only does social cohesion suffer, thereby placing democracy at risk, but so too does the economy" (*CV,* no. 32).

Challenging dualisms opens fascinating new paths of economic research and initiative. This is the case when *Caritas in Veritate* questions the dichotomy between profit and nonprofit enterprises (and the shortcut equating profit with "bad" and nonprofit with "good"): "When we consider the issues involved in the *relationship between business and ethics* . . . , it would appear that the traditionally valid distinction between profit-based companies and non-profit organizations can no longer do full justice to reality, or offer practical direction for the future. In recent decades a broad intermediate area has emerged between the two types of enterprise. . . . *The very plurality of institutional forms of business gives rise to a market which is not only more civilized but also more competitive*" (*CV,* no. 46).

Other commonsense juxtapositions are also challenged: economics versus politics, state versus market, market versus society. "The exclusively binary model of market-plus-State is corrosive of society" (*CV,* no. 39). "The Church has always held that economic action is not to be regarded as something opposed to society. . . . It must be remembered that the market does not exist in the pure state. It is shaped by the cultural configurations which define it and give it direction" (*CV,* no. 36); the same is clearly true for political institutions, which we are called to "be solicitous for" (*CV,* no. 7).[14] Human actions make the difference in shaping all sorts of institutions — which are not complex deterministic mechanisms, but the temporary and contingent configuration of actual interpersonal relations, with all their ambivalence.

Human actions bring with them the thickness of human experience: they occur *in* this world, here and now; but they are not confined *within* this time and space. Their meanings, and their actual consequences, exceed them. The encyclical warns against disconnecting history and eternal life (*CV,* nos. 7, 29, 34) and separating the material dimension of development from the spiritual: "Without the perspective of eternal life, human progress in this world is denied breathing-space" (*CV,* no. 11). "The supremacy of technology tends to prevent people from recognizing anything that cannot be explained in terms of matter alone. Yet everyone experiences the many immaterial and spiritual dimensions of life" (*CV,* no. 77). This claim is genuinely effective in discussing development: as a matter of fact, we can provide good "material" stories about how development occurred in the past, in a given region. Unfortunately, these stories seem to be unable to give us advice about how to produce material development by

14. "To take a stand for the common good is on the one hand to be solicitous for, and on the other hand to avail oneself of, that complex of institutions that give structure to the life of society, juridically, civilly, politically and culturally, making it the *pólis,* or 'city'" (*CV,* no. 7).

material incentives: we have to admit that most efforts along these lines have failed. Reasonably, we should at least consider the possibility that without the transcendent perspective "all of reality is transformed into an indecipherable enigma."[15]

Caritas in Veritate deals with human and global development as a "whole": for example, it points out the danger of separating human culture and human nature. As cultural exchange expands, human beings risk bouncing between uncritical cultural eclecticism, which kills the possibility of cultural dialogue, and homogenization of lifestyles. "What eclecticism and cultural levelling have in common is the separation of human culture from human nature. Thus, cultures can no longer define themselves within a nature that transcends them, and man ends up being reduced to a mere cultural statistic. When this happens, humanity runs new risks of enslavement and manipulation" (*CV*, no. 26).[16] Challenging this separation hints at the importance of a healthy plurality of cultures for global development. There is a parallel with the previously mentioned need of a "plurality of institutional forms" of enterprises for a healthy economic system: the plurality of local economic institutions, reflecting local cultures, is a potential richness for all.

The encyclical also denounces the practical separation of human rights, including the right to development, from the realm of duties: "It is important to call for a renewed reflection on how *rights presuppose duties, if they are not to become mere licence. . . .* If the only basis of human rights is to be found in the deliberations of an assembly of citizens, those rights can be changed at any time, and so the duty to respect and pursue them fades from the common consciousness" (*CV*, no. 43). Simply imagine what challenging the actual separation between the language of rights on the one side and the practice of duty on the other side would mean for realizing — for example — the right to food and to water (*CV*, no. 27).

15. Benedict XVI used this vigorous expression in the Inaugural Session of the Fifth General Conference of the Bishops of Latin America and the Caribbean, Shrine of Aparecida, May 13, 2007. "What is real? Are only material goods, social, economic and political problems 'reality'? This was precisely the great error of the dominant tendencies of the last century, a most destructive error. . . . Anyone who excludes God from his horizons falsifies the notion of 'reality' and, in consequence, can only end up in blind alleys or with recipes for destruction. . . . Yet here a further question immediately arises: who knows God? . . . only his Son, . . . true God, knows him. . . . If we do not know God in and with Christ, all of reality is transformed into an indecipherable enigma; there is no way, and without a way, there is neither life nor truth."

16. We could add that even fruitful scientific dialogue becomes impossible, with single disciplines or — worse — single methodologies colonizing single, fragmented topics. Private interests and logic of power are very quick at colonizing!

Facing these urgent needs, public debates often take the direction of supporting forms of international redistribution of income and wealth, so that all human beings may be granted access to the goods and services required for a decent life. In the encyclical, this conventional wisdom is also challenged: "it must be borne in mind that grave imbalances are produced when economic action, conceived merely as an engine for wealth creation, is detached from political action, conceived as a means for pursuing justice through redistribution" (*CV,* no. 36).[17] In particular, the encyclical sharply reaffirms the circulating oneness of justice and charity (*CV,* no. 6). The artificial separation between wealth creation and "pursuing justice through redistribution" is particularly dangerous, as it incorporates at the same time the efficiency-equity dualism and the state-market dichotomy. Benedict explores this topic further in section four of this essay.

Another striking aspect of this encyclical is its challenging of the separation between the private and the public dimensions of human life. "Charity is at the heart of the Church's social doctrine. . . . it is the principle not only of micro-relationships (with friends, with family members or within small groups) but also of macro-relationships (social, economic and political ones)" (*CV,* no. 2). This strong unitary vision leads to a radical message: "we need to affirm today that *the social question has become a radically anthropological question*" (*CV,* no. 75). This analytical statement has a clear ethical dimension: "At the foundation of society" we find "the married couple, man and woman . . . that is open to life. This is not a question of purely individual morality. . . . The Church forcefully maintains this link between life ethics and social ethics" (*CV,* no. 15). This remark applies also to the global social question: "To consider population increase as the primary cause of underdevelopment is mistaken,

---

17. "When both the logic of the market and the logic of the State come to an agreement that each will continue to exercise a monopoly over its respective area of influence, in the long term much is lost: solidarity in relations between citizens, participation and adherence, actions of gratuitousness, all of which stand in contrast with *giving in order to acquire* (the logic of exchange) and *giving through duty* (the logic of public obligation, imposed by State law)" (*CV,* no. 39). See also: "The continuing hegemony of the binary model of market-plus-State has accustomed us to think only in terms of the private business leader of a capitalistic bent on the one hand, and the State director on the other. In reality, business has to be understood in an articulated way. . . . [T]here exist various types of business enterprise, over and above the simple distinction between 'private' and 'public' . . . [I]t is appropriate to take account of this broader significance of business activity . . . [which] favours cross-fertilization between different types of business activity, with shifting of competences from the 'non-profit' world to the 'profit' world and vice versa, from the public world to that of civil society, from advanced economies to developing countries" (*CV,* no. 41).

even from an economic point of view. . . . *Morally responsible openness to life represents a rich social and economic resource"* (*CV,* no. 44). *Caritas in Veritate* here is touching a very sensitive issue; chapters five and six will argue that connecting openness to life and socioeconomic development is indeed analytically and practically convenient.[18]

Since private and public dimensions of human life should not be separated, *Caritas in Veritate* reclaims a clear public role for Church life and religion: "*the whole Church, in all her being and acting — when she proclaims, when she celebrates, when she performs works of charity — is engaged in promoting integral human development.* She has a public role over and above her charitable and educational activities" (*CV,* no. 11).[19] "The Christian religion and other religions can offer their contribution to development *only if God has a place in the public realm,* specifically in regard to its cultural, social, economic, and particularly its political dimensions. The Church's social doctrine came into being in order to claim 'citizenship status' for the Christian religion" (*CV,* no. 56). Catholic social doctrine is "*caritas in veritate in re sociali:* the proclamation of the truth of Christ's love in society" (*CV,* no. 5): announcing of the truth and realizing charitable deeds cannot be disconnected (*CV,* no. 11).[20]

And finally, let us not disconnect intelligence and love: "Charity and truth confront us with an altogether new and creative challenge, one that is certainly vast and complex. It is about *broadening the scope of reason and making it capable of knowing and directing these powerful new forces,* animating them within the perspective of that 'civilization of love' whose seed God has planted in every people, in every culture" (*CV,* no. 33).

---

18. The anthropological dimension, often formally unaddressed in socioeconomic research, remains inevitable. Inadequate anthropology, aware or unaware reduction of the human dimensions of social issues, eventually tends to show up under the form of incomplete or inadequate results. Hence, scientific inquiry is a strong ally in showing that life ethics matters to human and social development.

19. "In the truth, charity reflects the personal yet public dimension of faith in the God of the Bible, who is both *Agápe* and *Lógos:* Charity and Truth, Love and Word" (*CV,* no. 3). The very first step of interdisciplinary work consists in challenging the dualism between heart and brain, so to speak.

20. "The Church fulfills her mission to evangelize, for she offers her first contribution to the solution of the urgent problem of development when she proclaims the truth about Christ, about herself and about man, applying this truth to a concrete situation" (*Sollicitudo Rei Socialis,* no. 41). Translation at http://www.vatican.va/holy_father/john_paul_ii/encyclicals/documents/hf_jp-ii_enc_30121987_sollicitudo-rei-socialis_en.html. On this, see Simona Beretta, "Quale programma per lo sviluppo? Una nota a partire dalla Dottrina Sociale della Chiesa," *Rivista Internazionale di Scienze Sociali* 1-2 (2006): 21-36.

II. Toward Interdisciplinary Work: A Realistic Attitude

[Our] new and creative challenge . . . is about broadening the scope of reason and making it capable of knowing and directing these powerful new forces [of worldwide interdependence and globalization].

Caritas in Veritate, no. 33

Challenging dualisms opens the way for knowing and directing worldwide interdependence. In times of crisis, "the technical forces in play, the global interrelations, the damaging effects on the real economy of badly managed and largely speculative financial dealing, large-scale migration of peoples . . . , the unregulated exploitation of the earth's resources: all this leads us today to reflect on the measures that would be necessary to provide a solution to prob-lems . . . of decisive impact upon the present and future good of humanity. The different aspects of the crisis . . . require new efforts of holistic understanding and a *new humanistic synthesis*" (*CV*, no. 21).[21] "In view of the complexity of the issues, it is obvious that the various disciplines have to work together through an orderly interdisciplinary exchange" (*CV*, no. 30).

Interdisciplinary work is a clear vocation of research, in a university faith-ful to its name; unfortunately, we must admit that such work is often evoked but seldom realized. The interdisciplinary dimension, in fact, does not and could not emerge from putting together single pieces, as when composing a puzzle. Putting together independently preformed pieces, shaped along strict disciplinary lines, will very unlikely form a sensible overall picture. Each dis-ciplinary "piece" is at the same time valuable and incomplete: each piece, im-plicitly or explicitly, opens a larger question, pointing to something beyond it that needs to be explored. For a harmonious, well-rounded picture to form, orderly interdisciplinary exchange requires each piece be shaped with refer-ence to a common generative point: profound enough to be common across disciplines and robust enough to generate dialogue. Can we find it? Finding a solution requires, as a minimum, admitting the possibility of its existence.

The title of the encyclical provides a reasonable path to interdisciplinary work: *Caritas in Veritate* is very persuasive in arguing that truth and charity are at the center of disciplinary inquiry and interdisciplinary exchange. Sci-

---

21. See also *Caritas in Veritate*, no. 11: "*authentic human development concerns the whole of the person in every single dimension*" (*CV*, no. 11; *PP*, no. 14); "*Progress of a merely economic and technological kind is insufficient*" (*CV*, no. 23).

entists are called to "a commitment to *foster the interaction of the different levels of human knowledge* in order to promote the authentic development of peoples. . . . Knowledge is never purely the work of the intellect. It can certainly be reduced to calculation and experiment, but if it aspires to be wisdom . . . it must be 'seasoned' with the 'salt' of charity. . . . Charity in truth requires first of all that we know and understand, acknowledging and respecting the specific competence of every level of knowledge. Charity is not an added extra, like an appendix to work already concluded in each of the various disciplines: it engages them in dialogue from the very beginning. The demands of love do not contradict those of reason. . . . Intelligence and love are not in separate compartments: *love is rich in intelligence and intelligence is full of love*" (*CV,* no. 30).

This love that should engage interdisciplinary dialogue since the very beginning, where does it come from? It must come from experience. Why do I get passionate about a research topic? Because I bumped into it, I got fascinated by the encounter with reality. Reality, even material reality, is *given* despite the obsessive focus on production in modern culture. Reality is a fascinating sign: it brings with it the dynamic experience of the mysterious; it urges those who look at it with an open mind to move deeper and deeper; the discipline is challenged to adhere to its object.[22] Reality is genially complex: the closer the grip of disciplinary dominion over reality, the less we end up understanding reality itself. And finally: reality, in its truth, "is first of all *given* to us. In every cognitive process, truth is not something that we produce; it is always found, or better, received. Truth, like love, 'is neither planned nor willed, but somehow imposes itself upon human beings'" (*CV,* no. 34). Knowing is so much more than an intellectual endeavor: in the adventure of knowing, "charity is not an added extra, like an appendix to work already concluded in each of the various disciplines: it engages them in dialogue from the very beginning" (*CV,* no. 30).

Pope Benedict XVI, who so clearly loves to study, describes with moving words the experience of researching: "Knowing is not simply a material act, since the object that is known always conceals something beyond the empirical datum. All our knowledge, even the most simple, is always a minor miracle, since it can never be fully explained by the material instruments that we apply to it. In every truth there is something more than we would have expected, in the love that we receive there is always an element that surprises

---

22. "Realism requires a certain method for observing and coming to know an object, and this method . . . must be imposed by the object." Giussani, *The Religious Sense,* p. 5.

us. We should never cease to marvel at these things. In all knowledge and in every act of love the human soul experiences something 'over and above,' which seems very much like a gift that we receive, or a height to which we are raised" (*CV*, no. 77).[23]

Each researcher, each discipline, discovers this "superabundance" (*CV*, no. 34) in specific ways, but superabundance is there precisely because we do not *produce* reality. When studying human and global development, interdisciplinary research can build on the one reality we experience directly: the elementary experience of being human and being a member of the human family. The basic human experience is relational: living is constantly impacting reality; by appraising it, we get to appreciate more deeply what it is to be human.

Being human is being unique: humanity is not a set of identical, disconnected individuals; humanity, as a family, is not an undistinguished mass: the word "family" indicates a relational space, laden with all the ambivalence of human relations. "The world is in trouble because of the lack of thinking . . . a new trajectory of thinking is needed in order to arrive at a better understanding of the implications of our being one family. Thinking of this kind requires a *deeper critical evaluation of the category of relation.* This is a task that cannot be undertaken by the social sciences alone" (*CV*, no. 53).

Notice that the encyclical challenges us to explore the analytical, not simply the ethical, relevance of relations. Science and technology develop as a consequence of purposeful (ambivalent) human decisions and actions, and no one can seriously maintain that they develop independently from ethical evaluation. By acting, human beings reveal what is valuable to them: truly knowing reality, or gaining and preserving dominion over it.[24] This is why "moral evaluation and scientific research must go hand in hand, and . . . charity must animate them in a harmonious interdisciplinary whole, marked by unity and distinction" (*CV*, no. 31).

---

23. A previous passage says: "Gift by its nature goes beyond merit, its rule is that of superabundance" (*CV*, no. 33).

24. "The human journey never simply comes to an end; and the danger of falling into inhumanity is never totally overcome, as is only too evident from the panorama of recent history! The danger for the western world — to speak only of this — is that today, precisely because of the greatness of his knowledge and power, man will fail to face up to the question of the truth. This would mean at the same time that reason would ultimately bow to the pressure of interests and the attraction of utility, constrained to recognize this as the ultimate criterion." Address that Benedict XVI intended to give during a visit to La Sapienza University in Rome, January 17, 2008. Translation at http://www.vatican.va/holy_father/benedict_xvi/speeches/2008/january/documents/hf_ben-xvi_spe_20080117_la-sapienza_en.html.

III. How Does Development Occur?
Economics as If Elementary Economic Experience Mattered

When a society moves towards the denial or suppression of life, it ends up no longer finding the necessary motivation and energy to strive for man's true good.

Caritas in Veritate, no. 28

Caritas in Veritate offers a passionate and realistic perspective on the urgent need to promote development in the current time of globalization and impetuous change in national performance profiles. It is realistic in describing the situations: development theories and practices seem to be missing the target. It is passionate, in reminding all people of good will that development is a vocation for everybody: only by pursuing that vocation do we realize our freedom.[25]

For social scientists, it is indeed disturbing that development remains an "indecipherable enigma" after centuries of scientific inquiry into the "nature and the causes of the wealth of nations."[26] As a matter of fact, social scientists have been providing satisfactory accounts of how economic development historically happened in specific times and areas of the planet, but they patently appear not to have come up with any effective indications about what to do in order to generate economic development in a given place, in a given future. No mechanism, no simple recipes for development seem to be available, even when the notion of development is reduced to its easiest component — namely, increasing material wealth and GDP. To people considering only material explanations relevant to material events, it must be disturbing that material development remains an indecipherable enigma.

Accepting the invitation of the encyclical to broaden reason and working toward composing a "harmonious interdisciplinary whole," scientific work can rebuild a notion of development from elementary experience. Consider the following: isn't it curious that we commonly speak of economic miracles, when referring to unexpectedly rapid economic growth? Why should we bother about miracles, if we truly believed that economic development could be engineered by smart technocratic measures? In fact, development is akin to a "minor miracle" (*CV*, no. 77), as knowledge, love, and life itself are.

---

25. "A vocation is a call that requires a free and responsible answer" (*CV*, no. 17).

26. See the work by Adam Smith from 1776, *An Inquiry into the Nature and Causes of the Wealth of Nations* (New York: Modern Library, 1936).

Using a word that is dear to economists and social scientists, development is driven by innovation. Hence, understanding wealth creation requires focusing on how something *new* occurs: how personal decisions to work and invest come about, why people decide to form partnerships with others, how far they look into the future. Development is a story of innovation, exceeding and driving material production. Material development depends on *being,* not simply on doing. I would like to share with you a suggestive representation of two alternative accounts of how the economy works. One is about *doing (homo faber);* the second is about *acting (homo agens).*

The process of doing inserts the *res* in a process, in a logical sequence of physical and mental operations, conceived as a closed and autarchic system. Such operations can be analyzed in the categories of means and ends, causes and consequences, inputs and outputs; the measurable transformations they produce *(res extensa)* can be completely transformed in a logical sequence of mental operations *(res cogitans).* The process of doing can be repeated, reversed (un-done), and programmed: hence, it is dominated by a project that prescribes what to do with technical norms and operational manuals. *Homo faber* is lonely, individualist, and autarchic; he is interested in others as either means or obstacles to the functioning of the processes under his control. His freedom coincides with his power of control over means, and it is constantly menaced by the antagonistic power of others. Hence, *homo faber* does not create personal identity, history, or *polis;* he is rather structurally inclined to give up his freedom in exchange for security. . . .

While the process of doing can be expressed as a finite "mono-logical" process, acting takes the form of an open "dia-logical" relation. Acting for another person is both doing something for him but also with him: you could think about teaching, assisting, consulting, and also about the client-server relations that today tend to take place in all forms of work. Serving the external or internal client means listening to his needs, always new and unpredictable, to transform them in problems with reference to both theory and cumulated learning; it means searching for new solutions and comparing them with new questions deriving from previously proposed solutions, in an endless path. The point of view of the *homo agens* is "im-perfect" by definition: in order to face the new, unpredictable things, it is necessary to continuously and freely dare, try, experiment. *Homo agens* has to be interested in others, since his action is mandated by others and he himself demands from others.[27]

27. M. Martini, "Libertà Economica," in *Soggetto e libertà nella condizione postmoderna,*

From elementary experience, we recognize that our material existence occurs in time, under conditions of uncertainty, within objective interdependence. These facts of life make mechanistic ideas about economic decisions largely irrelevant. There obviously is a technical component in economic decisions, but we know by experience that it is very dangerous to take one component as if it were the whole. Following the typical textbook techniques for optimizing consumption and production decisions (let alone for policy decisions!) in everyday life would be the quick and ready recipe to disaster! Analytical perspectives where economic decisions occur in a-temporal, anonymous, institution-free settings (the space-free, timeless market of a basic economics textbook) provide at best limited insights, very far from a reasonable story of wealth creation and development. How much of economic life could you explain on the basis of *homo faber?* Production and consumption of some "stuff" may be explained — nothing about most other goods and preciously nothing about "care."[28]

Factors of time, uncertainty, and interdependence cause economic processes to be driven by free, open, ultimately unpredictable human actions; most of these actions consist in activating relations. While economic behavior is mechanistic and predictable, actions are open and unpredictable; they are based on beliefs, perceptions, and expectations; they are embedded in personalized and potentially durable relations. A simple look at personal experience allows us to assess how many of our economic decisions concern personalized and potentially durable relations; usually, the vast majority of them are: services, almost by definition (and they represent the largest share of GDP in most nations); but also material goods, which are tailor-made to the need of the buyers (think of specialized components firms require for production).

Interpersonal relations are very often needed for reaching one's goals, and at the same time they are justly feared: relations may consist in dependence

---

ed. Francesco Botturi (Milan: Vita e Pensiero, 2003), pp. 373-92. Translated into English by the author. Interestingly, Martini was a renowned Italian statistician who developed an innovative set of labor and production statistics for tertiary, knowledge-based societies. In working with him, I could appreciate how generative it is to look at reality with "intelligence full of love."

28. I take the expression from a very interesting book by Edward Hadas, *Human Goods, Economic Evils: A Moral Approach to the Dismal Science* (Wilmington: ISI, 2007), arguing that "stuff" and "care" identify two broad categories of goods that require different analytical approaches. Referring to standard economic analysis, "stuff" indicates the subset of goods whose production can be closely approximated by "doing": in case of little or no uncertainty in the production and consumption, practical irrelevance of informational asymmetries, no significant increasing returns, no requirement of personalized and durable relations.

and oppression, as well as partnership and support. In some cases, access to anonymous markets may have helped liberate individuals from oppressive personalized relationships, adding to their substantial personal freedom. "Ignoring the fact that man has a wounded nature inclined to evil gives rise to serious errors" (*CV,* no. 34).[29] The substantive quality of relations defines the substantive quality of economic transaction. Disconnecting ethics from economics is simply analytical nonsense.

Using elementary experience as the original focus for economic inquiry, we can easily recognize that perceptions, expectations, motivations, and hope are the driving force of material human actions: hence, no material development can dispose of its immaterial dimensions.[30] Consider how extremely poor people actually describe their experience of being poor: they use words such as "humiliation," "fear," "shame," and "despair."[31] Those words, coming from elementary experience, confirm the truth of the following: "*Integral human development presupposes the responsible freedom* of the individual and of peoples" (*CV,* no. 17).[32]

Human freedom ultimately also drives strictly material development, at both the micro- and the macro-levels. At the micro-level, any manager (including a housewife) can confirm that human motivations make the difference in work performance — in fact, managing human resources typically includes

29. See also *Catechism of the Catholic Church,* no. 407; Pope John Paul II, *Centesimus Annus,* no. 25. For example, one of the simplest, commonly observed forms of interpersonal relation is reciprocity: from *do ut des,* to *tit for tat* (up to "eye for eye, tooth for tooth"). In its strict sense, reciprocity is very ambivalent: it may sustain the pursuit of a decent social life, by reciprocating the "good" received within fraternal reciprocity; but it may also disintegrate society, through reciprocal retaliation.

30. The above remark helps us understand why spiritual development is a concrete issue, and does not express moralistic concerns. The "profound failure to understand the spiritual life" obscures the fact "that the development of individuals and peoples depends partly on the resolution of problems of a spiritual nature" (*CV,* no. 76).

31. "Poverty is humiliation, the sense of being dependent on them, and of being forced to accept rudeness, insults, and indifference when we seek help (Latvia 1998). Being poor is being always tired (Kenya 1996). Poverty is lack of freedom, enslaved by crushing daily burden, by depression and fear of what the future will bring (Georgia 1997). Poverty is pain; it feels like a disease. It attacks a person not only materially but also morally. It eats away one's dignity and drives one into total despair (Moldova 1997)." The above are powerful expressions of how poor people define poverty, taken from Deepa Narayan with Raj Patel, Kai Schafft, Anne Rademacher, and Sarah Koch-Schulte, *Voices of the Poor: Can Anyone Hear Us?* (New York: Oxford University Press, 2000).

32. From a different perspective, see A. Sen, *Development Is Freedom* (Oxford: Oxford University Press, 1999).

a massive effort to sustain workers' motivation, often with scant results, especially when extrinsic motivations such as pay and fringe benefits are used. At the macro-level, we find something similar: nations flourish and decay, with reasons that appear to be very loosely connected to material wealth and much related to the substantive set of expectations, beliefs, and motivations.[33]

The notion of economic action — free human dynamism, which affirms a value worth pursuing by the same act of pursuing it — seems to me especially powerful for rethinking from first principles what economic development is about. No deterministic story about development is adequate when it is fully scrutinized by reason. Revisiting elementary economic experience, we recognize that human actions make the difference. Machines and animals seem to perform better than humans in the field of efficient optimization; they do not seem to produce much innovation, though!

Here are some elementary features of economic development, consistent with the realization that human actions drive it. First, development consists of the *path* people are actually treading, in time and space, not in the abstract final destination they pursue. In fact, attempts at producing development as the outcome of some technocratic process typically end in near failure. Second, development is an intrinsically dynamic process, a story of wealth creation where static categories such as *means* and *ends* are totally inappropriate; hence, understanding the dynamism of development requires identifying appropriate dynamic categories. Third, economic development is a process we can recognize and measure by the fact that it goes *in crescendo,* with a precise sense: from less to more of "good" things. Any measurement of well-being, wealth creation, and development must obey a logic that comes from *outside* the measurement system.[34] For measuring development, we need criteria for judging what is good from what is bad, life from death, the "bettering of the human condition"[35] from its worsening. Furthermore, in a globalized world, we need these criteria to fit with human experience across the wide plurality of cultures.

We cannot dispose of the question about *sense,* when development is at stake. Elementary experience represents the possible grammar for human dialogue about the sense of development, across the rich plurality of cultures

33. Again, this is suggested by very different authors, from A. de Tocqueville, *Democracy in America* (1835-40), to M. Olson, *The Rise and Decline of Nations: Economic Growth, Stagflation, and Social Rigidities* (New Haven: Yale University Press, 1982).

34. This fact should not come as a surprise to scientific researchers: it is well known that in any axiomatic system there are propositions that cannot be proved or disproved within the axioms of the system!

35. Adam Smith, again!

and traditions that globalization makes possible for us to encounter. The words expressing the sense of development in elementary experience — love, truth, beauty, justice, and happiness — suffer from being dissected; they need to be well rounded. Elementary experience is especially fresh and powerful in children — they are widely open to reality, eager to detect its signs; they keep asking "how" and "why," about the origins and the destiny; they ask waiting for an answer; and they count on receiving a true answer (you do not easily quench their thirst with cheap answers). This is totally reasonable: they count on receiving because they are aware they live by receiving. Children have no doubts about what they want: they need love, and they need truth. Adults may at times forget the calling of love and truth. They may even argue that they are childish words; but you can be sure that they hate being despised, barely tolerated, misrepresented, cheated, and betrayed. They may maintain they do not believe truth and love exist, but they are too well aware of what it is to be disliked and betrayed.

In sum: to speak about development — even in the practical dimension of creating material wealth — we need to go back to well-rounded first principles: truth and love, vocation planted in our hearts and minds, gifts[36] we share with all human beings.

Caritas in veritate are words that all human beings understand, by elementary experience. Truth and love are definitely non-confessional words: "All people feel the interior impulse to love authentically: love and truth never abandon them completely, because these are the vocation planted by God in the heart and mind of every human person" (*CV,* no. 1).

IV. "Wealth Creation" versus "Wealth Distribution": Why It Is Convenient to Challenge This Dualism

It is not enough to increase the general fund of wealth and then distribute it more fairly.
                                                        Populorum Progressio, no. 34

In *Caritas in Veritate,* development is repeatedly defined with one intrinsically dynamic word: vocation.[37] It is the same word Paul VI used in his encyclical

---

36. "Truth, and the love which it reveals, cannot be produced: they can only be received as a gift" (*CV,* no. 52).

37. "Integral human development is primarily a vocation" (*CV,* no. 11); "To regard *devel-*

letter *Populorum Progressio* in 1967, where development is defined as a vocation to "do more, know more and have more in order to be more" (*CV,* no. 18, citing *PP,* no. 6).

This definition makes a lot of sense in elementary experience, but it is difficult to retrieve it in current analyses of development. A common idea about development is that it is a matter of policies, foreign aid, and international cooperation. The story goes: global wealth creation produces winners and losers, within and across countries; when the losers are the poor, wealth redistribution is required to counterbalance the negative effects of wealth creation on wealth distribution. There is a splinter of truth in this account, no doubt. The problem is when a splinter is taken to be the whole story; then, useful distinctions become useless (even dangerous) dichotomies.

A broadly diffuse idea is that ethics are called to intervene, *ex post,* as a correction of the negative side effects of technical decisions. In this view, wealth creation is seen as the outcome of (value-free) techno-economic decisions, while wealth distribution (within countries and across countries since winners and losers of wealth creation occur in both spaces) is an ethically relevant, value-laden policy determination. This view represents an international version of the traditional dichotomy "efficiency *versus* justice," which is unfortunate: justice concerns all the phases of production prior to income distribution: it obviously includes paying just wages, but autonomy, consideration, esteem, and participation are also important.[38]

The previous section took care of dismantling the separation between economic and ethical dimensions of human actions and interactions, which are driven by expectation, beliefs, and motivations and where ethics belong by definition. Here, it is fair to elaborate on the fact that inappropriately separating wealth creation and wealth distribution leads to very poor policy prescription. For example, consider the policy implications of the view that lack of devel-

---

opment as a vocation is to recognize, on the one hand, that it derives from a transcendent call, and on the other hand that it is incapable, on its own, of supplying its ultimate meaning" (*CV,* no. 16); "the humility of those who accept a vocation is transformed into true autonomy, because it sets them free" (*CV,* no. 17); "*integral human development as a vocation also demands respect for its truth.* The vocation to progress drives us to 'do more, know more and have more in order to be more'" (*CV,* no. 18); "Finally, the vision of development as a vocation brings with it the *central place of charity within that development*" (*CV,* no. 19); "the vocation to development . . . is an intrinsic part of a plan that is prior to us. . . . That which is prior to us and constitutes us — subsistent Love and Truth — shows us what goodness is, and in what our true happiness consists" (*CV,* no. 52).

38. These expressions, which have been chosen as the other side of how poor people describe poverty, are included in the definition of "decent" work (*CV,* no. 63).

opment of peoples and nations is due to lack of political will to redistribute existing income and wealth, as measured by the amount of foreign aid falling short with respect to both what is needed and what has been promised. Policy prescription would be as follows: more redistribution is required; official foreign aid should be aligned to the need of implementing agreed international targets (say, millennium development goals [MDGs]); let us do it in a clean, non-interfering way, by channeling official foreign aid through direct budget support.[39]

What is wrong with this? Funding is obviously necessary, but the efficient cause of development is not funding: it is what human beings decide about using material (and immaterial) resources — there is never a mechanical, necessary, automatic relation between material resources and outcomes. Human freedom, at all levels, makes the difference. As the epigraph at the opening of this section says (and that text was written in 1967), distributing a larger stock of wealth is simply "not enough." Necessary conditions may not be sufficient conditions, as in this case.

Consider the MDGs: do they fit with the assumption that more funding can effectively produce the desired outcome? The answer seems to be negative. Even the most basic goals such as food, health, and education are inherently relational economic goods. Hunger depends on *accessing* food (MDG1), not simply its material availability; effectively reaching children, pregnant women, and ill or infected people (MDG4, 5, and 6) with *personalized care* makes the difference between living or dying, not material availability of drugs; education (MDG2) is obviously not the same as enrolling children in schools, and it occurs only when teacher and pupil activate their relationship. Other MDGs are even more clearly relational in nature, such as gender equality (MDG3)[40] or partnership for development (MDG8); environmental sustainability (MDG7) is also essentially relational, although few people realize it.[41] Forgetting the fact that development is much more than *doing* leads to self-referential technocratic approaches, where poor people remain beneficiaries of redistribution policies and not partners in development.

---

39. The above is a drastic, but overall balanced, simplification of the conclusions that emerged from the international debate on the topic of official development financing in the past few years, from the Paris Declaration on Aid Effectiveness (2005) to the Accra Agenda for Action (2009).

40. See S. Beretta, *What Do We Know about the Economic Situation of Women and What Does It Mean for a Just Economy?* (Milan: Mimeo, forthcoming).

41. It takes awareness that the environment is a gift: "it is a wondrous work of the Creator containing a 'grammar' which sets forth ends and criteria for its wise use" (*CV*, no. 48).

Nurturing economic relations for creating wealth does require some form of *gift*, but that needs to be carefully distinguished from wealth redistribution (be it private or public). The former implies taking care of the relations that spring from the material act of giving; the latter, in principle, does not require it or it is explicitly designed to be anonymous. Take, as an example, the issue of how to sustain an unemployed individual. Purely redistributive measures would provide, for a given period, an income transfer to persons who find themselves in an objectively specified situation of unemployment (say — having been fired from a previous formal job; notice that only objective information matters in this case). As an alternative, consider providing personalized coaching to individuals who are out of work not by their choice (possibly including young people who have not had access to jobs yet, but do want to work — a subjective condition). They would receive temporary income transfers, along with the opportunity to be involved in tailored requalification activities, aimed at fostering personal participation in economic and social life. Both alternatives have pros and cons: it is less embarrassing to receive an anonymous subsidy than to enter a personalized relationship, but the second alternative is more likely to lead to job creation.

V. Ethics of Life versus Social Ethics: Why It Is Convenient to Challenge This Dualism

Openness to life is at the centre of true development.

Caritas in Veritate, no. 28

With an image that will be further explored, development can be represented as a vital story of *generation,* as opposed to a technocratic process of (enlarged) material *reproduction.*[42] Elementary experience can easily tell the difference between these two seemingly similar concepts. Think of a baby, to whom both concepts apply. Reproduction as such does not require a long involvement (from a few minutes to nine months maximum); as biotechnologies advance, the time of human involvement in reproduction may be further reduced. Gen-

---

42. "Simple reproduction" (steady state) and "enlarged reproduction" (growth) used to be common expressions in growth theory textbooks. More sophisticated versions of growth theories have been subsequently developed, including dynamics of so-called endogenous growth; but they never lost their mechanistic flavor.

eration exceeds reproduction: for a new human being to fully flourish we need personalized and durable relations, taking personal care of the baby and of the youngster. Generating is the free decision to love and keep loving, nurturing relations[43] up to their full symbolic and cultural dimensions. There is a clear analogy in confronting material growth and development: elementary experience can tell the difference. The former is mechanistic and objective. On the contrary, generation is a dynamic, relational notion; it is *acting,* not *doing.*

Economic growth can be reduced to technocratic "enlarged reproduction," resulting from wealth appropriation or wealth accumulation. These are powerful instruments for controlling material wealth, as human history illustrates all too well; but they tend to be temporary expedients, conducive to (slower or faster) decay of material wealth itself.[44] Development as a generative process includes economic growth but exceeds it: for something new to happen, for investing, discovering, innovating, we need generative actions. A plausible list of generative actions[45] includes economic actions (job creation, innovation, entrepreneurship, investment in physical, human, and social capital; and obviously childbearing), and political and societal innovation (institutional investment, promoting institutional diversity, societal openness, and pluralism).

The word "generation" comes from *genos,* origin — as the words "gender" (male-female) and "genealogy" (the individual "I" and his or her personal history).[46] Being generated is common to parents and child, to all parents and all children; it is a basic human experience. Reproduction can be seen as "power" (to give life, or to withhold it, through contraception) or as "right" (assisted fecundation); but there is something ultimately gratuitous (from *gratia,* grace) in generation. Elementary experience recognizes that a new life is *gratia,* an unfolding mystery in front of our eyes, well beyond power and rights.

Elementary experience also recognizes the logical priority of *receiving* life.

---

43. Love is a tricky word: it can be reduced to a temporary emotion; but the word "love" takes a powerful meaning when we use it in relation with the human experience of generating and being generated. Emotion is there (a lot of it!), but not by itself: with freedom of will, width of intelligence, profundity of time, awareness of belonging to a constitutive relationship. Gratuitous love is co-essential to generation.

44. Gold and silver from the Americas possibly hastened the economic decay of European empires; even the incredibly successful (and painful) experiment of Soviet technocratic growth lasted only a few decades.

45. These actions are relevant weak anticipatory signals of development because they require and signal the gift of reciprocal trust.

46. V. Cigoli and E. Scabini, *Family Identity: Ties, Symbols and Transitions* (Mahwah, N.J.: Lawrence Erlbaum Associates, 2006); E. Scabini, *Famiglia e procreazione oggi: contesto psicosociale odierno e sfide culturali* (Milan: Università Cattolica del Sacro Cuore, 2008).

You can give life because you first receive it: nobody asked for permission in giving us life, and none of us is born out of our own personal will. The other side of this recognition is equally strong: the decision of giving, withholding, or terminating life has nothing to do with rights (never to be disconnected from duties); such a decision boils down to the objective exercise of an asymmetric power. The same fact of giving life can be the gratuitous circulation of a received gift or the exercise of an asymmetric power. Whatever the intentions and whatever the advances in biotechnology, newborn babies would actually keep *being given* life.

The notion of generation is very relevant to social and economic ethics, for at least two reasons. One is the following: in a very true and basic sense, human beings are the most precious among economic resources for development. This idea was clear among the "fathers" of economics, with human labor at the core of their theory of value, but was soon forgotten in the discipline. Mainstream economics took other paths: more mechanistic and sophisticated, with human labor being reduced at best to an anonymous factor of production, among others. It took *Rerum Novarum* and the subsequent social encyclicals to explicitly affirm the ontological priority of labor over capital and the intrinsic economic value of human creativity — this obviously occurred well before the so-called knowledge society became fashionable. Currently, despite the abundant rhetoric about the crucial role of human resources in firms, and of human and social capital in development, you seldom feel that the discussion is about actual babies and youngsters. Still, to elementary experience it is so clear that their flourishing (human development) requires much more than food, shelter, and training: these would be enough just for social animals. Well-rounded human development requires meaningful relations, beauty and justice, the quest for understanding reality and for an overarching sense of life. Notice that the quest for sense is the most powerful (and the only durable) driver of innovation and progress: no sense, no notion of development!

The second reason why generation is important for social ethics concerns development. We used generation as a metaphor to capture the essence of development: a real path in time and space, treaded by people entering stable relations with each other, where material circulation of goods[47] is intertwined with the dynamics of gift. Intentional human gifts, as they occur in transmitting knowledge or material wealth, entail a free action by which the giver

---

47. Scientific and technical knowledge, all sorts of physical infrastructures, institutions, and so on, are materially handed down from generation to generation (we are dwarves on the shoulder of giants).

means to create or to consolidate a relationship; accepting a gift is also a free action, signaling the willingness of the recipient to enter into relationship with the giver. Giving is a tricky word,[48] like love. But we cannot dispose of it: we experience the importance of the symbolic, immaterial dimension of material exchange; actually, we know that the symbolic dimension of circulating goods can be more effective than the material dimension in spurring development. We know by experience that beliefs and motivations can make miracles out of material limitations. An initial gift sometimes generates a dynamics of reciprocal gifts, a story of social relations where objects and meanings circulate, inextricably connected with each other. This story of development can either be nourished, gratuitously taken care of, or it can be truncated, taking distance from the logic of gift and choosing different actions — accumulation, exploitation, depletion. Isn't it reasonable, at this point, to consider that openness to life is indeed at the center of development, including material wealth creation? Only good anthropology makes good economics.[49]

VI. Innovations for Development: Rooted in Gratitude, Driven by Hope

Economic, social and political development, if it is to be authentically human, needs to make room for the principle of gratuitousness.

Caritas in Veritate, no. 34

In the economic tradition, development as "bettering of the human condition" (A. Smith) is driven by innovations. Take division of labor and extension of the market (A. Smith again): both are social innovations, relational in their nature and expected to be durable to be able to make a difference (nobody would specialize in a tiny piece of production, unless she or he would expect to be able to safely trade and acquire all she or he needs). Something new occurs in development: new knowledge, new products, new jobs, new enterprises. Today, we say development occurs with innovation such as seizing new opportunities, anticipating weak signals of change, seeing a resource in some-

48. See J. Godbout, *Ce que circule entre nous. Donner, recevoir, rendre* (Paris: Seuil, 2007).

49. The Church's teachings on life do not find much praise; they are often severely criticized and dismissed as obsolete, especially in rich countries (maybe these countries are more worried about wealth distribution than wealth creation). Still, this disturbing witness can be enormously generative.

thing previously thought to be useless. Innovations are the subset of intuitions that become real because someone takes them seriously, nurturing relationships that can transform those intuitions into facts: they find partners, persuade potential financers, inform and involve potential buyers, and so on.

Innovation is taking care of intuitions. The decision to invest one's energies in realizing an intuition is an act of freedom, including a measure of gratuitousness that consists in not dumping, but circulating that intuition. Ultimately, taking care of intuitions is an act of giving: something gratuitously received is gratuitously circulated. Intuition is technically a grace; it is gratuitously received (what does it mean to deserve an intuition?). Intuition contains a promise: it hints at something "more," to something "better" coming along with developing it; it is reasonable to hope for that result. Hence, the decision to take care of an intuition matures on the basis of these two powerful, fully rational sentiments: gratitude and hope. They are not sentimental: they are very reasonable. These considerations help me clarify one aspect of the quote at the beginning of this section (*CV,* no. 34): we do need gratuitousness for economic, social, and political development because innovations are rooted in gratitude and are driven by reasonable hope.

Caritas in Veritate explicitly states that gratuitousness is needed for society to exist and develop;[50] but here comes a legitimate doubt: what if the gratuitousness *Caritas in Veritate* is talking about is just poetry? Can we see gratuitousness? Can we measure it? Sure enough, gratuitousness belongs to the immaterial dimension of human actions, and measuring "things" (hours of volunteer work in a community, number of not-for-profit initiatives) would be a very unsatisfactory shortcut. Acts of gratuitousness are not akin to cheap voluntarism; they involve the entire person, mind and deeds; they are acts of full-fledged reason, judging what is just and what is unjust; and acts of will, decidedly choosing what is just.

As with truth and love, we may find it hard to isolate gratuitousness, but we can easily detect *lack* of it, both in micro-situations, and macro-situations. We can detect lack of wealth-creating gratuitousness, whenever we observe the "all-consuming desire for profit" and the "thirst for power,"[51] which at best

---

50. In brief: no economic activity without gratuitousness, no justice without gratuitousness (*CV,* nos. 36, 38, 39).

51. "Without truth, without trust and love for what is true, there is no social conscience and responsibility, and social action ends up serving private interests and the logic of power, resulting in social fragmentation, especially in a globalized society at difficult times like the present" (*CV,* no. 5).

can be wealth-accumulating or wealth-appropriating. We can also detect it as lack of generative actions and of innovation.

Innovations of all kinds — social, economic, institutional, and so on — are the driving force of wealth creation and development. Job creation, enterprise formation, investment, finance for development, scientific research, and child-bearing all follow an initial intuition that could be ignored or refused; they drive development because they consist in taking care, here and now, of the future by pursuing a reasonable hope. Any investment is somehow a "jump in the void," risking material goods we could count on today, in the reasonable hope to better our conditions. Gratuitousness and hope back all investment: in physical capital (starting a new enterprise); in human capital (from the most obvious, giving birth to a child,[52] to taking care of people in transmitting knowledge, in teaching apprentices the job, etc.); in social capital (which also requires investment!); in being solicitous for "just" institutions, as opposed to exploiting existing institutions up to possible depletion of their contribution to the common good.

Conclusion

This encyclical, you must admit, is very innovative. It builds on gratitude for the most amazing gifts, charity and truth; and it follows a previous letter on hope. Now it is our turn, taking care of all the intuitions it suggests. It is time for innovation, and we are explicitly invited to become "creative minorities."

"I would say that usually it is creative minorities who determine the future," Pope Benedict said on September 26, 2009, during a flight to the Czech Republic, "and in this regard the Catholic Church must understand that she is a creative minority who has a heritage of values that are not things of the past, but a very lively and relevant reality."

---

52. Women, in childbearing, receive a very special kind of intuition (after all, an embryo is very much like an intuition: a gift, that contains a promise); if humanity is still alive, it is because that kind of intuition is taken care of. Obviously, gratuitousness does not enter the virtual totality of gender studies in economics and development. Should it be considered? As before, we can appreciate the effects of the *lack* of consideration for gratuitousness in gender studies by noticing their internal contradiction. On the one side, "best practices" in development typically target women in order to improve the lot of families and local communities, and gender studies show appreciation for this; on the other side, women are analyzed as undistinguished individuals, with no reference to the "relational" nature of the feminine and of the family. Why, then, does targeting women make sense? For exploiting their gratuitousness on taking care of intuitions, without acknowledging it?

The Logic of Gift: Practical Implications for the Corporation

Michael Naughton

> *Today's international economic scene, marked by grave deviations and failures, requires a profoundly new way of understanding business enterprise. Old models are disappearing, but promising new ones are taking shape on the horizon.*[1]
>
> Caritas in Veritate, no. 40

Our current financial crisis has caused a significant amount of pain and suffering for many people. It has also disoriented the most serious free market advocates of our economic system. While a painful and confusing moment, this is a great opportunity to do some rethinking about economics and in particular how we understand the business enterprise. Part of this rethinking is that our current crisis is not only a financial one, but also more fundamentally a cultural one that requires, as Benedict XVI explains, "new efforts of holistic understanding and a *new humanistic synthesis*" (*Caritas in Veritate [CV]*, no. 21). This synthesis "requires a *deeper critical evaluation of the category of relation*. This is a task that cannot be undertaken by the social sciences alone, insofar as the contribution of disciplines such as metaphysics and theology is needed if man's transcendent dignity is to be properly understood" (*CV*, no. 53). This essay is one such attempt at rethinking business and its purpose in light of this humanistic synthesis and deeper

---

1. Translation at http://www.vatican.va/holy_father/benedict_xvi/encyclicals/documents/hf_ben-xvi_enc_20090629_caritas-in-veritate_en.html.

insight into human relations, and to express what this rethinking practically looks like.[2]

If we are to take hold of this unique moment in history, what is needed is an engaged interdisciplinary exploration that brings to bear on the nature and purpose of business the "logic of gift" in *Caritas in Veritate*. It is precisely this logic that gives us the deep spiritual roots for "comprehensive moral thinking" concerning the firm.[3] The reality of gift provides the rich grounding on which businesspeople can make decisions that enable them to "see things whole." This theological thinking of gift moves us from seeing business as a "society of individuals" expressed in current shareholder (society of shares) and stakeholder (society of interests) models of business, which dominate the academic space of thinking on business, and moves us to seeing business as a "community of persons" grounded in a personalistic communitarian anthropology and ultimately a Trinitarian theology.

This seems to me to be one of Benedict's contributions to the Catholic social tradition — reconnecting us to the theological ground that is the fundamental resource not only to its intellectual understanding but also to its affective connection and willful acts. As I explain, this community of persons stands in contrast to the two dominant models of the corporation understood as the shareholder and stakeholder models. I do this by drawing on Benedict's "logic of gift," and its anthropological and theological underpinnings as the basis of business as a community of persons.

1. The Logic of Gift: The Theological Grounding of Love as Receiving and Giving

In his short essay, "Leisure and Its Threefold Opposition," Josef Pieper states that Christianity has been "well aware of the fact that the highest forms of applied goodness are indeed always effortless because they essentially flow from love." They are effortless because they are by nature gifts. He then states: "'Gifts' — this may well be the key concept."[4] He argues that the key to the moral and spiritual crisis of modern society is the refusal to accept such a gift.

---

2. For past attempts at this rethinking, see S. A. Cortright and Michael Naughton, eds., *Rethinking the Purpose of Business* (Notre Dame: University of Notre Dame Press, 2002).

3. See Kenneth E. Goodpaster, "Corporate Responsibility and Its Constituents," in *Oxford Handbook of Business Ethics,* ed. Tom Beauchamp and George Brenkert (Oxford: Oxford University Press, 2009).

4. Josef Pieper, *Josef Pieper: An Anthology* (San Francisco: Ignatius, 1989), p. 138.

While hedonism presents its own problems in a highly consumeristic and sexually saturated society, the larger problem, Pieper maintains, is "the strange propensity toward hardship that is engraved into the face of our contemporaries as a distinct expectation of suffering."[5] He asks whether this propensity toward work, toward career, toward achievement, toward technological solutions, is the deepest reason for the "refusal to accept a gift, no matter where it comes from?"[6] Have we lost the ability to receive gifts? Have we deluded ourselves that everything is acquired, earned, and achieved?[7]

I raise this particular line of reasoning because I have students read Pieper's essay in an M.B.A. course I teach called "The Great Books."[8] I find that this essay generates a perplexing attitude in my highly driven, goal-oriented students. One of my students in response to this essay stated, "I have a hard time accepting people's help, accepting their gifts." My students have a strong sense of working and giving themselves through their work, which sees relationships as quid pro quo exchanges. They have been brought up on heavy doses of careerism and athleticism within an increasingly technological culture.

What they find most perplexing about Pieper's essay is this notion of *receiving* and how it is actually the ground of their *giving*. What enables us to give authentically, in a way in which we do not exhaust ourselves, in ways that we do not give away ourselves too cheaply, in a way that we "find ourselves," is premised on how we receive. Many of my students feel an increasing alienation from those habits of receptivity, from silence, prayer, Sabbath, worship, and forms of service where they are with the poor rather than just doing things for them. This failure of receptivity is increasingly forming how they look at work, business, and the world. They also, as my student expressed, are uneasy when people give without expecting a return. Such acts do not easily conform to the exchange model they are used to.

There are few better than Nietzsche to explain the person who cannot receive. His "noble man" or "superman" is one who regards "*himself* as determining

---

5. Pieper, *An Anthology*, p. 138. See also Josef Pieper, *Leisure, the Basis of Culture* (South Bend, Ind.: St. Augustine's, 1998), p. 19. In many respects, the hedonism of consumerism and the hardness of careerism are two sides of the same coin often expressed in a common phrase — "work hard, play hard."

6. Pieper, *An Anthology*, p. 139.

7. See Pieper, *Leisure, the Basis of Culture*, chapter 2. Pieper sees this inability to receive as both an ethical and an epistemological problem. He explains that Kant's notion of knowledge work plays a destructive role in this significant problem of not receiving.

8. For a description of this course, see http://www.stthomas.edu/business/about/ethics/greatbooks.html.

values . . . he creates values," he does not receive them.[9] This notion of the person as only creative, active, constructive, distorts the place of the person within the cosmos as well as overrates the role of his own achievements and work within his life. It is in this receptivity, or as Pieper puts it "leisure," that we begin to understand that the human situation "calls not for a resolve but for a rescue," a rescue that can only be *received*. When we take by force those things that should only be received, we violate the divine image inherent within us. This refusal to receive is found in our origins, in the story of the fall of Adam and Eve, when God commands them not to eat "of the tree of the knowledge of good and evil" (Gen. 2:16-17). The moral law is given by God, which we can only receive. We cannot take it, manipulate it, or create it; we can only receive and accept it.[10] If we take and achieve when we should rather be accepting and receiving, we distort our place within God's order and our actions will increasingly be characterized by alienation, distrust, loneliness, and ultimately despair.[11]

Benedict is getting at this modern problem by helping us to see how this dynamic between receiving and giving must be informed by charity. He defines charity as "love received and given" (*CV*, no. 5). The phrase is the beginning of what we mean by a "logic of gift." This logic of receiving and giving is like the inhaling and exhaling of life. It begins to describe the dynamic relationship between the contemplative and active life within the person that informs the nature of relationships that make up communities. It is usually first formed in the experience of the family and nurtured in the church. Its ultimate theological expression is found in the Trinity, that community of Persons who perfectly realize the receiving and giving of relationships. Yet, this dynamic of receiving and giving is not contained only in the family and the church, but these communities inform and color all human activity, including economic activity (*CV*, no. 38). Within the realm of business, when these dimensions of giving and receiving are properly ordered, they create communions/common goods that form a "community of persons."[12] Before addressing the issues in relation to current business thinking, I want to highlight three particular

9. Friedrich Nietzsche, *Beyond Good and Evil* (Oxford: Oxford University Press, 1998), p. 154.

10. Pope John Paul II, *Veritatis Splendor* (Vatican City: Libreria Editrice Vaticana, 1993), nos. 35-37.

11. Pieper calls this despair *acedia*, the deep refusal to be who you were created to be (see *Leisure, the Basis of Culture*, chapter 3).

12. See Pope John Paul II, *Laborem Exercens* (Vatican City: Libreria Editrice Vaticana, 1981). This theme of a community of persons is significant in the thought of John Paul II since it is a term he applies not only to business but also to the family and the church.

claims that this dynamic and complex operation of receiving and giving brings with it, and how these claims inform how we understand business.

The *first* claim is that love as a dynamism of receiving and giving strikes at the heart of how we develop as persons. In the first sentence of the encyclical, Benedict explains that this charity "is the principal driving force behind the authentic development of every person and of all humanity" (*CV,* no. 1). These two fundamental dimensions of our lives, of giving and receiving, of action and contemplation, of work and rest, are not simply two isolated periods of time in human life, but rather they are, as Karl Rahner, S.J., explains, "moments in a person's self-realization which exist only in their relation with one another and are the primary constituents of human existence itself."[13]

The *second* claim, which is of critical importance to highlight in our current situation, is that the receiving dimension of this charity has a certain primacy. The structure of this love "expresses the primacy of acceptance over action, over one's achievement."[14] David Schindler expresses this well: "When we first experience our being as created, as being gifted life, this *receiving* enables us to see our *doing* and *having* . . . as ways of *giving* which they are meant to be."[15] This is why Benedict, as Cardinal Ratzinger, states that the person "comes in the profoundest sense to himself not through what he does but through what he accepts,"[16] not through what he achieves but what he receives. This primacy

13. Karl Rahner, "Theological Remarks on the Problem of Leisure," in *Theological Investigations,* vol. 4, trans. Kevin Smyth (Baltimore: Helicon, 1966), p. 379. Hans Urs von Balthasar explains that humanity's "calling is to *action* because the grace of God always charges him with a mandate or task to be carried out by his own efforts. In thus charging him, however, God draws the recipient of his grace into his confidence, reveals to him a part of the divine plan, and commissions him to realize a part of it by his own strength and ingenuity. . . . But man's calling to action is likewise a calling to contemplation [leisure] because the recipient of grace can understand and complete the task assigned to him only by holding all the more closely and exclusively to the thought of God in gratitude for the trust God has shown him, by undertaking no deed independently of God or that might run counter to God's plan, and by seeking, with his gaze fixed unwaveringly on God, to understand and accomplish the divine will in all things." Hans Urs von Balthasar, *The Christian State of Life,* trans. Sister Mary Frances McCarthy (San Francisco: Ignatius, 1983), p. 80.

14. Joseph Ratzinger, *Introduction to Christianity,* trans. J. R. Foster (San Francisco: Ignatius, 1990), p. 266.

15. David Schindler, "Christology and the Imago Dei: Interpreting Gaudium et spes," *Communio* 23 (Spring 1996): 159. Schindler goes on to explain that "receptivity thus seems to be the primary and indeed constitutive act of the creature's creatureliness. In a word, we have the primacy of the contemplative dimension; receiving (from the Father, in Jesus Christ) is the anterior condition for the creature's being (authentically) creative."

16. Ratzinger, *Introduction to Christianity,* p. 266.

of the receptive can be expressed in the following way: if we do not know how to receive, we will not know how to give; if we do not get leisure (in Pieper's sense) right, we will not get work right; if we do not get the Sabbath or the Lord's Day right, we will not get Monday right; if we do not understand the cultural crisis, we will not understand the financial crisis. As Newman puts it, "if we refuse what has been actually given, we shall be sure to adopt what has not been given" and we will find ourselves in a disordered world with disordered souls.[17]

The *third* claim, which builds on the prior two claims, is that if this deep receptivity fails to animate the economic order, that place where we give of ourselves, we will find ourselves in a disordered relationship in every exchange. This is why Benedict explains that

> the great challenge before us, accentuated by the problems of development in this global era and made even more urgent by the economic and financial crisis, is to demonstrate, in thinking and behaviour, not only that traditional principles of social ethics like transparency, honesty and responsibility cannot be ignored or attenuated, but also that in *commercial relationships* the *principle of gratuitousness* and the logic of gift as an expression of fraternity can and must *find their place within normal economic activity* (*CV*, no. 36).

One way to engage this "logic of gift" with business is to examine how we view the very nature and purpose of the corporation as a dynamic relationship of receiving and giving and then move to see the implications of this relationship. We need to be clear what "logic" animates this important social institution that we call business. A logic of the maximization (shareholder) and a logic of balance (stakeholder) will institutionalize different policies and practices and develop different relationships within business than a logic of gift (*CV*, no. 39). This is particularly of great concern for business schools that introduce and form students in one logic or another.

2. Society of Individuals: The Logic and Limitations of the Shareholder and Stakeholder Models in Light of *Caritas in Veritate*

The two reigning versions of the corporation that dominate the U.S. landscape are the shareholder and stakeholder models. These models of the corporation are two expressions of what I would call a *society of individuals*. While these

---

17. John Henry Newman, "Lectures on the Doctrine of Justification" (1838), http://www.newmanreader.org/works/justification/lecture13.html.

two models are different, they share similar first principles concerning the corporation as a society and the human as an individual. The theological grounding for a *community of persons* presupposed in *Caritas in Veritate* confronts their foundational first principle as a "society of individuals" and their failure to take seriously the primacy of receptivity in how they look at the corporation.

Shareholder Model (logic of profit maximization and the dominance of the market): In this view of the corporation, the shareholder is favored as the central player in the corporation. Those who manage and control the organization do not have the power to choose among values. They are agents to shareholders. Their fiduciary duty as executives is to maximize shareholder wealth. This duty dominates the moral relationship between management and shareholders, which makes the relationship a commodity exchange. Precisely because capital is described in commodity terms, labor, as well as customers, suppliers, and other stakeholders, are also described in commodity terms.[18] Because the corporation is largely seen as a pecuniary property exchange, namely a commodity, the firm is principally described as a "society of shares" where management is expected to discern the best means to achieve maximizing activities of capital.

Managers, then, are not responsible to customers or employees in the same sense that they are responsible to shareholders. They may and usually should respect employees or customers as one of their goals, not because of their dignity as human persons, but rather because respecting employees and customers generates greater return and less risk for shareholder wealth than not respecting them.

Often the general assumption within the shareholder model as a theory is that in a free market where corporations operate, wealth maximization aimed at shareholder value will produce the greatest amount of wealth in a society, which in the end will be the best good for all. The ability of corporations to make a profit for shareholders in a legal manner is the most important single measure of its contribution to society. The intentional pursuit of wealth maximization within the confines of the law and for the long term will produce the greatest good for society. Thus, profit maximization is seen as a means to the common good understood as maximal wealth generation.

This model of corporate life is problematic on several grounds in light of *Caritas in Veritate.* First, the model's notion of profit as an intentional end

---

18. See Louis Putterman, "The Firm as Association versus the Firm as Commodity," *Economics and Philosophy* 4 (1988): 2.

creates a self-referential character of the corporation. The purpose of the corporation is to maximize itself. When business refers to its purpose as the maximization of shareholder wealth, it has created the conditions for corruption since it fails to serve anything but itself, even though some proponents will argue that through the market mechanism this intention to maximize will mechanically contribute to the common good. While its proponents will speak of the constraints of the law or enlightened self-interests as the regulating dimensions of the model, these constraints along with a mechanical view of the overall social good are thin threads to the common good that will always be easily severed.

The problem with this view is that it cannot guarantee what it promises. When maximization logic dominates, you push the person and the firm to the limits of the law and they are one small step from immorality and illegality. It would be like walking on the edge of a cliff and you slip or a gust of wind pushes you off. While you did not intend to fall, you created the conditions to increase the probability of falling. The shareholder model does not intentionally promote illegality and unethical behavior, but it does create conditions for such behavior by providing a commodified and highly instrumental understanding of the firm. For Benedict, profit must be an intentional means not an end. He explains that "profit is useful if it serves as a means towards an end that provides a sense both of how to produce it and how to make good use of it. Once profit becomes the exclusive goal, if it is produced by improper means and without the common good as its ultimate end, it risks destroying wealth and creating poverty" (*CV,* no. 21). Once profit is the end, all relationships within the firm become ever more completely commodified, which increasingly reduces relationships to the thin thread of price.[19]

The second problem area for Benedict is that once profit is an end, the firm becomes dominated by a technical mindset that reduces rationality to its instrumental value and discounts virtue. Within the shareholder model, busi-

---

19. For an excellent example of the problems of commodification, see Cathleen Kaveny, "Living the Fullness of Ordinary Time: A Theological Critique of the Instrumentalization of Time in Professional Life," in *Work as Key to the Social Question* (Vatican City: Libreria Editrice Vaticana, 2002), pp. 111-27. Using lawyers as an example, she explains that the dominance of billable hours within the field of law has led to the commodification of time, which increasingly squeezes out other values such as mentoring, pro bono work, and the meaning of justice. "Its key feature is an ability to assign market value, to give a dollar equivalent of the commodified item. An hour of a lawyer's time is directly translatable into a substantial amount of money." While work has a commodity dimension to it, the danger arises when it becomes completely commodified.

ness is largely a technical activity to maximize wealth for the long term. While it asserts that wealth maximization will achieve the good of all in terms of enhanced GDP, it will do so largely through technical means. Virtues such as justice and practical wisdom are largely discounted since the mechanism of the market eventually guides the wealth-producing techniques to the best outcome. Benedict explains that "when technology is allowed to take over, the result is confusion between ends and means, such that the sole criterion for action in business is thought to be the maximization of profit, in politics the consolidation of power, and in science the findings of research" (CV, no. 71).[20]

When the corporation is perceived as a mere engine for maximum financial return to shareholders, consideration of the legitimate interests of stakeholders is reduced to an instrumental exercise in the strategy of the chessboard: interests are checked and balanced in order to channel the single-mindedly pecuniary interests of the corporation in those directions at once least objectionable to outside interests and most rewarding for shareholders. Its ways of thinking become dominated by an instrumental rationality that forms calculating souls who lose the capacity not only to serve society but to develop in an integral way. This is because a moral rationality of the virtues, especially prudence and justice, is discounted by the instrumental rationality of technique. The logic of means dominates the logic of ends. The leader in this model becomes the technocrat/bureaucrat whose criterion for truth is the measurement of efficiency and profitability, reducing all relationships to commodity exchanges, and when this happens "development is automatically denied" (CV, no. 70).

Third, for Benedict, the application of the shareholder model in our current global economic system reveals its fundamental inadequacy. He is particularly concerned about the maximization logic in relation to what Jeff Gates coined "disconnected capital," which is increasingly predominating publicly traded companies.[21] As "disconnected" capital searches for ever-increasing

20. See also John Paul II's understanding of alienation as the reversal of means and ends, *Centesimus Annus* (Vatican City: Libreria Editrice Vaticana, 1991), no. 41.

21. See Jeff Gates, *The Ownership Solution* (Reading: Addison-Wesley, 1998). In 1932 Berle and Means explained in part the reasons for this disconnection. "The spiritual values that formerly went with ownership have been separated from it. Physical property capable of being shaped by its owner could bring to him direct satisfaction apart from the income it yielded in more concrete form. It represented an extension of his own personality. With the corporate revolution, this quality has been lost to the property owner much as it has been to the worker through the industrial revolution." Adolf Berle and Gardiner Means, *The Modern Corporation and Private Property* (Houston: Transaction, 1932), pp. 64-65.

returns by impersonal forces of non-liable investors, the corporation limits its capacity for the common good. Benedict explains that "owing to their growth in scale and the need for more and more capital, it is becoming increasingly rare for business enterprises to be in the hands of a stable director who feels responsible in the long term, not just the short term, for the life and the results of his company, and it is becoming increasingly rare for businesses to depend on a single territory. . . . In recent years a new cosmopolitan class of *managers* has emerged, who are often answerable only to the shareholders generally consisting of anonymous funds which *de facto* determine their remuneration" (*CV,* no. 40). What particularly concerns Benedict is the impact of such an economy on culture, a culture that is becoming more materialistic, consumeristic, relativistic, technologically oriented, and disconnected.

One example of this disconnected phenomenon mentioned by Benedict is outsourcing production, which can "weaken the company's sense of responsibility towards the stakeholders . . . in favour of the shareholders." This disconnect happens on multiple levels. Final consumers are disconnected from those who produce products, often failing to realize the subliving wages, lack of rest, and poor working conditions that supplied such products. Suppliers, for example, often find themselves in increasing commodity relationships with their customers where practices such as reverse auctioning, extending payments to 120 days, shifting all risks to suppliers (tooling, materials, etc.), unilateral price reductions, and the like, completely commodify relations. These highly draconian demands on suppliers create a "cannibalizing" effect on their organizations, which makes it more difficult for these companies to become places where employees can develop. Such demands have significant multiplying effects since these suppliers are now pressured to squeeze out cost savings from their own suppliers, thus extending the commodifying disease.[22]

All of this is not to deny the fiduciary duty that managers owe to owners and investors, but such a duty cannot exhaust the moral relationship of the manager or the firm. The stakeholder model has done much to bring this forward.

Stakeholder Model (logic of balance [and equivalency] and dominance of contract): In the second view called the stakeholder model, the corporation as a "society of interests" favors a balanced mediation among various interests of stakeholders within the corporation such as employees, customers, suppliers, the broader community, and shareholders. In their classic work on the corporation, Berle and Means argue that "the 'control' of the great corporations

---

22. For a case on this situation, see Michael Naughton and David Specht, *Faithful Leaders in Difficult Times* (Mahwah, N.J.: Paulist, 2011), chapter 4.

should develop into a purely neutral technocracy, balancing a variety of claims by various groups in the community and assigning to each a portion of the income stream on the basis of public policy rather than private cupidity."[23] Management is charged with balancing the competing interests of a variety of groups that participate in corporations. While there are various types of interests in the corporation, for the most part interests are understood in terms of external goods such as monetary wealth. Here the firm is largely seen as an "equilibrating mechanism." Management arbitrates the conflicting claims and interests of the multiple stakeholders in the firm keeping the firm "in balance," which is seen as the optimum state of the firm, creating what we might call balancing or procedural mentalities.

This stakeholder model has produced helpful methods such as the "balance scorecard," triple bottom line reporting schemes, and other innovative programs to operationalize its perspective within corporations. While there are various schools within this stakeholder model, social contract theory has been a major influence on its normative claims, seeing the firm as a bundle of contracts. Instead of maximizing the profit for shareholders, "the firm maximizes the function that represents the solution to the negotiation game among all the stakeholders."[24]

As others have explained, the moral horizon of this view of the corporation is still stuck in a highly individualistic anthropology that fails to promote the common good.[25] While certainly a better model than the shareholder model, the stakeholder model tends to be dominated by a "logic of interests" rather than a "logic of responsibilities." Its focus is what individuals *have* in the firm (stakes) rather than how persons *are in relation* to the firm (community). Thus, all goods are *allocative* or distributed, diminished when shared, and there is little consideration of *participative goods* that are not diminished when shared. There is no deeper sense of the common good and the kind of *relations* that are necessary to create a community of persons that can foster this kind of good in the corporation. In the words of Benedict, the stakeholder model fails to provide "a *deeper critical evaluation of the category of relation*" (*CV*, no. 53).

While Benedict is not as direct in terms of his critique of the stakeholder model as he is of the shareholder model, he does express reservations over the

---

23. Berle and Means, *The Modern Corporation*, pp. 312-13.

24. Stefano Zamagni, "What CST Can Contribute to CSR," p. 6, available online at http://www.stthomas.edu/cathstudies/cst/conferences/thegoodcompany/Finalpapers/Zamagni%2005.10.06%2011.pdf.

25. See Helen Alford, "Stakeholder Theory," available online at http://www.stthomas.edu/cathstudies/cst/conferences/thegoodcompany/Finalpapers/Alford%2007.10.06%209.00.pdf.

current understanding of "business ethics" that is severed from a theological anthropology that has the capacity to bind people together. He explains that

> it would be advisable . . . to develop a sound criterion of discernment, since the adjective "ethical" can be abused. Much in fact depends on the underlying system of morality. On this subject the Church's social doctrine can make a specific contribution, since it is based on man's creation "in the image of God" (Gen. 1:27), a datum which gives rise to the inviolable dignity of the human person and the transcendent value of natural moral norms. When business ethics prescinds from these two pillars, it inevitably risks losing its distinctive nature and it falls prey to forms of exploitation; more specifically, it risks becoming subservient to existing economic and financial systems rather than correcting their dysfunctional aspects. (*CV,* no. 45)

The stakeholder model brings to light the importance of managing the firm in a way that is accountable to its key stakeholders, but what Benedict makes clear is that without a comprehensive moral vision of the person and the community in which that person fits, the moral conditions of the firm will always be prone to exploitation. Ken Goodpaster has noted this problem as well. He explains that without a richer and more comprehensive vision, stakeholder thinking will be prone to two risks: "(1) that it might accept uncritically the idea of stakeholder *satisfaction* as a surrogate for stakeholder *value,* and (2) that it might substitute *aggregation* of stakeholder satisfactions for normative principles that are less amenable to such a reductive methodology."[26] If moral principles such as human dignity and the common good do not inform the satisfactions of a corporation's stakeholders, there is a good chance, in the words of Benedict, that such a corporation will perpetuate "forms of exploitation" and "dysfunctional aspects."

Goodpaster provides an example of the exploitation and dysfunctionality of the stakeholder thinking within British American Tobacco (BAT). Its "Core Beliefs" are the following:

> We believe in creating long term shareholder value.
> We believe in engaging constructively with our stakeholders.
> We believe in creating inspiring working environments for our people.
> We believe in adding value to the communities in which we operate.
> We believe that suppliers and other business partners should have the opportunity to benefit from their relationship with us.

26. Goodpaster, "Corporate Responsibility and Its Constituents," p. 140.

Besides these stakeholders, the company also generously contributes a portion of its profits to various social causes. Its stakeholder orientation is further promoted with its customers since the company provides the "choice" to smoke or not. This choice premise is often associated with a defense of capitalism since it is an economic system that enhances our choices on a whole set of areas: tobacco, detergent, pornography, cereal, abortion, yogurt, guns, cars, euthanasia, and so on. While our choices are limited by restrictions they may have on the free choices of others (social contract, "my freedom to move my fist must be limited to the proximity of your chin"), no free choice can be normatively better than another, except in terms of choices that restrict the freedom of another person. Thus, "the only freedom which deserves the name is that of pursuing our own good in our way, so long as we do not attempt to deprive others of theirs."[27] Prescinding from the dignity of the person that has a transcendent vision of the human, the stakeholder thinking within the BAT fails to seriously consider the common good and the obvious moral consideration of diversifying away from tobacco products.[28]

At its best, the stakeholder model can bring greater equality and fairness than the shareholder model, but it cannot bring us a deeper bond of community. It can make us neighbors but not brothers and sisters (*CV*, no. 19). It can help us recognize our interdependence on each other but it cannot bring us solidarity. As Benedict explains, "Reason, by itself, is capable of grasping the equality between men and of giving stability to their civic coexistence, but it cannot establish fraternity" (*CV*, no. 19). The stakeholder model helps us to see the implications of the interactions of various stakeholders, but it does not have the capacity to see the deeper possibility of what a firm looks like as a "community of persons." This entails the logic of gift. This logic is not some gnostic seeing privileged to only a few. Benedict explains that this logic of gift, this charity in truth, is "received by everyone" and it "is a force that builds community" (*CV*, no. 34). It builds community by tapping us into the very foundation of love as receiving and giving. The logic of gift connects us with this deep sense of receptivity, that what I have is not mine, but a gift, which is first given and that as a gift its fulfillment is found in the deep need to give to another, in service to another. This deep sense of gift, of receiving and giving, of community, is first experienced in the family and nurtured in faith.

We come into the world not through a contract, but through a gift. The stakeholder model informed by a social contract theory is not robust enough

---

27. John Stuart Mill, *On Liberty* (New York: New American Library, 1962 [1859]), p. 138.
28. Goodpaster, "Corporate Responsibility," p. 141.

to tap into the "logic of gift," which reveals the deeper moral reality of the corporation as a community of persons bonded through the reciprocal relationship of receiving and giving. We need a view of the corporation and the person within it that opens us up *"to forms of economic activity marked by quotas of gratuitousness and communion"* (*CV*, no. 39). What is needed is an understanding of the firm not rooted in a logic of the market or of a contract, but a logic of gift nurtured in a moral and spiritual culture that has the capacity to see the fundamental giftedness of life. To this task we now turn.

3. Community of Persons: The Corporation Informed by the Logic of Gift

> *What life have you if you have not life together?*
> *There is no life that is not in community,*
> *And no community not lived in praise of God.*

T. S. Eliot[29]

This logic of gift, this love that is received and given, is the fundamental basis of integral human development and it is what enables us to participate in the relational structure of human living that gives us the possibility of going beyond the utilitarian, contractual, and calculative "society of individuals" that is increasingly dominating modern culture. This insight of the human dynamism of receiving and giving gives us the vision to challenge "the conviction that the economy must be autonomous, that it must be shielded from 'influences' of a moral character," of a deeper receptivity (*CV*, no. 34). It begins to overturn the radical separations between public and private, faith and work, spiritual and material, fact and value, normative and positive sciences, all of which compartmentalize human activity and further divide the human person. These divisions block the notion of a "community of persons" rooted in familial and religious experience; this community is barred from entering the economic sphere and is replaced by a society of individuals. If business is to be a

---

29. T. S. Eliot, *Choruses from The Rock* (London: Faber & Faber, 1934). The poem offers to the imagination the divine in what appears to be the empty and impersonal character of modern work life. Better than most poets, Eliot captures a fundamental truth in three lines, which will take me the rest of the essay to explain. We are made to live together not in an impersonal society, but as a community where we come to know each other as persons in relation to each other and to God.

place where people can integrally develop as persons, business must "make room" and provide space for a "logic of gift" that orients people to deeper levels of communion, solidarity, and fraternity.

While Benedict does not use the phrase "community of persons" to describe the business firm in *Caritas in Veritate,* he speaks throughout the document of the importance of relations, of communion, of community within economic life.[30] John Paul II was explicit in using this phrase. In *Centesimus Annus,* he explains that "the purpose of a business firm is not simply to make a profit, but is to be found in its very existence as a *community of persons* who in various ways are endeavoring to satisfy their basic needs, and who form a particular group at the service of the whole of society."[31] This personal and communal reality of the corporation has been a major theme within the Catholic social tradition.[32] While the phrase "community of persons" is rarely used in business literature today, it actually gets closest to what we mean by the word "company" and "corporation." The word "company" comes from "companions," *cum* — with and *panis* — bread, breaking bread together. The word "corporation" comes from the Latin *corpus,* which means "body," a *corps,* a group of people "united in one body." An *esprit de corps* is a shared spirit of companions who work for a common cause that is a force for good.

These etymologies clue us into the deeper meaning of the business firm, a meaning that has been too often suppressed by a distorted anthropology that has commodified relationships and instrumentalized rationality. The clue, however, is found not originally in business itself but in the place where we originally break bread together, where we are united as one body, where most people experience for the first time a community, namely, family and religion.[33]

30. Benedict did, however, use the phrase "community of persons" in reference to business in an address to Italian business leaders (see http://www.zenit.org/rssenglish-28687).

31. Pope John Paul II, *Centesimus Annus,* no. 35. Translation at http://www.vatican.va/holy_father/john_paul_ii/encyclicals/documents/hf_jp-ii_enc_01051991_centesimus-annus_en.html.

32. Jean-Yves Calvez and Michael Naughton, "Catholic Social Teaching and the Purpose of the Business Organization," in *Rethinking the Purpose of Business: Interdisciplinary Essays in the Catholic Social Tradition,* ed. S. A. Cortright and M. J. Naughton (Notre Dame: University of Notre Dame Press, 2002), pp. 3-19.

33. Culture, properly understood, *cultivates* within us a way of seeing the world, to see what is real, to make sense of reality. It creates in us, when it is operating well, a deep sensitivity to what is important and worthy of sacrifice. It forms within us what is moral and spiritual, what is most worthy in our lives, by helping us to understand the deep human reality of our origins and our destiny. It helps us to sort through all the data, all the ideas, all the alternatives, and land on what counts in life. Christopher Dawson explains that "culture is a common social

Business is a secondary institution and takes its cue from the primary institutions of family and faith. For this reason, business and the activity of work is a limited good and never exhausts the vocation of the person.[34] The person is first made for God and life eternal before he or she is a member of a firm. He or she is constituted as part of a familial society before being constituted to be part of an economic society (although in the past, these two societies were not institutionally separated).

Presupposed in *Caritas in Veritate* is that we need cultural institutions such as the church and family that provide us deep roots to remind us what we are created for (*CV*, no. 38). Family and religion are the two primary institutions of culture, and they ought to serve as the embedded soil out of which corporations humanly grow. When they are at their best, the family and religion give to the corporation its fundamental human form, precisely because it is in the family and religion where people learn to be a community of persons, where they learn how to relate and communicate to each other, where they learn virtue. This is the way culture animates and influences the corporate form and makes it human. The human form of a corporation does not primarily come from the market or the law, but from culture and its institutions. Once we sever this embedded cultural relationship, we fail to limit the economic system as well as inform such a system with moral and spiritual meaning.[35]

This is not as abstract as it seems. Many family and entrepreneurial businesses see this firsthand. Family businesses in particular live at a crossroads of the economy and culture. John Ward, in his study of family-run businesses, provides a helpful distinction between functional versus foundational principles that helps us to see the relationship between culture and business.[36] He explains that non-family businesses often base themselves on functional values

---

way of life — a way of life with a tradition behind it, which has embodied itself in institutions and which involves moral standards and principles." Christopher Dawson, *The Historic Reality of Christian Culture: A Way to the Renewal of Human Life* (New York: Harper & Brothers, 1960), p. 13.

34. Jacques Maritain, *The Person and the Common Good* (Notre Dame: University of Notre Dame Press, 1966), p. 66.

35. See S. A. Cortright, Ernest S. Pierucci, and Michael J. Naughton, "A Social Property Ethic for the Corporation in Light of Catholic Social Thought," *Logos* (Fall 1999): 138-54.

36. I heard this distinction in a talk by Ward. He used the word "values" rather than "principles." Unfortunately, I have not been able to track down the talk or any of his writings where he uses this distinction. Nonetheless, the distinction is implied in his writings. See Craig E. Aronoff and John L. Ward, *Family Business Values* (Marietta: Family Enterprise, 2001), chapter 1.

such as profits, teamwork, innovation, creativity, industriousness, and the like. These values are obviously important to running a business, but they do not touch the person in any profound fashion in relation to community, fraternity, or solidarity with the other, nor do they provide any kind of distinctive vision to the business itself. Family-run and entrepreneurial businesses are often informed by a richer understanding of principles that are more *foundational* and that often connect to the deeper meaning of the person. These families and entrepreneurs connect their existence as a business to their family, which often, although certainly not always, entails a religious dimension. Companies such as Cadbury (Quaker), Malden Mills (Jewish), Herman Miller (Calvinist), Service Master (Evangelical), Dayton Hudson, now Target (Presbyterian), Cummings Engine (Disciples of Christ), Mondragon (Catholic), and many others have had profoundly religious influence.[37] The founders and leaders of these companies were culturally embedded in a faith tradition. This religious culture imbued them with a theological vision and moral orientation that informed their practical decisions. They saw their company not as a society of shares or society of interests, but as a community of persons.

The rest of this section explores how some of these companies practically express this community of persons, and the underlying moral and theological premises for such a community of persons. Benedict mentions that economic and business life "needs works redolent of the *spirit of gift*" (*CV,* no. 37). While there is much more theoretical structure concerning the firm that needs to be done, it might be more helpful to see the practical expressions of a community of persons, which will give rise to the importance of the theoretical distinctions. At this juncture, then, we might learn more about this model by looking at practical experience.

4. Practical Expressions of a Community of Persons[38]

So what does a corporation as a community of persons look like? There are a lot of companies that live out this "community of persons" but that never use

37. See Patrick E. Murphy and Georges Enderle, "Managerial Ethical Leadership: Examples Do Matter," *Business Ethics Quarterly* (January 1995): 117-28. See also Jeffrey Cornwall and Michael Naughton, *Bringing Your Business to Life* (Ventura: Regal, 2008).

38. "Space also needs to be created within the market for economic activity carried out by subjects who freely choose to act according to principles other than those of pure profit, without sacrificing the production of economic value in the process. The many economic entities that draw their origin from religious and lay initiatives demonstrate that this is con-

the term. For many leaders and workers, their commitment to a community of persons is more intuitive and not conceptual. Nonetheless, what they ask in their own particular way is a very important question that clues us into this lived experience of a community of persons: *what carries the weight of a real relationship in regards to the practices and policies of a company?* Let me give two cases, one concerning layoffs and firings and the other concerning wages.[39]

What carries the weight of a real relationship in regards to the practice and policy of laying off and firing someone? There are all sorts of issues concerning whether one should lay off or fire and when (one company has described this as "the last alternative layoff policy"). Assuming the layoff or firing is just, how should one treat the person being laid off? At the Tomasso Corporation in Montreal, managers who lay off or fire employees must meet with those employees at least two times within a year after dismissal. This is policy. The reasons for this practice are multiple, but primarily they circle around two principles that serve as the pillars of a community of persons. The first is human dignity. Management needs to follow up to be sure that the former employees are alright and to see if they need further help. The second principle is the common good, especially in terms of reconciliation, that good which is shared in common with another. When dismissed employees leave a company, animosity and tension are usually the parting feelings. This conflict does not go away for both the dismissed employee and the manager who is dismissing, but rather becomes submerged in their deeper subconsciousness. Providing an opportunity for conversation furthers the common good by reconciling the conflicts and tensions.

This practice was developed by the former owner of Tomasso, Robert Ouimet, because as a Catholic he believed in the importance of spiritual reconciliation that was nurtured in him through the Sacrament of Reconciliation. Without this deep connection to this sacrament, there is little chance Ouimet would have even considered such a practice. If employees are seen as only individuals, forms of "human capital," there would be no need to follow up with them; however, if they are seen as *persons,* endowed with "human dignity," made in the image of God, destined for the kingdom, then the rela-

---

cretely possible" (*CV,* no. 37). See, for example, the companies associated with the Economy of Communion, family businesses, cooperatives, entrepreneurial ventures, and other types of firms inspired by faith. These communities of persons are not without their contracts and economic rationality, but these realities do not exhaust the meaning of such communities.

39. For the full cases of these two examples, see Naughton and Specht, *Faithful Leaders in Difficult Times.*

tionship between managers and laid-off employees demands the use of compelling practices that genuinely reflect the values of solidarity and reconciliation. This view of layoffs and employees is very different from that of a manager I interviewed who was facing her own set of layoffs. She said that the employees she was about to lay off would no longer be part of her company and she was no longer responsible for them. Those laid off were individuals who could take care of themselves. Her responsibilities were with survivors, not with those who were gone.

In terms of wages, we need to ask a similar question: *what carries the weight of a real relationship in regards to the practice and policy of compensation?* Reell Precision Manufacturing in St. Paul, Minnesota, operates on the practical application of Judeo-Christian values for the "growth of people."[40] Based on its mission, Reell believes that all its workers should at least be paid a "living wage" or what it calls a "target wage." In 1996 when Reell first developed the idea of a target wage, its estimate of a living wage in St. Paul was $11/hour ($22,000/year). The actual market wage or "sustainable wage" for assemblers in the company was $7/hour ($14,000/year). The $4 discrepancy between a living wage and a sustainable wage was a tension between two principles operating in the company: the principle of *need* and the principle of *economic order*. While the management of Reell desired to pay its employees not only their market worth, but also the worth of who they are (persons made in the image of God who deserve at least a minimum of need), management was all too aware that customers would only pay for the "instrumental value" of work, namely, the market wage. If Reell would pay $11/ hour while competitors paid $7, Reell's cost disadvantage would increase their likelihood of losing customers. Realizing that the *ought* of a living wage always implies the *can* of a sustainable wage, the company had to seriously rethink how it was doing business and act creatively.

This rethinking took place on several levels. First, Reell's leadership resisted capitulating their responsibilities to the mechanical force of labor markets or to simply contracts. They saw themselves as distributors of justice in the marketplace and not as mere technicians or contractarians. In order for there to be a "right relationship" between employee and employer, both need to recognize that work can never be reduced to the pay given, that is, the wage given can never fully account for the labor done, precisely because work is

---

40. See Michael Naughton, "Distributors of Justice: A Case for a Just Wage," *America*, May 2000, pp. 13-15. See Helen Alford and Michael Naughton, "Just Wages," in *Managing as if Faith Mattered* (Notre Dame: University of Notre Dame Press, 2001).

always "more" than its economic output or instrumental value. It is precisely this recognition that is a direct implication of the logic of gift.[41]

Second, Reell's leadership realized that every action has a reaction and that raising wage levels without changing the work process would have serious consequences on their cost structure. So in order to raise *labor rates* to pay a living wage, they would have to reduce their overall *total costs*. They eventually saw that low wages were merely a symptom of a much larger problem of how the company worked. When work is designed to use $7 of talent, it is difficult to pay people anything more than that amount. It is also difficult to have a real relationship with your employees when you as an employer cannot pay a wage that meets their basic needs. More than anything, it was this relational character that drove the revising of Reell's compensation system to include a target wage.

A corporation as a community of persons demands its leaders to embrace justice. It is difficult to believe, for example, that Reell could have developed a target wage policy if it was only concerned about employees' instrumental effect on shareholder value. Rather, the company saw employees as more than "factors of production" or simply "costs" to be reduced. Management saw employees as who they *really* are: persons made to be treated with human dignity because they are created in the image of God destined for glory. Wages are not simply economic exchanges, but rather are part of a much larger relationship that informs a community of persons.

For the founders and leaders of these two companies, however, justice is not some abstract social contract, but it comes from the deep human relationships expressed through family and nurtured through faith in the church. These leaders and their companies are far from perfect, but their operating premises open them up, subjecting a whole assortment of practices and policies within a firm to a community-of-persons question: do the practices and policies of job design, hiring, ownership, customer and supplier relationships, environmental practices, benefits, unionization, incentives, community giving, financing, and the like carry the weight of a real relationship that has the ca-

---

41. See *Caritas in Veritate*, no. 35: "In fact, if the market is governed solely by the principle of the equivalence in value of exchanged goods, it cannot produce the social cohesion that it requires in order to function well. *Without internal forms of solidarity and mutual trust, the market cannot completely fulfill its proper economic function.* And today it is this trust which has ceased to exist, and the loss of trust is a grave loss." See also Pieper, *Leisure, the Basis of Culture*, pp. 45-47, where the insight of the honorarium, which recognizes that "an incommensurability exists between performance [work] and recompense [pay], and that the performance cannot 'really' be recompensed," is the basis of a just wage.

pacity to create stronger bonds of communion to form an authentic community of persons?

Conclusion: Further Work

There is much more to be done to explore the logic of gift and its implications for business. First, to conceptually understand this idea of a corporation as a community of persons in contrast to a society of individuals, it is of critical importance to see the relationality among persons within this community in terms of a morally comprehensive picture. The comprehensiveness is found in the anthropological distinction between a *person* and an *individual* as well as between a *community* and *society*. If we inform these distinctions through the principles of human dignity and the common good we begin to see the difference between a community of persons and a society of individuals.

Second, we need to develop a more robust theological understanding of institutional life, because it is precisely a theological vision of organizational life that illumines its worthiness as a calling. The organization as a community of persons is deeply rooted in the personalist communitarian anthropology that is grounded in a Trinitarian and incarnational understanding of the world. As the Trinity is a community of persons, we who image this Trinitarian God reflect, however imperfectly, this community in the institutions in which we operate, principally and primarily in the family and church, but also in the corporation, the state, volunteering, and so on. Because we are made in the image of God, we are encoded with a spiritual and moral Trinitarian pattern. This Trinitarian pattern "will bring to our vision of the world a new criterion for interpreting it."[42] Understood as an image of this Trinitarian God, the person is viewed in his or her nature as a relational being and fulfilled in terms of a community of persons. If we continue, however, to sever this theological vision by always relegating it to the sidelines, we will find ourselves cut off from its source and subjected to the shareholder and stakeholder models, which will leave us unanchored from our deepest nature.

It is precisely here that *Caritas in Veritate*'s contribution lies — to remind us of our deepest nature. Thomas Rourke explains that at the root of Bene-

---

42. Pope John Paul II, *Sollicitudo Rei Socialis*, no. 40. Translation at http://www.vatican.va/holy_father/john_paul_ii/encyclicals/documents/hf_jp-ii_enc_30121987_sollicitudo-rei-socialis_en.html. See also Amelia J. Uelmen, "Toward a Trinitarian Theory of Products Liability," *Journal of Catholic Social Thought* 1 (2004): 603, 624-26 (reflecting on *Sollicitudo Rei Socialis*'s Trinitarian contribution to Catholic social thought and its application to product liability).

dict XVI's understanding of social doctrine is a "spirituality of communion." Rourke explains that it is "in the community of the divine persons that we discover the spiritual roots of the human community."[43] Key to this understanding of the person in community is the relationship between *receiving* and *giving*, which I described at the beginning of this essay. The Trinity reveals to us a perfect community of giving and receiving, of gift and receptivity, which models for us the pattern of social relationships within institutions that helps us to see what we and others look like when we are at our best.[44] Of course, our understanding and imitation of this perfect community are imperfect and will always be clouded by our own sinfulness. Yet, if we are not to ruin ourselves in our work, we must begin to appropriate this pattern of gift in our relationships at work.[45] The shareholder and stakeholder models are not robust enough to key us into this human reality of relationality, which is why a business as a community of persons needs a deeper reflection than what it has been currently given.

43. Thomas Rourke, *The Social and Political Thought of Benedict XVI* (Lanham: Lexington, 2010), p. 18.

44. Miroslav Volf explains that the modeling of the Trinity in whose image we are made should be understood analogously, not univocally. "As creatures, human beings can correspond to the uncreated God only in a *creaturely* way," and in particular a sinful creaturely way. Miroslav Volf, "'The Trinity Is Our Social Program': The Doctrine of The Trinity and the Shape of Social Engagement," *Modern Theology* 14 (1998): 403, 405.

45. Lorna Gold, *The Sharing Economy: Solidarity Networks Transforming Globalization* (Farnham, Surrey, U.K.: Ashgate, 2004), pp. 61-62.

Will Understanding the Principle of Gratuitousness Help Save the Soul of a Lapsed Economist?

Theodore Tsukahara Jr.

Product Warning Label

I have no formal training as a theologian or as a philosopher. My days as a practicing economist are in the distant past. When I entered the world of finance I was advised not to refer to myself as an economist because it would not give me much credibility in this new world. My return to academic life was built on the analytical tools I used in my business career. Although I continued to read economics after leaving my early career teaching it, I found myself increasingly being moved to the fringe of the discipline intellectually. The mathematics continued to be more arcane, the search for evidence more complex, and the conversations channeled into thinner silos. Also, please keep in mind that my teaching activities for almost the past decade have been in a Great Books–centered curriculum that influences not only my approach to academic inquiry but also to the charge for this session "to look at the theoretical work done by economists on the logic of the gift and lay out a program for furthering this critical area of research." Thus, if

I would like to thank my colleagues at Saint Mary's College for sharing their knowledge and perspective about the arguments in this presentation. Father John Morris, O.P., and Father Tom McElligott helped me appreciate the ideas of *Caritas in Veritate*. Conversations with Brother Donald Mansir, F.S.C., and Brother Raphael Patton, F.S.C., clarified themes in this presentation. I owe a debt to Steven Cortright for discussion of Rawls, Catholic social teaching, and Greek, and to Michael Riley for resurrecting my dormant Latin. Finally, I am grateful for the inspiration on Catholic intellectual tradition provided by Father John C. Haughey, S.J., Woodstock Theological Center. However, all errors of fact and of interpretation are mine.

you are seeking an analysis of *Caritas in Veritate (CV)* that most economists would recognize, perhaps what I present to you in the narrative that follows may not be it.

"Let us remember that we are in the holy presence of God." If this little prayer stirs old memories for you, then you and I share a history that makes us receptive to the theology of *Caritas in Veritate* and the practical challenges it raises for us. I first heard this call for reflection that traditionally began each activity at schools run by the Brothers of the Christian Schools when I entered Cathedral High School in Los Angeles as a freshman in 1954. My impression then as a non-Catholic with only an introduction to the basics of Catholicism according to the Baltimore Catechism in required lessons at the parochial elementary school I attended, was that I should be aware that my actions were being always evaluated by a watchful God. However, it did not take long for this phrase to become simply a reflexive mantra. Now with the benefit of old age and of a formal program of study of the Lasallian charism, I understand that this prayer is a purposeful nudge to remind me to look for God in each and every one I interact with in my daily activities. Furthermore, as a partner with the Brothers in their vocation to conduct schools "Together and by Association," I should faithfully direct my priorities to develop intellectual freedom and a desire to seek Truth in our students. After all, education is social justice.

Is Economic Theory Amoral?

What is the true subject of economics? The conventional view is that it is the "science" of exchange in society. The fundamental "law" is that efficiency in the exchange of goods and services will lead to distributional equity in their consumption that will result in collective societal satisfaction. The basic myth is the "free" market — that the dynamics of competition will correct naturally any short-term imbalances in market power in the long run. In *Caritas in Veritate* gift is inspired by charity, thus no exchange is expected. Does this mean that economists through careful analysis of economic theory can construct models that clearly address gift in a world of exchange, or should they simply hand the problem back to the theologians and philosophers for their continued study? If it is possible to incorporate a concept of gift consistent with *Caritas in Veritate,* how does it guide public policy? Is there a "moral foundation of economics"? Let us begin with the last question.

"Economics as a Moral Science"[1] was the title of the President's Lecture delivered by Kenneth Boulding during the annual meeting of the Allied Social Science Associations (ASSA) held in Chicago just after Christmas 1968. In his remarks, Boulding identified the "accidental" association of morality with economics via the "father" of this discipline, Adam Smith:

> Adam Smith, who has strong claim to being both the Adam and the smith of systematic economics, was a professor of moral philosophy, and it was at that forge that economics was made. . . . It can claim to be a moral science for its origin, if for no other reason. Nevertheless, to many economists the very term "moral science" will seem like a contradiction.[2]

As a young graduate student in economics, I was taught to view the discipline to be "value-free"; its axioms were readily defensible via the cold calculus of logical analyses. The theoretical underpinning of the discipline was presented to me cloaked in the language of multivariable calculus, linear algebra, and game theory. The scientific method to validate the claims of theory was rooted in the formal methods of probability and statistics. Thus, Boulding's observations about value in his lecture provided me with a very useful intellectual challenge:

> Every culture, or subculture, is defined by a set of common values, that is, generally agreed-on preferences. Without a core of common values a culture cannot exist, and we can classify society into cultures and subcultures precisely because it is possible to identify groups that have common values. Most tastes are in fact also common values and have been learned by the process by which all learning is done, that is, by mutation and selection.[3]

Boulding in an earlier essay cautioned that "theology and economics — along with all other theoretical frameworks — represent abstractions from reality, and hence we do not expect them to cover much of the same material."[4] Both theology and economics rely on the comfort of deductive methods that yield a sense of what may be possible for man even when reality may lead to

---

1. Kenneth Boulding, "Economics as a Moral Science," *American Economic Review* (March 1969): 1-12. Adapted version, chapter 6 in Kenneth Boulding, *Economics as a Science* (New York: McGraw-Hill, 1970). He was a devout Quaker.

2. Boulding, *Economics as a Science*, p. 117.

3. Boulding, *Economics as a Science*, p. 118.

4. Kenneth Boulding, *Beyond Economics: Essays on Society, Religion, and Ethics* (Ann Arbor: University of Michigan Press, 1970), p. 187.

hopelessness. Thus, Boulding finds a useful analogy to connect the practices guided by theology to those inspired by economics:

> To seek God is to find man. To live deeply with the life of Jesus, as revealed in the Gospels, is to know the glory, wonder, folly, and depravity of man in his fullness. Unless the economist has something of this sense of the fullness of man he will be in constant danger of misusing his abstraction, particularly as applied to the interpretation of history and in developing an appraisal of economic policy.[5]

Boulding seems to suggest that the economist who wants to put his beliefs into practice must discover his soul. The moral foundations of economics are embedded in the actors who inhabit this world,[6] for as Benedict XVI observes, "there is a convergence between economic science and moral evaluation. Human costs always include economic costs, and economic dysfunctions always involve human costs" (*CV,* no. 32).

Amartya Sen[7] makes a convincing case that *homo oeconomicus* must be transformed from a "rational fool" into a more tangible being.[8] He argues that for economics to become more socially productive, it must give explicit attention to the ethical considerations that shape human behavior and judgment. Thus it may be safe to conclude that conventional economic theory lacks any formal moral underpinnings.

An Economic Analysis of Love

Now let us turn to the question if economic theory is robust enough to accommodate the principle of gratuitousness. Boulding in the ASSA lecture cited

5. Boulding, *Beyond Economics,* p. 194.

6. A. Barrera, *Economic Compulsion and Christian Ethics* (New York: Cambridge University Press, 2005), provides an analysis of how negative externalities created by a market can compel economic agents to make undesirable and unintended choices. Chapter 6 applies his analysis to governmental policies to protect agricultural markets.

7. Sen is a Nobel Laureate (1998) and a past president of the American Economic Association (1994). His election gave some economists hope that the discipline had started a return to its moral philosophy roots.

8. This argument originates in A. Sen, "Rational Fools: A Critique of the Behavioral Foundations of Economic Theory," *Philosophy and Public Affairs* 6, no. 4 (1977): 317-44. I have adopted Barrera's spelling of *homo oeconomicus* for this text instead of the *homo economicus* used by most economists.

earlier defines a role for economics as an organizing influence of social systems. He suggests:

> I have elsewhere distinguished three kinds of social organizers which I have called the threat system, the exchange system, and the integrative system. Economics clearly occupies the middle one of these three. It edges over toward the integrative system insofar as it has some jurisdiction over the study of the system of one-way transfers of exchangeables, which I have called the "grants economy," for the grant, or one-way transfer, is a rough measure of an integrative relationship.[9]

Can his theory of grants economics provide the connection desired by Benedict XVI between economics and moral theology (*CV*, no. 32)?

Since the principles of grants economics are not "textbook" concepts, an outline of the basic ideas may be helpful. A "grant" may be defined as a one-way transfer of exchangeables.[10] In a grant situation, party A gives something to party B, but party B gives nothing in the way of a clearly defined exchangeable to party A in return. The net worth of the grantee, party B, is increased and the net worth of the grantor, part A, is decreased. By contrast, in a market situation, party A gives something to party B and party B recompenses party A. There is an exchange of equal values, thus no change in the net worth of either party. A grant, then, is a transaction in which there is no recompense in the traditional economic sense.[11] However, a transaction involving grants does not preclude the possibility that a grant from party A to party B may involve intangible transfers from party B to party A, such as prestige (gifts to your alma mater), status (gifts to your church), gratitude (gifts to disaster victims), friendship (gifts to your co-workers), or love (gifts to your family), for these are not exchangeables in the traditional economic sense.

Most transactions in the real world are a mixture of fair exchange (zero

---

9. Boulding, *Economics as a Science*, p. 123.

10. This summary of grants economics is a revision of the one prepared for Cortright and Tsukahara, "On the Economic Foundations of Catholic Social Thought," unpublished paper for Association for the Study of the Grants Economy session, "Economics and Theology: A Kenneth Boulding Retrospective," Allied Social Science Associations Annual Meeting, New York, 1999. The original formulation drew heavily on the description of grants economics in Kenneth Boulding, *The Economy of Love and Fear: A Preface to Grants Economics* (Belmont: Wadsworth, 1973).

11. Randall Wray has published a critique of the theory of grants economics that he says has been a "resounding failure"; see "Kenneth Boulding's Grants Economics," *Journal of Economic Issues* 28, no. 4 (December 1994): 1205-25, p. 1213.

percent grant) and pure (100 percent) grant or gift in the *caritas* sense. Thus, examples of the exchange of goods, services, factors of production, and the like at fair market prices involve no grants at all. Note that these exchanges are described as "fair" not "free" because the grants model assumes equal knowledge and circumstances between the parties involved in the exchange transaction, a rare case in real life. Equally difficult to find are examples of gift. Thus, fair exchange and gift are the polar cases in a market economy. And because we are speaking of transactions among humans can pure grants arise from agape?

According to Boulding there are two types of motivations for grants: one stems from expressions of benevolence and results in "gift"; the other originates in threat and results in "tribute." In an accounting sense, "gift" represents a transfer of net worth from the donor to the receiver. However, from the point of view of economics, the loss of "utility" to the donor resulting from the reduction of assets may be offset by the gain in "utility" arising out of perceived increases in the welfare of the recipient. An extreme example of a tribute-motivated transfer is when an armed robber gives you this choice: "Give me your money or give me your life." A more subtle form of tribute can be found in "free" market transactions when the seller has knowledge about the quality of his product that the buyer does not. In this case, the fact that exchange takes place is not enough evidence to suggest that the transaction was "fair" because asymmetric information is just an example of tribute. After all, isn't knowledge power?

Although threat plays a significant role in grants economics, gift, or the integrative element, is perhaps dominant in determining the pattern and structure of the grants economy. It is the integrative system, consisting of the set of social relations involving status, for example, community, legitimacy, love, loyalty, and trust, that, to a considerable extent, makes intelligible the grants economy.

Christophe Kolm provides another classification system to consider. He suggests there are "four modes of transfer: taking by force, giving, exchange, and reciprocity."[12] The first two cases have the same normative foundation as Boulding's threat and benevolence examples. The exchange case is the same for both. Reciprocity is the case of mutual grants: party A gives something to party B out of benevolence for B and party B gives to party A with similar motive. Boulding waggishly suggests that Christmas gifts are an example of reciprocity that often morphs into exchange.[13] The reciprocity case provides

---

12. S.-C. Kolm, "Introduction: The Economics of Reciprocity, Giving and Altruism," in *The Economics of Reciprocity, Giving and Altruism,* ed. L.-A. Gérarad-Varet et al. (New York: St. Martin's, 2000), p. 7.

13. Boulding, *The Economy of Love and Fear,* p. 25.

an opportunity to either cast gift into an exchange model as might be found in economic models of families and households or use the gift idea as an economic link to *philia* as expressed in *Caritas in Veritate* (nos. 34, 36). Kolm argues that "family life is mostly mutual givings, which can more or less depend on one another in reciprocity, and result from and manifest interrelated and often reciprocal sentiments . . . embedded in the set of gifts."[14]

Over the past couple of decades a common Christmas season news item has been a feature story of a "random act of kindness." The typical example, often a repeated annual event, is of a stranger who passes out money to people he passes on the street. When the identity of the stranger is discovered, it is not unusual to learn that his generosity was his way to repay a past kindness from another stranger. This situation describes what Boulding would call serial reciprocity where a gift from party A to party B creates a generalized sense of obligation on party B that is satisfied by a gift not to party A but to party C. In turn party C's sense of obligation is triggered and is not satisfied until a gift is made to a party other than B. Thus, it is quite possible that party A is the recipient of a gift as well in the chain of obligations they started.[15]

Have you experienced a random act of kindness? Did it set off the chain of obligation suggested by Boulding? I was the recipient of this type of gift one Christmas eve a number of years ago. My wife and I were on our way to pick up our older daughter at San Francisco International Airport. At the toll booth on the Bay Bridge, the attendant informed me that the driver of the car that had just left had paid our toll for us. Merry Christmas! I confess that to this day I have not passed on this gift to another driver on the Bay Bridge. I also admit that I have terminated the flow of many chain letters. Is one data point enough to call into question the validity of serial reciprocity? I do not believe so. It only suggests that a singular gift creates at best a weak sense of fraternity. As Kolm concludes, both reciprocity and gift-giving are important for economists to recognize, but can economics provide much guidance for public policy without agreement on the meaning of "good"?

> This is why reciprocity and gift-giving have a particularly important normative function. The normative evaluation of economic situations and transfers is classically a prime concern of economics. However, the good society is made of good acts, not only of productive actions and pleasurable

14. Kolm, "Introduction," p. 1.

15. Boulding, *The Economy of Love and Fear*, p. 26. Some kidneys supplied for transplants are the result of a sequence of "donations" that can eventually find a match for the desired patient.

gestures; it is also made of good social relations, not just of profitable exchanges; and it is made of good people and not just satisfied ones.[16]

The sense of reciprocity suggested in *Caritas in Veritate* rises above emotions such as sympathy or empathy that may not be captured by the usual market model. As Benedict XVI observed, "The market of gratuitousness does not exist, and attitudes of gratuitousness cannot be established by law. Yet both the market and politics need individuals who are open to reciprocal gift" (*CV*, no. 39).

The Political Economics of Gift

Do you recall when you received a gift or what has been described as a pure grant? Similarly, can you recall when you made a gift in the spirit of *Caritas in Veritate*? My life has been filled with the kindness of others almost from birth. My grandmother took me into her life when I was abandoned by my mother as an infant. This experience confirms for me the reality of "gift" in the world even though most gifts may be motivated more by a sense of fraternity than of *caritas* (*CV*, no. 34). I have been a blood donor independent of any emergency appeal program.[17] I would classify my act as a pure grant even though I consumed some of the available juice and cookies at the collection site. Reading *Caritas in Veritate* motivated me to elect the organ donor option when I recently renewed my driver's license. This decision is potentially a pure grant if at the time of my death anything suitable for transplantation can be found. Both of these examples are offered to illustrate how rare pure grants are for me.

Although my annual gift to Saint Mary's College is an act of solidarity with the next generation of students so that they can have a similar access to education that I experienced, I readily admit that the incentive provided in the income tax code makes this decision easier and sweeter since the gift reduces

---

16. Kolm, "Introduction," p. 2.

17. Richard M. Titmuss's study of blood donations in England concluded that a voluntary system works much more efficiently than a paid, that is, market-based system. He suggested that one factor could be the habit of donation that was formed by patriotic duty when England was at war. Much of the early work in the economics of altruism refers to Titmuss to support the rationality of giving. However, most of the blood collection today is purchased. One longtime fan of the Green Bay Packers was inducted into their Hall of Fame for his attendance history. This fan reported that he was able to buy tickets for the games because he was able to sell his blood.

my overall tax obligations. I am confident that very few of us voluntarily ignore this incentive to give if our incomes are large enough to benefit from itemized deductions. Saint Mary's in turn adds to making this an impure gift by providing special treatment for donors. I can, with the payment of a very small fee, have a parking space next to the arena for basketball games.

Few grants lie at one or the other end of the motivational spectrum. For example, taxes are paid under the threat of legal sanctions. The government may be characterized as sort of a robber in this sense. However, to the extent that the objectives of the tax system can be identified as payment for public services like public safety and defense, there is a surprising willingness to pay that accounts for the surprising efficiency of the self-accounting and reporting in the federal income tax system. The crucial element here is the legitimacy of the taxing organization in the eyes of the citizenry.

Ideally the grants economy should perform the function of a regulator of the exchange economy in instances where the normal operation of the market fails to attain social and economic goals (*CV*, no. 37). If prices established in the market do not lead to efficient allocation of resources or fail to cover costs transferred to parties not directly involved in the market transaction (e.g., negative externalities), there is a role for grants to play to offset these market imperfections. Wages paid to labor may provide a creative challenge for grants economics. If the labor market functions efficiently, but does not produce "just wages" for all workers, how can grants logic correct this situation?[18] Most economists may not choose to address the issue of "just wages" because it is a theologically based concept, so if the objective is changed to "living wage" then a response is necessary.

Benedict XVI correctly observed that "economic life . . . needs just laws and forms of redistribution governed by politics, and what is more, it needs works redolent of the spirit of gift" (*CV*, no. 37). Even if the test of commutative justice can be met, there is still the need to pursue distributive justice and social justice in the market economy (*CV*, no. 35). Just laws require what John Paul II calls an authentic democracy based on a "correct conception of the human person" (*CV*, no. 46). Is this possible in the modern liberal democratic state? If not, then how can the common good be achieved (*CV*, no. 37)?[19]

18. A discussion of just wage can be found in Cortright and Tsukahara, "On the Economic Foundations of Catholic Social Thought."

19. As the author of *Rerum Novarum*, Leo XIII is identified as the founder of Catholic social teaching. He should also be credited for his vision to bring Catholic philosophy back into dialogue with modern science. It is historically and intellectually interesting that *Aeterni Patris* was published prior to it. The evolution of Catholic social teaching from *Rerum Novarum*

Guidance from the "Gospel" of Euclid

The robes traditionally associated with the Brothers of the Christian Schools are not seen very often at Saint Mary's since the rules about public garb were relaxed by Vatican II. During my student days the commonly held view was how impractical the robes were especially if you needed to do something on the run. At Saint Mary's the Brothers who teach in the Integral Program of Liberal Arts, although not required to do so, wear their robes in the classroom. This practice gives our students a visual connection between the secular and the sacred that may also be a catalyst for an intellectual connection when the discussion for the day is a text by a pre-Christian author like Plato or Ptolemy or by a more modern one like Nietzsche, Kant, or Marx. At a recent social event I was reminded about the practical construction of the robe when a Brother arrived for the social hour, reached into the side pocket, and produced my favorite brand of single malt scotch. Of course, the deep pockets were not intended for easy transport of wine and spirits but to house the copy of the Gospels and the rosary that each Brother received when taking first vows. If a long day with difficult students was leading to despair, as was the case often at Cathedral High, all the Brother had to do was reach into his pockets for a spiritual refresher.

Recently I was the tutor for Senior Mathematics where our students are exposed to the foundational ideas of the calculus, non-Euclidean geometry, and relativity. Most of the students had studied Euclid with me as freshmen. One of my best Euclid students who was preparing to apply for law school was visibly troubled when we began the discussion of the possibility of parallel lines meeting. She finally asserted, "This is a waste of time! Euclid demonstrated that parallel lines cannot meet." I responded, perhaps rashly, that "there is no reason to look at Euclid like the Gospels. Euclid helps us appreciate the utility of deductive proof. But Euclid does not rise to the level of Truth." After class our conversation continued in my office where I believe she accepted that our work with Euclid provided us with the logic that guides the development of mathematics and mathematically influenced ideas. Furthermore, unlike natural science where seeing can influence thinking, mathematics helps us deal with abstraction — the unseen.

To illustrate the influence of Euclid let us recall that the purpose of this encyclical is to determine how the criteria of "justice and the common good"

---

to *Caritas in Veritate* is due in large part to the intellectual bridge that Catholic philosophical research gives to the Church about the influence of modern science on contemporary culture.

govern moral action (*CV,* no. 6). In Euclid assumptions accepted prior to analysis lead to the same geometric conclusion. However, there is no common agreement about assumptions that precede the discussion of justice or the common good. Bridging the different beginnings motivates Benedict XVI in the dialectic with the advocates of liberal social democracy — the conversation between the sacred and the secular, the dialogue of faith and reason.

For Benedict XVI, justice "prompts us to give the other what is 'his,' what is due to him by reason of his being or his acting," and "justice is inseparable from charity, and intrinsic to it" (*CV,* no. 6). His sense of justice is the virtue present in a society animated by charity that achieves a "commitment to the common good" that has "greater worth than a merely secular and political stand would have" (*CV,* no. 7). Rawls presents us with a political conception of justice that is independent of "wider comprehensive religious or philosophical doctrine, and this is elaborated in terms of fundamental political ideals viewed as implicit in the public political culture of a democratic society."[20] For him justice as fairness is the expected outcome of agreement among citizens to "conduct their fundamental discussions within a framework of what each regards as a political conception of justice based on values that the others can reasonably be expected to endorse and each is, in good faith, prepared to defend that conception as understood."[21]

A comparison of the Church's desire to inspire actions for the common good[22] with the Rawlsian aim to define the process that results in fair decisions reinforces another important difference about human behavior. As emphasized in *Gaudium et Spes,* the common good results from individuals acting from a view of rights and duties toward the whole human race.[23] Rawls's *homo civilis* acts from rights-centered motives that by assumption exclude any notion of

20. Rawls, *Political Liberalism* (New York: Columbia University Press, 1993), p. 223.

21. Rawls, *Political Liberalism,* p. 226.

22. Father Albino Barrera, O.P., is the leading American scholar of economics and Catholic social documents. He notes two gaps in the appeal to the common good and the need for new efforts to make the concept clearer. "First, the concept itself has to be made more accessible for practical use by describing its content with greater specificity. . . . There is need for a more precise enumeration, to the extent possible, of the requirements imposed by legal, distributive, and commutative justice operating within the confines of the common good. A second gap is the pressing need to systematize the various warrants used extensively in the social documents that follow in the wake of *Rerum Novarum.* The common good has been generally accepted to be the operative core of this tradition. In spite of this, very little has been done to show how its principles and norms flow from the common good." A. Barrera, *Modern Catholic Social Documents and Political Economy* (Washington, D.C.: Georgetown University Press, 2001), p. 288.

23. Vatican II, *Gaudium et Spes,* no. 26.

good to influence it.[24] Just as Euclid's postulate on parallel lines differs from Lobachevsky's, the source of dispute in any of these theories can usually be traced to a difference in the definition of key terms or assumptions about commonly held truths. In the case of theology and politics/economics the concept of human is the critical difference.[25]

Euclid requires close reading and reflection, a valuable habit for reading *Caritas in Veritate*. For example, Benedict XVI's use of "profit" (*CV*, no. 38) is the conventional economic understanding that the Church[26] accepts as legitimate since efficiency is a principle of justice.[27] However, he suggests that its use as the measure of business performance may be too narrow, adopting John Paul II's views that "profit is a regulator of the life of a business, but it is not the only one; other human and moral factors must also be considered which, in the long term, are at least equally important for the life of a business."[28] Would a sense of "profit" that accounted for all the costs of production, direct and indirect, yield a higher sense of justice? Would the use of just wage rather than market wage lead to just profit and business survival? Is the legal dichotomy of business, for example, in education or in health care, into "profit" and "non-profit" classifications necessary to achieve a just economy (*CV*, no. 41)?

Applying the Principle of Gratuitousness: Education

Because I live nearby, I generally attend Sunday Mass on campus rather than in my parish. One Sunday, when I entered the chapel I was approached by Father John Morris, O.P., the scheduled celebrant for the day, with this question: "Did you bring your glasses?" This was his usual greeting to me when he needed a reader for the Mass after I had once declined his invitation because

24. "Despite their various accounts of what rights we have, rights-oriented liberals agree that the principles of justice that specify our rights should not depend on their justification on any particular conception of the good life. This idea, central to the liberalism of Kant, Rawls, and many present-day liberals, is summed up in the claim that right is prior to the good." Michael Sandel, *Liberalism and the Limits of Justice* (New York: Cambridge University Press, 1998), p. 185.

25. Vatican II, *Gaudium et Spes,* no. 16; Pope John Paul II, *Fides et Ratio,* no. 98; Sandel, *Liberalism,* p. 188.

26. Pope John Paul II, *Centesimus Annus,* no. 35.

27. John J. Piderit, S.J., *The Ethical Foundations of Economics* (Washington, D.C.: Georgetown University Press, 1993), p. 214.

28. Pope John Paul II, *Centesimus Annus,* no. 35. Translation at http://www.vatican.va/holy_father/john_paul_ii/encyclicals/documents/hf_jp-ii_enc_01051991_centesimus-annus_en.html. See also *Caritas in Veritate,* no. 35.

I had forgotten to bring my glasses that I need for close reading. Getting old has its inconveniences! This time, I replied, "Yes," and agreed to do the second reading. When I went to the Lectionary to prepare, I recognized the text that concludes:

> For our knowledge is imperfect and our prophesying is imperfect; but once perfection comes, all imperfect things will disappear. When I was a child, I used to talk like a child, and think like a child, and argue like a child, but now that I am a man, all childish ways are put behind me. Now we are seeing a dim reflection in a mirror; but then we shall be seeing face to face. The knowledge that I have now is imperfect; but then I shall know as fully as I am known. In short, there are three things that last: faith, hope and love; and the greatest of these is love. (1 Cor. 13:9-13)[29]

What is the commitment that the whole Church should make to education? John Paul II gives us a partial answer to this question with respect to Catholic higher education when he invites "the entire ecclesial Community" to assist it in the process of "development and renewal" by offering "economic aid."[30] Benedict XVI outlines "the essential elements of Christian and ecclesial Charity" in *Deus Caritas Est,*[31] which suggests he has a more radical answer in the "logic of gift." The original schools founded by the Brothers of the Christian Schools and the Jesuits were gratuitous schools.[32] Perhaps this should be the goal for Catholic education at all levels. However, is it feasible for Catholic schools to return to this model of operation without the presence of a large number of vowed individuals? Is there hope for Catholic education available as an option for all children, especially the poor in the inner cities, by following the Christo Rey and San Miguel models? Can a case be made to overcome the strict separation of church and state to permit wider use of charter schools

---

29. Jerusalem Bible translation. Father Morris says that this reading is very popular with young couples planning their weddings in the college chapel.

30. Pope John Paul II, *Ex Corde Ecclesiae,* no. 11. Translation at http://www.vatican.va/holy_father/john_paul_ii/apost_constitutions/documents/hf_jp-ii_apc_15081990_ex-corde-ecclesiae_en.html.

31. Pope Benedict XVI, *Deus Caritas Est,* no. 31. See also no. 35: "Those who are in a position to help others will realize that in doing so they themselves receive help; being able to help others is no merit or achievement of their own. This duty is a grace." Translation at http://www.vatican.va/holy_father/benedict_xvi/encyclicals/documents/hf_ben-xvi_enc_20051225_deus-caritas-est_en.html.

32. Gratuitous schools may have been sponsored by groups following other charisms, but my research is limited to these two orders.

and vouchers based on education for the public good?[33] Without a positive response by the faithful to the principle of gratuitousness, can Catholic education survive the legislative assault underway on nonprofit institution tax benefits as a way to resolve state and local budget problems? Is a strategy to build endowments for Catholic education consistent with the logic of gift?

Final Observations

The path to the common good is very difficult since the Church and the state start from very different assumptions about the human person. The Catholic university can lead the way by guiding the dialectic between faith and reason closer together. At the minimum bringing the separate fields of moral and political philosophy together can create models of democratic institutions that will put secular and religious principles on more equal footing. Increased collaboration among the social and behavioral sciences could create a better understanding of social interactions that could inform better legislative actions. Charity and philosophy share the same root, *phil,* in Greek, which points to the model of fraternity for those of us following the vocation of education. Thus, informed conversations among all philosophers, that is, "lovers of wisdom," should lead to a richer conception of what it means to be human and ultimately, in the presence of *agape* to Logos.

As I grow older memories from my past are difficult to resurrect with fidelity. However, among the few that I have is of a warm spring evening when I was just sixteen. I am back in the old high school gym as part of the chorus for the annual spring concert. One hundred male voices foreshadow the truth in *Caritas in Veritate* as we sing:

> No man is an island far out in the blue
> We all look to One above
> Who our strength doth renew
> When I help my brother
> Then I know that I plant the seeds
> Of Friendship that will never die.[34]

33. In 2010 the Catholic Church was permitted to operate a public charter school in Indianapolis.

34. This is the last stanza of "No Man is an Island." The music is by Joan Whitney and the lyrics by Alex Kramer. This song is inspired by John Donne, Meditation 17. I thank Brother Richard Lemberg, F.S.C., research librarian, for his assistance.

PART IV: A GREEN POPE?
ECOLOGY IN *CARITAS IN VERITATE*

Human Ecology, Environmental Ecology, and *Ressourcement: Caritas in Veritate* in the Light of Philip Sherrard's Theandric Anthropology

Keith Lemna

A developing theological motif in the social magisterium of Pope Benedict XVI is the explicit recognition of the inextricable link between the demands of charity and care for the physical environment. In *Caritas in Veritate (CV)*, for instance, the Holy Father states that not only does respect for "human ecology" within society benefit "environmental ecology" (*CV*, no. 51), but that the former is the decisive factor in establishing a proper human relationship with physical nature. Understood in the full context of the Church's social doctrine, which ultimately elucidates the societal implications of the gift of charity, this would mean that it is only through the inculcation of the supernatural virtues in the life of the Church, which radiate outwardly into the social sphere, that a truly "deep ecology" can be nurtured. The gift of charity carries with it not only social but cosmic significance.

The Holy Father's linking together of the two ecologies of the created order in the perspective of charity is a transformation of most modern thought as it pertains to the relationship of creation to history. It calls to mind the patristic transformation of Greco-Roman microcosmism in the first millennium of the Church.[1] Pope Benedict XVI follows in the tradition of the pa-

---

1. On the patristic doctrine of man the microcosm, see Lars Thunberg, *Microcosm and Mediator: The Theological Anthropology of Saint Maximus the Confessor,* Acta Seminarii Neo-

---

This essay first appeared in *Logos* under the title "Human Ecology, Environmental Ecology, and a *Ressourcement* Theology: *Caritas in veritate* in the Light of Philip Sherrard's Theandric Anthropology," *Logos* 14, no. 3 (Summer 2011): 133-54. Used by permission.

tristic theologians in establishing the essential connection between the vocation and destiny of man and the sanctification of the physical universe. There were several twentieth-century *ressourcement* theologians who brought the patristic doctrine of man as microcosm and keystone of creation to the forefront again, precisely in order to recover the inextricable link between *anthropos* and *cosmos* in Christ.[2] One such theologian, who was also among the first twentieth-century intellectuals to sound the alarm of the environmental crisis, was the Greek Orthodox theologian, poet, and eminent English translator of many great spiritual and poetic creations of modern and pre-modern Greek literature Philip Sherrard (1922-95). Sherrard sought to recover a truly spiritual and metaphysical cosmology in the line of the great patristic tradition of Christian thought that elucidates the connection of (to use Pope Benedict XVI's language) "human ecology" to "environmental ecology." An exposition of Sherrard's work on this topic can shed a great deal of light on Pope Benedict XVI's *Caritas in Veritate,* especially if Sherrard's Eastern Christian polemic is, from the outset, scrutinized and tempered. My purpose in the present study is to use Sherrard's patristic "return to the sources," especially as found in his book *Human Image: World Image,* as a guide to uncover some of the wider implications of the Holy Father's suggestions. I focus in a first section on Sherrard's Christological and Trinitarian participationist metaphysics, or "theandric anthropology." In a second section I briefly expound his Christian Platonist epistemology. His evaluation of the human crisis at the root of the ecological crisis has both a metaphysical and an epistemological dimension. The two are necessarily linked.

I

Caritas in Veritate is founded on an explicitly Christological and Trinitarian perspective that sees the destiny of man and the world in the light of the innate connection of all creation to the supernatural. It remains a perpetual task for theologians to articulate fully this connection. Philip Sherrard's participationist metaphysics, or Christian theandric anthropology, exemplifies the sort of work

---

testamentici Upsaliensis 25 (Copenhagen: C. W. K. Gleerup, Lund und Einar Munksgaard, 1965).

2. See Louis Bouyer, *Cosmos: The World and the Glory of God,* trans. Pierre de Fontnouvelle (Petersham: St. Bede's, 1988); Dumitru Staniloae, *The Experience of God: Orthodox Dogmatic Theology, Volume II: The World: Creation and Deification,* trans. Ioan Ionita and Robert Barringer (Brookline: Holy Cross Orthodox Press, 2000).

that theologians are called to accomplish in this regard. Nevertheless, it is helpful, in expounding his theology, to abstract from his harshly expressed Eastern Christian polemic against the Western Church.[3] Sherrard rightly saw it as necessary, in order to combat modern naturalism, to recover the deepest metaphysical and anthropological implications of the Chalcedonian tradition. Yet he could see the mainstream, pre-modern Western tradition as little more than an obstacle standing in the way of such a recovery. He refused to recognize the mystical depths of the Western tradition, except in more marginal figures like Eckhart and Eriugena, and his analysis of the pre-modern West is deeply flawed as a result.[4] Even so, his theology as a whole is unique in connecting the recovery of Chalcedonian theandrism to the restitution of human ecology and environmental ecology. Moreover, few theologians in the modern age have been as bold as he to show the stark contrast between a Christian theandric view of man and a purely materialistic anthropology. We are now living in an age roiled by a resurgent naturalism, and his work has, as a result, taken on an increasing relevance. His tendentious reading of the pre-modern West need not detain us, as a Western theologian can, from the resources of his own tradition properly understood, concur with Sherrard's metaphysical and epistemological criticism of modern man's debased self-image.

Sherrard's theological work can be situated as both a neo-patristic *ressourcement* theology and as a type of unremitting anti-scientism inspired in great part by the French metaphysician and convert from Catholicism to Islamic Sufism René Guénon (1886-1951).[5] Guénon was one of the most radical

3. See Philip Sherrard, *The Greek East and Latin West: A Study in the Christian Tradition* (Limni, Greece: Denise Harvey, 1992). This book could serve as a primer on Eastern Orthodox complaints against the Western Church.

4. Henri de Lubac, Hans Urs von Balthasar, and Louis Bouyer had already thoroughly exculpated the Western tradition from radical critiques along the lines of Sherrard. The work of Dr. Jacques Albert Cuttat is also of enduring importance in showing the unique genius of the Western tradition in regard to its Christological and Trinitarian centering. Cuttat also deals with the Guénonians in general. See Jacques Albert Cuttat, *The Encounter of Religions*, trans. Pierre de Fontnouvelle (New York: Desclée, 1960). More recently, theologians of a "radically orthodox" bent have demonstrated anew the "theandric" depths of the theologies of St. Augustine and St. Thomas. See John Milbank and Catherine Pickstock, *Truth in Aquinas* (New York: Routledge, 2000); Michael Hanby, *Augustine and Modernity* (New York: Routledge, 2003).

5. For a wider perspective on Sherrard, see Kathleen Raine, *Philip Sherrard (1922-1995): A Tribute* (Birmingham: Delos, 1996). One can say that Sherrard's thinking is in line with the *ressourcement* theology of the twentieth century in his plea for the recovery of what Hans Boersma has called a "sacramental ontology." For the twentieth-century Western tradition in this regard, see Hans Boersma, *Nouvelle Théologie and Sacramental Ontology: A Return to Mystery* (New York: Oxford University Press, 2009).

and influential critics of modern scientism in the twentieth century.[6] He initiated a movement of thought whose goal was to restore what he took to be the perennial sacred cosmology of ancient religious humanity. Sherrard, though rejecting Guénon's preference for non-Christian Eastern modes of thought, wrote of Guénon's importance as a metaphysician in the strongest terms:

> If during the last century or so there has been even some slight revival of awareness in the western world of what is meant by metaphysics and metaphysical tradition, the credit for it must go above all to Guénon. At a time when the confusion into which modern western thought had fallen was such that it threatened to obliterate the few remaining traces of genuine spiritual knowledge from the minds and hearts of his contemporaries, Guénon, virtually single-handed, took it upon himself to reaffirm the values and principles which, he recognized, constitute the only sound basis for the living of a human life with dignity and purpose or for the formation of a civilization worthy of the name.[7]

The essay by Sherrard from which this quotation is taken is, in fact, a stirring defense of the Christian doctrine of the Trinity against Guénon's argument for the logical superiority of a Vedantic, non-dualist understanding of the Absolute. Nevertheless, the Guénonian influence on Sherrard is clear, particularly in regard to Sherrard's recovery of sacred cosmology.

Associates and followers of Guénon issued some of the earliest and most enduring analyses and refutations of the cultural and social forces that had brought, by the middle of the twentieth century, modern industrial civilization to the point of ecological crisis.[8] These Guénonian analyses differ greatly from most approaches to environmental ecology so prevalent among theologians and others in our own day. Whereas today's theological ecologists focus primarily on developing an environmental ethics that is hardly critical of sci-

---

6. For an historical account of Guénon's influence, see Mark Sedgwick, *Against the Modern World: Traditionalism and the Secret Intellectual History of the Twentieth Century* (New York: Oxford University Press, 2004). Sedgwick's work is journalistic and conspiratorial in tone, but it does give a sense of the scope of Guénon's influence.

7. Philip Sherrard, *Christianity: Lineaments of a Sacred Tradition* (Brookline: Holy Cross Orthodox Press, 1998), pp. 76-77.

8. It would be enough to inventory some of the names associated, either directly or indirectly, with Guénon — but all of whom acknowledge their indebtedness to his radical critique of scientism: E. F. Schumacher, Ananda Coomaraswamy, Henry Corbin, Fritjof Schuon, Aldous Huxley, Mircea Eliade, Titus Burckhardt (the great-nephew of Jacob Burckhardt), Seyye Hossein Nasr, Thomas Merton, Huston Smith, Wolfgang Smith, Jean Borella.

entism, the Guénonian school sought to recapture a religious vision of nature fully adherent to the metaphysical traditions of the world's religions, and as a result they were starkly critical of modern scientific cosmology.[9] Sherrard's goal is also to restore religious cosmology to a place of prominence, although he is not simply, like so many followers and associates of Guénon, a proponent of a perennialist religious philosophy. The religious vision of nature that Sherrard seeks to recover is specifically that of the tradition of Chalcedonian orthodoxy in Eastern Christian theology, and Sherrard's diagnosis of the modern situation, perhaps more than any other Guénonian analysis, stresses that the ecological crisis is rooted in a distorted anthropology. Truly, for Sherrard, "human ecology" has to be healed if "environmental ecology" is to have a foundation, for, as he says, "the ecological crisis is primarily a crisis about man and not about his environment."[10]

Sherrard's work helps us to see at a very deep level all of the relationships — moral and metaphysical — that the Holy Father has brought into consideration with his suggestions in *Caritas in Veritate.* His work is sharp and prophetic in this regard. He does not go in for half-measures. He is, like Guénon, a religious radical in the best sense, getting at the religious roots of the dilemma of modern man. His writings have the power to shake us from a self-delusional complacency. In many ways, his bold, Eastern-inspired Christian voice is just what the Western, post-conciliar Church needs to hear, as so many of her children are unduly submissive before the presumed authority of modern science.

It is important to grasp that modern culture is in fact rooted in religion and theology, and Sherrard's work is valuable in focusing our attention on this fact. He is thus able to show us that the ecological crisis goes far beyond the problem of global warming, or the depletion of the ozone layer, or any issue or concern that could be addressed by purely political or economic legislation. Current debates about whether there is such a thing as anthropogenic global warming deal only with tangential aspects of the ecological crisis. For Sherrard, the ecological crisis is not simply the issue of a consumer culture that refuses to use biodegradable goods and products, or that takes little regard for how economic expansion affects the physical environment of modern living. The existence of mountainous landfills and chlorofluorocarbons in the atmosphere is but a symptom of a much deeper disease. The ecological crisis has its foun-

---

9. Summing up the Guénonian school in this regard is the work of Seyyed Hossein Nasr. See Seyyed Hossein Nasr, *Religion and the Order of Nature* (New York: Oxford University Press, 1996).

10. Philip Sherrard, *The Rape of Man and Nature* (Cambridge: Golgonooza, 1987), p. 70.

dation, rather, in the desecration of sacral beauty within human culture, and the environmental injustices that have become so much of a concern for people in our own day ultimately flow from this desecration.[11]

Sherrard sees the absence of a transcendent religious presence at the center of modern life as the ultimate source of the environmental crisis. He argues that if man is to "save the environment," he requires first of all an explicit and central cultural recognition of the transcendent source and destiny of his being. This is to say that man needs to order his life once again by the insights of sacred wisdom. Ritual, doctrinal, and religious recovery is essential to heal his relationship with nature. The objective laws of sacred liturgical and artistic symbolism have to be protected, nurtured, and given a place of prominence in the daily life of the city.[12] Religious contemplation has to be valued as the most genuine source of a deep science of the cosmos. Non-sacral lines of interpretation of cosmic being have to be subjected to severe criticism, for they only deal with the exterior aspects of things and so do not convey a true knowledge of the cosmos. Man's essential link with the divine has to be expressed in culture, as the guide for everything that he does, if he is to recover from the manifest anthropological and cosmological injustices that have marred modern life.[13]

This call to a recovery of the religious dimension of our being, our deepest self, is the practical outcome of Sherrard's prescient insight that we can only have a truly respectful image of the world, and therefore a fully effective environmental ecology, if we recapture the sense of ourselves as God-informed beings.[14] Only a fully theological self-image can give rise to a world-image that inspires ecological justice. We are from God and are not merely "two-legged animals," and our relationship to the world depends on whether or not we realize this. Sherrard argues that full acknowledgment of the theological bearing of our nature requires a thoroughgoing, unstinting critique of secular humanist anthropologies that presume to be able to elucidate the nature of man on the basis of the findings of modern science:

> In the great creative [religious] cultures of the world, human beings do not regard themselves as two-legged animals, descended from the apes, whose needs and satisfactions can be achieved through pursuing social, political,

11. See Philip Sherrard, *The Sacred in Life and Art* (Cambridge: Golgonooza, 1990).

12. Sherrard, "The Meaning of Sacred Tradition," in *Christianity and the Lineaments of a Sacred Tradition*, pp. 1-26.

13. On this whole paragraph, see Sherrard, "The Meaning of Sacred Tradition," pp. 1-26.

14. This is the central thesis of his aforementioned book, *Human Image: World Image* (Cambridge: Golgonooza, 1992).

and economic self-interest in the material world and as though their life was confined to a material space-time dimension. On the contrary, they think of themselves first and foremost as descended from the gods, or from God, and as heirs to eternity, with a destiny that goes far beyond politics, society and economics, or anything that can be fulfilled in terms of the material world or by satisfying their mortal and physical desires and needs. They think of themselves as sacred beings, even as semi-divine beings, not in their own right, but because they are created in the divine image, in the image of God, of a transcendent more-than-human form of consciousness. They come from a divine source, and the divine world is their birthright, their true home.[15]

One often encounters theologians nowadays who talk about recapturing a sacramental image of the cosmos. From many theologians, who have not assessed as deeply as Sherrard the foundations of modern science, such talk can sound like a romantic dream, as if we can just choose to "re-enchant" nature on a whim. Sherrard's analysis is deeper than typical arguments for the "re-enchantment" of nature in that he realizes that the recovery of a sacramental vision of the universe requires a recovery of the tradition of the Christian sacred in its fullest manifestation. Contrary to the standard talk of contemporary theologians he argues that modern science is so essentially desacralizing in its fundamental motivation that it is difficult if not impossible to reconcile it with a sacramental vision of faith. There is a fine line, he argues, between modern science and pure scientism, the former having attained to a position of cultural dominance precisely because the latter has engulfed the modern Western mind. The recovery of a sacramental understanding of nature cannot be, then, merely a project of "re-enchantment." We cannot simply superimpose our dreams for what we think the world could or should be onto a physical foundation that we think in reality comprises purely mechanical parts or mathematically reducible quanta of mass and energy.

The recovery of a sacramental world-image requires a sense of nature that has nothing in common with the reductionist visions of Bacon, or Hobbes, or Descartes, or with any of their oftentimes unwitting postmodernist heirs. In recognizing this, we would be, with Sherrard, a far cry indeed from Sallie McFague's "eco-feminism" or Matthew Fox's concept of the cosmic Christ.[16]

15. Sherrard, *Human Image*, p. 4.

16. See Sallie McFague, *Models of God: Theologies for an Ecological, Nuclear Age* (Philadelphia: Fortress, 1987); Matthew Fox, *The Coming of the Cosmic Christ: The Healing of Mother Earth and the Birth of a Global Renaissance* (San Francisco: Harper & Row, 1988).

Both McFague and Fox give unquestioning allegiance to the modern scientific worldview. In contrast to these representative contemporary theologians, Sherrard recognizes that in order to understand the world sacramentally we must see its material "foundation" in integration with higher ontological planes. Indeed, it is these higher ontological planes, and not matter in and of itself, that are the foundational realities of cosmic being.

Sherrard realizes that a truly religious and therefore humane worldview would sharply contrast with modern, horizontalizing concepts of the world. Unlike McFague and Fox, he understands that the recovery of a truly sacramental cosmology requires that we be instilled with an awakened sense of the constitutive relationship of all things to their eternal, transcendent source. He realizes that it is precisely the sense of their relationship to their transcendent Creator that inspires religious men — and Christians most of all — to see the world in a sacramental way. Religious men do not "look upon what we call the outer world, the world of nature, as a mere chance association of atoms or whatever, or as something impersonal, soulless, inanimate, which they are entitled to manipulate, master, exploit and greedily to tamper and mess about with in order to gratify their greeds and their power lusts. They look upon nature, too, as a divine creation, as full of a hidden wisdom as they themselves are, as full of a personal, sensitive soul-life or psychic life as they themselves are."[17]

Many theologians today are deeply concerned with the problem of environmental ecology, but they tend to let political and economic concerns dominate their thinking. Sherrard's work is a fully theological rejoinder to any form of political or economic reductionism. His suggestions for sacramental recovery, if followed through on a wide scale, would spell the end of the technological imperative that propels modern civilization, with its concomitant conception of man as a purely political or economic creature. With this said, Sherrard does not recommend "back to nature movements." He is a proponent of high religious civilization, though not imperialist and colonialist, and there is as a result a strong sense in his writings of what the post-conciliar popes refer to as "integral human development." He is at pains to teach us, however, that any presumed human development that is not nourished by sacred wisdom carried in the context of sacramental tradition is ultimately dehumanizing.

Obviously, Sherrard's analysis of the human image that motivates modern scientific cosmology is uncompromisingly critical. Many readers of Sherrard have found him to be too one-sided in his assessment of modern science, but

17. Sherrard, *Human Image*, p. 4.

perhaps, as I have already suggested, it is precisely his sort of criticism that needs to have a greater hearing in our own day, when an increasing cultural prestige is accorded to socio-biologists, and trans-humanists, and eugenicists of varying degrees of self-awareness. It is no accident that the modern world, when it has not been directly ensconced in terror and bloodshed, has been always on the precipice of tyranny and holocaust, and Sherrard's analysis implies the clearly logical path that leads from the apotheosis of science and technology to the mass gallows, the gas chambers, the death camps, the abortion mills — and the destruction of the physical environment.

Sherrard forces us to ask ourselves how a "two-legged animal" could have an eternal moral value. If man is merely an accident or epiphenomenon of physical processes, how can we secure his dignity or his rights except on the basis of the shifting will of an increasingly vulgarized mass consciousness? And if man cannot see his own self in terms of the enduring dignity of his spiritual essence, how can he see anything else in that way? It is, again, no accident that he would turn his technology toward nature in the manner of brutal exploitation. It is no accident that humans who have come to see themselves as no more than "two-legged animals" would "deliberately blast out [nature's] guts through testing their atom and nuclear bombs, savage its skies with the din and stench of aeroplanes and space-craft, poison its rivers, its lakes, its seas, its underground waters through spilling chemicals into them or through the leaching of toxic wastes, or rape it in any of the thousands of ways in which we are now raping it."[18]

All of what I have expounded thus far implies that Sherrard is a forceful exponent for the recovery of the Christian Platonist tradition of theology. His work is indeed thoroughly suffused with the metaphysical wisdom of this tradition, in both its ancient and its modern guises. This gives his analysis a great force of philosophical depth that is entirely lacking in the superficial indictments of the monotheistic religions, and of Christianity most of all, issued by the likes of Arnold Toynbee and Lynn White.[19] For these men, the ecological catastrophe has its roots in the inspiration of classical Christian theology, which presumably sees man as a mere dominator of the natural world. It is not without pertinence to note, then, that the ecological crisis is, after all, a distinctly modern crisis. The age of its creeping advent in the mod-

18. Sherrard, *Human Image*, p. 5

19. See Arnold Toynbee, in *Ecology and Religion in History*, ed. David and Eileen Springs (New York: Harper & Row, 1974); Lynn White Jr., "The Historical Roots of Our Ecological Crisis," *Science* 155 (1967): 1203-7.

ern West corresponds precisely to the age of the advent of a cultural shift from the metaphysical perspective of classical Christian theism, with its fully participationist doctrine of creation, to the scientific dualism first foreshadowed in late medieval nominalism.

Sherrard is surely truer to history than Toynbee or White in seeing that the modern world has gone down its brutalizing path because it no longer understands finite being in terms of the Christian doctrine of creation.[20] How, after all, can we know or respect either ourselves or the world we live in if we ignore the very ground of our being? Desacralized man fancies himself completely autonomous, self-sufficient, and able to understand the cosmos solely by assessing its material and physical dimensions. Has not Sherrard taken precisely the correct tone in responding to this modern pretension with mocking derision, naming it for what it is — "barbaric" and "idiotic"?[21] Contemporary philosophers of an analytic persuasion consider it derisory to label one of their peers a Platonist.[22] But should a theologian be constrained, for fear of incurring such a superficial rebuke, to refrain from asking what must be for him the necessary question of how it is possible to know the plenary reality of anything without seeing it in the light of its share in God's eternal being?

The Chalcedonian tradition of Christian orthodoxy has taught us that it is indeed impossible to know any finite reality if we detach it in our speculative endeavors entirely from its eternal ground.[23] God's revelation in Christ has a meaning that encompasses all of reality. No finite being, as many church fathers and scholastic theologians understood, can be truly itself unless it is fully interpenetrated by its logos, or the idea that God has of it within himself, in his own eternal Logos, from all eternity.[24] We cannot know anything in full without knowing its logos. We cannot know any logos in full without knowing the Logos. The ideal and the real must come to correspond in any finite being if it is to shine forth in the full splendor of its truth. This implies the need, if

20. Sherrard, *Human Image*, pp. 147-81. Sherrard seeks the recovery of a doctrine of creation that balances the understanding that creation is from nothing with an understanding that creation is also from God, as is found, for instance, in some expressions of the tradition of the Rhineland mystics and the Christian Kabbalah.

21. See Sherrard, *Human Image*, p. 42.

22. See Alasdair MacIntyre's comments regarding the derisory nature of the epitaph "Platonism" as it is often used to describe Gottlob Frege's work in *Edith Stein: A Philosophical Prologue: 1913-1922* (New York: Rowman and Littlefield, 2006), p. 43.

23. See Louis Bouyer, *The Eternal Son*, trans. Simone Inkel and John F. Laughlin (Huntington: Our Sunday Visitor, 1979), pp. 295-301.

24. For a particularly good discussion of the implications of the Chalcedonian tradition in this regard, see Louis Bouyer, *Sophia; ou le Monde en Dieu* (Paris: Cerf, 1994), pp. 123-32.

we are to develop a fully coherent science, or to understand the beings of nature as they truly are, to be able to make reliable assessments of the relationships between matter and form, symbol and referent, inner and outer, and essence and manifestation. Modern science, in and of itself, does not give us the means for elucidating these relationships.

It was precisely René Guénon's intention to recover the ancient religious participationist cosmologies so that we might have the wisdom once again to understand the world in its exemplary relationships.[25] Sherrard has obviously learned from Guénon in this regard. Thus, like Guénon, he takes full account of the interplay between the "inner" and "outer" dimensions of finite beings. Sherrard, like Guénon, realizes that one does not reach to the truth of a being by focusing only on its outer appearance in the manner of modern empirical investigation.[26] One must, he realizes with Guénon, know its inner reality, even as this is made known through its appearance, and this will elucidate the meaning of its manifestation as well.[27] No being can be understood, then, without seeing it in connection with its archetypal meaning. Both Sherrard and Guénon understand that it is necessary to encourage a theology of symbol and manifestation or a truly sacramental ontology if we are to restore *scientia* to its ancient scope and therefore dignity.

On the other hand, unlike Guénon, Sherrard does not stop with a generically monotheistic doctrine of participation. His thinking is, again, fully Chalcedonian. He understands the participation of all things in God in a Christological and Trinitarian manner, and he focuses on the consummation of worldly being in the human person deified in Christ.[28] As for the great patristic and scholastic theologians so for Sherrard it is specifically Christ, the Second Person of the Trinity, the Archetypal Man and thus the Archetype of all archetypes, who is the beginning and end of all finite beings.[29] At the same time, Sherrard develops this ancient Christian tradition by using the language of the nineteenth-century Russian theologian and "sophiologist" Vladimir Soloviev.

---

25. See René Guénon, *The Reign of Quantity and the Sign of the Times*, trans. Lord Northbourne (Baltimore: Penguin, 1953).

26. Sherrard, *Human Image*, pp. 77-101.

27. Sherrard, *Human Image*, pp. 50-51.

28. For an account of Balthasar's "meta-anthropology" on this point, see Rodney A. Howsare, *Balthasar: A Guide for the Perplexed* (London: T&T Clark, 2009), pp. 50-53.

29. On the importance of Maximus the Confessor, Hans Urs von Balthasar's famous and groundbreaking study retains its immense importance. See Hans Urs von Balthasar, *Cosmic Liturgy: The Universe According to Maximus the Confessor*, trans. Brian Daley (San Francisco: Ignatius, 2003).

Like Soloviev, he speaks of the "divine-humanity" of Christ and of his "God-manhood."[30] These expressions serve to highlight the reality of Christ as the exemplary man, as the eternal fullness of humanity, "the first-born of all creation" (Col. 1:15), who perfects the human being by adopting him into his eternal filiation or sonship. Christ is the eternal model of the human being who, in his hypostatic union, shows forth and actualizes everything that man has it within himself to become.

This manner of understanding Christ's relationship with humanity stresses that there is reciprocity in God's communion with man. On the one hand, it places an emphasis on recognizing that if we are to be fully ourselves God must be the determinative element of our being, the innermost, active center of our existence. On the other hand, it teaches that there is a fulfilling potentiality in human nature that brings God to completion in the hypostatic union.[31] This sounds very Hegelian, but it would be truer to Sherrard's (and Soloviev's) fully traditional intention to place this idea in line with Hans Urs von Balthasar's understanding of the Trinitarian *perichoresis* in relation to creation than in the trajectory of a purely Hegelian mode of thought.[32] While lamenting the modern Western ecclesiastical theologian's undue fear of any sort of theological expression that can be even remotely associated with pantheism, Sherrard nevertheless fully recognizes the transcendence of God to finite being.[33]

Sherrard's point in this respect is ultimately a sound corrective to certain types of theology that fail to grasp the power of the grace of union by which God wills to establish communion with his creature. Sherrard in no way denies the eternal distinction of the natures in Christ.[34] He is a disciple of St. Maximus the Confessor and not a monothelite or monoenergist, however confusing his manner of expression may seem to be at first glance.[35] Without the "otherness" of the natures in Christ, he realizes, there could be no communion of inter-penetration between them. There could be no ecstatic self-completion. Christ's divinity radiates through his humanity, but this requires that he be both fully and "eternally human" (another expression that Sherrard derives ultimately from Soloviev) and fully and eternally divine. Christ fills his humanity with his Godhead, unlocking its inner potentialities from without and from within.

---

30. See Sherrard, *The Rape of Man and Nature*, p. 23.

31. See Sherrard, *The Rape of Man and Nature*, p. 25.

32. See Hans Urs von Balthasar, *Theodrama V: The Last Act*, trans. Graham Harrison (San Francisco: Ignatius, 1998), pp. 61-109.

33. Sherrard, *Human Image*, pp. 155-56.

34. Sherrard, *The Rape of Man and Nature*, p. 25.

35. Sherrard, *The Rape of Man and Nature*, p. 17.

On the other hand, his humanity gives his divinity the fullest mode of self-manifestation. There is both perfect otherness and perfect union in Christ's hypostatic subjectivity. God shows himself for who he is through the human nature that he assumes in the hypostatic union. But he could not do so if man, the highest exemplar of created alterity, refused to be the instrument for his manifestation.[36] In stressing the foregoing points, Sherrard's work thus takes on a profoundly Marian as well as Christological dimension, as Mary is the archetypal created personal "other" in relationship to Christ and the Holy Spirit.[37]

Christ's intimate union with man in the hypostatic union in no way diminishes the specific activity of either his divine or human nature, and this is what is meant by speaking in terms of theandric anthropology in describing Sherrard's theology. Though they exist in a relationship of interpenetration and *perichoresis,* the divine and human natures in Christ are nevertheless joined together without confusion or change. They work together in Christ as a full unity through the power of his divine subjectivity, each according to its own mode, but in a perfect, cooperative, theandric synergy.[38] Christ's theandric activity is the model for all human perfection. Through our own personal divinization in Christ, we imitate, by an interpenetrating participation or filiation in him, the unified activity of the unconfused natures in his personal unity. We do not lose our individual identity in Christ. Our personal identity, just as human nature as such, is perfected by our share in the Trinitarian life and by Christ's dwelling within us in his Spirit as the fullness of our being.[39]

Sherrard expounds the God-world relationship in terms of this just-described Chalcedonian "theandrism" in order to counter the modern idea that man and creation are self-sufficient and autonomous realities, with no final destiny transcending spatiotemporal immanence. Contemporary theologians could hardly be insistent enough to follow him on this point. If reality is collapsed, as it is by the scientism that dominates contemporary society, to the plane of contingent, horizontal movement in space and time, then it is no surprise that moral relativism should emerge in our day with such persistence. It is no surprise that we should, as a result, think that physical nature is just a field for exploitation by our unanchored, egocentric volition. Martin Heidegger was famously critical of modernity's technological ontology, but he was cap-

---

36. On all of the foregoing, see Sherrard, *The Rape of Man and Nature,* pp. 17-41.
37. Sherrard, *Human Image,* pp. 176-81.
38. Sherrard, *The Rape of Man and Nature,* p. 27.
39. Sherrard, *The Rape of Man and Nature,* p. 28.

tured by its non-teleological way of understanding the world, and his criticism of technological ontology thus tends to fall as flat as that ontology itself.[40] Sherrard, by contrast, moves our thinking in a more vertical direction, seeing that all reality is "grounded" in the eternal, non-contingent, enduring reality of God's Eternal Word.

The point needs to be highlighted, in the face of a certain extrinsicism that still persists in Catholic theology, that to see the world in these participationist terms is in no way a retreat to a merely philosophical Platonism. The incarnational centering of Christian doctrine links the eternal with the finite in a profound unity that surpasses the concepts of all purely philosophical metaphysics. Sherrard's theology makes this "Christian distinction" clear. But even the best Catholic theologians of the twentieth century realized that modern Western theology, having lost a sense of the universal scope of the profound unity of the eternal and the finite in Christ, should turn more in the direction of the traditional patristic emphasis on the participation or filiation of all things in the Eternal Word.[41] Thus, one could rightly interpret Sherrard's work as aligned with the Catholic Church's own recent and internally corrective renewal of its theological schools. Nevertheless, Sherrard could use a Western or Augustinian precision, for he does, it seems, display a tendency to collapse the order of redemption into the order of creation.

By issuing this caveat, I mean to say that Sherrard downplays the unique importance of Christ's personal mission of redemption in salvation history in order to emphasize Christ the Eternal Word and Creator who is always present in all things. Sherrard does effectively recapture the doctrine of St. Maximus the Confessor and others in the tradition according to which the incarnation of Christ is a perpetual reality that is not limited to his historical incarnation alone.[42] With the Confessor he can say that Christ "wills always to work the miracle of His Incarnation in all things."[43] This particular Christological emphasis does help us to see that there is nothing in our existence that is absolutely untouched by Christ's creative presence. It is important nevertheless to balance the emphasis on Christ the Pantocrator with an emphasis on Christ the Eternal Word fully and uniquely present in salvation history, whose crucifying cross is the only true path to personal and cosmic

40. See Robert Sokolowski's insightful comments on Heidegger in this regard in "Being My Way," *First Things* 89 (January 1999): 51-54.

41. As Boersma shows, this recognition is the founding insight of "la nouvelle théologie."

42. Sherrard, *The Rape of Man and Nature*, p. 17.

43. Sherrard, *Human Image*, p. 124.

re-creation.[44] As Hans Urs von Balthasar was at pains to insist — even as he himself recovered in a most sympathetic way the Christological, participationist theology of Pseudo-Dionysius — our participation in God is by grace and not by nature.[45]

II

If Sherrard is an advocate of "Christian Platonist" participationist metaphysics, or, more precisely, of "participationist Christology," as the preceding exposition shows, then it stands to reason that he would also urge the importance of recovering a Christian Platonist epistemology. And, indeed, throughout his writings, he emphasizes that it is only through our "spiritual consciousness," our *nous* or *intellectus,* that we can attain true knowledge. He consistently stresses that *dianoia* or *ratio* — discursive reason — requires contact with the transtemporal and trans-spatial realities of the Logos of God if it is to connect with the eternal meaning of finite beings and to carry out sound deductions.[46] Lacking contact with the archetypal realities of being, *ratio* becomes the base instrument of "ego-consciousness" and a mere tool for our self-gratification.[47] We can only see the hidden depths of being, Sherrard argues, if we are moved by the proper mode of consciousness, which must be shaped by intimate union with God through religious contemplation.

In many ways, Sherrard's emphasis on the primacy of the intellect over pure reason is similar to the uncovering of the "reasons of the heart" by the modern Augustinian tradition in the West, although Sherrard obviously sees himself as much more in the line of the Alexandrian tradition of Clement and

---

44. In *The Spirit of the Liturgy,* Cardinal Ratzinger (now Pope Emeritus Benedict XVI) gives a very important exposition in the context of a discussion of the theology of icons of the unique importance of the Western tradition of iconography, with its focus on the passion and the cross of Christ, in contradistinction to the Eastern tradition, with its focus on the cosmological and universal dimensions of Christ's glorifying self-revelation. Although stressing the need for a balance between East and West in this regard, the Holy Father has nevertheless always been insistent that the unique genius of the Western tradition, particularly as it is expressed in the medieval and early modern period, should not be denigrated for the sake of a purely archaeologistic return to the cosmological focus of the East. See Joseph Ratzinger, *The Spirit of the Liturgy,* trans. John Saward (San Francisco: Ignatius, 2000), pp. 115-35.

45. See Boersma's discussion of Balthasar, in *Nouvelle Théologie,* pp. 117-35.

46. See the discussion by Kallistos Ware in the foreword to Sherrard, *Christianity,* pp. xxiv-xxv.

47. Sherrard, *Human Image,* pp. 8-11.

Origen than in the line of St. Augustine. Sherrard insists on the recovery of Christian gnosis, which he considers to be a particularly Eastern Christian concern. He argues that the sacramental activation of *nous* or *intellectus* is a religious imperative: we must, he insists, seek to know the world truly in Christ.[48] The crisis of our time is for Sherrard (as for Guénon, in fact)[49] primarily a gnoseological crisis. Sherrard's doctrine emphasizes the noetic culmination of human experience in Christ. He does not, it is true, emphasize charity in the way that Pope Benedict XVI and the Augustinian tradition do, yet his theandric anthropology can easily be turned in support of this emphasis. After all, it is as true if not truer for St. Augustine as for any church father that charity is a gift that we receive only by incorporation into the Mystical Body of Christ through the power of the Holy Spirit. It is a general axiom of the church fathers, in both the East and the West, that in Christ and by the power of the Holy Spirit our perfection in knowledge coincides with our perfection in love. There is, moreover, an acknowledgment in Sherrard, as in Pascal, that purity of heart and love of truth are the necessary preconditions for knowing the truth, especially in the age of modern science.

Sherrard sees the idolatry of discursive reason — non-sacramental, a sham gnosis — as the worst of all sins besetting modern man. Having locked himself in his own immanence, modern man has pushed forth discursive reason as the highest faculty of knowledge, presuming that he can know the reality of cosmic being without being informed by the intellect's contact with supersensible or metaphysical realities.[50] He takes it as a dogmatic assumption that the way to get at the truth of the beings of nature is by means of mathematical analysis of the data of sensory experience.[51] His sense of the true reality of knowledge is, as a result, sorely misguided. He is operating in the wrong "mode of consciousness," allowing himself to be dominated by mathematical quantities.[52] The end result is to eliminate all meaningful existence, including human intelligence, from the category of the real.[53] In sum, Sherrard's epistemology contains a trenchant diagnosis of the modern tendency to reduce man to

48. See Sherrard, *The Rape of Man and Nature*, pp. 29-41.

49. See René Guénon, *The Crisis of the Modern World*, trans. Marco Pallis, Arthur Osborne, and Richard C. Nicholson (Hillsdale: Sophia Perennis, 2001).

50. Sherrard, *Human Image*, pp. 77-101.

51. Sherrard, *Human Image*, pp. 33-55.

52. Sherrard, *Human Image*, p. 2. The idea that man's "mode of consciousness" determines his capacity to see the depths of being was a common theme among the Guénonians as well as in Sherrard.

53. Sherrard, *Human Image*, pp. 39-40.

nothing more than a constructive or deconstructive subjectivity, no longer dwelling within a world of essential meanings and objective perceptions and experiences.

This diagnosis is a powerful jolt that forces us to confront the consequences of our self-banishment from the universe. What happens to us, or to the world, if we no longer understand our inner experiences as having an existence that is meaningfully compatible with the category of truth? This is ultimately the question we must face, having placed ourselves under "the reign of quantity." We can, given this situation of self-imposed exile, at best envision ourselves as a packet of fleeting whims and willfulness, whose only reason for being is to pursue those whims wherever they may lead us. All cosmic reality can be for us but mathematical limit or pattern, whose only "purpose" is to lie before our sovereign volition as a formless grid to be dissected and manipulated according to our basest desires. We are left only subjectively to impose values on the world where there is objectively nothing good to be discerned. There is no eternal, archetypal grounding for these imposed values. There is no standard of truth, goodness, or beauty that we must nurture in our use of the physical universe.

Sherrard compels us to see, as an essential precondition for the recovery of a sure-footed environmental ecology, that we must heal our human ecology by suffusing it once again with the undiminished sacred wisdom of our religious heritage. His critique is laden with positive suggestions and implications, but these are strong medicine. They would have us recognize that a Christian theologian who wishes to be a truly effective ecologist must be a proponent of the Chalcedonian orthodoxy and a defender of the high liturgical tradition that uplifts the intellect by contact with the archetypal realities that govern the universe. Sherrard prescribes prayer and contemplation as the medicine that we need most of all, the essential remedy that alone can heal our sick souls, our lost sense of humanity and of the world. The Eucharist of the Church, on his diagnosis and prescription, is not only "the medicine of immortality," as it has always been understood, but of participatory justice on earth.[54]

Sherrard thus has much to teach us about the relationship of human ecology to environmental ecology, and his work could give a fully theandric per-

---

54. I am in agreement with Kallistos Ware's assessment, in his foreword to Sherrard's *Christianity* (pp. ix-xlv), that Sherrard is, in the end, a fundamentally orthodox Christian thinker — in the tradition of Eastern Orthodoxy. Though the Eastern tradition conceives of the nature of the Church in more pneumatic terms than the Western Church does, it is nevertheless as true for the East as it is for the West that it is only through sacramental participation in the Eucharist of the Church that one can have full access to God's deifying grace.

spective to the Christological "integral humanism" that has become so explicitly a part of the Church's social doctrine, not least of all in *Caritas in Veritate*. Obviously, his analysis cannot be appropriated without criticism by the Western theologian. In addition to problematic aspects of it that I have already mentioned, it should be pointed out that his totalizing critique of modern science, however valuable in many respects, is obviously not fully in line with the more balanced suggestions in *Caritas in Veritate*. Nevertheless, Sherrard's "theoanthropocosmic" vision of reality and call for restitution of the Christian sacred is what is needed in our time, and, I might add, in some profound ways coheres with Pope Benedict XVI's larger theological project. It would not be too much to say that for the Holy Father, as for Sherrard, the Chalcedonian doctrine in its fullest implications and liturgical renewal are essential for the effective realization of social and ecological justice.

Nature, Soil, and God: Soils and the "Grammar of Nature"

Sister Damien Marie Savino, F.S.E.

Introduction

> *Normally we don't think too much about the ground that supports our feet, houses, cities, and farms. Yet even if we usually take it for granted, we know that good soil is not just dirt. When you dig into rich, fresh earth, you can feel the life in it. Fertile soil crumbles and slides right off a shovel. Look closely and you find a whole world of life eating life, a biological orgy recycling the dead back into new life. Healthy soil has an enticing and wholesome aroma — the smell of life itself.*
>
> *Yet what is dirt? We try to keep it out of sight, out of mind, and outside. We spit on it, denigrate it, and kick if off of our shoes. But in the end, what's more important? Everything comes from it, and everything returns to it.*[1]

What is this mystery we call soil, from which everything comes and to which everything returns? Believe it or not, a teaspoon of fertile soil contains between 100 million and 1 billion bacteria with 20,000 to 30,000 species,[2] several yards of fungal hyphae, several thousand protozoa, and a few dozen

---

1. David R. Montgomery, *Dirt: The Erosion of Civilizations* (Berkeley: University of California Press, 2007), p. 1.

2. Elaine R. Ingham, "Soil Biology: The Soil Biology Primer — Bacteria," U.S. Department of Agriculture, Natural Resources Conservation Service, http://soils.usda.gov/sqi/concepts/soil_biology/bacteria.html.

nematodes.[3] Soil ecosystems are mind-boggingly complex and incredibly rich in biodiversity, and without this thin skin of earth beneath our feet we would not have life as we know it. Indeed, the fate of humans has been inextricably linked to that of the soil since the dawn of human civilization, as cultures have risen and fallen with the health or depletion of the soil.[4] It is not exaggerating to say that healthy soils provide us with food and forests, clean air and water. They regulate water flows, cycle nutrients, support buildings, and filter pollutants.[5] Soils are tremendous engines of fertility. Without soils we would literally drown in our own wastes.

Even beyond the physical resources that soil provides, there is something about soil that is fundamental to the human experience. As anyone who has ever had a compost pile can testify, in an amazing way soils embody the mystery that life comes out of death. "Wherever there are decay and repose, there begins to be soil."[6] Soils are also linked to the origin and destiny of life. "You are dust, and unto dust you shall return."[7] Yet soils are often overlooked, and their essential significance for both natural and human development remains largely unexplored and underappreciated.

In *Caritas in Veritate (CV)*, Pope Benedict introduces an intriguing concept that may be a useful tool for redressing this situation. Focusing on environmental questions in chapter four, he speaks of what he calls the "grammar of nature":

> Nature is at our disposal . . . as a gift of the Creator who has given it an inbuilt order, enabling man to draw from it the principles needed in order "to till it and keep it" (Gen 2:15) . . . it is a wondrous work of the Creator containing a "grammar" which sets forth ends and criteria for its wise use, not its reckless exploitation. (*CV*, no. 48)[8]

---

3. Jeff Lowenfels and Wayne Lewis, "Teeming with Microbes — A Gardener's Guide to the Soil Food Web," http://www.goveganic.net/spip.php?article93.

4. See, for example, the cases discussed in Jared Diamond, *Collapse: How Societies Choose to Fail or Succeed* (New York: Penguin, 2005). A number of the cases he discusses speak to the collapse of civilizations due at least in part to soil denigration.

5. "Soil Quality Concepts — Overview," U.S. Department of Agriculture, Natural Resources Conservation Service, http://www.goveganic.net/spip.php?article93.

6. William Bryant Logan, *Dirt: The Ecstatic Skin of the Earth* (New York: The Berkley Publishing Group, 1995), p. 2.

7. Genesis 3:19.

8. Translation at http://www.vatican.va/holy_father/benedict_xvi/encyclicals/documents/hf_ben-xvi_enc_20090629_caritas-in-veritate_en.html.

The purpose of this essay is to apply this concept to soil — that is, to explore the notion of a "grammar of soil." This will be done by examining scriptural references to soil to see whether this approach can shed light on the fundamental mystery, or "inner grammar," of soil. If so, this kind of reflection could deepen our understanding of "the principles needed in order 'to till and keep [the soil]' " and meaningfully inform the principles and practices of contemporary environmental stewardship.

Scriptural References to Soil

Since the Near Eastern civilizations of the Scriptures were primarily agricultural, they were familiar with soil as a reality of daily life. It would have been natural for them to refer to it in their stories and parables. In the Scriptures the physical reality of soil assumed a spiritual significance, as the deeper symbolic or analogical dimensions became the focus of the scriptural message.

A query of the New American Bible (NAB) translation reveals that there are fifty-six references to the word "soil" in the Old and New Testaments.[9] Though there are many ways of analyzing these references, this essay identifies and focuses on three main themes. First, there is the association of soil with being, as portrayed in the second Genesis creation account in which man is created out the clay of the earth. Second, there is the relationship between soil and fertility, or more properly, the struggle for fertility, recounted in many stories and parables in the Old and New Testaments in which the health of the soil and the dispositions of the Israelites or Christians are related. Third, there is the connection between soil and virtue, found primarily in New Testament passages in which soil represents the process of conversion and the associated virtues of patience, faith, and the like. While these three themes are by no means exhaustive, it is interesting to explore how they point to some fundamental elements of the "grammar" of soil.

---

9. Older translations may include more than this, as the word has gone out of style somewhat in contemporary discourse, being replaced by more generic words such as "earth," "field," and the like. All Scripture quotes in this essay are from the New American Bible, translation approved by the United States Conference of Catholic Bishops, 1970.

Soil and Being

In Genesis 2:4b-7 the unique creation of man out of clay soil is recounted:

4b At the time when the LORD God made the earth and the heavens —

5 while as yet there was no field shrub on earth and no grass of the field had sprouted, for the LORD God had sent no rain upon the earth and there was no man to till the soil,

6 but a stream was welling up out of the earth and was watering all the surface of the ground —

7 [2]the LORD God formed man out of the clay of the ground and blew into his nostrils the breath of life, and so man became a living being.

Man was formed out of clay with the purpose of tilling the soil. Note 2 in the biblical commentary reminds the reader of the play on words in the original Hebrew, that God molds the body of man *(adam)* out of the clay of the ground *(adama)*.[10] Our bodies are portrayed as having their very origin in the soil of the earth; our being was given form out of it. As the commentary also indicates, the word "being" is literally "soul." The being (soul) of man was created when God breathed the breath of life into clay (soil). Note the connection between soil and the soul; this will be referred to again later.

It is interesting that one of the current hypotheses for the origin of life suggests that the first cells originated on clay surfaces. This is called the clay-life hypothesis. It was proposed by a Scottish chemist in 1986 and has been supported by more recent research.[11] Clays form in layers, and the theory proposes that clay layers, perhaps in the ancient oceans, could have provided the substrate and shelter needed for the biosynthesis of organic molecules. As clay crystals are highly variable and dimpled, this could have allowed many different permutations, the precursor of a genetic code. It is possible too that the clay matrix provided a container or hydrogel within which the earliest biomolecules found the shelter needed to form and persist, especially in the harsh ocean environment. The clay-life hypothesis reinforces from a scientific standpoint the importance of the connections between soil and being in relation to the "inner grammar" of soil.

10. Note 2: "God is portrayed as a potter molding man's body out of clay. There is a play on words in Hebrew between adam ('man') and adama ('ground'). Being: literally, 'soul.'"

11. A. G. Cairns-Smith and Hyman Hartman, eds., *Clay Minerals and the Origin of Life* (Cambridge: Cambridge University Press, 1986). And Dayong Yang and Songming Peng et al., "Enhanced Transcription and Translation in Clay Hydrogel and Implications for Early Life Evolution," *Scientific Reports* 3, no. 3165 (7 November 2013).

Soil and the Struggle for Fertility

The relationship between soil and fertility is a second common theme in the Scriptures. There are many passages, especially in the Old Testament, in which the fruit of the womb and the produce of the soil are linked to human flourishing. For example, see Deuteronomy 7:13; 26:2, 10, 15; 28:4; 30:9; Isaiah 30:23; and Ezekiel 34:27. Generally, the theme is that the soil and land will flourish when the Israelites listen to and heed the voice of God, as in Deuteronomy 30:9-10:

> 9 Then the LORD, your God, will increase in more than goodly measure the returns from all your labors, the fruit of your womb, the offspring of your livestock, and the produce of your soil; for the LORD, your God, will again take delight in your prosperity, even as he took delight in your fathers',
>
> 10 if only you heed the voice of the LORD, your God, and keep his commandments and statutes that are written in this book of the law, when you return to the LORD, your God, with all your heart and all your soul.

The soil represents fertility, the produce of the soil being associated with the fruit of the womb. Good soil by definition is fertile and in an almost miraculous way brings forth food that sustains human life. Anyone who gardens successfully is aware of this mystery. Part of the "grammar of soil" is its physical association with fertility — with the sprouting of the seed, the growth of the plant, and the harvesting of the produce.

There is also an analogical connection here, as exemplified in the famous parable of the soil recounted in Matthew 13:1-8, 18-23; Mark 4:1-8, 13-23; and Luke 8:4-15. In this parable, Jesus contrasts the various types of soil on which a seed may fall (on the path, on rocky ground with shallow soil, among thorns, and on rich soil) with the productivity of the harvest on each kind of soil. This image is one that would have been familiar to the Israelites, as described in note 2 of the commentary (referring to verses 3-8 of Matthew 13), which refers to the sowing practices at that time: "Since in Palestine sowing often preceded ploughing, much of the seed is scattered on ground that is unsuitable. Yet while much is wasted, the seed that falls on good ground bears fruit in extraordinarily large measure."[12]

---

12. New American Bible, Matthew 13:3, footnote 2.

The parable follows (Matt. 13:1-8):

1   On that day, Jesus went out of the house and sat down by the sea.
2   Such large crowds gathered around him that he got into a boat and sat down, and the whole crowd stood along the shore.
3   And he spoke to them at length in parables, [2]saying: "A sower went out to sow.[3]
4   And as he sowed, some seed fell on the path, and birds came and ate it up.
5   Some fell on rocky ground, where it had little soil. It sprang up at once because the soil was not deep,
6   and when the sun rose it was scorched, and it withered for lack of roots.
7   Some seed fell among thorns, and the thorns grew up and choked it.
8   But some seed fell on rich soil, and produced fruit, a hundred or sixty or thirtyfold."

When the disciples ask Christ what the parable means, he gives the following allegorical interpretation (Matt. 13:18-23):

18   [8]Hear then the parable of the sower.
19   The seed sown on the path is the one who hears the word of the kingdom without understanding it, and the evil one comes and steals away what was sown in his heart.
20   The seed sown on rocky ground is the one who hears the word and receives it at once with joy.
21   But he has no root and lasts only for a time. When some tribulation or persecution comes because of the word, he immediately falls away.
22   The seed sown among thorns is the one who hears the word, but then worldly anxiety and the lure of riches choke the word and it bears no fruit.
23   But the seed sown on rich soil is the one who hears the word and understands it, who indeed bears fruit and yields a hundred or sixty or thirtyfold.

As note 8 in the commentary indicates, the soil is a symbol for the inner dispositions of persons in response to the word of God. The different types of soil on which the seed falls represent various responses people can make to the preaching of Jesus:

- The seed falling on the path that never sprouts represents those who never understand or accept the word of God.
- The seed falling on rocky ground with shallow soil represents those who believe at first but then withdraw at the first signs of persecution.
- The seed falling among thorns represents those whose belief is choked out by worries and the lure of wealth and secular concerns.
- The seed falling on good soil represents those who truly listen to the word, respond to it in their actions, and produce abundant fruit in their lives.

In the parable, Christ draws a beautiful parallel between the fertility of the soil and the fertility of the soul. Those whose soil is not deep or whose interiority is choked by anxiety and desire for worldly goods will not be open to hearing the word of God and therefore will not be spiritually fruitful. Those persons, on the other hand, who are "good soil" will bear fruit abundantly, just as seed that falls into fertile soil bears fruit and yields a hundred- or sixty- or thirtyfold. If they have the proper dispositions of mind and heart, they will listen and respond to the word of God and put it into practice, and their lives will bear fruit as good soil does. The Greek word for soil in this passage, γῆν, or "gen," is the root for genesis, gene, or generation — meaning birth — again reinforcing the connection between soils and fertility.[13]

Other passages, especially in the Old Testament, go even further in linking the soil and the soul, by adding the notion that the *actual* fertility of the soil is dependent in some way upon how well the Israelites heed the voice of the Lord and keep his commandments. It is not just a symbolic or analogical connection, but also a real one in which the inner dispositions of the believer *actually* affect how productive the soil is. Those who turn away from God will experience the ravages of soil degradation and infertility. Those who turn toward God and are aligned with the commandments are not only symbols of good soil, but also agents of soil fertility, that is, their land will actually be more productive. This is indeed a radical proposition!

In the Old Testament, the land itself — the soil — is the sign of the covenant of God with his people.[14] When the Jewish people went into exodus, they were forced to spend forty years wandering in the wilderness. In their suffering they expressed their longing for God, a God who was connected to a particular place, to the "promised land." Much of the Old Testament is a re-

---

13. Online Greek Interlinear New Testament, available from http://interlinear.biblos.com/.

14. Personal communication, Sister Paula Jean Miller, F.S.E., professor of theology, University of St. Thomas, Houston, September 12, 2010.

counting of the longing of the Jewish people for the sacred soil of the promised land to which the Lord was calling them. The Lord their God would lead them to the fertile soil of the promised land, if only they would heed his voice and return to him with all their hearts and all their souls. The soil would be made fertile if the chosen people restored their relationship to the Lord. Note the radical connection, more than just symbolic, between faithfulness to the covenant and soil fertility. The land was the actual manifestation of the covenantal relationship of God with his people.

If, on the other hand, they strayed from God and disobeyed his commandments, the soil would be "stricken" (Jer. 14:4). There are also many stories of this in Scripture.[15] In these Old Testament passages, tilling the soil is a constant struggle, and the soil does not yield its fruits because of the arrogance, hubris, and idolatry of men.

The "curse" on the soil because of the sinfulness of man began when Adam and Eve disobeyed God. God cursed the soil *(adama)* from which they were formed and told them they would have to toil over it all the days of their lives (Gen. 3:17):

> 17 To the man he said: "Because you listened to your wife and ate from the tree of which I had forbidden you to eat, Cursed be the ground *(adama)* because of you! In toil shall you eat its yield all the days of your life."

The curse is reiterated to Cain after he murdered his brother Abel (Gen. 4:8b-12):

> 8b When they were in the field, Cain attacked his brother Abel and killed him.
> 9 Then the LORD asked Cain, "Where is your brother Abel?" He answered, "I do not know. Am I my brother's keeper?"
> 10 The LORD then said: "What have you done! Listen: your brother's blood cries out to me from the soil!
> 11 Therefore you shall be banned from the soil that opened its mouth to receive your brother's blood from your hand.
> 12 If you till the soil, it shall no longer give you its produce. You shall become a restless wanderer on the earth."

15. See, for example, Genesis 3:17; 4:12; 19:15; Leviticus 26:19; Deuteronomy 11:17; 29:22; Isaiah 32:13; Jeremiah 14:4; and Job 14:19.

Ever after, as the Hebrews struggled with their relationship with God, they were reminded that their struggle for fidelity would be reflected in the state of the soil. If they strayed from God, the soil would not yield its produce and the land would not support them, as in Deuteronomy 11:16-19:

16   But be careful lest your heart be so lured away that you serve other gods and worship them.

17   For then the wrath of the LORD will flare up against you and he will close up the heavens, so that no rain will fall, and the soil will not yield its crops, and you will soon perish from the good land he is giving you.

18   Therefore, take these words of mine into your heart and soul. Bind them at your wrist as a sign, and let them be a pendant on your forehead.

19   Teach them to your children, speaking of them at home and abroad, whether you are busy or at rest.

As meaningful as these words were for Old Testament times, they also merit reflection for today, as we suffer with global losses of soil fertility due to such issues as war, erosion, poor agricultural practices, poverty, and corrupt government, to name a few. In the United States, for example, the Dust Bowl resulted in huge soil losses due to poor land management practices driven by consumptive attitudes. Current erosion rates on farmlands as a result of poor soil management are reported to be 10 to 40 times the rates of natural soil formation, with erosion rates on forested land between 500 and 10,000 times the natural rates.[16] In his book, *Collapse: How Societies Choose to Fail or Succeed,* in which Jared Diamond considers how societies and even whole civilizations have "undermined themselves," soil problems are one of the eight categories he names as causes for the collapse.[17] Soil problems as he describes them include erosion, salinization, and soil fertility losses. The other categories include other land-related factors such as deforestation, overhunting, and overfishing. All of these reflect the links between degraded human attitudes and practices and degraded or "stricken" soil.

Soil is a nation's capital, providing the physical foundation for food, buildings, and the like, but also for human culture and interchange. Indeed, how we

16. Jared Diamond, *Collapse: How Societies Choose to Fail or Succeed* (New York: Penguin, 2005).

17. Diamond, *Collapse,* p. 6.

treat the soil says a great deal about our human condition. As the contemporary essayist Wendell Berry has said: "What we do to the land, we do to ourselves."[18] The reverse of this statement is also true: "What we do to ourselves, we do to the land," and the Old Testament Scriptures especially point to this mystery.

Further, the scriptural passages on soil and fertility suggest the rather radical idea that the actual fertility of the soil is enhanced not just by persons who know the physical techniques for cultivating it, but also by those who are attentive to their moral and religious status, that is, those whose "inner soils" are fertile. In other words, persons who are aligned with the commandments and are faithful to God will tend to foster and enhance the fertility of the land. So the virtuous man is not only a symbolic image of "good soil," but also the practical instrument and guardian of soil fertility.

Soil and Virtue

In light of this, it is interesting to look at the connections between soil and virtue in Scripture. Consider the parable of the fig tree (Luke 13:7-9):

6   [4]There once was a person who had a fig tree planted in his orchard, and when he came in search of fruit on it but found none,

7   he said to the gardener, "For three years now I have come in search of fruit on this fig tree but have found none. (So) cut it down. Why should it exhaust the soil?"

8   He said to him in reply, "Sir, leave it for this year also, and I shall cultivate the ground around it and fertilize it;

9   it may bear fruit in the future. If not you can cut it down."

In this passage, the process of improving the soil by manuring it so the fig tree can bear fruit represents a dual mystery: both the healing or conversion process necessary to help persons become spiritually fruitful, and the mercy and "continuing patience of God with those who have not yet given evidence of their repentance."[19] When manure is spread around a tree or plant, it un-

---

18. Quoted in Montgomery, *Dirt*, p. 1.

19. New American Bible, Luke 13:6-9, footnote 4: "Following on the call to repentance in *Luke 13:1-5*, the parable of the barren fig tree presents a story about the continuing patience of God with those who have not yet given evidence of their repentance."

dergoes a composting process that liberates nutrients and enriches the soil. In a mysterious and rather miraculous way, composting converts "spoils into soil,"[20] or garbage into a garden, through the activities of the literally millions of microorganisms in each teaspoon of soil. Nothing goes to waste, and all is transformed from unwanted scraps into rich humus. What a meaningful analogy for the personal conversion process!

The practical power of this process in soil has been widely recognized, as evidenced by the fact that the practice of composting has been employed by many cultures for thousands of years. A critical aspect of the composting process is that it requires time and patience. Likewise, the personal conversion process also requires time and patience — on the part of both the person and God. God is intimately involved in our conversion; in his generosity he is ultimately patient, ever waiting when we stray, ever desiring that our hearts be open to his word and seeking to fertilize our inner soils with his grace.

The word "patience" is derived from the Latin *pati,* meaning "to suffer or endure." Patience is a process of enduring and waiting, but it is not just bearing a process out of necessity. As a Christian virtue, patience is an exercise of the will. It is an act of trusting, hoping for, waiting in expectation, and with ears listening for the will of God. The process of manuring the soil around the fig tree and trusting that it will bear fruit in time exemplifies the virtue of patience. Indeed, it represents the process of acquiring any virtue, which is generally the fruit of a long, slow "composting" or conversion process.

There are practical implications here. Even Thomas Jefferson and other agrarians recognized that cultivating the earth fostered individual responsibility, freedom, and the virtuous life, as summarized in the following statement of agrarian ideals.

> Cultivating the earth confers a valid title to it. The ownership of the land, by making the farmer independent, gives him social status and dignity, while constant contact with nature makes him virtuous.[21]

The contemporary author Michael Pollen, in his book *Second Nature: A Gardener's Education,* speaks of composting as a model of ecological respon-

---

20. State of Connecticut Department of Environmental Protection, "Turn Your Spoils into Soil . . . Compost!" available from http://www.ct.gov/dep/cwp/view.asp?A=2718&Q=325370.

21. Karl Hess, *Visions Upon the Land: Man and Nature on the Western Range* (Washington, D.C.: Island, 1992), p. 32. Here he is quoting Henry Nash Smith from his book, *Virgin Land* (Cambridge: Harvard University Press, 1978).

sibility and a means by which we can redeem our broken human relationships with nature.[22] By allowing gardeners the privilege of participating in natural soil cycling processes, composting not only teaches patience and exemplifies the process of acquiring the virtues, but it also allows those participating to give back to the soil and to restore soil fertility. It is a way of counteracting the constant emphasis on "taking" so characteristic of modern society and of encouraging in its place a virtuous spirit of self-sacrifice and gift.

The "Grammar of Soil" and Environmental Stewardship

The scriptural themes discussed here — that of the relationship of soils to being, to fertility, and to virtue — help illumine the "grammar of soil" from a conceptual or symbolic standpoint. As recounted in the New Testament, Jesus used the reality of soil, as he did other natural realities, to teach his disciples the principles of the faith in parables. The mysteries in soil can help point persons beyond the created reality to the Creator.

While the Scriptures point us to analogical mysteries about soil, there is also the reality that laboring with the soil *actually* produces particular virtues in those who are true to the process. So the "grammar" is not just symbolic; as this essay has proposed, it is also real and in a sense dialogical. While the fertility of the soil symbolically represents the fertility of the soul, the fertility of the soul actually affects the fertility of the soil. There are real connections between the inner dispositions of the believer and the productivity of the soil, as the Old Testament readings bring to light so beautifully.

This offers interesting insights into the principles and practices of contemporary environmental stewardship. Stewardship has to do with careful stewardship of the soil, but it also has to do with the state of the soul. Scripture suggests that those with upright souls will be better stewards of the soil; they will be attentive to the "grammar of the soul" placed within it by the Creator. The inner order in their souls will resonate with the inner order of the soil because both orders were authored by God. A person who listens to and follows the word of God will more readily recognize and respect his handiwork in creation.

It is clear, then, that there is a need for a human ecology — an ecology of the soul, so to speak — and that human ecology and natural ecology are inti-

22. Michael Pollen, *Second Nature: A Gardener's Education* (New York: Dell, 1991), pp. 66-75.

mately connected. This is a theme the Holy Father has emphasized on numerous occasions and reiterates in paragraph 51 of *Caritas in Veritate*.[23] Virtuous environmental stewardship links the two.

As the encyclical indicates, nature expresses a design of love and truth (*CV*, no. 48). It is through learning its "grammar" that we come to better understand the Creator whose designs for us and for the world are those of love and truth. Soils in their inner structure and grammar speak to us of our origins and remind us of the overwhelming fertility of the earth — the "economy of gratuitousness" (*CV*, no. 38) present in the soil that could be an enlightening model for more virtuous interactions with the land and with others.

Is this achievable? St. Francis of Assisi, patron saint of ecology, is one model for us. In his integral holiness, he came to a profound understanding of the innermost grammar of creation, which is expressed beautifully in his famous Canticle of the Creatures. At the heart of this innermost grammar is praise and gratitude to the Creator for the gratuitousness of his creation. About the soil St. Francis says:

> All praise be yours, my Lord, through our Sister
> Mother Earth, who sustains us and governs us,
> and produces various fruits with colored flowers and herbs.[24]

---

23. See, for example, *Caritas in Veritate*, no. 51: "There is a need for what might be called a 'human ecology,' correctly understood. The deterioration of nature is in fact closely connected to the culture that shapes human existence: *when human ecology is respected within society, environmental ecology also benefits.* Just as human virtues are interrelated, such that the weakening of one places others at risk, so the ecological system is based on respect for a plan that affects both the health of society and its good relationship with nature."

24. St. Francis of Assisi, "Canticle of the Creatures," available from http://www.appleseeds .org/canticle.htm.

EPILOGUE

Loving in Truth for the Sake of Humanity

Cardinal Peter Kodwo Appiah Turkson

Clearly, recent global events awaken us to the importance of a sustained Christian reflection on the nature and soul of human development and economic life, both within our own society and in other parts of the world. It is in this context that Pope Benedict XVI, keenly aware of the dynamics of globalization and its impact on the human family, issued his third and greatly anticipated[1] encyclical letter, *Caritas in Veritate (CV)*. The encyclical identifies the twin call of love and truth on our lives as citizens, entrepreneurs, workers, and students, and, most fundamentally, as followers of Christ and subjects of reason.

In the different interventions on micro-credit and micro-financing, the economics of gift or the principle of gratuitousness and the logic of gift as an expression of the fraternity of humankind, the vocation of the human person and of all his activities to transcendence, the suggestion and thought of a world political authority to "watch over" a phenomenon whose presence and activities appear to supersede the competence of every single nation, the development and progress of people (social ethics), and respect for life (life ethics), the essays in this book have variously addressed and treated a good deal of the concerns the pope articulated in this encyclical, leaving some yet to be dealt with.

1. The reception of the encyclical has been great. It is a document that appears to have something for everybody to identify with. Within 30 days of its publication, Vatican Radio counted about 4,300 articles on the encyclical in English, French, Italian, Spanish, and Portuguese on the Web. The Meltwater Group, extending its survey to other languages, counted 6,000 articles on the encyclical. See Gianpaolo Salvini, S.J., "L'Enciclica Caritas in Veritate," *La Civiltà Cattolica*, September 9, 2009, p. 458.

To be sure, the domination of economic values and institutions embodied in the all-too-often unaccountable power of the World Trade Organization, World Bank, International Monetary Fund, large multinational companies, and financial institutions, for example, must be addressed. There is a need to articulate an alternative vision of development values and institutions capable of shaping a more just future. The fathers of 2009 Second Special Assembly for Africa of the Synod of Bishops believed indeed that "a new and just world order is not only possible but necessary for the good of all humanity. A change is called for with regard to the debt burden against poor nations, which literally kills children. Multinationals have to stop their criminal devastation of the environment in their greedy exploitation of natural resources. It is shortsighted policy to foment wars in order to make fast gains from chaos, at the cost of human lives and blood. Is there no one out there able and willing to stop all these crimes against humanity?"[2] We must, therefore, lay out the proper relationships of the institutions of the private and public sectors to achieve this alternative vision, and point toward how they should be organized and established. We need to extend this vision and our approaches toward establishing it in current areas of conflict and in global political arenas. We must promote solidarity, rather than competition and conflict, between workers and peoples of different nations.[3]

This essay offers a few observations on the encyclical as a social teaching, its papal authorship, its appeal to *faith* and *reason*, some of its main themes, and some of its striking features.

A Papal Teaching and a Teaching Pope

Announced in 2007, on the occasion of the fortieth anniversary of the encyclical letter *Populorum Progressio* of Pope Paul VI (1967) and the twentieth anniversary of the encyclical letter *Sollicitudo Rei Socialis* of Pope John Paul II (1987), *Caritas in Veritate* was originally intended to celebrate the memory of these two encyclicals, especially their treatment of the question of development. *Caritas in Veritate* originally intended to take up the issue of development in the new and changed situation of a globalized world. What was once a simple "social issue" in the days of Pope Paul VI and Pope John Paul II has

2. Second Special Assembly for Africa of the Synod of Bishops, "Message to the People of God," October 23, 2009, no. 33.

3. See James E. Hug, S.J., "Economic Justice and Globalization," in *Globalization and Catholic Social Thought,* ed. John A. Coleman and William F. Ryan (Maryknoll: Orbis, 2005), p. 61.

now become a "global issue." The economic crisis of 2008-9 invited the pope to treat the issue and the ethics of economics in the context of human development in greater detail. This delayed the completion of the encyclical letter somewhat, but on June 29, 2009 (feast of Sts. Peter and Paul), the pope signed the new social encyclical and promulgated it on July 7, 2009 (month of St. Benedict), just before the meeting of the G-8 in L'Aquila, Italy.

Caritas in Veritate is a social encyclical like many others before it, beginning with Pope Leo XIII's *Rerum Novarum* (1891).[4] In it the insights of theology, philosophy, economics, ecology, and politics have been harnessed coherently to formulate the great need to place the human person (his total and integral development) at the center of all world systems of thought and activity. The human person (his salvation) was at the center of the mission and ministry of Jesus Christ: as the revelation of the love of the Father (John 3:16) and the truth of man's creation in God's image and of his transcendent vocation to holiness and to happiness with God. This is the setting of the two concepts, love and truth, which drive the encyclical. Love and truth do not only lie at the heart of the mission and ministry of Jesus; they also correspond to and describe the essential character of the life of the human person on earth, namely, as a gift and love of God to become gift and love too.

In specifying love and truth as the premise and scope of human development, the encyclical may appear to be idealistic, but "this is a method the Social Teachings of the Church constantly follow, namely: to take the high road, not to distance us from reality, but to draw our attention to the essential point. It is then up to individuals, in their countries, in their profession, in their personal life, to follow through with concrete practice."[5] This dynamic of charity

---

4. Counting the letter of the Sacred Congregation of the Council to Bishop Liénart, of Lille, France, June 5, 1929, two documents of Vatican II, *Gaudium et Spes* and *Dignitatis Humanae*, the second half of the encyclical letter, *Deus Caritas est*, and the instruction *Dignitas Personae*, on certain bioethical questions from the Congregation for the Doctrine of the Faith (December 8, 2008), one may reckon with twenty-two official documents on the social teaching of the Church; see *Le Discours social de l'Eglise Catholique; De Léon XIII à Benoit XVI* (Montrouge: Bayard, 2009). On the various uses of encyclicals by the popes, Wikipedia's entry on the matter ("papal use of encyclicals") is useful. While some popes have made use of encyclicals to address issues of social concern, others have simply made use of addresses/speeches at papal audiences.

5. "C'est une method constant de la doctrine social de l'Eglise: prendre de la hauteur, non pour nous éloigner de réel, mais pour nous rapprocher de l'essentiel. Ensuite, à chacun, dans son pays, dans son métier, dans sa vie personnelle, d'en tirer les consequences practiques." J.-Y. Naudet, "Caritas in Veritate. La doctrine sociale de l'Eglise: un unique enseignement . . . ," *Annales de Vendée*, no. 5 (2009): 140.

received and given is what gives rise to the Church's social teaching, which is *caritas in veritate in re sociale* (*CV*, no. 5).

Human society, the reference of the Church's social teaching, has changed over the years from the misery of workers in the days after the Industrial Revolution and the emergence of Marxism (Pope Leo XIII), the crisis of 1929 (Pope Pius XI), decolonization and the appearance of third worldism (Pope John XXIII and Pope Paul VI), the fall of the Berlin Wall and political changes in Eastern Europe (Pope John Paul II) to globalization, underdevelopment, and the financial, economic, moral, and anthropological crisis of Pope Benedict XVI (*CV*, no. 75). In these changing situations, the social encyclicals of the popes have fulfilled the need to actualize the same principles of the Church's social teaching. "The Church's social doctrine illuminates with an unchanging light the new problems that are constantly emerging" (*CV*, no. 12).[6] From illuminating merely social problems and challenges in the past, the Church's social doctrine in *Caritas in Veritate* illuminates the social, global, economic, entrepreneurial, political, anthropological, and ecological problems and challenges of our world-society.

Thus, *Caritas in Veritate* preserves the tradition of the pope or church councils, presided over by the pope, offering teachings that reflect the prophetic and teaching office of the pope and that are meant to guide the Church's living of the gospel's values and message in the world (social doctrine). In this sense, Pope Pius XII is believed to have held that papal encyclicals, even when they are not *ex cathedra,* can nonetheless be sufficiently authoritative to end theological debate on a particular question.[7]

This long tradition of papal teaching does not only locate *Caritas in Veritate* in the living stream of Church life and practice. It also roots the figure of the teaching pope equally deeply in the Church's life and history, and the significance of this must not be overlooked. As the author of an encyclical, the pope is a religious figure, constituted pastor, leader, and prophet, according to the faith of the Church, by Jesus Christ, the Son of God and founder of the

---

6. See also Pope John Paul II, *Sollicitudo Rei Socialis,* no. 3.

7. "It is not to be thought that what is set down in encyclical letters does not demand assent in itself because in this the popes do not exercise the supreme power of their magisterium.... Usually what is set forth and inculcated in encyclical letters already pertains to Catholic doctrine. But if the supreme pontiffs in their acts, after due consideration, express an opinion on a hitherto controversial matter, it is clear to all that this matter, according to the mind and will of the same pontiffs, cannot any longer be considered a question of free discussion among theologians" (Pope Pius XII, *Humani Generis,* no. 20). Translation at http://www.vatican.va/holy _father/pius_xii/encyclicals/documents/hf_p-xii_enc_12081950_humani-generis_en.html.

Church. Like the apostle Peter, his predecessor, whom he succeeds in the pastoral care of Christ's sheep and lambs (John 21:15-17), the pope shares in Christ's prayer for Peter: "I have prayed for you that your faith may not fail, and you . . . strengthen your brothers" (Luke 22:31-32). As the spiritual and pastoral leader of the Catholic Church, the pope is prayed for universally by the Church. No Eucharist is celebrated without a prayer for the pope, and the pope himself is a man of deep personal prayer,[8] who seeks God's face and the mind of Christ (see 1 Cor. 2:16) in prayer. Like the Church which he is made a pastor of by Jesus (John 21:15-17), the pope is, therefore, a figure in whom heaven and earth meet and whose mission is to form and inform the earthly with the heavenly. He is a figure who represents an openness to the divine and the transcendent, and who accordingly invites the world to a similar experience of openness to the transcendent and the divine. His is a leadership that is exercised in the power of the Spirit, and it is rooted in the long and ancient tradition of the exercise of religious leadership in Scripture and in the history of the Church. Thus, like the prophets of old, the pope cultivates an openness to God during which "his ears are awakened" (Isa. 50:4-5) to hear a saving message for humanity and the world and during which "the Lord gives [him] the tongue of a teacher to sustain the weary with a word" (Isa. 50:4). He can be resisted and rejected, persecuted and disgraced, but for this, he is also given a "flint face" (see Isa. 50:7; Ezek. 3:9) to teach "in and out of season" (2 Tim. 4:2).

This is not an apologia for the pope. It is what Roman Catholics believe about their leader and pope, who teaches them and all men and women of good will in *Caritas in Veritate,* the encyclical under study.

Appeal to Faith and Reason

Caritas in Veritate, like all the other social encyclicals, is addressed to Catholics and non-Catholics: all men and women of good will. Recognizing the pluriformity of confessions and mental postures (agnostics, atheists, freethinkers, etc.) in human society, the social encyclicals seek to invite all the components of society to come together to develop a more human and better society.

The two basic groups addressed, Catholics and non-Catholics (men and women of good will), also explain the encyclical's reference and appeal to faith and reason: faith for those who believe in Christ and reason for nonbelievers.

---

8. See the prayer life of Pope John Paul II in *Varcare la Soglia della Speranza* (Milan: Arnoldo Mondadori, 1994), pp. 20-26.

Thus, the pope reminds us that the social doctrine of the Church is a "truth of faith and of reason" (*CV*, no. 5). Indeed, the dynamic of charity received and given, which gives rise to *caritas in veritate in re sociale* is the proclamation of the truth of Christ's love in society, and it is rooted in truth: the truth of faith and of reason (*CV*, no. 5). For, just as a person, on the order of nature, is led by the light of reason to the discovery of natural law, to the understanding of rights of people, and to a reflection on social issues, so are Christians, as objects of God's love and on the order of grace, called on to become subjects of charity, pouring forth God's charity and weaving networks of charity. So, the underlying affirmation of social encyclicals addressing Catholics and men and women of good will is the perfect compatibility between faith and reason, even if faith always challenges reason to open up to transcendence. Thus, though distinct in their cognitive characters and fields, faith and reason still converge in *Caritas in Veritate* and in the other social encyclicals to cast their prophetic regard on society, on its institutions, and on its structures, condemning ideologies and social systems that deny humanity its freedom and dignity and affirming those that promote the true nature of the human person — for example, by supporting justice with the culture of love to establish a civilization of love and to uphold the primacy of ethics over technique and all forms of manipulation of life, utilitarianism, economics, and politics.

An Integral Model of Human Development

Caritas in Veritate proposes an integral model of human development in the context of globalization, "the expansion of worldwide interdependence," and calls for a "person-centered and community-oriented process of integration." As has been aptly pointed out, although globalization has indeed lifted millions of people out of poverty, primarily by the integration of the economies of developing nations into international markets, the unevenness of this integration leaves us deeply concerned about the flagrant disregard for human dignity, inequality, poverty, food insecurity, unemployment, social exclusion, violations of religious freedom, and materialism that continue to ravage human communities with destructive consequences for the future of our planet and for our human family (*CV*, no. 21).

A key element of *Caritas in Veritate,* and one that Catholic social teaching has consistently affirmed, is that economic life is not amoral or autonomous per se. Business and economic institutions, including markets themselves, must be marked by internal relations of solidarity and trust. This means that profit, while a necessary means in economic life, cannot be the exclusive end for truly human economic flourishing. Instead, as Pope Benedict points out, the social enterprise — that is, business efforts — must transcend the dichotomy of for-profit and not-for-profit and pursue social ends while covering costs and providing for investment (*CV*, no. 21). More broadly, the Holy Father is urging business educators and practitioners to rethink who must be included among corporate stakeholders and what the moral significance of investment is (*CV*, no. 40). *Caritas in Veritate* is not an economic policy paper with the primary intention of advocating for any particular institutional program. In fact, the pope goes to great lengths to stress from the beginning that its central concept is not economic development per se, but "integral human development," or the understanding of true human progress as a "vocation." For Benedict, a proper understanding of the challenges to our moral development requires further and deeper reflection on the economy and its goals, to be sure, but this is only a first step toward bringing about a "profound cultural renewal" that cannot fully be captured by the technical language or categories of academic economics (*CV*, nos. 8-9).

The Centrality of the Human Person:
The Continuity of Catholic Social Doctrine

For Pope Benedict, the phenomenon of globalization, with its positive and negative consequences, is not the result of blind and impersonal historical forces, but rather the organic outgrowth of our deep longing for spiritual unity (*CV*, no. 42). While the family — and by extension, the local community — are the most natural stages for moral flourishing, we are "constitutionally oriented towards 'being more'" (*CV*, no. 18), always striving to further approximate the image of God in which we are made. This basic inclination toward transcendence expresses itself in the technological inventiveness of our freedom and is evidenced by our ceaseless attempts to conquer and control the forces of nature by our own efforts. And yet, as the Holy Father points out, the "cultural and moral crisis of man," which comes about by "idealizing" either economic or technological progress as the ultimate human goals, leads to a detachment of these goals from moral evaluation and responsibility. Both of these idealizations produce the intoxicating sensation of our own self-sufficient "autonomy" and a misguided notion of "absolute freedom." Our gravitational pull toward "being more" should never be confused with the possibility of "being anything" or having everything.

Catholic reflection on what it means to be authentically human in history and culture goes back to the fathers of the church in the second and third centuries. Throughout the course of history, the Church has never failed, in the words of Pope Leo XIII, to speak "the words that are hers" with regard to questions concerning life in society. The proclamation of Jesus Christ — the "Good News" of salvation, love, justice, and peace — is not readily received in today's world, which is devastated by wars, poverty, and injustices. For this very reason, people everywhere have a greater need than ever of the gospel: of the faith that saves, the hope that enlightens, the charity that loves.[9] When the bishops of Africa gathered in synod in October 2010, they expressed the same need of their continent for Christ, saying, "We are therefore committed to pursuing vigorously the proclamation of the gospel to the people of Africa, for 'life in Christ is the first and principal factor of development,' as Pope Benedict XVI says in *Caritas in Veritate* (*CV*, no. 8). For a commitment to development comes from a change of heart, and a change of heart comes from conversion to the Gospel."[10]

It has often been said that the Church is an *expert* in humanity, and the Church's expertise is rooted in its active engagement in human affairs, ceaselessly looking toward the "new heavens" and the "new earth" (2 Pet. 3:13), which she indicates to every person, in order to help people live their lives in the dimension of authentic meaning. *Gloria Dei vivens homo:* The glory of God is man and woman alive! This sentiment is the reason why the Church teaches, not only Catholics but people of good will everywhere, about the things that truly matter in life. The concerns of the Church include an immersion in a web of relationships that are continuously connected with work, family, the economy, civil society, and the state. In the context of faith, the social doctrine of the Church is an instrument of evangelization because it places the human person and society in relationship with the light of the gospel of Jesus Christ.[11]

It is in this light that men and women are invited above all to discover themselves as transcendent beings, in every dimension of their lives, including those related to social, economic, and political matters. As Christians, for example, we believe that faith brings fullness to the meaning of the family, which, founded on marriage between one man and one woman, constitutes the first and vital cell of society. Faith also sheds light, for example, on the dignity of

---

9. See Pontifical Council for Justice and Peace, *Compendium of the Social Doctrine of the Church* (Washington, D.C.: United States Conference of Catholic Bishops, 2004), pp. xx-xxv.

10. Synod of Bishops, "Message to the People of God," no. 15.

11. Synod of Bishops, "Message to the People of God," no. 15.

work, which ennobles people in their daily activity and confirms their rightful claim to share in the fruits that result from work (*CV*, no. 25). The social teaching of the Church reveals the importance of moral values, founded on the natural law written on every human conscience; and every human conscience is hence obliged to recognize and respect this law. Every believer must learn to obey the Lord with the strength of faith, following the example of St. Peter: "Master, we have worked all night and have caught nothing! But at your word, I will let down the nets again" (Luke 5:5). In short, Catholic social doctrine offers a sound approach to thinking about economic and financial realities based on fundamental moral and spiritual principles that speak to the truth of the human person and the centrality of the human family in world affairs.[12]

Moral Responsibility and the Need for Solidarity

Preferential love for the poor is part of the most basic Christian tradition, dating from the practice and teaching of Jesus: "As you did to one of the least of these my brethren, you did it to me" (Matt. 25:40; *CV*, no. 27). This has been the central thread of the Christian tradition throughout history, expressed visibly by charitable works and defense of the poor. It was pursued in the midst of the people of Israel (Deut. 15:1-11; cf. Leviticus 25), and it was the exemplary life of the early Christians, so that "no one was in need" (Acts 4:32-37).

But going beyond this duty of helping the poor, the principle of solidarity reflects the broader conviction that the human person is necessarily a social being: what Africans would express as *sumus ergo sum*. Human society does not exist by accident or by a chance coming together (*CV*, no. 38). This conviction is at the heart of the many questions that the Church raises about economic activity and, in particular, in relation to the development of the financial sector and the just distribution of power and wealth (*CV*, no. 24). In this respect, it seems to me that there are several related issues that will require ongoing reflection: (1) the excessive concentration of power; (2) the inequality between countries; (3) the distribution of economic resources that conflicts with the wider requirements of the universal destination of earthly goods; and (4) the use of resources by those who control them that does not take sufficient account of the need for social justice.

(1) Pius XI was the first to set out a critical interpretation concerning the concentration of economic power. In 1931 he wrote to those engaged in the

---

12. See *Compendium*, pp. xx-xxv.

financial sector: "In the first place, it is obvious that not only is wealth concentrated in our times but an immense power and despotic economic dictatorship is consolidated in the hands of a few, who often are not owners but only the trustees and managing directors of invested funds which they administer according to their own arbitrary will and pleasure."[13] He went on to write that "this power becomes particularly irresistible when exercised by those who, because they hold and control money, are able also to govern credit and determine its allotment, for that reason supplying, so to speak, the lifeblood to the entire economic body, and grasping, as it were, in their hands the very soul of production, so that no one dare breathe against their will."[14] While the style of the language may be rather dated, it remains true that the Church is asking a universal question concerning the concentration of power associated with financial development that stems from its understanding of human solidarity, and we hear a powerful echo here from the African synod, where its message made this appeal: "To the great powers of the world, we plead: treat Africa with respect and dignity. Africa has been calling for a change in the world economic order, with unjust structures piled heavily against her. Recent turmoil in the financial world shows the need for a radical change of rules. But it would be a tragedy if adjustments are made only in the interest of the rich and again at the expense of the poor."[15]

(2) Inequalities among countries must also be addressed squarely in light of the need for solidarity in this context. In order to be just, the interdependence between countries should give rise to new and broader expressions of solidarity that respect the equal dignity of all peoples, rather than lead to domination by the strongest, to national egoism, to inequalities and injustices. The monetary and financial issue therefore commands attention today in an urgent and new way (CV, no. 43).

(3) The Church holds that there is a universal destination of earthly goods, whereby the earth's resources are provided for the use of all human beings, so that their right to life can be respected in a way that provides for both the dignity of the individual and the needs of family life. This principle, however, raises certain problems for the economist. In a market economy, financial intermediation has a major role in the allocation of resources. The savings of some are used to finance the investment needs of others, in the hope that the

---

13. Pope Pius XI, *Quadragesimo Anno*, no. 105. Translation at http://www.vatican.va/holy
_father/pius_xi/encyclicals/documents/hf_p-xi_enc_19310515_quadragesimo-anno_en.html.

14. Pope Pius XI, *Quadragesimo Anno*, no. 106.

15. Synod of Bishops, "Message to the People of God," no. 32.

proper functioning of this financial circuit will play its part in attaining an optimal economic growth. A serious question lies at the heart of this financial strategy: does this process lead toward the effective implementation of the universal destination of earthly goods? The answer to this question is not easy to discern, but it must nevertheless be pondered, and often, when investment decisions are being made (*CV,* no. 42).

(4) This leads to the fourth consideration in the context of the need for solidarity. Since financial activity can involve important risks, it can lead to very large profits for both individuals and companies. In this context, the Church has usually restricted itself to pointing out in general terms some basic principles to be followed and the need for each individual to exercise his or her discernment. Yet, the individual must never lose sight of the fact that even those resources he possesses belong not only to him but also to the wider community. They should be used not only for his profit but also for that of others.[16]

The enterprise of business education and business practice must always be understood in conjunction with our moral responsibility, rooted in a recognition of that which limits us. In this regard, effective governance and aid that provides support for development are needed in charting a path toward more integral development. The challenge to "humanize" or "civilize" globalization through the mechanism of business education and practice does not necessarily mean more government. It does, however, demand *better* government — the rule of law, the development of strong institutions of governance, the restoration of the balance between competing interests, the eradication of corruption. *Caritas in Veritate* properly recognizes that states are not to relinquish their duty to pursue justice and the common good in the global economic order, but also that subsidiarity and solidarity must be held in tandem. Ethical business practice demands fairer and freer trade and assisting the poor of the world to successfully integrate into a flourishing global economy.

Pope Benedict is not so much concerned with globalization as an economic phenomenon, but rather the "underlying anthropological and ethical spirit" of the economic order, globalization, the business world, and their "theological dimensions" (*CV,* no. 42). Indeed, this is what the pope seems to mean when he contends that "every economic decision has a moral consequence" (*CV,* no. 37). The question of business, therefore, becomes a social and radically anthropological one: when it comes to business, we are called to respect not only profit, but also the moral conditions of those who pursue it. If we engage in this effort, recognizing our call to do the truth in love, we will authentically

16. See Vatican II, *Gaudium et Spes,* no. 69.

continue to respond to the Great Commission to "make disciples of all the nations."

Some Striking Features[17]

The effort, as observed above, to address social, global, economic, financial, entrepreneurial, political, anthropological, and ecological issues as they impact on the human person and his total and integral development is certainly a striking feature of *Caritas in Veritate*. The challenging task of presenting a synthetic vision of all the problems of human society, full of tensions, contradictions, and pitfalls, but also with positive signs of hope, in the light of faith and in the light of natural ethics and reason is certainly new.

It is equally striking how benignly and pastorally sympathetic the encyclical treats even those issues that are considered problematic, unethical, and unfavorable to humanity's growth and development. There is no demonization of economics, market, technology, globalization, trade, and other economic activities — the structures and activities of man and society that impact negatively on the dignity and vocation to development of the person. There is rather a commendation for development, entrepreneurship, market, technology, and the like, as expressions of the human spirit and per se not evil. It is their abuse in the hands of sinful humanity against humanity's good that the encyclical cautions against.

It is also noteworthy how the encyclical enriches the deposit of the social teaching of the Church with a series of notions and realities, hitherto unknown in the magisterium of the Church, such as notions about finance, voluntarism, ethics in economics *(economia etica)*, reasonable use of natural resources, responsible procreation, and gratuitousness and the logic of gift in economics (where until now the overriding concern has been profit-making). These are ideas that are gaining currency in discussions among economists, believers and nonbelievers alike. The encyclical also invites the state and politics to promote economic freedom and initiative, and not to suppress them. It calls for the recognition of the role of intermediate bodies and groups, guided by a principle of fiscal subsidiarity, to give voice to people in the determination of the life and conduct of the economy.

17. Father Gianpaolo Salvini, S.J., prefers to describe these striking features of the encyclical as "le novità dell'enciclica," and the ideas expressed here are taken from him. See "L'Enciclica Caritas in Veritate," pp. 469-70.

Another discernible thrust of the encyclical is the evangelization of reason and of social, economic, financial, political, and technological structures with a view to making them more human and open to transcendence. The appeal to the reality of the brotherhood of the human family and the consequent sense of solidarity and reciprocity aims at restoring hope to humanity's sense of being a family.

Conclusion

In the final analysis, it is fundamentally the issue of the ultimate goals of humanity that should underline the concern of governments, nongovernmental organizations, and individuals alike. Faced with the choices involved in finance and in economics at every level, there can be no purely financial and economic response. We must look higher!

If, in the end, our goal is to reach "the integral development of man and of all men," according to Popes Paul VI, John Paul II, and Benedict XVI, the response to these challenges from a Christian standpoint must go beyond the simple question of management, however efficient this may be. Since social relations also have a spiritual dimension, the true response must be both moral and spiritual. It must pass through a conversion implying renewed fidelity to the gospel and an unshakeable determination to do nothing that could undermine the divine calling of humanity.

To respect this openness to conversion, political action and financial advisors should be both more modest — since they can never replace the discernment of each conscience — and less ambitious. Individuals, financial specialists, managers of companies, politicians, and administrators are in very different situations. But each one has a necessary moral commitment to make in economic life.

At the end of the day, the encyclical *Caritas in Veritate* calls all and sundry to the development of a serious sense of moral responsibility for humanity, for its world, for its integrity (anthropology), and for its vocation. Such a sense of responsibility can be developed only in the experience of love, which comes from God and is destined to be the nature and attribute of us all. Either as the nature and attribute of God, or as an endowment of the human person, love is true to its nature only when it is free. Only a free being can love, and it is truth that makes one free. "The truth shall make you free" (John 8:32). Thus, ultimately, it is only in truth that one can love!

Contributors

J. Brian Benestad became the D'Amour Professor of Catholic Thought in the Department of Theology at Assumption College in the fall of 2013. He previously taught for thirty-seven years at the University of Scranton. He received a Ph.D. from Boston College in Boston, Massachusetts; an S.T.L. from the Gregorian University in Rome, Italy; and a B.A. from Assumption College in Worcester, Massachusetts. His teaching and research interests include moral theology, Catholic social thought, St. Augustine, St. Thomas Aquinas, the Italian novelist Alessandro Manzoni, and the writings of Joseph Ratzinger and Avery Dulles. He has authored more than fifty articles for various journals and magazines, written numerous book reviews, and edited several books. With the Catholic University of America Press he published in 2011 *Church, State, and Society: An Introduction to Catholic Social Doctrine*.

Simona Beretta is an Ordinary Professor of International Economics and Policy, Political Science Faculty at the "Sacro Cuore" Catholic University, Milan. Her degrees include a laurea in economics from the Catholic University and an M.Sc. in economics from the London School of Economics and Political Science. She is the director of the joint Postgraduate Program in European Studies and Global Affairs, ASERI (Postgraduate School of Economics and International Relations), at Catholic University, Milan, and Pázmány Péter University, Budapest. She is a member of the editorial board of the *Rivista Internazionale di Scienze Sociali*, a consultant of the Pontifical Council for Justice and Peace, and a member of the ad hoc group on Global Governance, COMECE (Commission of Catholic Bishops' Conferences of the European

Community). Her publications and research activities concern international policy-making; trade structure and trade policies; exchange rate dynamics, exchange rate intervention, and macroeconomic policies; and capital flows liberalization and financial organization.

MICHAEL BUDDE is a senior research fellow in the Center for World Catholicism and Intercultural Theology and professor of Catholic studies and political science at DePaul University. He was the former chair of the Political Science Department and former director of DePaul's Center for Church-State Studies and currently chairs Catholic studies. Budde's areas of research focus on interactions between ecclesiology and political economy, especially, but not exclusively, as such relate to Catholicism and Christianity as transnational communities. He has authored the following books: *The Two Churches: Catholicism and Capitalism in the World System* (Duke University Press), *The (Magic) Kingdom of God: Christianity and Global Culture Industries* (Westview Press), *Christianity Incorporated* (Brazos Press), and *The Borders of Baptism: Identities, Allegiances, and the Church* (Cascade). He also co-edited (with Karen Scott) *Witness of the Body: The Past, Present, and Future of Christian Martyrdom* (Eerdmans). He has also published several edited volumes and articles in scholarly journals, including *Studies in Christian Ethics, Sociology of Religion,* and *World Policy Journal.*

PATRICK CALLAHAN (B.A., M.A., Northern Illinois University; Ph.D., Ohio State University) is a professor of political science at DePaul University and has served three terms as chair of that department. His scholarly work and teaching are in the areas of international ethics and American foreign and national security policy. In additional to teaching courses in political science, he teaches two courses in Catholic studies. He received a teaching excellence award in 1991.

PAULO FERNANDO CARNEIRO DE ANDRADE is vice dean at Pontifícia Universidade Católica do Rio de Janeiro (PUC-Rio), where he has been a member of the faculty of the Graduate Program in Theology since 1989. He was born in Rio de Janeiro, Brazil, in 1958 and received a doctor in theology at the Pontifical Gregorian University of Rome. Andrade is a member of the Board of Globethics, a global network of institutions and people that work with applied ethics. He works with the base ecclesial communities and the Popular movement. Andrade is also a past president of SOTER (Brazilian Society of Theology and Religious Studies), one of the founders of the World

Forum for Theology and Liberation, and a former vice president of INSeCT (International Network of Societies for Catholic Theology). Andrade has written more than sixty academic publications. A few of his most recent include "Popular Leadership in a Context of Oppression: A Latin American Liberation Perspective," in *Responsible Leadership: Global and Contextual Ethical Perspectives,* ed. C. Stückelberger and J. Mugambi (Geneva: WCC Publications, 2007), pp. 324-31; "Ciudadanía y Derechos Humanos," in *Tejiendo redes de Vida y Esperanza: Cristianismo, sociedad y profecia en America Latina y el Caribe,* ed. Amerindia and SOTER (Bogotá: Indo-American Press Service Ltda, 2006), pp. 155-72; "Debito Sociale ed Economia di Mercato," *Prospettiva Persona* 12, no. 44 (2003): 34-38; and "A crise da modernidade e as possibilidades de uma nova militância cristã," in *Terra Prometida: Movimento Social, engajamento cristão e teologia,* ed. L. C. Suzin (Petrópolis: Vozes, 2001), pp. 213-24.

PETER J. CASARELLA is an associate professor of systematic theology at the University of Notre Dame. He received his Ph.D. in 1992 from the Department of Religious Studies at Yale University after completing a dissertation on the theology of the word of the fifteenth-century Catholic thinker Nicholas of Cusa. He spent two years as an assistant professor of theology at the University of Dallas before assuming a similar position at the Catholic University of America. In 2007 he was appointed as a professor in the Program of Catholic Studies at DePaul University in Chicago. In 2008 he was named the founding director of the Center for World Catholicism and International Theology. He has written essays in scholarly journals on a variety of topics, including medieval Christian Neoplatonism, contemporary theological aesthetics, and the Hispanic/Latino presence in the U.S. Catholic Church. He has co-edited several volumes: with Raúl Gómez, S.D.S., *Cuerpo de Cristo: The Hispanic Presence in the U.S. Catholic Church* (Academic Renewal, 2003), and with George Schner, S.J., *Christian Spirituality and the Culture of Modernity: The Thought of Louis Dupré* (Eerdmans, 1998). In 2006 the Catholic University of America Press published a volume that he edited: *Cusanus: The Legacy of Learned Ignorance.* In 2011 he co-edited (with Will Storrar and Paul Metzger) *A World for All? Global Civil Society in Political Theory and Trinitarian Theology* with Eerdmans. He served in 2005-6 as president of the Academy of Catholic Hispanic Theologians in the U.S. (ACHTUS) and from 2009 to 2014 as president of the American Cusanus Society. He is also on the editorial board of *Communio, Cultural Encounters, Asian Perspectives in the Arts and Humanities,* and *Nova et Vetera.*

WILLIAM T. CAVANAUGH is a research professor in the Center for World Catholicism and Intercultural Theology and the Department of Catholic Studies at DePaul University. He received a B.A. in theology from Notre Dame in 1984 and an M.A. from Cambridge University in 1987. After working as a lay associate with the Holy Cross Order in a poor area of Santiago, Chile, Cavanaugh worked at the Center for Civil and Human Rights at the Notre Dame Law School. He then studied at Duke University, where he received a Ph.D. in religion in 1996. He has taught at the University of St. Thomas since 1995. Cavanaugh specializes in political theology, economic ethics, and ecclesiology. In addition to many journal articles, he has published the following books: *Torture and Eucharist* (Blackwell, 1998), *Theopolitical Imagination* (T&T Clark, 2002), *Being Consumed* (Eerdmans, 2008), and *The Myth of Religious Violence* (Oxford University Press, 2009). He is also the co-editor of the *Blackwell Companion to Political Theology* (Blackwell, 2004) and the forthcoming *Eerdmans Reader in Contemporary Political Theology.* His books have been translated into French and Spanish. Cavanaugh is co-editor of the journal *Modern Theology.* He is a popular speaker, having given invited talks at dozens of universities in the United States, as well as in Australia, Canada, England, Belgium, Spain, Italy, and Sweden.

MARYANN CUSIMANO LOVE is a tenured associate professor of international relations in the Politics Department of the Catholic University of America in Washington, D.C. She is also a fellow at the Commission on International Religious Freedom, where she is writing materials for the Foreign Service Institute, professional military education schools, and universities. She teaches graduate and undergraduate international relations courses at Catholic University and the Pentagon, such as Security, Just Peace, Terrorism, Globalization, and The Problem of Sovereignty. Her recent international relations books include *Beyond Sovereignty: Issues for a Global Agenda* (4th ed., 2010), *Morality Matters: Ethics and the War on Terrorism* (forthcoming at Cornell University Press), and "What Kind of Peace Do We Seek?" a book chapter in the forthcoming volume with Notre Dame Press, *The Ethics and Theology of Peacebuilding.* She serves on the United States Catholic Bishops' International Justice and Peace Committee, where she advises the bishops on international affairs and U.S. foreign policy, and engages in advocacy with the U.S. government; the Advisory Board of the Catholic Peacebuilding Network, a network of practitioners, academics, clergy, and laity from around the world in the field of Catholic peacebuilding; and the board and Communications Committee of Jesuit Refugee Services, an international refugee relief and advocacy group active in more than sixty countries. An alumna of the Johns Hopkins University (Ph.D.), the University of Texas at Austin (M.A.), and St. Joseph's University in Philadelphia (B.A.), she is a frequent speaker on international affairs issues, as when she addressed the United Nations at the request of the Vatican on the topic of Religious Peacebuilding. She is a columnist for *America* magazine and a recipient of the 2009 Best Columnist Catholic Press Award. As a former Pew faculty fellow and a current consultant for Georgetown's Institute for the Study of Diplomacy, she regularly gives faculty development workshops on religion and world politics and on case and participatory teaching techniques. Dr. Maryann Cusimano Love lives on the Chesapeake Bay outside of Washington, D.C., with her husband, Richard, and three young children, Maria, Ricky, and Ava, who inspired her *New York Times* best-selling children's books, *You Are My I Love You, You Are My Miracle, You Are My Wish,* and *Sleep, Baby, Sleep.*

DANIEL K. FINN is professor of theology and the William E. and Virginia Clemens Professor of Economics and the Liberal Arts at St. John's University in Collegeville, Minnesota. He is a past president of the Catholic Theological Society of America, the Society of Christian Ethics, and the Association for Social Economics. He is the director of the True Wealth of Nations research project at the Institute for Advanced Catholic Studies and is working on a project to engage the Catholic Church in Latin America to work with civil society organizations to confront government corruption. He has provided leadership on affordable housing in the five-city St. Cloud, Minnesota, area for the Great River Interfaith Partnership, a faith-based community organization. He has received the Monica Hellwig Award for Outstanding Contributions to Catholic Intellectual Life from the Association of Catholic Colleges and Universities, the Thomas F. Divine Award for Lifetime Contributions to Social Economics and the Social Economy from the Association for Social Economics, and the Robert L. Spaeth Teacher of Distinction Award from Saint John's University. His most recent books are *Christian Economic Ethics: History and Implications* (Fortress), *Distant Markets, Distant Harms: Economic Complicity and Christian Ethics* (Oxford), *The True Wealth of Nations: Catholic Social Thought and Economic Life* (Oxford), and *The Moral Ecology of Markets: Assessing Claims about Markets and Justice* (Cambridge). He earned a B.S. from St. John Fisher College and an M.A. and Ph.D. from the University of Chicago.

ROBERTO GOIZUETA is the Margaret O'Brien Flatley Professor of Catholic Theology at Boston College. He has served as president of both the Catholic

Theological Society of America and the Academy of Catholic Hispanic Theologians of the United States. His book *Caminemos con Jesús: Toward a Hispanic/Latino Theology of Accompaniment* received a Catholic Press Association Book Award. In 2009 he published *Christ Our Companion: Toward a Theological Aesthetics of Liberation* with Orbis Press.

LORNA GOLD currently works as policy and advocacy manager for Trócaire, the Irish Catholic Agency for International Development (Caritas Ireland). She holds an M.A. and Ph.D. in economic geography from the University of Glasgow. Prior to joining Trócaire in 2002, she held the Joseph Rowntree and ESRC (Economic and Social Research Council) Research Fellowships in the Department of Politics, University of York, where her research was on the political economy of overseas aid. Her thesis research on the philosophical underpinnings of the Focolare movement's Economy of Communion was published as *The Sharing Economy* by Ashgate in 2004 and in numerous academic papers. In her current role she researches, writes, and advises on the policy implications of Catholic social thought for international development. She was a member of the International Commission for an Economy of Communion from 2000 to 2008 before stepping down because of family commitments. Her updated book on the Economy of Communion, *New Financial Horizons — The Focolare Movement's Economy of Communion,* was published by New City Press, New York, in the fall of 2010.

KEITH LEMNA is assistant professor of systematic theology at Saint Meinrad Seminary and School of Theology. He has taught at the Catholic University of America, Belmont Abbey College, and Saint Joseph College. Since completing his dissertation in 2007, in which he explored the Trinitarian theological cosmology of the French theologian Louis Bouyer, he has continued to research the meeting of Trinitarian metaphysics, cosmology, and culture in modern theology. He has explored the interrelation of these themes in Bouyer, Hans Urs von Balthasar, and John Henry Newman, among others. Since the time of his dissertation, he has published or been accepted for publication in *The Heythrop Journal, Nova et Vetera, Communio, International Philosophical Quarterly,* and *Antiphon.* He has contributed to the revised edition of *The New Catholic Encyclopedia* (2010) and to *The Encyclopedia of Catholic Social Thought, Social Science, and Social Policy.*

D. STEPHEN LONG is professor of systematic theology at Marquette University. Previously he worked at Garrett-Evangelical Theological Seminary, St. Joseph's

University, and Duke Divinity School. He is an ordained United Methodist and served churches in Honduras and North Carolina. He has published eight books and numerous essays. The books are *Living the Discipline: United Methodist Theological Reflections on War, Civilization, and Holiness* (Eerdmans, 1992), *Tragedy, Tradition, Transformism: The Ethics of Paul Ramsey* (Westview Press, 1993), *Divine Economy: Theology and the Market* (Routledge, 2000), *The Goodness of God: Theology, Church and Social Order* (Brazos Press, 2001), *John Wesley's Moral Theology: The Quest for God and Goodness* (Kingswood, 2005), *Calculated Futures: Theology, Economics and Ethics* (Baylor, 2007), *Theology and Culture* (Cascade, 2008), *Speaking of God: Theology, Language and Truth* (Eerdmans, 2009), *Christian Ethics: A Very Short Introduction* (Oxford, 2010), *Hebrews: A Theological Commentary on the Bible* (Westminster John Knox Press, 2011), and *Saving Karl Barth: Hans Urs Von Balthasar's Preoccupation* (Fortress, 2014). Steve is married to Ricka and they have three children.

ARCHBISHOP CELESTINO MIGLIORE is Titular Archbishop of Canosa and Apostolic Nuncio to Poland. He previously served as Permanent Observer of the Holy See to the United Nations. He is a native of Cuneo, in the Piedmont region of Italy. His Excellency Archbishop Celestino Migliore was born in 1952 and ordained a priest in 1977. Having obtained his master's degree in theology, Archbishop Migliore pursued his studies at the Pontifical Lateran University, where he was awarded the doctorate in canon law. In 1980, after graduating from Pontifical Academy for Ecclesiastical Diplomacy, he joined the Holy See's diplomatic service. He served at the apostolic nunciatures in Angola (1980-84), Washington, D.C. (1984-88), Egypt (1988-89), and Poland (1989-92). In April 1992 he was appointed Permanent Observer of the Holy See to the Council of Europe in Strasbourg, France, and from December 1995 to October 2002 served as under-secretary of the Section for Relations with States of the Secretariat of State, at the Vatican. While in Rome, he also taught ecclesiastical diplomacy at the Pontifical Lateran University in Rome as a visiting professor.

MICHAEL NAUGHTON is a full professor and holds the Moss Chair in Catholic Social Thought at the University of St. Thomas (Minnesota). As a faculty member with a joint appointment in the Departments of Catholic Studies (College of Arts and Sciences) and Ethics and Law (Opus College of Business), he is also the director of the John A. Ryan Institute for Catholic Social Thought, which examines Catholic social thought in relationship to business. As director he has organized international conferences in the United States, Europe, Asia, and Latin America on the theme of Catholic social thought and management as well as various faculty and administrative seminars on the mission and identity of Catholic universities. His most recent books are *Leading Wisely in Difficult Times: Three Cases on Faith and Work* (2011; co-author David Specht), *Bringing Your Business to Life: The Four Virtues that Will Help You Build a Better Business — and a Better Life* (2008; co-author Jeff Cornwall), *Managing as if Faith Mattered: Christian Social Principles in the Modern Organization* (2001; co-author Helen Alford — translated into Chinese, Spanish, Russian, and Hungarian), *Rethinking the Purpose of Business: Interdisciplinary Essays in the Catholic Social Tradition* (2002; co-editor S. A. Cortright), and *Rediscovering Abundance: Interdisciplinary Essays on Wealth, Income and Their Distribution in the Catholic Social Tradition* (2005; co-editors Helen Alford, Charles Clark, and S. A. Cortright). He serves on several boards of directors for profit and nonprofit organizations, including Reell Precision Manufacturing (profit) and the Center for Seeing Things Whole (nonprofit). He is the editor of the series entitled Catholic Social Tradition from the University of Notre Dame Press and he serves on the editorial board for the *Journal of Catholic Social Thought.* He received a Ph.D. in theology and society from Marquette University and an M.B.A. from the University of St. Thomas. Besides authoring and editing eight books, Naughton has also published more than sixty articles in a wide variety of journals. His course on Faith and Entrepreneurship (team taught with Jeff Cornwall) was the recipient of the 2002 National Outstanding Course Award from the United States Association for Small Business and Entrepreneurship. In 2009 he was awarded an honorary degree of doctor of humane letters from the Dominican School of Philosophy and Theology in Berkeley, California, and was inducted into the school's College of Fellows. He is married with five children.

JULIE HANLON RUBIO is currently associate professor of Christian ethics at St. Louis University. In her research, she aims to bring together Catholic social teaching and Christian theology on marriage and family. Her articles have appeared in *Theological Studies, Journal of the Society of Christian Ethics, Horizons,* and *Josephinum.* Her first book, *A Christian Theology of Marriage and Family* (Paulist Press, 2003) received a Catholic Press Association award. With Charles E. Curran, she is the co-editor of *Readings in Moral Theology* No. 15: *Marriage* (Paulist Press, 2009). *Family Ethics: Practices for Christians,* was published by Georgetown University Press in 2010. Her new book *Between the Personal and the Political: Catholic Hope for Common Ground* will be published by Georgetown Univeristy Press in 2015. Dr. Rubio lives in St. Louis with her husband and three sons.

SISTER DAMIEN MARIE SAVINO, F.S.E., is associate professor and chair of the Environmental Science and Studies Department at the University of St. Thomas, Houston. She is a member of the Franciscan Sisters of the Eucharist and received her master of science degree in soil science from the University of Connecticut in Storrs, Connecticut, her master of arts degree in theology from the Catholic University of America, and her Ph.D. in environmental engineering also from the Catholic University of America. Her doctoral research applied an interdisciplinary approach, integrating ecology and theology, to the restoration of the Anacostia River in Washington, D.C. It has since been published as a book entitled *The Contemplative River: The Confluence Between People and Place in Ecological Restoration*. Sister Damien Marie holds a joint appointment in Theology. Prior to coming to Houston, she taught natural resource management at Grand Valley State University in Allendale, Michigan. She has also worked as an environmental consultant and in the environmental remediation group at United Technologies Corporation.

DAVID L. SCHINDLER is Dean Emeritus and Edouard Cardinal Gagnon Professor of Fundamental Theology for the Pontifical John Paul II Institute for Studies on Marriage and Family at the Catholic University of America. Formerly a Weaver Fellow and a Fulbright Scholar (Austria), Professor Schindler taught for thirteen years in the Program of Liberal Studies at the University of Notre Dame, where he received tenure in 1985 and, before that, for four years at Mount St. Mary's College, where he received tenure in 1978. Since 1982 he has been editor-in-chief of the North American edition of *Communio: International Catholic Review*, a federation of journals founded in 1972 by Hans Urs von Balthasar, Joseph Ratzinger (Pope Benedict XVI), Henri de Lubac, and other European theologians. He serves as editor of the series Ressourcement: Retrieval and Renewal in Catholic Thought, published by Eerdmans. Professor Schindler has published more than eighty articles in the areas of metaphysics, fundamental theology, biotechnology, and the relation of theology and culture. Professor Schindler is author of *Ordering Love: Liberal Societies and the Memory of God* (Eerdmans) and *Heart of the World, Center of the Church* (T&T Clark and Eerdmans). His edited collections include, with Doug Bandow, *Wealth, Poverty, and Human Destiny* (ISI) and *Love Alone Is Credible: Hans Urs von Balthasar as Interpreter of the Catholic Tradition* (Eerdmans). Pope John Paul II appointed Professor Schindler a consultor for the Pontifical Council for the Laity in 2002.

THEODORE TSUKAHARA JR. is a tutor and former director of the Integral Program of Liberal Arts, director of the John F. Henning Institute, and professor of economics at Saint Mary's College of California. He is a graduate of Saint Mary's (1962) with a B.S. in economics and business administration. He earned an M.S. in quantitative business analysis from the University of Southern California (1964) and an M.A. (1967) and Ph.D. (1970) in economics from Claremont Graduate University. He was a National Endowment for the Humanities Post-Doctoral Fellow in Bioethics at the Hastings Center in 1974-75. Before entering the business world in 1976, Ted taught mathematics at inter-city Catholic high schools in Oakland, California, and Los Angeles, California, and economics at the college level, completing his earlier academic career as a tenured associate professor of economics at Pomona College and Claremont Graduate University. From 1976 to 1986 he held executive positions in finance and planning with divisions of Atlantic Richfield Company (ARCO) — ARCO Petroleum Products in Los Angeles and ARCO Chemical Company in Philadelphia. Ted returned to academic life in September 1992 when he joined the faculty of Saint Mary's College, California, to teach economics and quantitative methods principally in the Executive MBA Program. His research interests are in the economic analysis of altruism, especially the informal care of the elderly, higher education management issues, and Catholic social teaching. He is chair, domestic board of directors, and former president of the Association for the Study of Generosity in Economics and serves as a member of the editorial board of the Journal of Gambling Studies. At Saint Mary's he has twice served as chair of the Academic Senate and Faculty representative to the board of trustees, interim dean of the School of Economics and Business Administration, and director of the Bay Area Consortium for Higher Education Project funded by the James Irvine Foundation. He chaired the original Housing Task Force for the city of Claremont, California. Ted has been married to Victoria Fujita for forty-six years.

CARDINAL PETER KODWO APPIAH TURKSON is president of the Pontifical Council for Justice and Peace. His Eminence was born October 11, 1948, in Nsuta Wassaw (in the western region of Ghana, Africa). On July 20, 1975, he was ordained to the priesthood in the Cathedral of Saint Francis de Sales in Cape Coast, Ghana. Eighteen years later, on March 27, 1993, in the same cathedral, he was ordained and installed as the archbishop of Cape Coast. On September 28, 2003, Pope John Paul II named him to the Sacred College of Cardinals, and he was created a cardinal in the public Consistory of October 21, 2003, at the Vatican. He studied at St. Teresa's Seminary in Amisano from 1962 to 1967. From 1969 to 1971, he studied at the regional Seminary of St. Peter in Pedu. Later he traveled to the United States for further studies in theology at

St. Anthony's on Hudson, in Rensselaer, New York. Five years later, he was assigned to study at the Pontifical Biblical Institute in Rome, first for a licentiate in Sacred Scripture (1976-80) and again in 1987 at the doctoral level in Sacred Scripture, during which time he was nominated to be the archbishop of Cape Coast (in 1993). He served on the faculty of St. Teresa's Seminary of Amisano, and of St. Peter's Regional Seminary in Pedu. He also served as part-time lecturer at the Department of Religious Studies at the University of Cape Coast (1981-87), and as visiting lecturer at the Catholic Major Seminary of Anyama, Côte d'Ivoire (1983-86). During those years, Father Turkson also served as chaplain for the Catholic community of the University of Cape Coast (1984-86). As the archbishop of Cape Coast, His Eminence was president of the Ghana Catholic Bishops' Conference (1997-2004), chancellor of the Catholic University of Ghana, and an appointed member of several institutions of the Roman Curia: the Pontifical Commission for Methodist-Catholic Dialogue (1997-2007), the Pontifical Council for Christian Unity (2002-present), the Pontifical Commission for the Cultural Patrimony of the Church (2002-present), the Pontifical Congregation for Divine Worship (2005-present), the International Secretariat of the Pontifical Mission Societies (2006-present). Cardinal Turkson was appointed to the Pontifical Council for Justice and Peace in 2007 and has been president since 2009. He has been a member of the governing council of the University of Ghana in Legon (2001-6), a member of the board of directors of CEDECOM (2002-present), treasurer of the Symposium of Episcopal Conferences of Africa and Madagascar (SECAM) (2007-present), chairman of the Ghana Chapter of The Conference of Religions for Peace (2003-7), and chairman of the Ghana National Peace Council (2006-present).

Horacio Vela is a Ph.D. candidate in biblical studies at the University of Notre Dame and assistant professor of biblical studies at the University of the Incarnate Word in San Antonio, Texas. He has published "Philo and the Logic of History," *The Studia Philonica Annual* 22 (2010): 165-82, and is currently completing a dissertation as a Hispanic Theological Initiative Doctoral Fellow on "The Inner Person: The Transformation of a Platonic Metaphor in Ancient Judaism and Early Christianity."

Index of Names and Subjects

Index of Scripture References